AF762998

Suicide and Self-Harm

Note

Health and social care practice and knowledge are constantly changing and developing as new research and treatments, changes in procedures, drugs and equipment become available.

The authors, editor and publishers have, as far as is possible, taken care to confirm that the information complies with the latest standards of practice and legislation.

Suicide and Self-Harm: an evidence-informed approach

John Cutcliffe and Jose Carlos Santos

QUAY BOOKS
A division of MA Healthcare Ltd

Quay Books Division, MA Healthcare Ltd, St Jude's Church, Dulwich Road, London
SE24 0PB

British Library Cataloguing-in-Publication Data
A catalogue record is available for this book

ISBN-10: 1 85642 433 2
ISBN-13: 978 1 85642 433 2

Printed by Mimeo, Huntingdon, Cambridgeshire

Contents

Acknowledgements

The authors wish to offer their thanks to Ana Margarida for her cooperation in translation.

Some sections of this book have been adapted or reproduced from original work authored by Professor Cutcliffe and Professor Santos.

While we have included specific acknowledgements to the publishers of these original works and reference details in the chapters where this is the case, we wish once more to offer our most profound and heartfelt thanks to the following publishing houses:

- Blackwell Science Ltd, for allowing the use of papers published in the *Journal of Psychiatric and Mental Health Nursing*; and the *International Journal of Mental Health Nursing.*
- Churchill Livingstone/Elsevier Ltd, for allowing the use of the paper published in *General Hospital Psychiatry* and for some sections included in the text *Care of the Suicidal Person* (2007).
- Hogrefe Publishing Ltd, for allowing the use of papers published in *Crisis: The Journal of Crisis Intervention and Suicide Prevention.*

Chapter 10

The authors also wish to acknowledge the research team who undertook the research in this chapter:

At the time of undertaking the study, **John Cutcliffe** held the 'Acadia Professorial Chair in Psychiatric and Mental Health Nursing at the University of Maine, United States of America. He also holds Adjunct Professor of Nursing positions at the University of Ulster, UK, the University of Coimbra, Portugal and the University of Malta. He continues to work on a number of federally funded suicide-focused research studies with colleagues from Canada, the United Kingdom, Ireland and Norway.

Paul Links is the Arthur Sommer Rotenberg Chair in Suicide Studies at St. Michael's Hospital, Toronto, Ontario, Canada; he is a Professor of Psychiatry in the Department of Psychiatry, Faculty of Medicine, University of Toronto, and the Centre for Research in Inner City Health in The Keenan Research Centre, Li Ka Shing Knowledge Institute, St Michael's Hospital, Toronto, Ontario, Canada.

Henry Harder is Professor and Chair of Health Sciences Programs at the University of Northern British Columbia. He is a registered psychologist. His research interests are in workplace mental health, suicide and aboriginal health.

Ken Balderson is a staff psychiatrist, Medical Director of the Inpatient Mental Health Unit at St Michael's hospital and an Assistant Professor, Department of Psychiatry, University of Toronto. His clinical work is in general and HIV psychiatry, and he provides mental health consultation in Nunavut. He is also physician lead responsible for developing and implementing Medication Reconciliation at St. Michael's.

Yvonne Bergmans is a Suicide Intervention Consultant and Lecturer in the Department of Psychiatry at the University of Toronto. Her work involves clinical, research and education primarily in the area of people with recurrent suicide attempts. She is the lead facilitator and lead for the groups psychotherapy intervention: Psychosocial /Psychoeducational Intervention for People with Recurrent Suicide Attempts (PISA).

Rahel Eynan is a Research Coordinator with the Suicide Studies Research Unit at St Michael's Hospital and the President of the Ontario Association for Suicide Prevention (OASP).

Munazzah Ambreen is a researcher at St. Michael's Hospital, who worked with Arthur Sommer Rotenberg Chair in Suicide Studies from January 2008 to January 2010. Munazzah received her MD from Pakistan and MSc in Genetics from McGill. Her current research focuses on mental health issues in homeless populations.

Rosane Nisenbaum is a scientist in the Keenan Research Centre of the Li Ka Shing Knowledge Institute of St. Michael's Hospital, Toronto, Canada and an Assistant Professor at the Division of Biostatistics, Dalla Lana School of Public Health, University of Toronto. She has experience of over 20 years as a Senior Biostatistician working in the United States and Canada in projects related to population-based studies of chronic illnesses, neighbourhood effects on mental health, homelessness and housing, and suicide studies.

Rosane Nisenbaum gratefully acknowledges the support of the Ontario Ministry of Health and Long-Term Care. The views expressed in this publication are the views of the authors and do not necessarily reflect the views of the Ontario Ministry of Health and Long-Term Care.

This book is dedicated to
Dr Maryla Cutcliffe, João Santos and Rita Santos

These individuals add meaning to our lives

CHAPTER 1

Introduction

> Suicide is functional because it abolishes painful tension…[it is a form of] intolerable suffering. (Murray, 1981, p. 216)

> Given intense and irremediable sufferings, there is nothing irrational about the act of suicide. It is irrational only to those who stand outside of it. (Murray, 1981, p. 491)

Introduction

For many people, suicide is bewildering. Why would a person – any person – wish to deliberately bring their existence to a premature end? How would a healthcare practitioner understand such a choice, let alone know how to bring about a change of view in the suicidal person? And even if I, as a healthcare practitioner, wanted to help the suicidal person, what evidence is there available to me to inform my practice? These are the principal questions and issues that we shall concern ourselves with in this book.

Take a moment to look back over human history and, regrettably, you will see suicide. You will see it occurring for people from all walks of life; people of every ethnicity, gender, race, socio-economic status or political persuasion. Suicide, it seems, is closely inter-twined with the human experience. However, despite its ubiquity, an honest appraisal of our understanding of why any particular individual takes his or her own life is that this comprehension is far from complete; it may only be just beginning. Or, more precisely, it is difficult to reconcile that we have a comprehensive understanding of suicide, and that this has led to global reductions in the rate of suicide, with the reality that, since 1950, the global trend in suicide rates has risen!

What most practitioners appear to be particularly lacking is evidence-informed literature that guides the practice of nurses (and others) in terms of day-to-day, hour-by-hour, minute-by-minute care of suicidal people. As a result, this book specifically focuses on theory and practice to help inform and guide the clinical interactions of healthcare professionals wherever they encounter suicidal people. It hopes in some small way to provide comprehensive and contemporary literature that will act as a 'balm', helping practitioners to recognise and deal with the powerful emotional responses to suicide, ranging from anger, to fear, to bewilderment and to confusion.

Nursing-sensitive outcomes and suicide

Rightly or wrongly, the relationship between healthcare and evidence-informed or evidence-based practice is a reality that we all have to deal with. The epoch of evidence-informed practice is upon us and it has profound implications for the way(s) in which we carry out our business of caring for/with people. One such implication is the perpetual contentious need for, and associated efforts of, healthcare organisations to balance cost-effectiveness and quality of care, given the increased attention being given to identifying, measuring and reporting on outcomes for clients, healthcare professionals and employers. At the same time, within healthcare settings, there is a growing emphasis on evidence-based decision-making regarding staff mix and care delivery models, which has prompted considerable research on identifying outcome indicators sensitive to nursing interventions and staffing levels.

The discipline of nursing only started to have more robust scientific evidence to demonstrate the difference that it makes in healthcare since the 1990s, when studies were undertaken to bridge the gap in knowledge and identify nursing-sensitive outcomes (Doran, 2011). Despite the fact that nurses are the single largest discipline involved in healthcare[1] (Benner *et al*, 2009), but nursing is often absent from health policy decision and descriptions of healthcare. While some literature is available regarding nursing sensitive outcomes in acute (medical/surgical) care (Yang *et al*, 1999; Doran *et al*, 2006; Tourangeau *et al*, 2006; Blegen *et al*, 2011), and to a lesser extent in long-term care (Head *et al*, 2004; Castle, 2008), it is extremely limited in the area of psychiatric/mental health (P/MH) nursing. In some small way, this book attempts to contribute to rectifying this limitation by providing an evidence-informed approach (not least by considering nurse-sensitive outcomes) to caring for and working with suicidal people.

Identifying nursing-sensitive patient outcomes

What do we mean when we are referring to nursing-sensitive outcomes? When patient outcomes tend to focus on how people and their health problems are

1 In terms of numbers of clinicians; furthermore, the same 'picture' is evident when one examines international and global data on this issue.

affected by nursing interventions, then these (it can be argued) are references to nursing-sensitive patient outcomes. Maas *et al* (1996, p. 295) define nursing-sensitive patient outcomes as

> ...measurable changes in a patient's state of health or condition as a result of nursing interventions and for which nurses are responsible.

Nursing-sensitive patient outcomes are within the scope of nursing practice. They are coherent with the processes of nursing care and can be evidenced by an empirical link between nursing interventions and the patient condition (Given *et al*, 2004).

The need to move towards an international consensus on a set of measures to best capture the quality of hospital-based P/MH nursing care have been acknowledged in the extant literature and there are two predominant perspectives on the investigation of nursing-sensitive patient outcomes. The first involves the investigation of outcomes according to a process model of care, whereby

> outcomes are affected not only by the care provided but also by the factors related to the patient, to the interpersonal aspects of care and to the setting or environment in which care is provided. (Irvine et al, 1998, p. 58)

The second perspective encompasses P/MH nursing-sensitive patient safety outcomes which include the unintended effects of inadequate P/MH nursing care, such as medication errors, patient falls, nosocomial infections, violence, absconsion, and relapse (McGillis-Hall, 2004). Nursing's independent role concerns the functions and responsibilities for which only nurses are held accountable – activities initiated by nurses which do not require a physician's order (Irvine *et al*, 1998). They are interventions developed and initiated by nurses in response to a so-called nursing diagnosis, or also autonomous actions based on scientific rationale performed by the nurses to benefit the patient, ie. to obtain a nursing-sensitive outcome (McCloskey and Bulechek, 2000).

As a result, we present a great deal of material in this book that can be characterised as aspects of the nurse's independent role, function and/or responsibility, in addition to other material where there is perhaps, for want of a better expression, a shared or collaborative responsibility, function or role with other (mental) healthcare professionals.

Structure of the book

Many countries now have national prevention or action plans to attempt to combat and subsequently reduce suicide rates. For many nations, lowering rates of suicide (and more specifically in certain groups or populations who hitherto were not known for being high risk groups – eg. young men) has become a national health policy target. These policy positions, prevention programs and action plans (such as they are), quite rightly adopt a broad and wide-ranging approach to tackling suicide, recognising that effectively combating suicide requires a comprehensive approach; it needs a more comprehensive response than 'tinkering' with formal mental health services. Reducing suicide rates also appears to require consideration of social services, family dynamics/support, education and training for young men, access to means, conceptualisations of and how suicide is portrayed in the mass media, atypical primary prevention programs (such as using formerly suicidal people and suicide survivors as a resource), and addressing societal-based stigma to name but a few. As a result, Chapter 2 focuses on National Suicide Prevention Strategy documents and suicide prevention policies (where they exist). Areas or themes that share commonality are identified and consideration of what direction these provide to healthcare professionals are included. While national suicide prevention strategies and polices are often more capacious and capture more than clinical practice *per se*, we pay particular attention to how such policies, plans and strategies inform and might impact upon the day-to-day, hour-by-hour clinical practice of caring for (with) suicidal people.

Leading logically from the examination of policies, plans and strategies, Chapter 3 is dedicated to risk assessment of suicide and self-harm. While there seems to be little or no debate regarding the necessity of thorough and accurate assessment as a prerequisite for or antecedent of effective care of the suicidal person[2,3], it is perhaps counter-intuitive to realise that the evidence indicates that we (mental health practitioners) often fall some way short of best practice when it comes to assessing suicide and/or self-harm. In the first instance, comprehensive assessment of suicide risk is merely the beginning of the care of the suicidal person; such assessments have to lead to meaningful and effective interventions. Secondly, such formal and informal assessments are bedevilled by conflating suicide with self-harm. Thirdly, some practitioners report that they do not believe that standardised instruments scales are clinically helpful, that scales take too much time to use, and that they have not been trained in the use of such measures. Moreover, despite the existence of a substantial body of work in this area, our assessments (and associated instrumentation) remain far from perfect. Accordingly, this chapter reviews and draws attention to a wide range of instruments and considers so-called

2 Indeed, an argument could be made that assessment is a prerequisite

3 Similarly, locating this chapter where we have, early in this book, also seems logical and in keeping with current approaches to organising care.

'up-stream' and 'down-stream' risk factors. We situate the use of risk assessment instrumentation in the broader, more comprehensive 'picture' of assessment *per se* and, importantly, link the identification of high-risk clients with different levels (intensities) of intervention, engagement and care.

In Chapter 4 we focus on suicide in hospital settings and pay particular attention to if/how the physical environment and unit/ward milieu (or atmosphere) can be managed to reduce the chance of suicidal acts. Particular attention is paid to recommendations for the possible prevention of suicidal behaviours in hospital settings through the means or medium of 'managing the physical environment and ward milieu'. And we draw attention to how families and significant others might be 'mobilised' as a further healing resource for suicidal people. Although nurses have significant responsibilities in this domain and should be mindful of how these phenomena might be managed to enhance care, environmental safety is only one piece of the puzzle (Sullivan *et al*, 2005).

Defensive practices are concerned with the physical integrity of the person and do little or nothing to address the genesis (and/or exacerbation) of the person's suicidal thoughts or feelings (Cutcliffe and Stevenson, 2008). In Chapter 5 we identify the most common defensive practices – containment, seclusion, observations, removal of objects and no-suicide contracts – and examine each of these approaches/interventions, especially as despite their lack of supporting evidence (in many cases), these remain common practices that nurses engage in on the ward/unit as a means to (purportedly) prevent suicide. In this chapter we analyse the efficacy and legitimacy of these practices based on evidence-based data and discuss some implications of these practices from the point of view of users and nurses. Finally, we address alternatives to these practices, as we believe that the evidence indicates that it is necessary for us to move away from defensive strategies as a matter of urgency.

Rather than discussing the issue of prescription of medication by nurses *per se*, or exploring/arguing/identifying the most appropriate pharmacological treatment for the prevention of suicidal behaviours, Chapter 6 aims to explore the existing evidence-based practice related to pharmacological 'treatment' for suicidal people. At the outset, it should be taken into account that medication is only one measure among many others to 'treat' or help suicidal people, and it may or may not be a priority. However, in certain parts of the world, even despite the evidence pertaining to the questionable efficacy of pharmacological interventions for treating suicide (see van Praag, 2003), pharmacological 'treatment' or intervention is the mainstay of 'care' offered to suicidal people, in some places being the only 'care' that suicidal people receive. So while the chapter does indeed consider the wider evidentiary context of pharmacology, we do also review and explore some of the more common pharmacological 'treatments' provided to suicidal people. In this way, this chapter is expected to contribute to a more profound discussion about pharmacological interventions for suicidal people among nurses (and other formal caregivers).

The centrality of, for want of a better expression 'talk therapy', in helping suicidal people, leads logically to the focus of Chapter 7. The chapter begins by reviewing common elements and aspects of psychotherapeutic attempts to help suicidal people. Given the existing evidence (such as it is) pertaining to the efficacy of cognitive therapy (or approaches) for suicidal people, we examine such approaches in some detail. Similarly, the chapter then focuses on dialectical behaviour therapy (DBT) as a means for working with certain groups of suicidal people. We draw the chapter to a close by reviewing the empirical evidence pertaining to these psychotherapeutic approaches.

As we have pointed out in previous chapters, even a cursory survey of mental health facilities in most parts of the (so-called) 'developed' world will show that the current standard *modus operandi* for the nursing care of suicidal people is to place the person 'under observation'[4]. This book also highlights how woefully inadequate such practices often are; how they do little or nothing to help alleviate the suicidal person's psychache and/or genesis of his/her suicidal ideation. Further evidence previously provided also shows how observations often fail in even their most basic function: keeping the person physically safe. Yet it would be remiss of the authors of this book to point out the serious and significant limitations of this current practice without, at the same time, offering an alternative. Accordingly, Chapter 8 focuses on such an alternative; one that has been termed the 'engagement/inspiring hope – reconnecting the person with humanity' approach (see for example Cutcliffe and Barker, 2002; Cutcliffe and Stevenson, 2007). The chapter begins by drawing the reader's attention to the literature, which has repeatedly shown how suicidal people feel a sense of disconnection. It then proceeds to underscore this experience with reference to the literature linking suicide with isolation/loneliness and then highlights the links between a sense of disconnection and Shneidman's psychache. Following this, we present the findings of a recent federally funded study that explored how P/MH nurses work with suicidal people (see Cutcliffe *et al*, 2006; Cutcliffe and Stevenson, 2007). A summary of the three-stage process is provided, explaining how P/MH nurses work day-by-day, hour-by-hour and minute-by-minute with suicidal people.

---

4 Or whatever vernacular term is used to connote keeping the suicidal person under some form of surveillance.

While Chapter 8 introduces the reader to and provides an overview of the 'engagement – reconnecting the person with humanity' approach to caring for suicidal people, Chapter 9 provides a more comprehensive and detailed account of this approach. It provides a detailed account of each of the three stages and illustrates the key psychosocial care practices and the process therein by drawing on participant quotes (from formerly suicidal clients) which were procured during the study.

While much of this book focuses on the assessment, care and management of suicidal people during their 'acute' period of increased risk of suicide, often (but not always) involving some form of hospitalisation, there is a compelling body of evidence which indicates that people whose mental health problems lead them to require psychiatric hospitalisation are at a significantly increased risk of suicide (Appleby *et al*, 1999; Pirkola *et al*, 2005; Troister *et al*, 2008). However, hospitalisation for people at risk of suicide is only 'part of the bigger picture'; the period of time immediately following discharge after such hospitalisations appears to be a particularly high risk time (see Goldacre *et al*, 1993; Geddes and Juszczak, 1995; Geddes *et al*, 1997; Lawrence *et al*, 2001; Ho, 2003; Yim *et al*, 2004; Troister *et al*, 2008). Accordingly, Chapter 10 highlights how a number of variables have been shown to be significantly related to suicide after recent discharge, such as previous suicide attempts (Fernando and Storm, 1984; King *et al*, 2001a,b; McKenzie and Wurr, 2001; Yim *et al*, 2004); presence of affective disorder/depressive symptoms (King *et al*, 1995); unplanned discharge (Ho, 2006); and experience of negative life events following discharge (Pokorny and Kaplan, 1976). Conflicting findings exist regarding the link between duration of hospitalisation and increased risk (Qin and Nordentoft, 2005; Ho, 2006). It also shows that while there is consensus within the limited literature concerning the existence of this increased period of risk, our understanding of the particular experience(s) that contribute to this risk is far from complete. Accordingly, Chapter 10 reports on findings from a federally funded, mixed-methods study which sought to better understand the observed increased risk for suicide following discharge from an inpatient psychiatric service. Ultimately, the theoretical understanding of this specific high-risk period will lead to the development of selective prevention strategies that will decrease the risk of suicide and suicidal behaviour (Knox *et al*, 2004).

It is both interesting and disturbing to note that only a limited literature exists regarding practitioners' reactions to loss of a client due to suicide, very little of which focuses on P/MH nurses or general nurses. When one considers the worldwide prevalence of suicide and the estimates of how many people are affected by a single suicide (numbers ranging from 6 to 28), the under-developed nature of this associated literature is a puzzle. The immaturity of this literature may be all the more counter-intuitive given the increasing attention since the 1980s to 'Suicide Survivors' *per se*. Conceptual and methodological limitations notwithstanding, the extant studies on mental health clinicians' exposure to suicidal behaviours indicate that P/MH nurses report rates of 58.3% (Itoh, 2006) and 32.4% (Itoh, 2005). For psychotherapists this exposure was found to be around 33%; and for psychiatrists a figure of 51% was discovered (Valente, 1994). However, some authors have advanced the argument that these figures may be significant understatements (see, for example, Ruskin *et al*, 2004).

There exists a widely accepted and fairly well developed body of work that shows how a completed suicide can lead to a variety of mental health challenges for 'survivors' of a suicide – including increasing the survivor's own risk of suicide (Jobes *et al*, 2000). So when one considers how practitioners working in mental health settings (e.g. P/MH nurses, psychiatrists, psychologists, ministers/priests, general nurses) can and do form close relationships with suicidal people, there is a logical intuitive position that the death by suicide of a person under one's care can have major effects on the (mental) health and wellbeing of the practitioner. Accordingly, Chapter 11 begins by examining and problematising the definitions and conceptualisations of Suicide Survivors and goes on to make the case for considering that mental health practitioners who lose a client to suicide can be thought of as Suicide Survivors. The chapter then focuses on embracing (and ultimately implementing) clinical supervision as one means to help such practitioners deal and cope with their reactions to client suicide. It closes by examining the case for regarding a client's suicide as a Critical Incident, and goes on to make the case for the potential utility in providing Critical Incident Debriefing in such instances.

Lastly, in Chapter 12 we focus our attention on what lies ahead: what are the challenges we might consider addressing in the future in order to enhance our care of suicidal people and ultimately save lives. We draw attention to the need for additional conceptual clarity, addressing the conceptual confusion *vis-à-vis* restricting our thinking to suicide as *exclusively* a mental health problem and the continuing problem of conflating suicide with self-harm. The chapter then focuses on the practice challenges and developments that lie ahead of us. It reminds us of the need to keep talking as the centrepiece of care of the suicidal person, of the need to move away from defensive, surveillance and containment-orientated measures. It looks at the need to pay more attention to what can/should happen *after* a risk assessment is completed, the need to re-examine our initiatives regarding reducing access to lethal means, and (by no means least) what the evidence-informed options are before considering re-thinking and re-configuring mental healthcare service delivery for the suicidal person.

References

Appleby L, Shaw J, Amos T, McDonnell R, Kiernan K, Davies S, Harris C, McCann K, Bickley H, Parsons R (1999) Suicide within 12 months of contact with mental health services: national clinical survey. *British Medical Journal*, **318**: 1235–9.

Benner P, Sutphen M, Leonard V, Day L (2010) *Educating Nurses: a Call for Radical Transformation*. Jossey-Bass, San Francisco.

Blegen MA, Goode CJ, Spetz J, Vaughn T, Park SH (2011) Nurse staffing effects on patient outcomes: safety-net and non-safety-net hospitals. *Medical Care* **49**(4): 406–14.

Benner P, Stephen M, Leonard V, Day L (2009) *Educations Nurses: A call for radical transformation*. Jossey-Bass, San Francisco.

Canadian Association for Suicide Prevention (2009) *Blueprint for a Canadian National Suicide Prevention Strategy*, 2nd edn). Available from: http://www.suicideprevention.ca/wp-content/uploads/2009/11/2010strategy-final-september.docx (accessed 25 June 2012).

Canadian Institute for Health Information (2004) *National Trauma Registry Analytic Bulletin: Hospitalization Due to Suicide Attempts & Self-Inflicted Injury in Canada, 2001–2002*. Available from: https://secure.cihi.ca/estore/productFamily.htm?pf=PFC1361&lang=fr&media=0 (accessed 25 June 2012).

Castle NG (2008) Nursing home caregiver staffing levels and quality of care: a literature review. *Journal of Applied Gerontology* **27**(4): 375–405.

Cutcliffe JR, Barker P (2002) Considering the care of the suicidal client and the case for 'engagement and inspiring hope' or observations. *Journal of Psychiatric and Mental Health Nursing*, **9**(5): 611–21.

Cutcliffe JR, Stevenson C (2008a) Never the twain? Reconciling national suicide prevention strategies with the practice, educational, and policy needs of mental health nurses (part one). *International Journal of Mental Health Nursing*, **17**: 341–50.

Cutcliffe JR, Stevenson C (2007) *Care of the Suicidal Person*, Elsevier, London.

Cutcliffe JR, Stevenson C (2008) Never the twain? Reconciling national suicide prevention strategies with the practice, educational and policy needs of Psychiatric/Mental Health Nurses: part one. *International Journal of Mental Health Nursing*, **17**: 341–50.

Cutcliffe JR, Stevenson C (2008) Never the twain? Reconciling national suicide prevention strategies with the practice, educational and policy needs of Psychiatric/Mental Health Nurses: part two. *International Journal of Mental Health Nursing*, **17**: 351–62.

Cutcliffe JR, Stevenson C, Jackson S, Smith P (2006) A modified grounded theory study of how psychiatric nurses work with suicidal people. *International Journal of Nursing Studies*, **43**(7): 791–802.

Doran D (2011) *Nursing Outcomes: State of the Science*, 2nd edn. Jones & Bartlett Learning, Toronto.

Doran DM, Harrison MB, Laschinger HS, Hirdes JP, Rukholm E, Sidani S, McGillis Hall L, Tourangeau AE (2006). Nursing-sensitive outcomes data collection in acute care and long-term-care settings. *Nursing Research*, **55**(2S), S75–S81.

Fernando S, Storm V (1984) Suicide among psychiatric patients of a district hospital. *Psychological Medicine*, **14**: 661–72.

Geddes JR, Juszczak E (1995) Period trends in rate of suicide in first 28 days after discharge from psychiatric hospital in Scotland, 1968–92. *British Medical Journal*, **311**: 357–60.

Geddes JR, Juszczak E, O'Brien F, Kendrick S (1997) Suicide in the 12 months after discharge from psychiatric inpatient care, Scotland 1968–92. *Journal of Epidemiological Community Health*, **51**: 430–4.

Given B, Beck S, Etland C, Holmes Gobel B, Lamkin L, Marsee VD (recovered March 2012) *Nursing-Sensitive Patient Outcomes – Description and Framework*. http://www.ons.org/Research/NursingSensitive/Description.

Goldacre M, Seagrott V, Hawton K (1993) Suicide after discharge from psychiatric inpatient care. *Lancet*, **342**: 283–6.

Head BJ, Lober Aquilino M, Johnson M, Reed D, Maas M, Moorhead S (2004). Content validity and nursing sensitivity of community-level outcomes from the Nursing Outcomes Classification (NOC). *Journal of Nursing Scholarship*, **36**(3): 251–9.

Ho TP (2003) The suicide risk of discharged psychiatric patients. *Journal of Clinical Psychiatry*, **64**: 702–7.

Ho TP (2006) Duration of hospitalization and post discharge suicide. *Suicide and Life Threatening Behavior*, **36**(6): 682–8.

Irvine D, Sidani S, McGillis Hall L (1998). Linking outcomes to nurses' roles in health care. *Nursing Economics*, **16**(2): 58–64, 87.

Itoh O (2005) Suicide cases encountered by clinical psychiatric nurses – research and study for participants in the study meeting for registered nurses for psychiatric emergency units and acute patients. *Suicide Prevention and Crisis Intervention*, **26**(1): 32–9.

Itoh O (2006) Suicide incidents encountered by clinical psychiatric nurses (Part 2). *Suicide Prevention and Crisis Intervention*, **27**(1): 64–70.

Jobes D, Luoma J, Hustead L, Mann R (2000) In the wake of suicide: survivorship and postvention. In: Maris RW, Berman A, Silverman M (eds.) *Comprehensive Textbook of Suicidology*. Guilford Press, New York, pp. 536–61.

King CA, Segal H, Kaminski K, Naylor MW (1995) A prospective study of adolescent suicidal behavior following hospitalization. *Suicide Life Threatening Behavior*, **25**(3): 327.

King EA, Baldwin DS, Sinclair JMA *et al* (2001a) The Wessex recent in-patient suicide study, 1: Case-control study of 234 recently discharged psychiatric patient suicides. *British Journal of Psychiatry*, **178**: 531–6.

King EA, Baldwin DS, Sinclair JMA, Campbell MJ (2001b) The Wessex recent in-patient suicide study, 2: Case-control study of 59 in-patient suicides. *British Journal of Psychiatry*, **17**: 537–42.

Knox KL, Conwell Y, Caine ED (2004) If suicide is a public health problem, what are we doing to prevent it? *American Journal of Public Health*, **94**: 37–45.

Lawrence D, Holman CDJ, Jablensky AV *et al* (2001) Increasing rates of suicide in Western Australian psychiatric patients: a record linkage study. *Acta Psychiatrica Scandinavia*, **104**: 443–51.

Maas M, Johnson M, Moorehead S (1996) Classifying nursing-sensitive patient outcomes. *Journal of Nursing Scholarship*, **28**(4): 295–301.

McCloskey JC, Bulechek GM (eds.) (2000) *Iowa Interventions Project Nursing Interventions Classification (NIC)*, 3rd edn.

McGillis-Hall L (2004) Nursing staff mix models and outcomes. *Journal of Advanced Nursing*, **44**: 217–26.

McKenzie I, Wurr C (2001) Early suicide following discharge from psychiatric hospital. *Suicide and Life Threatening Behavior*, **31**(3): 358–63.

Murray HA (1981) Outline of a conception of personality. In: Shneidman E (ed.) *Endeavors in Psychology: Selections From the Personology of Henry A. Murray*. Harper & Row, New York, p. 216.

Pirkola S, Sohlman B, Wahlbeck K (2005) The characteristics of suicides within a week of discharge after psychiatric hospitalization – a nationwide register study. *BMC Psychiatry*, **5**: 32.

Pokorny AD, Kaplan HB (1976) Suicide following psychiatric hospitalization. *Journal of Nervous and Mental Disease*, **162**(2): 119–25.

Qin P, Nordentoft M (2005) Suicide risk in relation to psychiatric hospitalization – evidence based on longitudinal registers. *Archives of General Psychiatry*, **62**: 427–32.

Ruskin R, Sakinofsky I, Bably RM *et al* (2004) Impact of patient suicide on psychiatrists and psychiatric trainees. *Academic Psychiatry*, **28**: 104–110.

Sullivan A, Barron C, Bezmen J, Rivera J, Zapata-Vega M (2005) The safe treatment of the suicidal patient in an adult inpatient setting: a proactive preventive approach. *Psychiatric Quarterly*, **76**(1): 67–83.

Tourangeau AE, Doran DM, McGillis Hall L, O'Brien Pallas L, Pringle D, Tu JV, Cranley LA (2006) Impact of hospital nursing care on 30-day mortality for acute medical patients. *Journal of Advanced Nursing*, **57**(1): 32–44.

Troister T, Links P, Cutcliffe JR (2008) Review of predictors of suicide within 1 year of discharge from a psychiatric hospital. *Current Psychiatry Reports*, **10**: 60–5.

Valente SM (1994) Psychotherapist reactions to the suicide of a patient. *American Journal of Orthopsychiatry*, **64**: 614–21.

Van Praag HM (2003) A stubborn behaviour: the failure of antidepressants to reduce suicide rates. *World Journal of Biological Psychiatry*, **4**: 184–91.

Yang KA, Simms LM, Yin JT (1999) Factors influencing nursing-sensitive outcomes in Taiwanese nursing homes. *Online Journal of Issues in Nursing*, **4**(2). Available at: http://www.nursingworld.org/MainMenuCategories/ANAMarketplace/ANAPeriodicals/OJIN/TableofContents/Volume41999/No2Sep1999/ArticlePreviousTopic/TaiwaneseNursingHomes.aspx.

Yim PHW, Yip PSF, Li RHY *et al* (2004) Suicide after discharge from psychiatric inpatient care: a case-control study in Hong Kong. *Australian and New Zealand Journal of Medicine*, **38**(1–2): 65–72.

CHAPTER 2

A review of suicide and self-harm prevention policies and national suicide prevention strategies

> Given the multi-determined nature of suicidal behavior, many interventions tend to be multifaceted and it is not clear which components produced the desired outcomes (John Mann and Dianne Currier, 2011, p. 79)

Introduction

Suicide and suicidal behaviours are a major public health issue. Each year approximately one million people worldwide complete suicide and ten million attempt to do so (WHO, 2011). Estimates indicate that these numbers will increase if preventive and treatment efforts are not forcefully supported by legislative and economic measures (Wasserman and Wasserman, 2009).

Suicide prevention has become an important task in today's society. Perhaps the first formal example of this development was the Lemberg Volunteer Rescue Society (1893–1906) and, later on, the National Save-A-Life League (New York, USA) and the constitution of a Suicide Prevention Department by the Salvation Army, in London, UK, both founded in 1906 (Pompili, 2011; De Leo, 2011). Nowadays, a large number of countries have prevention plans or actions for suicide and suicidal behaviours, and producing such plans has become a priority for many governments. However, according to the WHO (2011), suicide prevention has not been adequately addressed, due in essence to a lack of awareness of suicide as a major public health problem and the taboo in many societies about discussing or talking openly about it. We begin to attempt to remedy this (in some small way) by starting our open dialogue about suicide by presenting and reviewing some global issues regarding suicide prevention policies and national suicide prevention strategies, in so doing drawing attention to the roles of nurses in this domain.

Suicide prevention plans

In order to help combat the phenomenon of suicide, a wide range of suicide prevention programs have been developed (see for example Gould *et al*, 2003; Mann *et al*, 2005; Mann and Currier, 2011). Nevertheless, there is a lack of sustainable evidence-based prevention programs (Mann *et al*, 2005; Althaus and Hegerl, 2003). As mentioned by the Suicide Prevention Action Network (SPAN) in the USA,

> the single greatest obstacle to effective prevention of suicide is the lack of evaluation research (SPAN USA, Inc., 2001, p. 19).

This may be a result of the methodological difficulties involved in evaluating prevention interventions using suicide as a primary outcome due to its low base rate. Other issues are common to the multidimensional level of interventions: the difficulty in identifying which action or component produces the desired outcome, and the lack of a system to review the effectiveness of suicide prevention programs (Rodgers *et al*, 2007; Mann and Currier, 2011). From an international perspective, the existence of different healthcare systems, and the unequal availability of health services and specialised mental healthcare, may also contribute to these methodological difficulties.

A number of efforts have been made to produce evidence from robust and rigorous methods and research designs, so as to evaluate the effectiveness of prevention plans and identify the best suicide prevention practices: Prevention Effectiveness and Evaluation (SPAN, 2001), the Evidence-Based Practices Project (EBPP) (Rodgers *et al*, 2007), and Optimizing Suicide Prevention Programs and Their Implementation in Europe (OSPI-Europe) – an evidence-based multi-level approach (Hegerl *et al*, 2009). One of the aims of the SPAN project is to provide the basic tools needed to create effective suicide prevention plans (SPAN, 2001). The EBPP's primary goals are to review suicide prevention programs and, based on those reviews, to create an online registry of evidence-based suicide prevention programs (Rodgers *et al*, 2007). The aim of OSPI-Europe is to provide diverse regional policy makers and the European Commission with an evidence-based, efficient concept for suicide prevention, along with the corresponding materials and instruments for multi-faceted intervention and guidelines for the implementation process (Hegerl *et al*, 2009).

Five central areas emerge in suicide prevention programs: education and awareness for the general public and for professionals; screening tools for at-risk individuals; treatment of psychiatric disorders; restriction of access to lethal means; and responsible media reporting of suicide (Mann *et al*, 2005; Mann and Currier,

Table 2.1 Common areas for policy development contained within national suicide prevention strategies. (Adapted from WHO (2007), with permission; source: Cutcliffe and Stevenson, 2008a)

- Public awareness campaigns to increase awareness of suicide as a preventable problem, development of broad-based support for prevention efforts, and stigma reduction
- Community development and implementation of suicide prevention programmes
- Improved access to services for people who are suicidal and their loved ones
- Support of service delivery through development of guidelines and linkages
- Media education to improve reporting and portrayals of suicide in the media
- Training for caregivers to improve recognition of at-risk behaviour and delivery of effective treatments
- Incorporation of licensing standards for professional caregivers
- Development and promotion of effective clinical and professional practices
- Initiatives to reduce access to lethal means and methods of self-harm
- Support of research and evaluation
- Improve surveillance systems
- Evaluation of the effectiveness of new or existing suicide prevention interventions

2011). Based on the WHO prevention plans, Cutcliffe and Stevenson (2008a,b) identified five policy directions which have implications for the practice and/or educational needs of mental health nurses: training for caregivers to improve recognition of at-risk behaviour; development and promotion of effective clinical and professional practices; initiatives to reduce access to lethal means; improved surveillance systems; and training for caregivers to improve delivery of effective treatments. These authors summarise the WHO recommendations for national suicide prevention strategies, and these are displayed in Table 2.1.

In all recommendations and plans, three main areas have emerged as priorities: education (of the general public, professionals and those involved in a suicidal situation); community and policy challenges; and clinical practice. In these three areas, the following aspects should be taken into consideration:

- **Education**: campaigns to increase public awareness of suicide as a preventable problem, to develop broad-based support for prevention efforts, and to reduce stigma; training for caregivers to improve recognition of at-risk behaviour and delivery of effective treatments; initiatives to reduce access to lethal means and methods of self-harm; media education to improve reporting and portrayals of suicide in the media

- **Community and policy challenges**: community development and implementation of suicide prevention programs; evaluation of the effectiveness of new or existing suicide prevention interventions; and support of research and evaluation
- **Clinical practice**: support of service delivery through the development of guidelines and linkages; development and promotion of effective clinical and professional practices and improvement of surveillance systems; and improved access to services for people who are suicidal and their loved ones

In light of the importance of these issues, they should be analysed separately.

Education

This is an important and central issue in terms of a public approach to suicide prevention. Low levels of mental health literacy are directly associated with stereotypes that do not promote professional help-seeking behaviours and which create barriers to treatment seeking. Stigma is one of the most powerful obstacles to accessing healthcare and an important issue in suicide prevention efforts (Goldsmith *et al*, 2002).

Promotion of mental health literacy, such as knowledge and beliefs about so-called mental disorders or mental health/behavioural problems which aid their recognition, management or prevention, is necessary for appropriate health decision-making. Particularly in the field of suicide, some ideas such as 'suicide is inevitable' and 'we cannot do anything' or 'it is an act of courage or heroism' or 'it is the only solution for life's problems' can create difficulties in dealing with these behaviours.

Some public education and destigmatisation programs focus on so-called mental illness, mostly depression, rather than specifically on suicide prevention, in part due to concerns about over-exposure to suicide which may normalise or inadvertently encourage suicidal behaviour (Mann and Currier, 2011). This can be explained by the existing myth that talking about suicide gives the person 'the idea' or leads to an increase in the number of cases.

Although education and awareness appear to be good strategies, proving their efficacy seems more difficult. In fact, large-scale public education campaigns focused on depression suggest modest effects on attitudes regarding the causes and treatment of depression which become more evident when suicide rates are compared (see Table 2.2). Studies on suicide education and awareness campaigns have confirmed that, despite better knowledge of depression, this knowledge

Table 2.2 Awareness and education intervention campaigns.

Authors	Country	Target
Regier *et al* (1988)	USA	Community
Paykel *et al* (1998)	UK	Community
Akroyd and Wyllie (2002)	New Zealand	Community
Hegerl *et al* (2003)	Germany	Community
Hickie (2004)	Australia	Community

does not lead to changes in attitudes regarding suicide risk factors and treatment adherence. It is even harder to prove the efficacy of these studies on suicide because it is a rare phenomenon.

However, there is an example of partial effectiveness. The Nuremberg Alliance Against Depression (Hegerl *et al*, 2006) reported declines in suicide attempts of 26.5% (mostly in high-risk methods: hanging, jumping, shooting), in the intervention region in comparison with the control region. Unfortunately, there are no significant differences in completed suicides compared to the control region. Nonetheless, the decline in suicide attempts is quite significant, since those individuals who make suicide attempts have emerged as an identifiable high-risk population that is characterised by ongoing mental health problems and high mortality (Beautrais, 2004a,b).

Although these results are valuable, it is necessary to understand what can be improved. Goldney and Fisher (2008) conducted a naturalistic study in Australia between 1998 and 2004 on a random and representative population sample to examine the changes in mental health literacy and treatment-seeking of those with major depression, both with and without suicidal ideation, and those who were neither depressed nor suicidal. Results indicated that there was marked improvement in mental health literacy in all three groups, although there was less change for those most in need of intervention, ie. those with major depression and suicidal ideation and in situations in which there was a major risk of suicide. This study highlights the limitations of broad-based community education programs and the authors argue that more focused suicide prevention initiatives are required, specifically for those who are depressed and suicidal.

Considering both technicians and gatekeepers, all studies emphasise the role of primary care physicians or general practitioners as a priority in suicide prevention strategies. This is explained by the fact that approximately 83% of those who die by suicide have had contact with a primary care physician within a year of their death, and up to 66% within a month (Andersen *et al*, 2000; Luoma *et al*, 2002). In addition, a pattern of contacting more than one general practitioner per quarter occurred significantly more often in the suicide quarter than during the year before, predominantly in those older than 60 (Deisenhamer *et al*, 2007). Indeed, every member of the care community staff is important and so are the nurses and their education, training, responsibility and role.

As Titelman and Wasserman (2009) pointed out, a difference must be made between having an immediate impact on conscious attitudes and the more difficult challenge of influencing less conscious individual and cultural ambivalent attitudes to suicide prevention. Attitudes towards patients who deliberately self-harm are complex and multidimensional, demanding professional skills, an emphatic approach and confidence. This is crucial for dealing with prevention.

In this field, nurses are recognised for their proximity to patients and their empathy, comprehension and positive attitudes to people who self-harm (McLaughlin, 1994; Anderson, 1997; Crawford *et al*, 2003; Anderson and Standen, 2007; Sun *et al*, 2007; Dip and Gijbels, 2010), even when compared with different professionals (Ramon *et al*, 1975; Catalan *et al*, 1980; Hawton *et al*, 1981; Mackay and Barrowclough, 2005). However, the evaluation of patients, which is very elucidatory, may be more important. As Talseth *et al* (1997, 1999) found, nurses made a concerted effort to communicate a sense of acceptance rather than condemnation. The nurses focused on listening without prejudice, and this appears to be very important in order to understand and build a therapeutic relationship. Thus mental health nurses have a central role in this field to provide education and awareness for other professionals in health settings and the general public in community care.

To sum up, and based on the reasons mentioned above, it is difficult to evaluate the campaigns in this domain. Nonetheless, the programs seem more effective if they are integrated into a multilevel and multifaceted intervention, can create synergistic effects with different partners, and consider the public's cultural specificity.

In this section, the initiatives to reduce access to lethal means and methods of self-harm and media education to improve reporting and portrayals of suicide in the media will also be presented. These issues are not specifically part of the role of mental health nurses, but any nurse can advocate or/and lobby for these aspects, which are considered effective in preventing suicide in almost all literature. The reduction of access to lethal means and methods will be analysed in another chapter on the safe environment.

Community and policy challenges

Regarding community and policy challenges, suicidal behaviours should be addressed as a public health problem and discussed openly. It is necessary to plan actions so as to identify the real magnitude of the problem. In some countries there is a trend towards under-reporting suicidal behaviours, both completed and attempted (Bertolote, 2001; De Leo *et al*, 2002; Sakinofsky, 2003; Andriessen, 2006; Mäkinen, 2006). Other countries, namely some of the 70 least developed countries (mostly in Africa, but also in Southeast Asia), do not maintain vital registration systems because of the lack of means to collect and process data (Bertolote and Fleischmann, 2009). Due to the variety of concepts around this phenomenon (suicide ideation, parasuicide, self-harm, self-cutter, self-injury, attempted suicide), some countries lack reliable data on suicidal behaviours, which occur in ratios that are generally around 20 or even 30 per suicide among young people and 3 or less per suicide among the elderly (Wasserman and Wasserman, 2009).

These differences and classification difficulties can be an obstacle to research and, more importantly, to the development and evaluation of suicide prevention plans (in terms of their effectiveness) because the full impact of these phenomena, and consequently how the interventions modify behaviours and improve results, is still unknown.

According to SPAN (2001), the Principles of Suicide Prevention Effectiveness are the following:

- prevention programmes should be designed to enhance protective factors. They should also work toward reversing or reducing known risk factors. Risk for negative health outcomes can be reduced or eliminated for some or all of a population
- prevention programmes should be long-term, with repeat interventions to reinforce the original prevention goals
- family-focused prevention efforts may have a greater impact than strategies that focus only on individuals
- community programmes that include media campaigns and policy changes are more effective when individual and family interventions accompany them
- community programmes need to strengthen norms that support help-seeking behaviour in all settings, including family, work, school, and community
- prevention programming should be adapted to address the specific nature of the problem in the local community or population group
- the higher the level of risk of the target population, the more intensive the prevention effort must be and the earlier it must begin

- prevention programmes should be age-specific, developmentally appropriate, and culturally sensitive
- prevention programs should be implemented with no or minimal differences from how they were designed and tested (SPAN USA, Inc., 2001, p. 12)

It can be concluded that it is necessary to understand the population, respect their culture and specificities, and act with all of the elements in mind in order to obtain better results. As the IASP theme for the World Prevention Day states:

Think globally, plan nationally, act locally (IASP, 2008).

There is some evidence on screening tools for at-risk individuals. However, some concerns arise with this issue. There are many more risk factors than there are people who have suicidal behaviours. Many false positives, which can demoralise technicians and give them a false perception of some symptoms or signs, can be found. On the other hand, it does not guarantee that identified individuals will move into treatment (Mann and Currier, 2011). However, this can be effective in specific at-risk populations because of their age (eg. adolescents), context (eg. school) or history (eg. history of suicidal behaviours). Nurses can lead intervention projects in this field of community care (schools, work settings), but also inside hospitals, where the risk of suicide among technicians (nurses and physicians) increases.

Despite the methodological issues referred to, research studies should be developed to evaluate the impact of the prevention programmes. However, more variables need to be considered, such as suicidal behaviours and wellbeing. Systematic reviews and meta-analyses with discussion of validity and confidence intervals; randomised controlled trials with discussion of validity, magnitude, and clinical significance; cohort studies; case-control studies; cross-sectional surveys; and case reports can help to achieve the best global practices in suicide prevention. The lack of an evidence base is common, and all experiences across cultures should also be considered. Much of the research being conducted continues to be clinical or epidemiological in nature. More research focusing on prevention activities is needed (Suicide Prevention Resource Center and SPAN USA, 2010).

Support research in this field is imperative, but all funding should demand that an evaluative component be included in the program so that the activity that has been funded can be evaluated (Lester, 2011). Unfortunately, suicide prevention stakeholders consider the relative paucity of both public and private sector funding for research to be one of the most serious challenges which the suicide prevention community faces (Suicide Prevention Resource Center and SPAN USA, 2010).

Clinical practice

Clinical practice is central to suicide prevention. Practitioners should use evidence-based interventions when these are available, and

> focus should be on what patients feel rather than on how they can be categorized (Pompili, 2011, p. 21).

Clinical practice is the setting where technicians deal with major problems and where the risk of suicide is higher. In fact, suicide attempters are the population with the highest risk of re-attempting suicide and dying by suicide (Mishara, 2007). It is estimated that 4–7% of the 32,000 suicides in the USA each year occur in inpatient psychiatric settings (Wolfersdorf, 2000). The use of interventions based on research brings more confidence and certainty into the field. Unfortunately, the lack of evidence-based interventions for working with people with suicidal behaviours is real (Cutcliffe and Stevenson, 2008a,b) and can be one of the most significant obstacles in suicide prevention (Pompili, 2011). These difficulties are greater in the clinical setting, where a trial with internal validity demonstrates the efficacy of an intervention, but the findings are difficult to apply to real clinical settings (Cimpean and Drake, 2010). As Michel (2010, p. 4) points out:

> clinical suicide prevention thus demands approaches that reduce the likelihood of suicidal behavior beyond the simple calculation of odds based on risk factors elicited in a usual impersonal clinical interview.

Addressing suicide in the clinical encounter with a suicidal patient requires a different therapeutic attitude, and hospitals should handle suicide more effectively (Michel, 2010; Pompili, 2011). Suicidal behaviour is not a psychiatric diagnosis, such as depression or schizophrenia, but it is an act (or action) that always has its very personal and individual inner truth (Michel, 2010).

Some authors write that about 90% of individuals who attempt or complete suicide meet diagnostic criteria for a psychiatric disorder, most often mood disorder, substance use disorders, psychoses, and personality disorders (Henriksson *et al*, 1993; Bertolote *et al*, 2004; Lönnqvist, 2009). Nevertheless, there are other authors who do not confirm this idea. Maris *et al* (2000) state that most people who have completed suicide are sad, but not necessarily clinically depressed[1]. Hence suicide and depression or so-called mental illness cannot be automatically associated, although this can happen (Cutcliffe and Stevenson, 2008a,b). However, the experience of putting patients who have attempted suicide into groups according to their characteristic profiles can lead to errors (Rapeli and Botega, 2005).

1 Which echoes Shneidman's views.

Once again, what is important is that the person has received quality care, which implies treatment that is person-centred, not diagnosis-centred (Leenaars, 2004). Moreover, many features have been associated with suicide risk, but no single factor has been demonstrated to be necessary or sufficient to cause suicide (Pompili, 2010). A patient-oriented approach is crucial and a narrative-based approach is not a contradiction to evidence-based practice (Jobes, 2010; Greenhalgh and Hurwitz, 1999; Michel and Valach, 2010). In fact, narratives provide a medium for the education of both patients and health professionals and may also expand and enrich the research agenda (Greenhalgh and Hurwitz, 1999).

Another issue is the right time to act directly with patients in a collaborative approach. Michel (2010) stated that the fundamental importance of a collaborative professional relationship – the alliance – tends to be neglected, particularly in the age of managed care, time pressures, and the tendency to reduce human suffering to mere diagnostic entities. As a result of this context, we are witnessing a change from long-term inpatient hospitalisations to short-term inpatient stays (Cutcliffe and Stevenson, 2008a,b).

These changes raise the importance of an interpersonal approach, brief interventions and community mental healthcare services (if these are available). Nurses have a role to play in this field if they consider interpersonal relationships to be central to effective mental health nursing, as defined by Altschul (1972).

Past studies have shown that nurses are available to connect/engage with suicidal people in order to reconnect the person with humanity (Talseth *et al*, 1997, 1999; Sun *et al*, 2005; Cutcliffe *et al*, 2006; Cutcliffe and Stevenson, 2007).

In Norway, using a qualitative methodology (phenomenological-hermeneutic method inspired by Ricoeur), Talseth *et al* (1997, 1999) studied 21 patients who had thought about, expressed the wish or even attempted to commit suicide and who narrated their experiences of receiving care from mental health nurses. Two main themes with subthemes were found: *Conforming*: attending to the patient's basic needs; seeing the patient; having time for the patient; being with the patient; listening to the patient without prejudice; being open with the patient; accepting the patient's feelings; communicating hope to the patient; and *Lack of conforming*: overlooking the patient's basic needs; not seeing the patient; not having time for the patient; leaving the patient to himself or herself; listening to the patient with prejudice; not being open with the patient; denying the patient his or her feelings; communicating hopelessness to the patient.

Regarding nurses, 17 Norwegian and two Danish registered nurses specialised in psychiatric nursing narrated their experiences in caring for suicidal psychiatric inpatients. Two main themes with subthemes were found: *Distance*, which included compassion without emotional identification, mistrusting the patient, being responsible for the patient's actions, feelings of guilt, rejecting the patient, being rejected by the patient, and focusing on the nurse; and *Closeness*, which included compassion with emotional identification, trusting the patient through contact, responsibility for the patient making his or her own agenda, being temporarily rejected by the patient, listening to the patient, and focusing on the patient.

In Taiwan, Sun *et al* (2005, 2006) developed a suicide nursing care theory. A qualitative approach using grounded theory was adopted. A total of 15 people who had either had suicidal ideas or had attempted suicide and 15 psychiatric nurses were interviewed and observed. Four categories surfaced in the nursing care theory related to the nurses' action/interaction strategies: the holistic assessment of people who are suicidal (vigilant observations, interviewing skills, warning signals of suicide and information sharing); providing protection (monitoring and supervising patients, protecting patients from dangerous items, protecting patients' safety and preventive strategies in crisis situations); providing basic care (mental and emotional care and physical care); and providing advanced care (compassionate art of nursing, nurses' roles, communication skills and instilling hope).

Similarly, Cutcliffe *et al* (2006) and Cutcliffe and Stevenson (2007) studied 20 patients from South Yorkshire and Newcastle who had had a suicidal crisis in the past. They used a modified grounded theory method. The psychosocial central key of this theory is 'reconnecting the person with humanity'. The subcategories are: 'reflecting an image of humanity' (stage one) – experiencing intense, warm, care-based human-to-human contact; implicitly challenging suicidal constructs as a result of encountering contrary experiences; 'guiding the individual back to humanity' (stage two) – nurturing insight and understanding; supporting and strengthening pre-suicidal beliefs; encountering a novel interpersonal, helping relationship; and 'learning to live' (stage three) – accommodating an existential crisis, past, present and future; going on in the context set by the existential relationship with suicide.

These studies in different regions share some common ideas, especially the necessity and subsequent therapeutic value of co-presencing (and all the micro-skills and qualities that such a phrase captures) in the care of the person with suicidal tendencies (Cutcliffe and Stevenson, 2008a,b), but they also confirm patients' recognition of the nurses' central role in this field.

To sum up, the priority should be a patient-oriented approach in order to explore and understand the 'death-oriented' position with a sense of acceptance rather than condemnation, in a non-judgmental and supportive environment so as to connect people to life and bring them to a 'life-oriented' position. Nurses become more comfortable with effective co-presencing and listening (Cutcliffe and Stevenson, 2008a,b), and sometimes giving some time and attention is the most important thing.

In addition, can nurses deal with people who attempt suicide without feeling some discomfort? This nurse–patient interaction can bring nurses some discomfort and stress. These feelings can be intensified if the patient completes suicide, so that the idea of failure increases. When the individual risk signs come together with this suffering, it is the clinician who is often at risk of suicide (Jobes *et al*, 2000). These feelings can explain, but not justify, a less defensive, less risk management-oriented position (Cutcliffe and Stevenson, 2008a,b). On the one hand, although some literature confirms the idea that many nurses have difficulties dealing with death and suicide, on the other hand, more frequent contact with suicide-prone patients among nurses has been found to be related to more positive attitudes towards attempted suicide patients (Samuelsson *et al*, 1997). In addition, 'a positive correlation between the level of client and/or clinician interpersonal engagement (and associated emotional investment) and the extent of emotional load experienced by the clinician' can also occur (Cutcliffe and Stevenson, 2008a, p. 347).

Mental health nurses need to have a high level of self-awareness and use it as a tool for clinical practice. They should know and reflect upon their own attitudes towards suicide so that they are able to stay close, emotionally, psychologically and physically, to the person with suicidal behaviours (Santos, 2001; Cutcliffe and Stevenson, 2008a,b).

Developing self-awareness is a very important task, built in a process of dialectic interaction with the other person (Hegel, 1977). Self-awareness is also being conscious of our attitudes and presence, and knowing how they can influence the other person's behaviour. As Michel (2010) points out, nothing threatens the whole question of clinical suicide prevention more than professional fear, lethargy, cynicism, and doubt in the face of suicidal risk.

To avoid these feelings and attitudes, regular clinical supervision of nurses can help them to improve their performance and clinical practices, as well as their wellbeing. In addition, this can also promote self-awareness and training for nurses so that they can deal with suicidal patients in situations in which death and suicide are more frequent.

References

Akroyd S, Wyllie J (2002) *Impacts of National Media Campaign to Counter Stigma and Discrimination Associated with Mental Illness: Survey 4*, Publication 9-20-0004. New Zealand Ministry of Health, Wellington.

Andriessen K (2006) Do we need to be cautious in evaluating suicide statistics? *European Journal of Public Health* **16**: 445–7.

Althaus D, Hegerl U (2003) The evaluation of suicide prevention activities: state of the art. *World Journal of Biologyical Psychiatry* **4**: 156–65.

Altschul A (1972) *Patient–Nurse Interaction: A Study of Interaction Patterns in Acute Psychiatric Wards*. Churchill Livingstone, Edinburgh.

Andersen U, Andersen M, Rosholm J, Gram L (2000) Contacts to the healthcare system prior to suicide: a comprehensive analysis using registers for general and psychiatric hospital admissions, contacts to general practitioners and practising specialists and drug prescriptions. *Acta Psychiatrica Scandinavia* **102**: 126–34.

Anderson M (1997) Nurses' attitudes towards suicidal behavior: a comparative study of community mental health nurses and nurses working in an accident and emergency department. *Journal of Advanced Nursing* **25**(6): 1283–91.

Anderson M, Standen P (2007) Attitudes towards suicide among nurses and doctors working with children and young people who self-harm. *Journal of Psychiatric and Mental Health Nursing* **14**(5): 470–7.

Beautrais A (2004a) Further suicidal behaviour amongst medically serious suicide attempters. *Suicide and Life Threatening Behavior* **34**(1): 1–11.

Beautrais AL (2004b) Subsequent mortality in medically serious suicide attempts: a 5 year follow-up. *Australian and New Zealand Journal of Psychiatry* **37**(5): 595–9.

Bertolote J (2001) Suicide in the world: an epidemiological overview, 1995–2000. In: Wasserman D (ed.) *Suicide: An Unnecessary death*. Martin Dunitz, London, pp. 3–10.

Bertolote J, Fleischmann A (2009) A global perspective on the magnitude of suicide mortality. In Wasserman D, Wasserman C (eds.) *Oxford Textbook of Suicidology and Suicide Prevention. A Global Perspective*. Oxford University Press, Oxford, pp. 91–8.

Bertolote J, Fleischmann A, De Leo D, Wasserman D (2004) Psychiatric diagnoses and suicide: revisiting the evidence. *Crisis* **25**(4): 147–55.

Catalan J, Marsack P, Hawton K, Whitwell D, Fagg, J, Bancroft J (1980) Comparison of doctors and nurses in the assessment of deliberate self-poisoning patients. *Psychological Medicine* **10**(3): 483–91.

Cimpean D, Drake R (2011) Evidence-based medicine in mental health: general principles. In: Pompili M, Tatarelli R (eds.) *Evidence-Based Practice in Suicidology*. Hogrefe Publishing, Cambridge, MA, pp. 27–44.

Crawford T, Geraghty W, Street K, Simonoff E (2003) Staff knowledge and attitudes towards deliberate self-harm in adolescents. *Journal of Adolescence* **26**(5): 619–29.

Cutcliffe J, Stevenson C (2007) *Care of the Suicidal Person*. Elsevier, Edinburgh.

Cutcliffe J, Stevenson C (2008a) Never the twain? Reconciling national suicide prevention strategies with the practice, educational, and policy needs of mental health nurses (part one). *International Journal of Mental Health Nursing* **17**: 341–50.

Cutcliffe J, Stevenson C (2008b) Never the twain? Reconciling national suicide prevention strategies with the practice, educational, and policy needs of mental health nurses (part two). *International Journal of Mental Health Nursing* **17**: 351–62.

Cutcliffe J, Stevenson C, Jackson S, Smith P (2006) A modified grounded theory study of how psychiatric nurses work with suicidal people. *International Journal of Nursing Studies* **43**(7): 791–802.

De Leo D (2011) The World Health Organization: approach to evidence-based suicide. In: Pompili M, Tatarelli R (eds.) *Evidence-Based Practice in Suicidology*. Hogrefe Publishing, Cambridge, MA, pp. 55–64.

De Leo D, Bertolote J, Lester D (2002) Self-directed violence. In: Krug E, Dahlberg L, Mercy J *et al* (eds) *World Report on Violence and Health*. World Health Organization, pp. 183–212.

Deisenhammer E, Huber M, Kemmler G, Weiss E, Hinterhuber, H (2007) Suicide victims' contacts with physicians during the year before death. *European Archives of Psychiatry Clinical Neuroscience* **257**: 480–5.

Dip L, Gijbels H (2010) An examination of emergency department nurses' attitudes towards deliberate self-harm in an Irish teaching hospital. *International Emergency Nursing* **18**: 29–35.

Goldsmith SK, Pellmar TC, Kleinman AM, Bunney WE (eds.) (2002) Reducing Suicide: a National Imperative. National Academies Press, Washington, DC. http://www.nap.edu/openbook.php?isbn=0309083214 (accessed 6 October 2011).

Goldney R, Fisher L (2008) Have broad-based community and professional education programs influenced mental health literacy and treatment seeking of those with major depression and suicidal ideation? *Suicide and Life-Threatening Behavior* **38**(2).

Gould MS, Greenberg TDM, Shaffer D (2003) Youth suicide risk and preventive interventions: a review of the past 10 years. *Journal of the American Academy of Child and Adolescent Psychiatry* **42**: 386–405.

Greenhalgh T, Hurwitz B (1999) Why study narratives? *British Medical Journal* **318**: 48–50.

Hawton K, Marsack P, Fagg J (1981) The attitudes of psychiatrists to deliberate self-poisoning: comparison with physicians and nurses. *British Journal of Medical Psychology* **54**: 341–8.

Hegel GWF (1807/1977) *Phenomenology of Spirit, Part B*. Oxford University Press, Oxford.

Hegerl U, Althaus D, Schmidtke A, Niklewski G (2006) The alliance against depression: 2-year evaluation of a community-based intervention to reduce suicidality. *Psychological Medicine* **36**(9): 1225–33.

Hegerl U, Wittenburg L, Arensman E *et al* (2009) Optimizing Suicide Prevention Programs and Their Implementation in Europe (OSPI-Europe): an evidence-based multi-level approach. *BMC Public Health* **9**, 428.

Henriksson M, Aro H, Marttunen M, Heikkinen M, Isometsä E, Kuoppasalmi K, Lönnqvist J (1993) Mental disorders and comorbidity in suicide. *American Journal of Psychiatry* **150**(6): 935–40.

Hickie, I (2004) Can we reduce the burden of depression? The Australian experience with beyond blue: the national depression initiative. *Australasian Psychiatry: Bulletin of*

Royal Australian and New Zealand College of Psychiatrists **12**(suppl.): S38–46; PMID: 15715829.

International Association for Suicide Prevention and World Health Organization (2008) *Suicide Prevention*. http://www.iasp.info/wspd/pdf/2008_wspd_flyer_english.pdf (accessed 25 June 2012).

Jobes D (2010) Summary, next steps, and conclusion. In: Michel K, Jobes, D (eds). *Building a Therapeutic Alliance with the Suicidal Patient*. American Psychological Association, pp. 379–94.

Jobes D, Luoma J, Hustead L, Mann, R (2000) In the wake of suicide: Survivorship and postvention. In: Maris, RW, Berman A, Silverman M (eds). *Comprehensive Textbook of Suicidology*. Guilford Press, New York, pp. 536–61.

Leenaars A (2004) *Psychotherapy with Suicidal People: A Person-centered Approach*. Wiley, Chichester.

Lester D (2011) Evidence-based suicide prevention by helplines: a meta-analysis. In: Pompili M, Tatarelli R (eds.) *Evidence-Based Practice in Suicidology*. Hogrefe Publishing, Cambridge, MA, pp. 139–52.

Lönnqvist J (2009) Major psychiatric disorders in suicide and suicide attmepters. In Wasserman D, Wasserman C (eds.) *Oxford Textbook of Suicidology and Suicide Prevention. A Global Perspective*. Oxford University Press, Oxford, pp. 275–86.

Luoma J, Martin C, Pearson J (2002) Contact with mental health and primary care providers before suicide: a review of the evidence. *American Journal of Psychiatry*, **159**: 909–16.

Mackay N, Barrowclough C (2005) Accident and emergency staff's perceptions of deliberate self-harm: attributions, emotions and willingness to help. *British Journal of Clinical Psychology* **44**: 255–67.

Mäkinen J (2006) Suicide mortality of Eastern European regions before and after the communist period. *Social Science and Medicine* **63**: 307–19.

Mann J, Currier D (2011) Evidence-based suicide prevention strategies: an overview. In: Pompili M, Tatarelli R (eds.) *Evidence-Based Practice in Suicidology*. Hogrefe Publishing, Cambridge, MA, pp. 67–88.

Mann J, Apter A, Bertolote J *et al* (2005) Suicide prevention strategies: a systematic review. *Journal of the American Medical Association* **294**: 2064–74.

Maris RW, Berman AL, Silverman MM (2000) *Comprehensive Textbook of Suicidology*. Guilford Press, New York.

McLaughlin C (1994) Casualty nurses' attitudes to attempted suicide. *Journal of Advanced Nursing* **20**(6): 1111–18.

Michel K (2010) Introduction. In: Michel K, Jobes, D (eds). *Building a Therapeutic Alliance with the Suicidal Patient*. American Psychological Association, pp. 3–10.

Michel K, Valach L (2010) The narrative interview with the suicidal patient. In: Michel K, Jobes, D (eds). *Building a Therapeutic Alliance with the Suicidal Patient*. American Psychological Association, pp. 63–80.

Mishara B (2007) Foreword. In Cutcliffe J, Stevenson C (2007) *Care of the Suicidal Person: XIII–XIV*. Elsevier, Edinburgh.

Paykel S, Hart D, Priest R (1998) Changes in public attitudes to depression during the Defeat Depression Campaign. *British Journal of Psychiatry* **173**: 519–22.

Pompili M (2011). Evidence-based practice in suicidology: what we need and what we need to know. In: Pompili M, Tatarelli R (eds.) *Evidence-Based Practice in Suicidology*. Hogrefe Publishing, Cambridge, MA, pp. 3–26.

Ramon S, Bancroft J, Skrimshire A (1975) Attitudes towards self-poisoning among physicians and nurses in a general hospital. *British Journal of Psychiatry* **127**: 257–264.

Rapeli C, Botega, N (2005) Clinical profiles of serious suicide attempters consecutively admitted to a university-based hospital: a cluster analysis study. *Revista Brasileira de Psiquiatria* **27**(4): 285–9.

Regier D, Hirschfeld R, Goodwin F, Burke J, Lazar J, Judd L (1988) The NIMH Depression Awareness, Recognition, and Treatment Program: structure, aims, and scientific basis. *American Journal of Psychiatry* **145**(11): 1351–7.

Rodgers P, Sudak H, Silverman M, Litts D (2007) Evidence-Based Practices Project for suicide prevention. *Suicide and Life-Threatening Behavior* **37**(2): 154–64.

Sakinofsky I (2003) Suicide: the persisting challenge. *Canadian Journal of Psychiatry* **48**, 289–291.

Samuelsson M, Sunbring Y, Winell I, Asberg M (1997) Nurses' attitudes to attempted suicide patients. *Scandinavian Journal of Caring Sciences* **11**: 232–7.

Santos J (2001) A atitude dos enfermeiros perante o indivíduo para-suicida. *Revista de Psiquiatria Clínica* **22**(1): 101–11.

SPAN USA, Inc. (2001) *Suicide Prevention: Prevention Effectiveness and Evaluation.* SPAN USA, Washington, DC.

Suicide Prevention Resource Center and SPAN USA (Litts D ed.) (2010) *Charting the Future of Suicide Prevention: A 2010 Progress Review of the National Strategy and Recommendations for the Decade Ahead.* Education Development Center, Inc., Newton, MA. Available at: http://www.sprc.org/.

Sun FK, Long A, Boore J, Tsao LI (2005) Nursing people who are suicidal on psychiatric wards in Taiwan: action and interaction strategies. *Journal of Psychiatric and Mental Health Nursing* **12**(3): 275–82.

Sun FK, Long A, Boore J, Tsao LI (2006) A theory for the nursing care of patients at risk of suicide. *Journal of Advanced Nursing* **53**(6): 680–90.

Sun F, Long A, Boore J (2007) The attitudes of casualty nurses in Taiwan to patients who have attempted suicide. *Journal of Clinical Nursing* **16**(2): 255–63.

Talseth AG, Lindseth A, Jacobson L, Norberg A (1997) Nurses' narrations about suicidal psychiatric inpatients. *Nordic Journal of Psychiatry* **51**: 359–64.

Talseth AG, Lindseth A, Jacobson L, Norberg A (1999). The meaning of suicidal in-patients' experiences of being cared for by mental health nurses. *Journal of Advanced Nursing* **29**(5): 1034–41.

Titelman D, Wasserman D (2009) Suicide prevention by education and the moulding of attitudes. In Wasserman D, Wasserman C (eds.) *Oxford Textbook of Suicidology and Suicide Prevention. A Global Perspective*. Oxford University Press, Oxford, pp. 509–14.

Wasserman D, Wasserman C (2009) Preface. In Wasserman D, Wasserman C (eds.) *Oxford Textbook of Suicidology and Suicide Prevention. A Global Perspective*. Oxford University Press, Oxford, pp. vii–viii.

Wolfersdorf M (2000) Suicide among psychiatric inpatients. In: Hawton K, van Heeringen K (eds.) *The International Handbook of Suicide and Attempted Suicide*. John Wiley and Sons, Chichester, pp. 457–66.
World Health Organization (2007) *Depression/suicide*. Available at: http://www.int/health_topics/suicide/en/.
World Health Organization (2011) *Suicide Prevention.* http://www.who.int/mental_health/prevention/suicide/suicideprevent/en/ (accessed 25 June 2012).

CHAPTER 3

Assessing risk of suicide and self-harm

> Suicide risk assessment is an integral part of the psychiatric examination, yet is rarely performed systematically... (Simon, 2011, p. 9)

Introduction

It is important to preface this chapter on the assessment of risk of suicide and self-harm by noting that there is a well-documented, important and significant relationship between suicidal and self-harming acts and people experiencing mental health problems[1] (Tanney, 2000). It also important to note that these behaviours are in no way exclusive to this population, as suicide and self-harm are also found in the general population. While caution should be exercised in any interpretation of epidemiological studies of the prevalence of suicide, due to the epistemological and methodological limitations of such studies, and acknowledging major fluctuations in recorded rates over time (and by country), evidence indicates that 2.9% of the adult population attempts suicide at least once during their lifetime (Clark, 1992). Recent epidemiological evidence provided by the United States Centers for Disease Control (recovered 2011) shows that the overall rate was 11.3 suicide deaths per 100,000 people, whereas numerous studies, both contemporary and those with a recognised vintage, repeatedly show the overall rate for suicide deaths in people with mental health diagnoses/problems range from 37 per 100,000 (Tanney, 2000) to 279 per 100,000. As a result, we can acknowledge with a degree of empirical confidence that people with certain mental health problems have a much higher rate of suicide than the general population (Troister *et al*, 2008).

Furthermore, those who require psychiatric hospitalisation are at an even more increased risk of suicide (Pirkola *et al*, 2005). It should not be surprising then that

1 The authors deliberately do not use the terms mental illness, mental disorder or other such synonyms for these terms. In our view, it is conceptually prudent not to further conflate or associate 'suicide' with so-called mental illness, mental disorder etc.

Psychiatric/Mental Health (P/MH)[2] nurses are highly likely to encounter people who present with an increased risk of suicide and/or self-harm. Accordingly, the requirement for such nurses to be highly conversant with and competent in risk assessment of both suicide risk and risk of self-harm seems both obvious and logical. What may be counter-intuitive then is the somewhat disturbing evidence which shows the inadequacy of much/many suicide risk assessments in formal mental healthcare (Simon, 2011). Zimmerman and McGlinchley's (2008) survey of 314 psychiatrists, for example, found that more than 80% of this sample indicated that they did not routinely use scales to monitor outcome when treating depression. The most frequent reasons that psychiatrists gave for not using scales were that they did not believe scales would be clinically helpful, that scales take too much time to use, and that they were not trained in the use of such measures.

Risk assessment, as several authors have highlighted (see for example Cutcliffe and Stevenson, 2007; Maris, 2007; Simon, 2011) in and of itself, is only the beginning of care for the suicidal person. In order for risk assessment to be a meaningful rather than tokenistic act, it has to result in action(s); it should be an antecedent to evidence-based interventions to attempt to reduce the suicidal risk in the person. The utility of judicious suicide risk assessment notwithstanding, it remains the case that it is a complex and imperfect 'science', one bedevilled with conceptual difficulties, methodological limitations and operational problems.

A further common and potentially misleading/unhelpful practice is the automatic conflation of suicide and self-harm, positing these as isomorphic phenomena. At the outset it needs to be acknowledged that there are significant differences between suicide and self-harm and not only a difference in the outcome (see Favazza, 1996); self-harm is not necessarily a failed suicide attempt[3]. While it should be noted that distinctions between forms of self-harm and suicide are problematic, fundamental differences have been well documented and we would advance the argument that it is inaccurate and misleading to conflate the two. Perhaps the most fundamental difference between suicide and self-harm is the following: *self-harm is a life-orientated, coping-driven act and suicide is a death-orientated act* (our emphasis). Such conflation is, for the authors of this book, little more than a methodological or conceptual 'sleight of hand'. Maris *et al*, 2000, pp. 427–8) capture this distinction succinctly when they state:

---

2 'While 'Psychiatric nursing' and Mental Health nursing' may not be the same phenomenon, we use the conflated term 'P/MH nursing' conservatively given that this term is used commonly in the extant literature.

3 Though there is evidence to suggest that it patently can be.

> As a starting point, we must distinguish indirect self-destructive behaviours from behaviours more directly suicidal. Self-destructive behaviours take many forms.... In marked contrast, there are however, a vast number of behaviours that are self-harming, frequently injurious, self-negating, and self-defeating in which the individual engages but in which there may be no intention to die...

Similarly, Favazza (1996) clearly differentiates between self-harm and suicide, stating that self-mutilation is the deliberate alteration of body tissue *without conscious suicidal content or intent* (our emphasis). Fulwiler *et al* (1997) advance similar arguments stating that non-lethal forms of self-injury are often discussed together with suicide attempts as though they belonged on a continuum of self-harm. Their 1997 findings further support the differences between suicide and self-harm whereby they highlight how prison self-mutilators and suicide attempters had very different clinical presentations and histories. Similarly, numerous mental health service users groups and associated self-help groups draw clear distinctions between suicide and self-harm, drawing specific attention to how self-harm should not be regarded as a failed suicide attempt.

However, there are authors (see for example Anderson and Jenkins, 2006) who deliberately posit these two distinct phenomena as one and the same; merely different points on a continuum of lethality. Indeed, Anderson and Jenkins (p. 645) suggest that given the methodological and ethical issues involved in research on 'treatments' for suicide, we should simply substitute a population of people who self-harm for the 'missing' population of suicidal people, given that:

> interventions following self harm/suicidal behaviours are more amenable to evaluation.

A thorough examination of the literature in this substantive area will indicate that, historically, some definitions constructed for suicide and self-harm did indeed overlap with one another. Furthermore, self-harm questions have been included in some suicide risk assessments (Stuart, 2001, for example.) Undoubtedly, links between the two phenomenon do exist; sadly there is evidence to suggest that some people who self-harm do go on to take their own lives (Platt *et al*, 2005; Cooper *et al*, 2005). Nevertheless, there is a wealth of empirical evidence that shows that 95% and over of people who self-harm do not go on to take their own lives (see for example Santa Mina and Gallop, 1998; Anderson, 2000; Welch, 2001). Therefore this chapter acknowledges the differences between self-harm and suicide and deals with them separately.

Definitions

A review of the extant literature will show that determining and identifying fundamental dissimilarities between self-injurious actions and suicide, and thus arriving at delineating definitions for these phenomena, is problematic. While a person's intent to die has repeatedly been shown to be one such dissimilarity, there are significant difficulties in determining the person's intent (Kinmond and Bent, 2000). As a result, construction of a precise definition that clearly differentiates between self-harm and suicide is difficult, though this may be helped by the recently published proposed nomenclature for the study of suicide (Silverman *et al*, 2007). Be that as it may, several definitions have been advanced.

Professor Ed Shneidman (1973, 1985), who is often credited as the founder of suicidology as a discrete area of healthcare-focused science, undertook some preliminary work towards producing a definition of suicide. In his 1973 work, Shneidman defined suicide as the human act of self-inflicted, self-intentioned cessation of life. In his later 1985 work, he developed and extended this definition stating that,

> suicide is a conscious act of self-annihilation, best understood as a multi-dimensional malaise in a needful individual who defines an issue which suicide is the best solution. (Shneidman, 1985, p. 3)

Contrast these preliminary definitions of suicide with those of self-harm. Kreitman's (1977) important contribution to the literature, penned around the same time as Shneidman's work, defines self-harm as

> any non-fatal act in which an individual deliberately causes self-injury or ingests a substance in excess of any prescribed or generally recognised therapeutic dose. (Kreitman, 1977, p. 8)

A more recent definition has been offered by Favazza (1996), who refers to self-harm as the deliberate alteration of body tissue without conscious suicidal content or intent. Santa-Mina and Gallop (1998) propose a definition which, in the view of the authors, captures both the nature of self-harm while simultaneously alluding to its relationship with suicide, stating as they do that

> Self-harm is commonly defined as an individual's intentional damage to a part of his or her body, without a conscious intent to die, although the result might be fatal.

Assessing risk of self-harm

Before highlighting variables (risk factors) that have been found to indicate an increased risk of self-harm, and looking at several existing instruments for rating this risk, a few important contextual points need to be stated. Firstly, rates of self-harm in populations are not static; patterns of self-harming behaviour change over time (McLoone and Crombie, 1996; Hawton, 1997; Kinmond and Bent, 2000; Welch, 2001; Cooper *et al*, 2005; Soomro, 2008). The much over-used stereotypical portrayal of self-harmers as typically Caucasian, middle-class, teenage girls only reflects part of the clinical epidemiological reality. Numerous large-scale registration studies and surveys (see Welch, 2001, for an excellent summary of these studies) show significant variation over different sites and over time. While these findings continue to detect higher rates of self-harm in women than in men, and higher rates in younger (15–24) than older women, significant rates of self-harm have also been found in males, particularly the 25–34 age group (Welch, 2001). As a result, it would be rash for nurses to constrict their view(s) on at-risk populations.

Secondly, while these studies provide valuable information regarding 'conventional risk factors', there is a growing recognition that assessing for conventional risk factors alone is likely to be insufficient and potentially misleading, and is unlikely to improve the current predictive criteria, given the heterogeneous nature of the population who engage in self-harm (Sidley *et al*, 1999).

Thirdly, a number of authors (see for example Burrow, 1992; Platt *et al*, 2005) have drawn attention to limitations in current (epidemiological) attempts to identify risk factors (in self-harm). These authors argue that the individual risk factor approach and emphasising patient characteristics can only produce insufficient/incomplete 'pictures' of the risk of self-harm. In addition to these factors, 'upstream' (eg. non-proximal) risk factors such as history, culture and socioeconomic factors also need to be considered. Platt *et al* (2005, p. 54) conclude that:

> Individual-level health outcomes cannot be adequately studied by reference to the characteristics of individuals alone. It is also necessary to examine the characteristics of the social groups to which they belong, or the neighborhoods where they live and to acknowledge the interactions between individuals and contexts.

Similarly, Anderson (1999) advances a compelling argument for consideration of the internal and external factors and their interactions in the person's life, in that they allow shape and depth to be added to the assessment. Thus, checking for the presence of certain risk factors should form one part of a more composite and thorough clinical assessment. To examine 'proximal' risk factors first, Welch's (2001) review of the extant literature on the epidemiology of self-harm in the general population provides a useful summary. The following variables were found to be linked to increased risk of self-harm. These include:

- being single or divorced
- being unemployed
- having a recent change in living situation (particularly moving from a stable living situation to living alone, living in an unstable situation or living in an institution)
- having a so-called 'mental disorder'
- having a low socioeconomic situation
- having a previous self-harm incident.

Read's (1997) study of trends in the adolescent/young adult self-harm population who present at a psychiatric emergency unit identified the following variables as indicative of high risk of self-harm:

- high incidence of so-called psychiatric illness (affective disorders in particular)
- psychiatric co-morbidity
- family distress
- sexual abuse
- physical abuse.

A study that explored the specificity of risk assessment for self-harm found that the most potent short-term predictor of self-harm repetition was a high score on the Beck Hopelessness scale; whereas, in the longer term, the number of previous self-harm incidents was the major predictor (Sidley *et al*, 1999). Several other studies have also reported that previous incidents of self-harm are perhaps the clearest indicator of current/future risk of self-harm (see for example Burrow, 1992; Kreitman and Casey, 1988). However, other compelling (and widely confirmed) evidence indicates that a history of childhood sexual abuse appears to be the clearest indicator of increased risk of self-harm. This is particularly the case if the duration of the abuse is long, if the perpetrator is known to the victim and if force/penetration were used (Santa Mina and Gallop, 1998; Berliner and Elliott, 1996; Gratz *et al*, 2002; Van der Kolk *et al*, 1991; Zlotnick *et al*, 1996; 1999). Accordingly, there appears to be a substantial evidence base and a fair degree of consensus that these two variables (eg. previous incident of self-harm and history of childhood sexual abuse) represent the most significant predictors of further incidences of self-harm.

As stated above, while a thorough assessment of risk of self-harm ought to include consideration of these items/variables, the 'upstream' (eg. non-proximal) risk factors such as history, culture and socioeconomic factors as described by Platt *et al* (2005, p. 54) should also be considered in a comprehensive assessment. We will highlight the additional 'shape and depth' of assessment that these factors can bring using the study findings described in Platt *et al* (2005). These findings highlight how significant numbers of people presenting with self-harm issues have 'problematic' early family experiences. In the main, these were issues of dysfunctional interpersonal and/or family dynamics and relationships rather than poverty, low socio-economic conditions or material disadvantages. Experiences of sexual abuse, alcohol-related problems in the self-harming person and his/her family, and poor, damaging parenting practices passed on from one generation to the next were all found to be highly prevalent in the population who engaged in repeated self-harm. Then, during their adult lives, this population was found to be linked with insecure interpersonal relationships and 'rollercoaster' up-and-down, on-off relationships. This population was also characterised by low-income, low-skill jobs, and many were unemployed; these factors and experiences then led to financial worries and further interpersonal tensions with partners. Not surprisingly, many had low self-esteem and low levels of hope.

Platt *et al* (2005) conclude that further qualitative (phenomenological) research is needed to better understand the particular lived-experiences that contribute to these alarmingly high rates of self-harm. We concur; a thorough assessment of risk of self-harm needs to include listening acutely to the self-harming person's accounts; to their lived experiences. As Platt *et al* (2005) succinctly state, these accounts document how perceptions of key influences across the life-course contributed to their current life circumstances and decisions to engage in self harm.

Numerous instruments have been designed to assess (or measure) the risk of self-harm. Sansome and Sansome (2010) provide a very useful summary of these instruments. A list of them, their authors and a summary overview is provided in Table 3.1.

Further, in many cases, self-injurious acts have a symbolic meaning; the form of self-harm should not be regarded as a random act. As a general rule, self-injurious behaviour, particularly in people who have been given the diagnostic label of 'multiple personality disorder' or 'borderline personality disorder' is a coping (and communication) orientated act rather than a death-orientated act (Marmer and Fink, 1994). Although it would be unwise for practitioners to adopt a 'cavalier' attitude towards suicide attempts in such clients, these clients have

Table 3.1 Instruments for assessing risk of self-harm.

Instrument name	Authors	Brief overview
Chronic Self-Destructiveness Scale (CSDS)	Kelley *et al* (1985)	■ 73 items, with Likert-style response options ■ Items attempt to explore high-risk behaviours that are commonly indicative of impulsivity ■ Instrument includes items that are focused on general health-related issues ■ Gender-specific scoring key ■ Studies (eg. Sharp and Schill, 1995) conclude that this instrument is better (or more accurately) described as a measure of impulsiveness, poor judgment and immediate gratification, rather than a measure of Self-Defeating Personality
Self-Harm Behaviour Survey*	Favazza (1986) Favazza (1987) Favazza and Conterio (1988) Favazza (1996)	■ Over 170 individual items that have a variety of response options ■ Sub-sections or areas covered in this instrument include demographic information, family history of so-called mental illness, religious background, family relationships and self-harm behaviours
Self-Injury Survey	Simpson *et al* (1994)	■ Condensed instrument containing 31 self-harm items ■ Conflates suicide and self-harm risk assessment as it contains elements referring to suicide attempts, suicide ideation and self-harm
Impulsive and Self-Harm Questionnaire	Rossotto (1997)	■ Condensed instrument containing 14-items, with Likert-style response options ■ Explores impulsive, self-destructive behaviours and suicide attempts ■ Limited clinical exposure
Self-Injury Questionnaire (SIQ)	Vanderlinden and Vandereycken (1997)	■ 54-item, self-report questionnaire ■ Various response options, including Likert-style and multiple-choice selections ■ No items/queries about suicide attempts
Deliberate Self-Harm Inventory (DSHI)	Gratz (2001)	■ 17-item, yes/no, self-report questionnaire ■ Items related to frequency, severity, and duration of self-harm events ■ No items relating to suicide attempts

Table 3.1 (*continued*)

The Self-Harm Inventory	Sansome *et al* (1998)	■ 22 items, related to ration of self-harm events. ■ Yes/no responses

*Recognised as a seminal contributor to the substantive area of self-harm (Favazza 1986, 1987, 1988) and for some, author of the first psychiatric textbook on the topic of self-harm, Favazza produced the 'The Self-Harm Behavior Survey' (1986). Given Favazza's clearly stated position on the differences between suicide and self-harm, it is perhaps not surprising that this instrument does not contain any items regarding suicide attempts. For the authors of this book, this is a comprehensive instrument (and we applaud the exclusion of reference to suicide attempts), though it is perhaps somewhat unwieldy and time-consuming.

offered a range of reasons for self-harming behaviour and each of these dynamics has been repeatedly shown to have a strong association with a history of self-harming. Thus, risk assessment for future risk of self-harm should therefore also determine the presence and influence of the following intra-personal dynamics:

- self-harming as a means to release intra-personal tension
- self-harming as an expression of 'letting the badness flow out'
- self-harming to assuage a sense of guilt
- self-harming to harm the rejecting object (eg. the abuser) by harming what is dear to them, ie. the self-harmer
- self-harming as a way to interrupt the person's feelings of 'internal deadness' or 'invisibility'; a way of still 'feeling alive'
- self-harming as a metaphor for 'blood-letting'
- self-harm as a means of exercising control in a life that otherwise feels out of control.

Assessing risk of suicide

Suicide is a multi-faceted, complex phenomenon. A handful of uni-factorial theories (or single factor theories) have been advanced, with perhaps the uni-factorial theory with the most widely acknowledged cogency being that of suicide as 'psychache'[4] (Shneidman, 1993). Nevertheless, even for those scholars who highlight the centrality of psychache to suicide (such as Joiner, 2007)[5] there is broad consensus in the international suicidology community that suicide is a multi-dimensional, complex phenomenon that cannot be completely understood or explained using a uni-factorial theory. Indeed, numerous theoretical perspectives

4 With psychache conceptualised as severe, pervasive and unremitting psychological pain.

5 Who suggests that 'psychache is necessary but not sufficient for suicide' (Joiner, 2007, p. 38).

and explanations of suicide have been advanced and some of the key theories are listed in Table 3.2.

Concomitantly, given this complexity and multi-dimensionality, effective care of the suicidal person requires a pluralistic, multi-dimensional and multi-professional response (Shea, 1999; Maris *et al*, 2000; Cutcliffe and Stevenson, 2007). This point of view is emphasised by Maris *et al* (2000, p. 28) when they state:

> While suicidologists give lip service to the multi-disciplinary study of suicide, in actual fact most of us have very narrow and specialised domain assumptions – usually those relating to our professional training and sub-disciplinary paradigms.

For the authors of this book, this complexity and multi-factorial nature is mirrored in the assessment of suicide risk, wherein precise assessment of the extent of risk is extremely difficult to achieve (Morgan, 1994; Shneidman, 2004). Accurate and reliable assessment of suicide risk is further bedevilled by the absence of *any* pathognomonic indicators or variables for risk of suicide. As with almost all mental health problems[6],

> the psychiatrist, unlike the general physician does not have laboratory tests and sophisticated diagnostic instruments available to assess the suicidal patient (Simon, 2005, p. 40).

Another dynamic (or behaviour) which further diminishes the utility and accuracy of suicide risk assessment is when instruments are used in a cross-sectional manner; that is, when risk assessment is conceptualised as a singular event rather than a process (see also Simon, 2005). It may be interesting to note that, especially when used in isolation, suicide risk assessment instruments may produce accurate findings over the long-term, but can be unspecific and insensitive over the short term (Morgan, 1994), creating a large number of false positives (people regarded to be at high risk of suicide when they are not) and false negatives (people regarded to be at low risk of suicide when they are actually at high risk).

A further critical point that should be acknowledged is that of the function of suicide risk assessment instruments within the broader context of comprehensive risk assessment practices. Our view is congruent with the consensus viewpoint (see for example, Shea, 1999; Cutcliffe and Barker, 2004; Simon, 2011), namely

6 We recognise that suicide is not a mental health problem *per se*, though it is very clearly related to mental health problems.

Table 3.2 Theoretical perspectives and explanations of suicide (adapted from Cutcliffe and Stevenson, 2007).

Theoretical perspectives and explanations	Examples and authors
Biological	Genetic predisposition: Brezo *et al* (2008) Altered (lowered) serotonin levels (Brown *et al*, 1982)
Psychological	Cognitive theories, eg. constricted thinking (see Weishaar and Beck, 1992) Psychoanalytical theories, eg. suicide is motivated by intentions within the person's unconscious
Intra-psychic	The presence and influence of pervasive, unbearable psychological pain or 'psychache' (Shneidman, 1993)
Sociological	Social learning, eg. suicide is a learned behaviour. Suicide results from one's childhood experiences and from the forces and factors encountered in the environment. For these theorists, suicide is thus a shaped behaviour; it has been reinforced in the suicidal person's environment and especially through the person's experiences of being reared as a child (Joiner, 2005) Suicide as sociological, 'product' – based on degrees of imbalance of two social forces: social integration and moral regulation (Durkheim, 1897/1951)
Cultural	Some have even posited the possibility of a *suicidogenic* national character (see Maris *et al*, 2000). Such groups are posited as those who are set apart from others on the basis of key cultural differences (eg. attitudes, meanings attached to the act, customs, language) towards or about suicide
Philosophical/existential	Frankl (1959) writes that a person may consider suicide as a result of an 'existential vacuum'. This refers to the experience of a total lack, or loss, of an ultimate meaning to one's existence that would make life worthwhile
Lifespan theories; suicide pathways or trajectories	Maris (1981, 1990) has advanced the idea of a '*pathway(s)*' or '*trajectory(s)*' of suicide, in which he posits the developmental-existential perspective of suicide Maris (1981) argues that this is predicated as a person's inability or refusal to accept the terms of the human condition, as the endpoint of long-term difficulties (Morttunen *et al*, 1992)

that the fundamental basis of risk assessment must be a full and thorough clinical assessment of each individual and that isolated, cross-sectional scores obtained from any suicide risk assessment instrument should not be counted or relied upon as the sole basis for any clinical decision regarding suicide risk (Hawton, 1994; Morgan, 1994; Shea, 1999). That being said, an assessment of suicidal risk can be enhanced or augmented by the use of structured suicide risk assessment instruments (Morgan, 1994; Cutcliffe and Barker, 2004; Simon, 2011). However, while we regard this position as axiomatic, there are two important caveats to consider:

1. Comprehensive, rigorous and 'sensitive' clinical assessments require a significant degree of 'clinical judgement'. While the precise mechanism(s) of acquiring/developing sophisticated clinical judgement remains only partially understood (Benner, 1984; Standing, 2008), there appears to be little (if any) disagreement that clinical judgement is, at least in part, predicated by clinical experience. That is to say, in order to develop the clinical acumen, inexperienced clinicians need time, the ability/opportunity for reflection, and 'first-hand' exposure to, and experience of, working with clients (in this instance, clients deemed to be at high risk of suicide).
2. The current emphasis on 'evidence-based practice' would suggest that full and thorough clinical evaluations of individuals are perhaps best served when they are underpinned with evidence. Accordingly, prudence perhaps dictates, particularly in instances where the practitioner's clinical judgement is only partially developed, that the clinical judgement should be supplemented and/or complemented by using a suicide risk assessment instrument.

While the limitations of any/all suicide risk assessment instruments are a matter of record (Shea, 1999; Morgan, 1994; Joiner, 2005; Simon, 2011), as Shea (1999) purports, assessing for the presence of risk factors can alert the clinician to suspect that the client *may* (original emphasis) be at higher risk. This view is supported by Morgan (1994) and Simon (2011), who assert that instruments can provide useful checklists and can help guard against complacency and overconfidence. Consequently, in keeping with these arguments, and considering the two-stage caveat described above, the remainder of this chapter focuses on the Nurses' Global Assessment of Suicide Risk instrument (Cutcliffe and Barker, 2004).

Background to the development of the Nurses' Global Assessment of Suicide Risk instrument

Studies with a noted vintage (Motto *et al*, 1985; Goldstein *et al*, 1991; Morgan and Priest, 1991) and more contemporary work (Thomas *et al*, 2006; Sullivan and Bongar, 2006; Zimmerman and McGlinchley, 2008) have shown that the detection of suicide risk in populations of psychiatric clients poses many problems. Mindful of these problems, the first author, while working in the UK as a Practice Development Nurse during the 1990s[7], wished to enhance the practice of assessment of suicide risk. The first author was enthusiastic about designing and introducing an evidence-based suicide risk assessment tool and yet was also anxious to communicate that this would augment the clinical judgement of the nurses; particularly in the cases of the less experienced practitioners. Where experienced P/MH nurses had, through the processes of experiential learning and reflecting on practice (Menghella and Benson, 1995), developed their clinical judgement, it was stressed that the tool would not replace the experienced clinician's own judgement, but serve to augment it. As Motto *et al* (1985) point out,

> a scale can only be a supplement to clinical judgement and should not, on its own, override contradicting information.

On its own, risk assessment does not necessarily constitute evidence-based practice. However, as noted, specific variables are associated with increased risk of suicide (see for example Motto *et al*, 1985; Fawcett *et al*, 1987; Goldstein *et al*, 1991; Morgan and Priest, 1991; Weisharr and Beck, 1992; Joiner, 2005), with some variables having a stronger positive statistical correlation than others (Joiner, 2005). A risk assessment instrument that enables P/MH nurses to assess for the presence and influence of these predictor variables then means that part of their assessment becomes evidence-based. Importantly, *à propos* Shea's (1999) view, utilising such an instrument also had the influence of raising the nurses' awareness of the problem of suicide and factors associated with increased risk, with a corresponding increase in their vigilance.

A crucial problem in constructing any suicide risk assessment tool lies in the fact that high-risk issues for an individual cannot be generalised into a larger population. Similarly, high-risk factors for large populations do not necessarily translate and apply to the individual (Motto *et al*, 1985; Young *et al*, 1994). However, even an imperfect instrument can serve a useful purpose, especially

7 At least in part in response to the requests from psychiatric hospital ward-based Psychiatric/Mental Health nurses.

for those who are less confident or experienced with their suicide risk assessment skills (Simon, 2011). Such a view is supported by the study undertaken by Malone *et al* (1995), who found that having clinicians augment their assessment with an instrument improved both their documentation and detection of lifetime suicidal behaviour. Indeed, more recently a number of authors (see for example, Lamberg, 2007; Mossman, 2008; Swanson, 2008) have advanced the argument that the use of risk assessment instruments[8] should or may soon become the standard of care[9].

The Nurses' Global Assessment of Suicide Risk (NGASR) instrument takes the form of a simple scoring scale with 15 items (see Table 3.3). The instrument was designed so that all the information necessary to score each of the predictor variables would be able to be extracted during the admission interview and/or from each subsequent clinical encounter/assessment. By highlighting the variables that are pertinent to the client (and his/her experiences) and totalling the scores, a single final score or rating is arrived at. This score then correlates with an (estimated) indication of the level of potential suicide risk and also corresponds to a suggested level of engagement (see Table 3.4). Additionally, subsequent risk assessment ratings, aided by the use of the tool, mean that all the formal and informal collection of data (eg. observations of the client's mood and behaviour, records of interactions with nurses, other clients and additional healthcare staff) could be 'summarised' and repeated on a regular basis, providing an indication of changes in apparent risk of suicide. As to the question of how often reassessments should be undertaken, the view of the authors is that suicide risk assessment using the NGASR should follow the standard approach for determining frequency of re-measurement depending on level of acuity. In other words, it is common practice to increase the frequency of measurement in more acute (higher risk) cases. Thus when a suicide assessment indicates that a client is scored at high risk or very high risk, then this should logically be followed by more frequent re-assessments than a client who scores low/intermediate.

The NGASR was based on a review of the relevant empirical literature, which indicated that the presence (and influence) of variables appeared to suggest a higher degree of risk than some of the other variables. Thus, unlike many other suicide risk assessment instruments, not all variables of increased suicidal risk were given the same 'weighting' or score. The most significant variables in the NGASR – those with a reported, higher statistical correlation with – are weighted with a score of three, the remainder being allocated a score of one (for further

8 Or to use the parlance of these authors – 'actuarial risk assessment instruments'.

9 It should be noted that much of this research has been conducted in the domain of assessing risk of violence not suicide.

Table 3.3 Nurses' Global Assessment of Suicide Risk.

VARIABLE THAT INDICATES POSSIBLE INCREASED RISK OF SUICIDE	VALUE
PRESENCE/INFLUENCE OF HOPELESSNESS	3
RECENT STRESSFUL LIFE EVENT eg. Job loss, stressful family situation, sexual and/or interpersonal violence, pending legal action, natural/man-made disasters	1
EVIDENCE OF PERSECUTORY VOICES/BELIEFS	1
EVIDENCE OF DEPRESSION/LOSS OF INTEREST OR LOSS OF PLEASURE	3
EVIDENCE OF WITHDRAWL	1
WARNING OF SUICIDAL INTENT	1
EVIDENCE OF A SPECIFIC PLAN FOR SUICIDE	3
FAMILY HISTORY OF SERIOUS PSYCHIATRIC PROBLEMS OR SUICIDE	1
RECENT BEREAVEMENT OR RELATIONSHIP BREAKDOWN	3
HISTORY OF PSYCHOSIS	1
WIDOW/WIDOWER	1
PRIOR SUICIDE ATTEMPT	3
HISTORY OF SOCIO-ECONOMIC DEPRIVATION	1
HISTORY OF ALCOHOL AND/OR SUBSTANCE USE/MISUSE	1
PRESENCE OF TERMINAL ILLNESS	1
TOTAL = (a maximum score of 25)	

Table 3.4 NGASR and corresponding levels of risk and suggested engagement.

Score of 5 or less = low level of risk estimated. Suggested level of engagement = level four
Score between 6 and 8 = intermediate level of risk. Suggested level of engagement = level three
Score between 9 and 11 = high level of risk. Suggested level of engagement = level two
Score 12 or more = very high/extreme level of risk. Suggested level of engagement = level one

information see Beck *et al*, 1974; Pokorny, 1983; Motto *et al*, 1985; Fawcett *et al*, 1987; Goldstein *et al*, 1991; Weisharr and Beck, 1992; Young *et al*, 1994; Shea, 1999; Powell *et al*, 2000; Shneidman, 2004; Joiner, 2005).

An additional difficulty in designing a risk assessment instrument involves determining the demarcations between degrees of risk. As previously noted, suicide is a complex phenomenon and unsophisticated models that suggest that one can either be at risk or not at risk of suicide are simplistic and inappropriate. As a result of participating as a co-investigator in a study involving attending over 75 formal suicide coroner's inquests, reviewing each set of case notes and in-depth interviews with the families (see Cutcliffe and Ramcharan, 2002), the first author felt that there should be four discrete levels of suicidal risk. Two polarised opposite levels of risk were clear: very high or extreme risk and very little risk. 'Very high risk' refers to that state of being that might be likened to a state of 'psychiatric emergency'. The person is extremely vulnerable; requires the highest degree of engagement and input from the P/MH nurse; and would present with a number of high risk factors (variables) and maybe some other risk factors too. Since it would not be prudent for P/MH nurses to claim that a client presents with no risk of suicide, the first author described the category that represents the least risk as 'low risk of suicide'. These individuals would thus score low and present with few (if any) of the risk factors. A further two categories were added: 'intermediate' and 'high risk'. Again, given the complexity of suicide and the multiple factors that can be involved in predicting risk, a single third category was felt to be rather simplistic and unsophisticated, not allowing sufficiently for the interplay of risk factors/variables and the cumulative degree of risk that multiple factors/variables combined indicated.

Empirical evidence and rationale to support each of the 15 key variables

1. Presence/influence of hopelessness

There is a well-established body of empirical evidence that indicates how a sense of (or feeling of) hopelessness is highly correlated with increased suicide risk (see 'vintage' studies such as Beck *et al*, 1975; Wetzel, 1976; Wetzel *et al*, 1980; Kazdin *et al*, 1983; Motto *et al*, 1985; Drake and Cotton, 1986; Fawcett *et al*, 1987; Hill *et al*, 1988; Morgan and Priest, 1991; Cooper-Patrick *et al*, 1994). These studies indicate that feelings of hopelessness, sometimes (but not always) associated with a depressive state, are a more accurate indicator of increased risk than the depressive state itself. More recent findings have confirmed those of these earlier studies. For example, in the study undertaken by Chochinov *et al* (1998) hopelessness was correlated more highly with suicidal ideation than was the level of depression. Furthermore, these authors point out that multiple linear regression analyses have indicated that hopelessness contributed uniquely to the prediction of suicidal ideation when the level of depression was controlled for. The recent study undertaken by Britton *et al* (2008) further underscores the relationship between hopelessness and increased suicide risk. Moreover, hopelessness is not isolated or unique to depressive states; people with recurrent forms of mental and/or physical distress, personal problems or social problems, can and do develop a sense of pervasive hopelessness. If the P/MH nurse wishes to assess this area in more detail, in order to verify his/her initial assessment, he/she might draw upon one of the well-established and validated instruments for estimating hope/hopelessness.

2. Recent stressful life event

Stressful life events (and/or traumatic life events) have been found to be positively correlated with increased suicide risk; notably this may be more significant in younger people. The findings have been shown to be relatively consistent over time, across different geographical populations and in families of low, middle and high income. These findings can be located in earlier studies such as Paykel *et al* (1974), Paykel (1976), Slater and Depue (1981), Tishler *et al* (1981), Cohen-Sandler *et al* (1982), Gispert *et al* (1985), Compas (1987), Burt *et al* (1988) and Pfeffer (1989); and also in more recent studies such as those undertaken by DeVanna *et al* (1990), Asarnow (1992) and Adams *et al* (1996). More recently, Stein *et al* (2010) have drawn on data pertaining to trauma exposure and subsequent first onset of suicidal behaviour collected from 102,245 households in 21 countries participating in the World Health Organization World Mental Health Surveys. Their findings confirm those of earlier studies, whereby a range of traumatic events are associated with suicidal behaviour, with sexual and interpersonal violence consistently showing the strongest effects. Their findings also indicate that these associations are, in the main, consistent across high, middle and low-income countries. Also, according to the authors, these data reinforce the importance of traumatic exposures as a risk factor for suicide ideation and attempts, particularly when there are cumulative stressful/traumatic life events.

3. Evidence of persecutory voices/beliefs

There exists a body of evidence which indicates that an increased risk of suicide for those people experiencing (so-called) schizophrenia. Studies with a recognised vintage such as Caldwell and Gottesman (1990) and more recently Inskip *et al* (1998) put this increased risk as affecting 4–13% of that population, whereas more contemporary evidence depicts the rate at around 5% (see Palmer *et al*, 2005). Needless to say, while the precise elevated risk may well fluctuate over time, these and other studies repeatedly show that there is an elevated risk of suicide when compared to the 'general public'. While it should be noted that people experiencing (so-called) schizophrenia are not the only population who hear voices (see for example the 'Hearing Voices' network, Romme *et al*, 1992), recent literature highlights how there may indeed be a sub-group of people experiencing (so-called) schizophrenia whose increased risk is motivated primarily by their psychotic symptoms, such as hearing voices (Acosta *et al*, 2006). In addition to the reasonably well documented sense of despair than can arise (at least in part) from such 'symptoms' (Kim *et al*, 2003), when such voices take on a persecutory tone or content or such voices/beliefs contain explicit messages of self-harm or destruction this can further exacerbate the increased risk (Shea, 1999).

4. Evidence of depression, loss of interest or pleasure

Since the seminal paper by Barraclough *et al* (1974) (methodological issues notwithstanding), which stated that of the 100 cases of suicide investigated, 85% were described as suffering from depression or alcoholism, many other studies have found a strong relationship between depression and increased suicide risk (Pokorny, 1983; Fawcett *et al*, 1987; Young *et al*, 1994; Powell *et al*, 2000; Arsenault-Lapierre *et al*, 2004). Indeed, the meta-analysis undertaken by Arsenault-Lapierre *et al* (2004) found that the most common diagnostic affective disorders were diagnosed in 43.2 % of suicide cases. When depression is accompanied with the person expressing a loss of interest or pleasure (anhedonia), this can be regarded as further indication of potential suicidal risk (see for example, Malik, 2000).

5. Evidence of withdrawal

Some research into risk factors in suicide has indicated that a withdrawal from interpersonal and social interactions/activities can be associated with increased risk (Charlton *et al*, 1992; Suicide Resource Prevention Centre, recovered 2011). In some population groups – such as college/university students – changes in patterns of interaction with pronounced increased in withdrawal and more social isolation can be one of the first warning signs that the person is contemplating suicide. We need to add a caveat here: clearly one should not automatically conclude that a person who wishes to spend time alone is *ipso facto* contemplating suicide or even at increased risk of suicide. It is more a matter of changes in patterns of interpersonal and social interaction; a change in the balance of time spent alone against time spent with others (Cutcliffe and Barker, 2004).

6. Warning of suicidal intent

Verbalisations of one's intent to take one's own life are a further risk factor for suicide; though perhaps counter-intuitively, such verbalisations are not *always* conclusive evidence of genuine intent (see Morgan, 1994). It has to be acknowledged, particularly in cases where a 'learned behaviour' has been acquired, that some people can use verbalised threats of suicide or verbalisations of suicide ideation as a mechanism to influence (some might say 'manipulate') certain outcomes. However, even while acknowledging the existence of this dynamic, it would be imprudent to adopt a 'cavalier' attitude towards such warnings; they should not be ignored and can indeed be genuine and clear indications of increased suicide risk. Consider for example how numerous studies have indicated that in some cases, warnings[10] and/or verbalisations of intent have been uttered, but alas have passed by unnoticed (see for example, Morgan and Priest, 1991; Luoma *et al*, 2002; Thomas *et al*, 2006.)

7. Evidence of a specific plan for suicide

Any evidence of a specific plan to take one's own life represents a major risk factor. This may even be more the case if the person attempted to keep the plan secret (Motto *et al*, 1985; Shea, 1999; Joiner, 2005). Indeed, the DSM IV (American Psychological Association, 2000) identifies four discrete degrees of suicide risk, ranging from 'thoughts that life is not worth living' to 'specific plans for committing suicide'. More recent research findings continue to identify how having a specific plan is a key predictor of a suicide attempt. Hodgins *et al* (2006) study found in their sample that those people who actually made an attempt on their life were significantly more likely to have a plan (66%) than those people with suicide ideation only (43.6%).

8. Family history of serious psychiatric problems or suicide

There exists a body of evidence which shows that psychiatric problems and suicide acts can and do 'run in families' (see Maris *et al*, 2000; Powell *et al*, 2000). Accordingly, having a 'family history' of suicide and/or psychiatric problems is associated with an increased risk of suicide. While the international suicidology community is in broad agreement on this risk factor, what we are currently unsure about is whether this effect is due to genetics (ie. a genetically inherited increased risk – see Science Daily, 2011) or modelling (CDC, recovered 2011). When family members, significant others or friends have died by suicide, this can, inadvertently, serve as a role model and lead to the so-called 'contagion effect'.

9. Recent bereavement or relationship breakdown

In Powell *et al*'s (2000) relatively recent study of 117 inpatient suicides, the two variables which showed the highest statistical correlation with completed

---

10 'Cries for help'

suicide were having a first-degree relative who completed suicide and a recent bereavement. Such findings were uncovered in previous related studies (see Motto *et al*, 1985; Fawcett *et al*, 1987; Petronis *et al*, 1990; Kessler *et al*, 1999). The relationship between recent bereavement and increased suicide risk was again found in the study undertaken by Erlangsen *et al* (2004). They found that while a small proportion of people who complete suicide have experienced a recent bereavement, there is a significant increase in the suicide risk during the first year after a bereavement, especially for men.

10. History of psychosis

Since Barraclough *et al* (1974) published their important study, suicide has repeatedly been found to be one of the major causes of premature death for people with psychosis. Further, it is noteworthy that this increased risk has been detected in different countries and repeatedly during different time periods (see for example, Petronis *et al*, 1990; Kessler *et al*, 1999; Shea, 1999, Powell *et al*, 2000; Preti *et al*, 2009; Simon 2011). This literature indicates that the lifetime risk of suicide for people with schizophrenia is estimated to be significantly higher than the general population, ranging from 5–15 per cent. Although it is accepted as an axiom that not all people who endure and live with a psychosis also experience suicidal thoughts, the evidence indicating increased risk needs to be acknowledged.

11. Widow/widower

Some empirical studies with a noted vintage (Wenz, 1977; Motto *et al*, 1985; Goldstein *et al*, 1991) as well as more contemporary studies (see Erlangsen *et al*, 2004; Luoma and Pearson, 2002) have shown that when the person is a widow/widower her/his risk of suicide is increased. This may be particularly the case if the person has not reached any 'resolution' to their bereavement or has not 'adapted' to their loss. It is important to remember that in contemporary society this predictive variable also includes the loss of 'common law' spouse and the loss of a homosexual life partner.

12. Prior suicide attempt

The relevant empirical literature is consistent in showing that if a person has evidence of a prior suicide attempt, then he/she is at much greater risk for eventual completed suicide (Petronis *et al*, 1990; Gunnell and Frankel, 1994; Kessler *et al*, 1999; Shea, 1999; Maris *et al*, 2000; Moscicki, 2001; NIMH, recovered 2011). Joiner's (2005) work on the 'acquired ability' also points to how previous serious attempt on one's life can be a significant indicator of current/future suicidal risk. Two important caveats should be noted, however. Firstly, even in the presence of this significantly increased risk, Maris *et al* (2000) estimate that 85% (or over) of people with a previous suicide attempt do not go on to take their own lives, and secondly, the assessing practitioner needs to attempt to determine whether a so-called previous suicide attempt was indeed a genuine attempt to end one's life or whether the 'attempt' can more accurately be categorised as a form of self-harm: self-injurious behaviour where there was no real intent to die.

13. History of socio-economic deprivation

Suicide is a multi-factorial event that does not happen in isolation from the world in which the person lives in (Maris, 1997). Thus, it can be precipitated by both internal phenomenon and external events, in addition to external circumstances. As a result, it may not be entirely surprising that, in many cultures, a history of socio-economic deprivation (eg. poor housing, unemployment, low quality of life) appears to be associated with increased risk of suicide (Gunnell and Frankel, 1994; Li *et al*, 2011).

14. History of alcohol and/or substance use/misuse

Further studies have supported the findings of Barraclough *et al* (1974) and continue to suggest that a history of alcohol and/or substance misuse is associated with a higher risk of suicide (Shea, 1999; Joiner, 2005; Pompili *et al*, 2010); though it is also accurate to point out that considerable variation in the degree of increased risk associated with alcohol is to be found in the various studies. This effect may be a result of interactions between alcohol and serotonin levels; or/and disruptions to impulse control (most commonly lowering of impulse control); and/or disruptions in the person's social support structure or interpersonal relationships (Maris *et al*, 2000).

15. Presence of terminal or serious physical illness

Finally, some people who are suffering from a serious physical or terminal illness engage in suicide (Hawton, 1994; Maris *et al*, 2000). The literature suggests that such individuals engage in suicide as a means of dealing with physical pain; or as a means of taking an element of control/dignity; or as a way of dealing with the prospect of further holistic deterioration and loss. Bazalgette *et al*'s (2011) research found findings that support these earlier findings. These authors found that at least 10 per cent of the suicides that take place in the UK are by people who are chronically or terminally ill.

Developing an evidence base for suicide risk assessment.

The clear consensus within the psychiatric and suicidology clinical and academic 'academe' is that formal assessment tools for estimating the risk of suicide constitute only one part of the assessment process. That being said, there is also consensus that they constitute an invaluable component of the 'bigger picture' of suicide risk assessment *per se*, particularly in the case of less clinically experienced and/or 'junior' staff. In addition to formal risk assessment tools, a full clinical assessment (we would argue) may include some (or all) of the following:

- the clinical judgement of all practitioners involved. Particular value may be attached to the judgement of a clinician that has established a strong/close relationship with the client; or someone who has spent long periods of time in the company of the client
- ongoing or repeated assessments and evaluations (whether based on a risk assessment tool or not) that piece together to form a cumulative 'picture' of the person's potential risk; 'stand-alone' or 'cross-sectional' assessments have limited utility
- data/information gained during the initial admission interview and subsequent interviews with the client, family and/or significant others.

Having identified that formal interviews (admission interviews and subsequent assessment interviews) can also play a key part in arriving at more accurate assessments of a person's risk of suicide, it is necessary to consider some of the questions that might be asked in such interviews (see Table 3.5). Each interview will have to be conducted with extreme sensitivity and empathy, and should conclude with an emphatic declaration of support, care and concern for the individual. Also, while there appear to be a range of questions that have potential application and utility to all suicide risk assessments, each interview is likely to be unique, since it will involve the unique situation, personality and presenting needs of the particular client. That is to say, the questions need not necessarily be asked in the same order for each clinical interview; additional supplementary questions may also be asked. Therefore, the questions included in Table 3.5 should be regarded as guidelines and not a 'check list' of questions that the P/MH nurse should follow unthinkingly.

In conclusion

It is important to be realistic and recognise the limitations of self-harm and suicide prevention (Hawton, 1994). A number of authors have pointed out the ubiquitous nature of suicide and its omnipresence throughout history (see, for example, Rosen, 1971; Alvarez, 1974; Cutcliffe and Stevenson, 2007). Furthermore, as pointed out in previous chapters, if one examines the global 'picture' of suicide over the last sixty years, the clear trend is an increase in the global rate of suicide – despite

Table 3.5 Suggested questions for suicidal risk assessment interviews (adapted from Morgan, 1994; Barker, 1999; Shea, 1999; Simon 2011).

- When you think about your current situation and difficulty, do you think that it can improve, that things can turn out well?
- Where does it hurt? Are you in psychological pain (psychache)?
- How much pleasure do you gain from your life, from those activities and relationships that used to give you pleasure?
- How hopeful do you feel? Do you feel that you still have hope on a day-to-day basis?
- At the start of the day, how do you feel about the day to come and how you will be able to cope?
- Does your current situation make you question the point or purpose of it all; of your situation or even your life/existence?
- Would you describe yourself as feeling desperate or experiencing a sense of despair?
- How does the thought of having to face another day make you feel?
- How you ever thought or felt that you are a burden, and if so, could you say in what way; a burden to whom?
- Have you ever thought about or wished that it would all end?
- Have you ever thought that death would be a relief; an end to your psychological pain; that death would present a way out or ever wished that you were dead?
- Have you ever thought about ending your life? How often do you have these thoughts and are you having them at the moment? How compelling or pressing are they?
- Have these thoughts ever led you to make an attempt to take your own life? When did this happen? Have you made more than one attempt?
- Have you ever made a plan about how you would take your own life? Do you have such a plan at the moment?
- If you experience pressing thoughts about taking your own life, how are you able to resist them? How might we be able to help you when you experience such thoughts?
- How serious are your thoughts, your intent to harm yourself?
- Do you feel the need for extra interpersonal support and security right now? What would this look like? Please tell me what you need.
- How easy is it for you to ask for help, particularly when you are feeling vulnerable of harming yourself?
- How do feel right now?
- How can I help you right now?
- What degree of interpersonal support and security do you feel you need right now?

the concerted research and clinical efforts made during the corresponding time to reduce the rate. Accordingly, while in no way advocating a case for complacency, it might be prudent to acknowledge that the complete eradication of suicide is highly unlikely. Nevertheless, methodological limitations notwithstanding, historical and contemporary epidemiological data *vis-à-vis* suicide and self-harm clearly indicate that there is a great deal more that formal mental healthcare services (including P/MH nurses) can do to reduce the rate of suicide, and better manage a person's self-harming behaviour(s), both of which are prefaced by accurate risk assessment.

While acknowledging that risk assessment instruments are only one aspect of a more thorough assessment of risk, the NGASR provides P/MH nurses with an instrument which can assist them with this assessment process, and it can be argued that the instrument has particular utility for less experienced (and student) nurses. The NGASR is now utilised in the UK, Canada, Australia, the USA, China, New Zealand, Portugal, Holland, Germany and Switzerland. It has been translated into German, Dutch, Chinese and Portuguese. It is reported as being used in a variety of clinical settings, including acute psychiatry, older adult psychiatry, substance use/misuse units, community psychiatric nursing, Emergency Rooms/Accident and Emergency rooms (see Mitchell *et al*, 2005); it is woven into or included in various 'Best Practice Guidelines' (see British Columbia and Ontario, Canada). The instrument is also woven into the Tidal Model (Barker and Buchanan-Barker, 2005) and has numerous (albeit hitherto unpublished) quantitative validations that underscore the instrument's reliability and validity; further international empirical validation of the instrument is currently under way in the USA and Holland.

Acknowledgement

Some sections of this chapter have been adapted or reproduced, with the kind permission of Blackwell Science Ltd, from the peer-reviewed paper published in the Journal of *Psychiatric and Mental Health Nursing*. Full reference details of this article are:

Cutcliffe JR, Barker P (2004) The Nurses' Global Assessment of Suicide Risk (NGASR): developing a tool for clinical practice. *Journal of Psychiatric/Mental Health Nursing* **11**: 393–400.

References

Acosta FJ, Aguikar EJ, Cejas MR *et al* (2006) Are there subtypes of suicidal schizophrenia? A prospective study. *Schizophrenia Research* **86**: 215–20.

Adams D, Overholser J, Spirito A (1996) Suicide attempts and stressful life events. *The Prevention Researcher* **3**(3): 5–8.

Alvarez A (1974) *The Savage God: A Study of Suicide*. W. W. Norton, New York.
American Psychological Association (2000) *Diagnostic and Statistical Manual of Mental Disorders IV*. APA, Arlington.
Anderson M (1999) Waiting for harm: deliberate self-harm and suicide in young people – a review of the literature. *Journal of Psychiatric and Mental Health Nursing* **6**(2): 91–100.
Anderson R (2000) Assessing the risk of self-harm in adolescents: a psychoanalytic perspective. *Psychoanalytic Psychotherapy* **14**(1): 9–21.
Anderson M, Jenkins R (2006) The national suicide prevention strategy for England: the reality of a national strategy for the nursing profession. *Journal of Psychiatric and Mental Health Nursing* **13**(6): 641–50.
Arsenault-Lapierre G, Kim C, Turecki G (2004) Psychiatric diagnoses in 3275 suicides: a meta-analysis. *BMC Psychiatry* **4**: 4–37.
Asarnow J (1992) Suicidal ideation and attempts during middle childhood: associations with perceived family stress and depression among child psychiatric inpatients. *Journal of Clinical Child Psychology* **21**: 35–40.
Barker P (1999) *Developing the Security Plan: Guidance Notes*. Newcastle City Health Trust, Newcastle.
Barker P, Buchanan-Barker P (2005) *The Tidal Model: A Guide for Mental Health Professionals*. Brunner-Routledge, Hove and New York.
Barraclough B, Bunch J, Nelson P, Sainsbury P (1974) A hundred cases of suicide: clinical aspects. *British Journal of Psychiatry* **125**: 355–73.
Bazalgette L, Bradley W, Ousbey J (2011) *The Truth About Suicide*. Demos, London. http://www.demos.co.uk/publications/thetruthaboutsuicide (accessed 26 June 2012).
Beck AT, Weissman M, Lester D, Trexler L (1974) The measurement of pessimism: the hopelessness scale. *Journal of Consulting and Clinical Psychology* **42**: 861–5.
Beck AT, Kovacs M, Weissman A (1975) Hopelessness and suicidal behavior. *Journal of the American Medical Association* **234**: 1146–9.
Benner P (1984) *From Novice to Expert: Excellence and Power in Clinical Nursing Practice*. Addison-Wesley, Menlo Park, California.
Berliner L and Elliott DM (1996) Sexual abuse of children. In Briere J, Berliner L, Bulkey J, Jenney C, Reid T (eds.) *The APSAC Handbook on Child Maltreatment*. Sage, Newbury Park, CA.
Brezo J, Klempan T, Turecki G (2008) The genetics of suicide: a critical review of molecular studies. *Psychiatric Clinics of North America* **31**(2): 179–203.
Britton PC, Duberstein PR, Conner KR, Heisel MJ, Hirsch JK, Conwell Y (2008) Reasons for living, hopelessness, and suicide ideation among depressed adults 50 years or older. *American Journal of Geriatric Psychiatry* **16**(9): 736–41.
Brown GL, Ebert MH, Goyer PF, Jimerson DC, Klein WJ, Bunney WE, Goodwin FK (1982) Aggression, suicide, and serotonin: relationships to CSF amine metabolites. *American Journal of Psychiatry* **139**: 741–6.
Burrow S (1992) The deliberate self-harming behaviour of patients within a British special hospital. *Journal of Advanced Nursing* **17**(2): 138–48.
Burt C, Cohen L, Bjorck J (1988) Perceived family environment as a moderator of young adolescents' life stress adjustment. *American Journal of Community Psychology* **16**, 101–21.

Caldwell CB, Gottesman H (1990) Schizophrenics kill themselves too: a review of risk factors for suicide. *Schizophrenia Bulletin* **16**, 571–89.

Centers for Disease Control and Prevention, National Center for Injury Prevention and Control (recovered 2011) *Suicide Contagion and the Reporting of Suicide: Recommendations from a National Workshop.* http://www.cdc.gov/mmwr/preview/mmwrhtml/00031539.htm.

Charlton J, Kelly S, Dunnell K, Evans, B, Jenkins R (1992) Trends in suicide deaths in England and Wales. *Population Trends* **69**: 6–10.

Chochinov HM, Wilson KG, Enns M, Lander S (1998) Depression, hopelessness, and suicide ideation in the terminally ill. *Psychosomatics* **39**: 366–70.

Clark DC (1992) Rational suicide and people with terminal conditions or disabilities. *Issues in Law and Medicine* **8**: 147–66.

Cohen-Sandler R, Berman A, King R (1982) Life stress and symptomatology: Determinants of suicidal behavior in children. *Journal of American Academy Child Psychology* **21**: 178–86.

Compas BE (1987) Stress and life events during childhood and adolescence *Clinical Psychology Review* **7**: 275–302.

Cooper J, Kapur N, Webb R, Lawlor M, Guthrie E, Mackway-Jones K, Appleby L (2005) Suicide after deliberate self-harm: a four year cohort study. *American Journal of Psychiatry* **162**(2): 297–303.

Cooper-Patrick L, Crum RM, Ford DE (1994) Identifying suicidal ideation in general medical patients. *Journal of the American Medical Association* **272**: 1757–62.

Cutcliffe JR, Barker P (2004) The Nurses' Global Assessment of Suicide Risk (NGASR): developing a tool for clinical practice. *Journal of Psychiatric/Mental Health Nursing* **11**: 393–400.

Cutcliffe JR, Ramcharan P (2002) Levelling the playing field: considering the 'ethics as process' approach for judging qualitative research proposals. *Qualitative Health Research* **12**(7): 1000–10.

Cutcliffe JR, Stevenson C (2007) *Care of the Suicidal Person.* Elsevier, London.

DeVanna M, Paterniti S, Milievich C, Rigamonti R, Sulich A, Faravelli C (1990) Recent life events and attempted suicide. *Journal of Affective Disorders* **18**: 51–8.

Drake RE, Cotton PG (1986) Depression, hopelessness and suicide in chronic schizophrenia. *British Journal of Psychiatry* **148**: 554–9,

Durkheim E (1951) *Suicide: a Study in Sociology*. Free Press, Glencoe, IL (original work 1897).

Erlangsen A, Jeune B, Bille-Brahe U, Vaupel JW (2004) Loss of partner and suicide risks among oldest old: a population-based register study. *Age and Aging* **33**(4): 378–83.

Favazza AR (1986) *Self-harm Behavior Survey*. Columbia, MI.

Favazza AR (1987) *Bodies Under Siege: Self-mutilation in Culture and Psychiatry*, 1st edn. Johns Hopkins University Press, Baltimore.

Favazza AR (1996) *Bodies Under Siege: Self-mutilation and Body Modification in Culture and Psychiatry*, 2nd edn. Johns Hopkins University Press, Baltimore.

Favazza A, Conterio K (1988) The plight of chronic self-mutilators. *Community Mental Health* **24**: 22–30.

Fawcett J, Scheftner W, Clark D, Hedeker D, Gibbons R, Coryell W (1987) Clinical predictors of suicide in patients with major affective disorders: a controlled prospective study. *American Journal of Psychiatry* **144**(1): 35–40.

Frankl V (1959) *Man's Search for Meaning*. Hodder & Stoughton, London.

Fulwiler C, Forbes C, Santangelo SL, Folstein, M (1997) Self-mutilation and suicide attempt: distinguishing features in prisoners. *Journal of the American Academy of Psychiatry Law* **25**(1): 69–77.

Gispert M, Wheeler K, Marsh L, Davis M (1985) Suicidal adolescents: factors in evaluation. *Adolescence* **20**: 753–62.

Goldstein RB, Black DW, Nasrallah A, Winokur G (1991) The prediction of suicide: sensitivity, specificity and predictive value of a multivariative model applied to suicide among 1906 patients with an affective disorder. *Archives of General Psychiatry* **48**: 418–22.

Gratz KL (2001) Measurement of deliberate self-harm: preliminary data on the Deliberate Self-Harm Inventory. *Journal of Psychopathological Behavioural Assessment* **23**: 253–63.

Gratz KL, Conrad SD, Roemer L (2002) Risk factors for deliberate self-harm among college students. *American Journal of Orthopsychiatry* **72**: 128–40.

Gunnell D, Frankel S (1994) Prevention of suicide: aspirations and evidence. *British Medical Journal* **308**: 1227–33.

Hawton K (1994) Causes and opportunities for prevention. In: Jenkins R, Griffiths S, Wylie I *et al* (eds.) *The Prevention of Suicide*. Department of Health, HMSO, London, pp. 34–45.

Hawton K (1997) Attempted suicide. In: Clarke DM, Fairburn CG (eds.) *Science and Practice of Cognitive Behavioural Therapy*. Oxford University Press, Oxford, pp. 285–312.

Hill RD, Gallagher D, Thompson LW *et al* (1988) Hopelessness as a measure of suicidal intent in the depressed elderly. *Psychological Aging* **3**: 230–3.

Hodgins DC, Mansley C, Thygesen K (2006) Risk factors for suicide ideation and attempts among pathological gamblers. *American Journal of Addiction* **15**: 303–10.

Inskip HM, Harris EC, Barraclough B (1998) Lifetime risk for suicide attempts among patients with schizophrenia. *Psychiatric Services* **49**: 1353–5.

Joiner T (2005) *Why People Die by Suicide*. Harvard University Press, Cambridge.

Kazdin AE, French NH Unis, AS *et al* (1983) Hopelessness, depression and suicidal intent among psychiatrically disturbed inpatient children. *Journal of Consulting Clinical Psychology* **51**: 504–10.

Kelley K, Byrne D, Przybyla DPJ, Eberly C, Eberly B, Greendlinger V, Wan CK, Gorsky J (1985) Chronic self-destructiveness: conceptualization, measurement, and initial validation of the construct. *Motivation and Emotion* **9**: 135–51.

Kessler RC, Borges G, Walters EE (1999) Prevalence of and risk factors for lifetime suicide attempts in the National Comorbidity Survey. *Archives of General Psychiatry* **56**(7): 617–26.

Kim CH, Jayathilake K, Meltzer HY (2003) Hopelessness, neurocognitive function, and insight in schizophrenia: relationship to suicidal behavior. *Schizophrenia Research*, **60**: 71–80.

Kinmond KS, Bent M (2000) Attendance for self-harm in a West Midlands A and E department. *British Journal of Nursing* **9**(4): 215–20.

Kreitman N (1977) *Parasuicide*. Wiley, Chichester.

Kreitman N, Casey P (1988) Repetition of parasuicide: an epidemiological and clinical study. *British Journal of Psychiatry* **153**: 792–800.

Lamberg L (2007) New tools aid violence risk assessment. *Journal of the American Medical Association* **298**(5): 499–501.

Li Z, Page A, Martin G, Taylor R (2011) Attributable risk of psychiatric and socio-economic factors for suicide from individual-level, population-based studies: a systematic review. *Social Science Medicine* **72**(4): 608–16.

Luoma JB, Pearson J (2002) Suicide and marital status in the United States, 1991–1996: is widowhood a risk factor? *American Journal of Public Health* **92**(9): 1518–22.

Luoma JB, Martin CE, Pearson J (2002) Contact with mental health and primary care providers before suicide: a review of the evidence. *American Journal of Psychiatry* **159**: 909–16.

McLoone P, Crombie IK (1996) Hospitalisation for deliberate self-poisoning in Scotland from 1981–1993: trends in rates and types of drugs used. *British Journal of Psychiatry* **169**: 816.

Malik SMA (2004) *Anhedonia: a Study in Depression, Apathy and Suicide*. Cosmophobia Theory Monographs no. 58. Roseneath Scientific, New York.

Malone KM, Katalin S, Corbitt EM, *et al* (1995) Clinical assessment versus research methods in the assessment of suicidal behavior. *American Journal of Psychiatry* **152**: 1601–7.

Maris RW (1981) *Pathways to Suicide*. Johns Hopkins University Press, Baltimore.

Maris RW (1990)The developmental perspective of suicide. In: Leenaars A (ed.) *Life-span Perspectives on Suicide*. Plenum Press, New York.

Maris R (1997) Social forces in suicide: a life review. In: Maris RW, Silverman MM, Caneto SS (eds.) *Review of Suicidology 1997*. Guilford Press, New York, pp. 42–60.

Maris RW (2007) Foreword. In: Cutcliffe JR, Stevenson C (eds.) *Care of the Suicidal Person*. Elsevier, Edinburgh, pp. x–xii.

Maris RW, Berman AL, Silverman MM, Farberow N (2000) Indirect self-destructive behavior. In: Maris RW, Berman AL, Silverman MM (eds.) *Comprehensive Textbook of Suicidology*. Guilford Press, New York, pp. 427–55.

Marmer SS, Fink D (1994) Rethinking the comparison of borderline personality disorder and multiple personality disorder. *Psychiatric Clinics of North America* **17**(4): 743–71.

Menghella E, Benson A (1995) Developing reflective practice in mental health nursing through critical incident analysis. *Journal of Advanced Nursing* **21**(2): 205–13.

Mitchell AM, Garand L, Dean D, Panzak G, Taylor M (2005) Suicide assessment in hospital emergency departments. *Topics in Emergency Medicine* **27**(4): 302–12.

Morgan G (1994) Assessment of risk. In: Jenkins R, Griffiths S, Wylie I *et al* (eds.) *The Prevention of Suicide*. Department of Health, HMSO, London, pp. 34–45.

Morgan HG, Priest P (1991) Suicide and other unexpected deaths among psychiatric in-patients. The Bristol confidential inquiry. *British Journal of Psychiatry* **158**: 368–74.

Morttunen M, Aro H, Lonnqvist J (1992) Adolescent suicide: endpoint of long-term difficulties. *Journal of the American Academy of Child and Adolescent Psychiatry*, **31**(4): 649–54.

Moscicki EK (2001) Epidemiology of completed and attempted suicide: toward a framework for prevention. *Clinical Neuroscience Research* **1**: 310–23.

Mossman D (2008) Violence risk: is clinical judgment enough. *Journal of Family Practice* 7(6). http://www.jfponline.com/Pages.asp?AID=6258 (accessed 26 June 2012).

Motto JA, Heilbron DC and Juster RP (1985) Development of a clinical instrument to estimate suicide risk. *American Journal of Psychiatry* **142**(6): 680–6.

Palmer BA, Pankratz VS, Bostwick JM (2005) The lifetime risk of suicide in schizophrenia: a reexamination. *Archives of General Psychiatry*, **62**: 247–53.

Paykel ES (1976) Life stress, depression and attempted suicide. *Journal of Human Stress* **2**: 3–12.

Paykel E, Prusoff B, Myers J (1974) Suicide attempts and recent life events: a controlled comparison. *Archives of General Psychiatry* **32**: 327–33.

Petronis KR, Samuels JF, Moscicki EK, Anthony JC (1990) An epidemiologic investigation of potential risk factors for suicide attempts. *Social Psychiatry and Psychiatric Epidemiology* **25**(4): 193–9.

Pfeffer C (1989) Life stress and family risk factors for youth fatal and nonfatal suicidal behavior. In: Pfeffer C (ed.) *Suicide Among Youth: Perspectives on Risk and Prevention.* American Psychiatric Press, Washington, DC, pp. 143–64.

Pirkola S, Sohlman B, Wahlbeck K (2005) The characteristics of suicides within a week of discharge after psychiatric hospitalization – a nationwide register study. *BMC Psychiatry*, **5**: 32.

Platt S, Davis S, Sharpe M *et al* (2005) Contextual effects in suicidal behaviour: evidence, explanation and implications. In: Hawton, K (ed.) *Prevention and Treatment of Suicidal Behaviour: From Science to Practice*. Oxford University Press, Oxford, pp. 53–70

Pokorny AD (1983) Prediction of suicide in psychiatric patients: report of a prospective study. *Archives of General Psychiatry* **40**: 249–57.

Pompili M, Serafini G, Innamorati M, Dominici G, Ferracuti S, Kotzalidis GD, Serra G, Girardi P, Janiri L, Tatarelli R, Sher L, Lester D (2010) Suicidal behavior and alcohol use. *International Journal of Environmental Research and Public Health* 7(4): 1392–431.

Powell J, Geddes J, Hawton K (2000) Suicide in psychiatric hospital in-patients. *British Journal of Psychiatry* **176**(3): 266–72.

Preti A, Meneghelli A, Pisano A, Cocchi A (2009) Risk of suicide and suicidal ideation in psychosis: results from an Italian multi-modal pilot program on early intervention in psychosis. *Schizophrenia Research* **113**(2–3): 145–50.

Read GFH (1997) Trends in adolescent and young adult parasuicide population presenting at a psychiatric emergency unit: a descriptive study. *International Journal of Adolescent Medicine and Health* **9**(4): 249–69.

Romme M, Hoing A, Noorthoorn E, Escher A (1992) Coping with hearing voices: an emancipatory approach. *British Journal of Psychiatry* **161**: 99–103.

Rosen G (1971) History in the study of suicide. *Psychological Medicine* **1**: 267–85.

Rossotto E (1997) Bulimia nervosa with and without substance use disorders: a comparative study. *Dissertation Abstracts International* **58**: 4469.

Sansome RA, Sansome LA (2010) Measuring self-harm behavior with the Self-Harm Inventory. *Psychiatry (Edgmont)*, 7(4): 16–20.

Sansome RA, Wiederman MW, Sansome LA (1998) The Self-Harm Inventory (SHI): development of a scale for identifying self-destructive behaviours and borderline personality disorder. *Journal of Clinical Psychology* **54**: 973–83.

Santa Mina EE, Gallop R (1998) Childhood sexual and physical abuse and adult self-harm and suicidal behaviour: a literature review. *Canadian Journal of Psychiatry* **43**(8): 793–800.

Science Daily (recovered 2011) *Genetic Link to Attempted Suicide Identified.* http://www.sciencedaily.com/releases/2011/03/110328131258.htm (accessed 26 June 2012).

Sharp M, Schill T (1995) Chronic self-defeating personality: similarities and differences. *Journal of Personality Assessment* **64**(2): 270–8.

Shea SC (1999) *The Practical Art of Suicide Assessment: A Guide for Mental Health Professionals and Substance Abuse Counsellors.* John Wiley, New York.

Shneidman ES (1973) Suicide. In: *Encyclopaedia Britannica* **21**: 383–5. Williams Benton, Chicago.

Shneidman ES (1985) *Definition of Suicide*. John Wiley, New York.

Shneidman E (1993) *Suicide as Psychache: A Clinical Approach to Self-destructive Behavior*. Jason Aronson Inc., Northvale, NJ.

Shneidman ES (2004) *Autopsy of a Suicidal Mind.* Oxford University Press, Oxford.

Sidley GL, Calam R, Wells A *et al* (1999) The prediction of parasuicide repetition in a high-risk group. *British Journal of Clinical Psychology* **38**(4): 375–86.

Silverman MM (1997) Current controversies in suicidology. In: Maris RW, Silverman MM, Canetto SS (eds.) *Review of Suicidology 1997*. Guilford Press, New York, pp. 1–21.

Simon RI (2005) *Preventing Patient Suicide: Clinical Assessment and Management*. American Psychiatric Publishing Inc., Arlington.

Simpson E, Zlotnick C, Begin A *et al* (1994) *Self-Injury Survey*. Providence, RI.

Slater J, Depue R (1981) The contribution of environmental events and social support to serious suicide attempts in primary depressive disorder. *Journal of Abnormal Psychology* **90**: 275–85.

Soomro GM (2008) Deliberate self-harm (and attempted suicide) *Clinical Evidence Online*. http://www.ncbi.nlm.nih.gov/pmc/articles/pmc2907980/ (accessed 26 June 2012).

Standing M (2008), Clinical judgement and decision-making in nursing – nine modes of practice in a revised cognitive continuum. *Journal of Advanced Nursing* **62**: 124–134. doi: 10.1111/j.1365-2648.2007.04583.x.

Stein DJ, Chiu WT, Hwang I, Kessler RC, Sampson N *et al* (2010 – recovered 2011) Cross-national analysis of the associations between traumatic events and suicidal behavior: findings from the WHO World Mental Health Surveys. *PLoS One* 13;5(5):e10574. http://www.ncbi.nlm.nih.gov/pubmed/20485530 (accessed 26 June 2012).

Stuart G (2001) Self-protective responses and suicidal behaviour. In: Stuart G, Laraia MT (eds.) *Principles and Practices of Psychiatric Nursing*, 7th edn. Mosby, New York, pp. 381–400.

Suicide Prevention Resource Centre (recovered 2011) *Featured Resources for College Students*. http://www.sprc.org/featured_resources/customized/college_student.asp.

Sullivan GR, Bongar B (2006) Psychological testing in suicide risk management. In: Simon RI, Hales RE (eds.) *The American Psychiatric Publishing Textbook of Suicide Assessment and Management*. American Psychiatric Publishing, Washington, DC, pp. 177–96.

Swanson JW (2008) Preventing the unpredicted: managing violence risk in mental healthcare. *Psychiatric Services* **59**: 191–3.

Tanney B (2000) Psychiatric diagnoses and suicidal acts. In: Maris RW, Berman AL, Silverman MM (eds.) *Comprehensive Textbook of Suicidology*. Guilford Press, New York, pp. 311–40.

Thomas S, Ferrier N, Watkinson H, Lewis G *et al* (2006) *Avoidable Deaths: Five Year Report of the National Confidential Inquiry into Suicide and Homicide by People with Mental Illness*. University of Manchester, Manchester.

Tishler C, McKenry P, Morgan K (1981) Adolescent suicide attempts: some significant factors. *Suicide Life-Threatening Behavior* **11**: 86–92.

Troister T, Links P, Cutcliffe JR (2008) Review of predictors of suicide within 1 year of discharge from a psychiatric hospital. *Current Psychiatry Reports*, **10**: 60–5.

Van der Kolk BA, Perry JC, Herman JL (1991) Childhood origins of self-destructive behavior. *American Journal of Psychiatry* **148**: 1665–71.

Vanderlinden J and Vandereycken W (1997) *Trauma, Dissociation and Impulse Dyscontrol in Eating Disorders*. Taylor & Francis, New York.

Weisharr ME, Beck AT (1992) Hopelessness and suicide. *International Review of Psychiatry* **4**: 177–84.

Welch SS (2001) A review of the literature on the epidemiology of parasuicide in the general population. *Psychiatric Services* **52**(3): 368–75.

Wenz FV (1977) Marital status, anomie, and forms of social isolation: a case of high suicide rate among the widowed in an urban sub-area. *Diseases of the Nervous System* **38**(11): 891–5.

Wetzel RD (1976) Hopelessness, depression and suicide intent. *Archives of General Psychiatry* **33**: 1069–73.

Wetzel RD, Margulies T, Davis R, *et al* (1980) Hopelessness, depression and suicide intent. *Journal of Clinical Psychiatry* **41**: 159–60.

Young MA, Fogg LF, Schefter WA, Fawcett,JA (1994) Interactions of risk factors in predicting suicide. *American Journal of Psychiatry* **151**(3): 434–5.

Zimmerman M, McGlinchley JB (2008) Why don't psychiatrists use scales to measure outcome when treating depressed patients? *Journal of Clinical Psychiatry* **69**: 1916–19.

Zlotnick C, Shea MT, Pearlstein T, Simpson E, Costello E, Begin A (1996) The relationship between dissociative symptoms, alexithymia, impulsivity, sexual abuse, and self-mutilation. *Comprehensive Psychiatry* **37**: 12–16.

Zlotnick C, Mattia JI, Zimmerman M (1999) Clinical correlates of self-mutilation in a sample of general psychiatric patients. *Journal of Nervous and Mental Disease* **187**: 296–301.

CHAPTER 4

Managing the physical environment and the milieu

> In hospital settings, it is the psychiatric or mental health nurses who are the most available to engage in more extensive interactions with suicidal individuals. The nursing staff is also responsible for creating a therapeutic hospital environment to help decrease the suicide risk and prepare the patient for life outside the hospital setting (Brian Mishara, 2007, p. xiii)

Introduction

In this chapter, we will address suicide in hospital settings, ie. where the risk is higher, and pay particular attention to if/how the physical environment and unit/ward milieu (or atmosphere) can be managed to reduce the chance of suicidal acts. We will talk about both professional and institutional issues and characterise the most common types of suicide. We will discuss some recommendations for the prevention of suicidal behaviours in hospital settings through the means or medium of 'managing the physical environment and ward milieu'. Finally, we draw attention to how families and significant others might be 'mobilised' as a further healing resource for suicidal people. Although nurses have significant responsibilities in this domain and should be mindful of how these phenomena might be managed to enhance care, environmental safety is only one piece of the puzzle (Sullivan *et al*, 2005).

Suicidal ideation and suicide in hospital

Consideration and management of the physical environment is important in efforts to prevent suicidal behaviours. In addition to the more broad, 'macro' level prevention measures, such as public awareness and education, restriction of access to lethal means and careful media reporting of suicide in the community (Mann and Currier, 2011), specific measures related to managing the physical environment and milieu on a treatment ward are crucial (Lieberman *et al*, 2004; Yeager *et al*, 2005; Joint Commission Resources, 2007; Cardell *et al*, 2009; Mills and Bagian, 2009; Tishler and Reiss, 2009).

Some existing data depict a clinical picture whereby approximately 50–60% of psychiatric inpatient admissions are related to suicidal ideation/intent (Jacobs, 1999), and the proportion of patients at acute risk of completing suicide is thought to be approximately 30% (Ritzel and Kornek, 1983). For more than 100 years there have been reports of suicides by inpatients in hospital settings (Damerow, 1856; Edel, 1891; both cited by Wolfersdorf, 2000). It is argued that patients with so-called mental disorders who require hospitalisation have an increased risk of suicide, sometimes ten times higher than the general population (Baxter and Appleby, 1999; Powell *et al*, 2000; Mortensen *et al*, 2000; Eagles *et al*, 2001). Data indicate that between 100 and 400 inpatients per 100,000 admissions complete suicide (Proulx *et al*, 1997; Martin, 2000; Powell *et al*, 2000; Dong *et al*, 2005; Kapur *et al*, 2006; Neuner *et al*, 2008). Suicide rates in general hospitals are lower: 5–15 per 100,000 admissions (Shapiro and Waltzer, 1980; Dong and Kan, 2005). However, in comparative studies, non-psychiatric inpatients had less suicidal communication, performed suicidal acts more rapidly after admission and used more violent methods than psychiatric inpatients (Cheng *et al*, 2009). This situation can be partly explained by the lack of experience of the general hospital's team, as it is particularly focused on the physical issues.

Although recent studies estimate suicide rates based on the number of admissions, there are still estimates based on the number of discharges per year or the number of patients a year at risk. Available data indicate an increase in the number of suicides worldwide (Wolfersdorf, 2000), despite the fact that there may be an under-enumerated number of cases of inpatient suicide (Blain and Donaldson, 1995). Given the consequences of these behaviours, a number of authors have argued that suicide assessments and systematic patient safety protocols in psychiatric hospitals should both be priorities (Yeager *et al*, 2005; Cardell *et al*, 2009). However, it was only in the 1950s that the concern for a decrease in the number of suicides became stronger (Farberow, 1981). According to Wolfersdorf (2000), this increase in inpatients can only be explained based on untested (or rather unverified) hypotheses, given the difficulty of testing them because of ethical and methodological issues. Be that as it may, Wolfersdorf (2000) has advanced a summary of explanations for the increase inpatient suicidal behaviours and these are collated in Table 4.1.

It is possible that some of the reasons are related to a 'disease-focused model' and to difficulties in adapting to structural changes in hospitals and to social changes regarding the view on suicide, as well as to less availability to provide care. The same author also mentions some predisposing factors for suicide, such as those related to the ward environment and milieu, and these are summarised in Tables 4.2 and 4.3.

Table 4.1 Possible explanations for the increase in suicidal behaviours in psychiatric inpatients (adapted from Wolfersdorf, 2000).

- Structural changes in psychiatric hospitals in the last few decades
- A lack of internal structure in mixed psychiatric wards
- Changes in patient groups which are felt to be increasingly difficult to manage, and are more demanding and suicidal
- Changes in societal attitudes towards mental illness and chronic illness, with an increased acceptance of suicidal behaviour
- Depression induced by the traditional or typical neuroleptic drugs
- So-called forced rehabilitation
- The lack of protection as a result of the increased reduction in the amount of time spent in care
- Greater liberty in terms of the freedom and holiday time permitted to patients

Table 4.2 Factors related to the ward's milieu (adapted from Wolfersdorf, 2000).

Organisational:

- frequent staff turnover (loss of personal relationships, particularly in long-term wards; exposure to traumas and instability)
- rehabilitation pressure (over activation)

Professional:

- poor ward atmosphere, insufficient integration of patients
- isolation and loneliness, especially among long-term patients
- frequent change of treatment strategies
- diagnostic errors, especially in the diagnosis of suicidality

Organisational and professional:

- nursing shortages are reported in around a quarter of inpatient suicides (Appleby *et al*, 1999)
- premature or insufficiently prepared vacations, premature free outings
- too short a duration of patient treatment, insufficiently prepared aftercare
- too early discharge
- deficits in education and continuing education of staff, particularly involving estimation of suicidality and in the handling of suicidal patients
- lack of, or insufficient, therapeutic supervision and lack of support from hospital management (inadequate policies for the management of suicidal patients)

Table 4.3 Factors related to the ward's physical environment (adapted from Wolfersdorf, 2000).

Organisational:
- oversized or undersized treatment wards (excessive emotional pressure or lack of emotional security)
- insufficiently prepared renovation and change of wards (hospital instability; change of social relationships; compulsion to reorientation)
- poor architectural design (such as unsafe shifts and stairwells, windows which can be easily opened; access to pipes and similar structures...)
- difficulties in observing patients because of ward design (Appleby *et al*, 1999)

Professional:
- careless handling of instruments and objects potentially usable in suicide in wards; opportunities for access to such objects

Organisational and professional:
- insufficient safeguarding strategies (organisational, mechanical, human – safeguarding through relationships)

These tables show that most factors are related to the organisation. However, nurses also have an important role in this matter as a group of people who can influence the organisations' decisions and the management of professional issues, particularly in terms of relationship management and the organisation of safe wards. Unfortunately, nursing shortages are a crucial problem which can hinder the implementation of a safe environment.

Characteristics of suicidal behaviour in psychiatric hospitals

Most psychiatric inpatient suicide attempts and completions actually take place outside the physical boundaries of the ward (Appleby, 1992; Neuner *et al*, 2008). However, inside the ward, hanging/strangulation and jumping/multiple injuries are the most common methods of suicide, while self-poisoning is the most common method of suicide attempt. According to the United Kingdom's National Confidential Inquiry into Suicide and Homicide (NCISH) (2006), between April 2000 and December 2004, there were 856 suicides among inpatients, the largest number of them through hanging/strangulation (44%), followed by jumping/ multiple injuries (25%) and self-poisoning. With regard to diagnoses, most patients showed affective disorders (bipolar disorder and depression, 53%) or schizophrenia and other delusional disorders (30%).

In a more detailed analysis, the most common objects used in hanging were: a belt (45%), a sheet, a towel etc. (16%), shoelaces (10%), clothing (tie, scarf, tights etc.); and the ligature points were a hook or handle (42%), a door (18%), a window

(13%), a bed head (10%), other rails (eg. toilet rail, wardrobe rail), shower fixtures (eg. shower head, tap), and a bed curtain rail. Thirty-five per cent occurred during the period when discharge was being planned and 15% took place in the first week after admission, with suicides that occurred on the ward being more common (41%) in the evening and night (NCISH, 2006).

In places where a certain method has been found to be common and very accessible, small changes can have an impact on suicide rates (Florentine and Crane, 2010). If we consider suicide as a process starting from triggering events, distress, ideation or attempts to suicide, we can intervene by limiting cognitive access in the ideation phase and then limiting physical access between ideation and suicide (Florentine and Crane, 2010). Thus, when we talk about physical environment and milieu, we are only talking about this intervention in the chain of the suicidal process. However, in hospitalisation, it acquires greater importance since the other phases may have already been completed and they justify hospitalisation. Moreover, this limitation of access to the methods can create a rupture in the suicidal process. Some studies indicate a substitution of the methods, but this substitution in a safe hospital environment becomes even more difficult, if not impossible[1]. Even when an intervention is successful in limiting physical availability, it is important to note that this cannot work in isolation as a suicide prevention strategy (Florentine and Crane, 2010).

Physical environment

In a major independent review of inpatient (hospital) suicides, the physical environment was identified as one of the root contributing factors to 84% of the suicides that occurred, and an overwhelming majority of incidents involved environmental concerns. Seventy-five per cent occurred in bathrooms, bedrooms and closets (Joint Commission Resources, 2007).

The goals of environmental safeguards in psychiatric institutions are to limit the means that inpatients may use to physically harm themselves, and to provide external control over inpatients through staff interventions until the inpatients are able to reestablish internal control over their suicidal impulses (Cardell *et al*, 2009). Considering the ways and means used in suicidal behaviours, the following summary tables (Tables 4.4–4.8) are presented with general recommendations for the prevention of hanging; prevention of jumping; prevention of self-poisoning; and prevention of damages with personal objects.

---

1 Though substitution of method(s) post-discharge remains a distinct possibility in some cases.

Table 4.4 General environmental recommendations.

- Psychiatric wards with safety features (Tishler and Reiss, 2009)
- Define the most appropriate/safest wards in hospitals and admit suicidal patients accordingly (Lieberman *et al*, 2004)
- Install breakaway bars, namely shower curtain rods, closet rods etc. (Lieberman *et al*, 2004)
- Redesign or enhance security strategies such as door-locking mechanisms, patient monitors and alarms (Rose, 2000)
- Find alternatives to plastic trash can liners (Rose, 2000)
- Use non-sharp dining utensils and non-breakable plates and glasses (Lieberman *et al*, 2004)
- Use rooms closest to nursing stations for high-risk patients (Lieberman *et al*, 2004)
- Install non-breakable glass or plastic mirrors and windows (Lieberman *et al*, 2004)
- Conduct environmental rounds using active observation skills and a comprehensive checklist of potential environmental hazards (Mills and Bagian, 2009)
- Update or establish procedures to educate hospital visitors about patient suicide risks and visitors' role, particularly with regard to bringing in restricted items (Lieberman *et al*, 2004)
- Update patient information transfer procedures (Wysocker, 2000)
- Eliminate doors when not required by code (Mills and Bagian, 2009)
- Provide unlockable patient bathroom doors (Oregon Association of Hospitals and Health Systems, 1999)
- Lock doors that may provide access to sharp objects (Oregon Association of Hospitals and Health Systems, 1999).

Table 4.5 Recommendations for hanging prevention.

- Inpatient units should remove (or make inaccessible) all likely ligature points (Department of Health, 2001)
- When installing structural or utilitarian items, it should be made sure that they cannot support a human body (Lieberman *et al*, 2004; Yeager *et al*, 2005; Cardell *et al*, 2009);
- Remove items that can be used as hanging or strangulation devices such as drapery cords, belts, shoelaces, ties, handkerchiefs, bathrobe sashes, drawstring pants and bras (Lieberman *et al*, 2004)
- Bedrails should be avoided when possible (Cardell *et al*, 2009)
- Remove doors on wardrobe cabinets and replace rods and hangers with shelves (Mills and Bagian, 2009)

Table 4.6 Recommendations for jumping prevention.

■ Locate psychiatric wards on the ground floor
■ Install safety barriers when wards are located on the upper floors
■ Install windows that do not open from the inside, or use windows that have locks or locked interior safety screens (Lieberman *et al*, 2004)

Table 4.7 Recommendations for self-poisoning prevention.

■ Ensure there is a protocol in place to eliminate access to drugs that could be used for an overdose (Mills and Bagian, 2009)
■ Avoid leaving portable cleaning carts unattended (Lieberman *et al*, 2004)
■ Total control of the nursing office and of access to medication
■ Use nontoxic cleaning agents
■ Do not use cleaning products, such as common toxic cleaning and maintenance solutions, that include acetate, butyl alcohol, paint thinner, floor and carpet-cleaning solutions

Table 4.8 Recommendations for prevention of harm with personal belongings.

■ Check all objects in the patient's ward
■ Eliminate belts, shoelaces and safety razors, shave high-risk patients or observe while shaving (Mills and Bagian, 2009)

In a study conducted in Ireland, O'Donovan (2007) identified some of the nurses' practices in terms of environment management to prevent suicidal behaviours. The primary methods outlined for ensuring a service user's safety were the removal of sharp objects from the service use and requesting that they remain in their night clothes. Also, razors and scissors, pens, combs, matches, lighters, phone chargers, glass bottles, aerosol sprays, photo frames, nail clippers, medication and anything that could be used as a ligature, including shoelaces, were removed. However, some nurses expressed discomfort with this practice because of patients' rights; indeed, some patients expressed dissatisfaction with this practice as it erodes personal dignity and choice.

These concerns are congruent with other studies which argue that we have been witnessing a clear move to a mental healthcare model influenced by a more controlling and coercive mental health policy (Heffern and Austin, 1999; Hannigan and Cutcliffe, 2002). This is currently the dominant way of thinking and the policies are related to a 'medical' or 'disease model', coupled with the management and treatment of these 'disorders' (Hannigan and Cutcliffe, 2002; Szasz, 2007). Therefore, this is a model in which control and containment practices emerge as a result of a shift from a focus on care to a focus on control, underlining the role of the illness and the therapist and decreasing the patient's role. As a result, the 'problem of suicide' is seen to reside in individuals who thus need to be controlled, contained and/or managed, and this inevitably means controlling and/ or containing and/or managing the risk. Further, in such policies, the 'solution' to the person's suicidality is seen to reside in the hands of the psychiatrist; not necessarily in the people themselves (Cutcliffe and Stevenson, 2008). Influenced by phenomena such as stigma, mental health illiteracy and the very little power of patients' associations, there is a strengthening of the idea of control rather than self-determination, or a focus on the individual's potential.

On the other hand, failure to protect patients from harming themselves is one of the most common reasons for lawsuits and/or legal action brought against healthcare organisations (Simon and Shuman, 2007), which leads to an effective penalisation of hospitals. Thus the prevalence of healthcare focused on risk management is not surprising; whether or not this produces the best results for clients is an entirely different matter. In addition, the deinstitutionalisation movement (through the shutdown of hospitals and the need for hospitalisation based on risk levels); civil rights and patient rights (calling for a greater need to identify the levels of dangerousness to the self and others); and involuntary (civil) complement proceedings have also led to an increased focus on risk management (Yeager *et al*, 2005).

According to Cutcliffe and Stevenson (2008), we need to encourage suicide policy literature to reflect upon a less defensive, less risk management-oriented position. This is important because, as mentioned by Paterson *et al* (2008), predicting suicide risk in psychiatric inpatients in order to make informed risk management decisions is compromised by the poor predictive validity of the available models. In addition, although psychiatrists and nurses appear to agree on the characteristics of patients[2] who are considered to be at higher or lower risk of suicide, the consistency of judgments is low because clinicians often use cues that have been associated with suicide in traditional predictive models based on epidemiological studies and short-term factors that may be particularly

2 For the most part.

relevant to acute psychiatric settings. Alternative approaches need to incorporate a phenomenological perspective on suicide risk management into practice (Paterson *et al*, 2008).

Environment and milieu as a puzzle piece in a suicide prevention plan

When considering the most therapeutic setting(s) for suicidal people, the need for privacy and a therapeutic environment needs to be considered. Environmental safety is only one piece of the puzzle, and ongoing assessment and staff communication are critical (Sullivan *et al*, 2005). In order to prevent suicidal behaviours during inpatient stays, some authors have attempted to identify the necessary/useful procedures during hospitalisation. According to Wolfersdorf (2000), it is important to have: a detailed assessment of risk at the time of admission; the formation of close therapeutic relationships with staff (namely by ensuring that each patient has one or two named nurses who are his/her key workers); repeated assessment of risk, especially at times of crises; adequate treatment of so-called mental illness; and elimination of environmental features which contribute to increased risk (eg. hooks on walls).

The UK Department of Health (2001) has also issued some recommendations on the prevention of suicide in hospital settings, namely: inpatients going on leave should have close community follow-up; patients under non-routine observations should not normally be allowed time off the ward or leave; inpatient services should ensure that there are no gaps, however brief, in one-to-one observation; and all discharged inpatients who have a so-called severe mental illness or a recent (less than three months) history of suicidality should have a follow-up within one week.

More recently, the NCISH (2006) in a five-year report of the national confidential inquiry into suicide and homicide by people with mental illness, suggested some recommendations on suicide prevention regarding inpatients: reduce absconding from inpatient units; strengthen the transition from the ward to the community; respond robustly when care plans break down; accept that prevention is possible in many cases, particularly regarding inpatient suicides; strengthen observation procedures in wards; further improve the physical environment in wards; develop services for dual diagnosis patients; and give greater emphasis to risk management in older people's services.

The authors will not belabour the obvious emphasis in these documents: namely how these recommendations are part of a defensive model focused on risk management. Taking into account that the number of inpatients completing suicide has increased worldwide, the predominantly defensive and risk management-focused model does not appear to have had the hoped-for (expected) outcome, so an alternative approach to caring for suicidal inpatients is needed[3].

Although several factors were identified to be strongly associated with suicide, in terms of predictive power, their clinical utility is limited by low sensitivity and specificity, combined with the rarity of suicide, even in this high-risk group (Powell *et al*, 2000).

We cannot place the environment, the illness or risk management at the centre of healthcare: rather we should be concerned with the patients and their singularity and specificity and, above all, their ability to deal with the situation, and what we, as P/MH nurses, might be able to do to help.

Next to the ward's door: families as contributors to the environment or milieu

The burden on families with a person who has a severe so-called mental illness has been extensively analysed, initially among relatives of schizophrenic patients, but then generalised. Among other things, it has been examined in connection with the major changes in psychiatric services towards community-based services (Brown *et al*, 1962; Fadden *et al*, 1987; Östman and Hannson, 2000; Kjellin and Östman, 2005). Also, changes in burden on the families as the deinstitutionalisation process proceeded, with more care provided in patients' homes, are also largely uninvestigated (Östman and Hansson, 2000).

In the overall panorama of psychiatric patients, a highly significant behaviour in the individual and family dynamics emerges: suicidal behaviours. This issue can be analysed from two different perspectives. On one hand, in terms of their consequences (which may result in death or permanent sequelae from the family's point of view), and on the other (concerning hospital and community care), follow-up and sometimes hospitalisation are not a synonym for problem-solving. Suicide is sometimes completed after discharge.

Östman and Hannson (2000) have analysed the burden on relatives of patients hospitalised in acute psychiatric wards. Around half (46%) of the relatives experienced severe concerns about whether the patient would attempt suicide. Parents are the group that was most concerned about whether the patient would attempt suicide or not. While comparing data between 1986 and 1991, the same authors found that, despite the fact that most burden indicators had decreased, the indicators related to the relatives' concerns about whether the patient would

3 Interestingly, one in which nurses have a key, important role.

attempt suicide had increased. This situation was also observed in 2005, in which the fear of suicide attempts was more often a source of concern, especially among relatives of patients who had one or more suicide attempts within a month prior to admission recorded in their medical records (Kjellin and Östman, 2005). Studies which have been carried out with families of individuals who had suicidal behaviours concluded that families show high expressed emotion through over-involvement, criticism or hostility (Pollard, 1996; Wedig and Nock, 2007; Santos *et al*, 2009). These studies reinforce the need to further include families in healthcare provision, reducing expressed emotion particularly through psycho-education.

Among those in the general population who complete suicide, up to 41% may have contact with psychiatric inpatient care in the year prior to death and up to 9% may complete suicide within one day of discharge (Pirkis and Burgess, 1998). This issue is further developed and explored in Chapter 10. For these reasons, family burden increased among relatives of patients who had attempted suicide, and the need for support was higher for relatives of patients with suicidal behaviour. The results corroborate the need for psychiatric services to involve and support relatives of psychiatric patients with suicidal behaviour (Kjellin and Östman, 2005).

References

Appleby L (1992) Suicide in psychiatric patients: risk and prevention. *British Journal of Psychiatry*, **161**: 749–58.

Appleby L, Shaw J, Amos T, McDonnell R, Kiernan K, Davies S, Harris C, McCann K, Bickley H, Parsons R (1999) Suicide within 12 months of contact with mental health services: national clinical survey. *British Medical Journal* **318**: 1235–9.

Baxter D, Appleby L (1999) Case register study of suicide risk in mental disorders. *British Journal of Psychiatry* **175**: 322–6.

Blain PA, Donaldson LJ (1995) The reporting of in-patient suicides: identifying the problem. *Public Health* **109**: 293–301.

Brown GW, Birley JLT, Wing JK (1972) Influence of family life on the course of schizophrenic disorders; a replication. *British Journal of Psychiatry* **121**: 241–58.

Cardell R, Bratcher K and Quinnett P (2009) Revisiting 'Suicide Proofing' an inpatient unit through environmental safeguards: a review. *Perspectives in Psychiatric Care* **45**(1): 36–44.

Cheng I, Hu F, Tseng M (2009) Inpatient suicide in a general hospital. *General Hospital Psychiatry* **31**: 110–15.

Cutcliffe J, Stevenson C (2008). Never the twain? Reconciling national suicide prevention strategies with the practice, educational, and policy needs of mental health nurses (part one). *International Journal of Mental health Nursing* **17**: 341–50.

Department of Health (2001) *Safety First. Five-Year Report of the National Confidential Inquiry into Suicide and Homicide by People with Mental Illness*. Department of Health, London.

Dong J, Ho T, Kan C (2005) A case-control study of 92 cases of in-patient suicides. *Journal of Affective Disorders* **87**: 91–9.

Eagles J, Klein S, Gray N, Dewar I, Alexander D (2001) Role of psychiatrists in the prediction and prevention of suicide: a perspective from north-east Scotland. *British Journal of Psychiatry*, **178**: 494–6.

Fadden G, Bebbington P, Kuipers L (1987) The burden of care; the impact of functional psychiatric illness on the patient's family. *British Journal of Psychiatry* **150**: 285–92.

Farberow N (1981) Suicide prevention in the hospital. *Hospital and Community Psychiatry* **32**(2): 99–104.

Florentine J, Crane C (2010) Suicide prevention by limiting access to methods: a review of theory and practice. *Social Science and Medicine* **70**: 1626–32.

Hannigan B, Cutcliffe JR (2002) Challenging contemporary mental health policy: time to assuage the coercion? *Journal of Advanced Nursing* **35**(5): 477–84.

Heffern WA, Austin W (1999) Compulsory community treatment: ethical considerations. *Journal of Psychiatric and Mental Health Nursing* **6**: 37–42.

Jacobs D (1999) *The Harvard Medical School Guide to Suicide Assessments and Interventions*. Jossey Bass, San Francisco, CA.

Joint Commission Resources (2007) *Suicide Prevention: Toolkit for Implementing National Patient Safety Goal 15A*. Oakbrook Terrace, IL.

Kapur N, Hunt I, Webb R, *et al* (2006) National confidential inquiry into suicide and homicide: suicide in psychiatric in-patients in England, 1997–2003. *Psychological Medicine* **36**: 1485–92.

Kjellin L, Ostman M (2005) Relatives of psychiatric inpatients – do physical violence and suicide attempts of patients influence family burden and participation in care? *Nordic Journal of Psychiatry* **59**: 7–11.

Lieberman D, Resnik H, Holder-Perkins V (2004) Environmental risk factors in hospital suicide. *Suicide and Life-Threatening Behavior* **34**(4): 448–53.

Mann J, Currier D (2011) Evidence-based suicide prevention strategies: an overview. In Pompili M, Tatarelli R (eds.) *Evidence-Based Practice in Suicidology*. Hogrefe Publishing, Cambridge, MA, pp. 67–88.

Martin BA (2000) The Clarke Institute experience with completed suicide: 1966 to 1997. *Canadian Journal of Psychiatry* **45**: 630–8.

Mills P, Bagian J (2009) Response to Tishler and Reiss' review of inpatient suicide. *General Hospital Psychiatry* **31**: 589.

Mishara B (2007) Foreword. In: Cutcliffe J, Stevenson C (eds.) *Care of the Suicidal Person*. Churchill Livingstone/Elsevier, Edinburgh, pp. xiii–xiv.

Mortensen PB, Agerbo E, Erikson T, Qin P, Westergaard-Nielsen N (2000) Psychiatric illness and risk factors for suicide in Denmark. *Lancet* **355**: 9–12.

NCISH (2006) *Five Year Report of the National Confidential Inquiry Into Suicide and Homicide by People with Mental Illness*. National Confidential Inquiry into Suicide and Homicide by People with Mental Illness, London.

Neuner T, Schmid R, Woldersdorf M, Spiebl H (2008) Predicting inpatient suicides and suicide attempts by using clinical routine data? *General Hospital Psychiatry* **30**: 324–30.

Oregon Association of Hospitals and Health Systems (1999) *Helpful Hints on Preventing Inpatient Suicide*.

O'Donovan (2007) Pragmatism rules: the intervention and prevention strategies used by psychiatric nurses working with non-suicidal self-harming individuals. *Journal of Psychiatric and Mental Health Nursing* **14**: 64–71.

Östman M, Hansson L (2000) The burden of relatives of psychiatric patients. Comparisons between parents, spouses, and grown-up children of voluntarily and compulsorily admitted psychiatric patients. *Nordic Journal of Psychiatry* **54**: 31–6.

Paterson B, Cassels C, Dowding D, Morrison D, Niven C (2008) Managing the risk of suicide in acute psychiatric inpatients: a clinical judgement analysis of staff predictions of imminent suicide risk. *Journal of Mental Health*, **17**(4): 410–23.

Pirkis J, Burgess P (1998) Suicide and recency of healthcare contacts: a systematic review. *British Journal of Psychiatry* **173**: 462–74.

Pollard CW (1996) *Attempted Adolescent Suicide and Expressed Emotion*. Doctoral Dissertation, The Catholic University of America, Washington, DC.

Powell J, Geddes J, Deeks J, Goldacre M, Hawton K (2000) Suicide in psychiatric hospital in-patients: risk factors and their predictive power. *British Journal of Psychiatry* **176**: 266–72.

Proulx F, Lesage A, Grunberg F (1997) One hundred in-patient suicides. *British Journal Psychiatry* **171**: 247–50.

Ritzel G, Kornek G (1983) Förden Freizügige und individuelle Therapie und Klinikführung den Suizid? *Psycho*, **9**: 7–80.

Rose N (2000) Six years' experience in Oxford: review of serious incidents. *Psychiatric Bulletin* **24**: 243–6.

Santos J, Saraiva C, Sousa L (2009) The role of expressed emotion, self-concept, coping, and depression in parasuicidal behavior: a follow-up. *Study Archives of Suicide Research* **13**: 358–67.

Shapiro S, Waltzer H (1980) Successful suicides and serious attempts in a general hospital over a 15-year period. *General Hospital Psychiatry* **2**: 118–26.

Simon R, Shuman D (2007) *Clinical Manual of Psychiatry and the Law*. American Psychiatric Publishing, Washington, DC.

Sullivan A, Barron C, Bezmen J, Rivera J, Zapata-Vega M (2005) The safe treatment of the suicidal patient in an adult inpatient setting: a proactive preventive approach. *Psychiatric Quarterly* **76**(1): 67–83.

Szasz T (2007) *The Medicalisation of Everyday Life – Selected Essays*. Syracuse University Press, Syracuse, New York.

Tishler C, Reiss N (2009) Inpatient suicide: preventing a common sentinel event. *General Hospital Psychiatry* **31**: 103–9.

Wedig M, Nock M (2007) Parental expressed emotion and adolescent self-injury. *Journal of American Child and Adolescent Psychiatry* **46**: 9.

Wolfersdorf M (2000) Suicide among psychiatric inpatients. In: Hawton K, Van Heeringen K (eds.) *The International Handbook of Suicide and Attempted Suicide*. Wiley, Chichester.

Wysocker A (1999) Suicide: risk management strategies. *Journal of the American Psychiatry Nurses Association* **5**(5): 164–6.

Yeager R, Saveanu R, Roberts A, Reissland G, Mertz D, Cirpili A, *et al* (2005) Measured response to identified suicide risk and violence: what you need to know about psychiatric patient safety. *Brief Treatment and Crisis Intervention* **5**: 121–41.

CHAPTER 5

Custodial 'defensive' practices such as containment, seclusion, observations, and no-suicide contracts

> I deeply believe that the principal function of a mental health facility (and the staff member within it) and of psychotherapists generally after the obvious need to protect people from their own self-destructive impulses is assured – is to assess and evaluate psychological pain as it relates to frustrated psychological needs, and then to act as anodynes. (Edwin Shneidman, 1996, p. 151)

Introduction

It can be argued that so-called defensive practices have become generalised from a risk management perspective and in so doing are more concerned with avoiding (or limiting) damage resulting from the problem, rather than actually solving the problem. Defensive practices are concerned with the physical integrity of the person and do little (or nothing) to address the genesis (and/or exacerbation) of the person's suicidal thoughts or feelings (Cutcliffe and Stevenson, 2008). The most common defensive practices are: containment, seclusion, observations, removal of objects and no-suicide contracts. In this chapter, we will examine each of these approaches/interventions, especially as despite their lack of supporting evidence (in many cases), they remain common practices that nurses engage in on the ward/unit as a means to (allegedly) prevent suicide. In this chapter we analyse the efficacy and legitimacy of these practices based on evidence-based data and discuss some implications of these practices from the point of view of users and nurses. Finally, we address alternatives to these practices, as the authors believe that the evidence indicates that it is necessary for us to move away from defensive strategies as a matter of urgency.

A close look at close observations

The first question which should be clarified is what we mean when we speak of 'close observations'. Close observations involve having someone, sometimes a nurse, with the patients at all times, sometimes 'at arm's length' (Rooney, 2009), or the formal assigning of nursing staff to maintain a clearly defined degree of observation or supervision over a patient who is assessed as representing some degree of risk to self and/or others on the basis of a single or multiple variables (Nielson and Brennan, 2001). Also, according to Ward and Jones (2007), observation is a commonly used P/MH nursing intervention for patients at risk and involves the allocation of one nurse (or sometimes two) to one patient for a prescribed length of time in order to 'provide intensive nursing care'.

Close observations are also described as: 'maximum observation', 'constant supervision', 'continuous observation', 'specialling', 'maximum observation', 'constant observation', 'observation one-to-one', 'individual observation' and 'special observation' (Duffy, 1995; Fletcher, 1999; Horsfall and Cleary, 2000; Nielson and Brennan, 2001; Sullivan *et al*, 2005; Rooney, 2009). The plethora of terms may very well be indicative of a general confusion and a lack of consistency (Duffy, 1995). In an attempt to provide a response to this confusing and ambiguous terminology, which lacks a clear definition and is often subject to individual staff interpretation, several authors have made efforts to address this issue. These efforts include those advanced by the Standing Nursing and Midwifery Advisory Committee (1999), as well as by Bowers *et al* (2000) and Neilson and Brennan (2001). Neilson and Brennan (2001), for example developed a special observation record sheet (SORS). According to them, the special observation policy was originally written for use within the psychiatric intensive care unit (PICU), and it comprises four levels: red, amber, blue and green (Box 5.1).

Box 5.1 Special Observation Policy (adapted from Neilson and Brennan, 2001)

Level	Characterisation
Red	Is the most intrusive and restrictive, and reserved for the most disturbed individuals
Amber	Allows staff a little more flexibility in terms of minimising the intrusiveness to the patient
Blue	Provides for staff contact with patient at specified frequencies
Green	Provides for a general level of observation

Other models indicate an observation of 1:1 (arm's length observation), every 15 or 30 minutes, then moving on to close observation in situations of low and moderate suicidality risk, while those with higher risk were maintained in a 1:1 observation (Sullivan *et al*, 2005).

Neilson and Brennan (2001) conducted an audit to assess the use of the SORS system and found that it

> provides clear evidence that the special observation policy is not being implemented and adhered to in practice as was intended, and raises a number of important issues that both clinicians and managers need to address. One of the challenges facing both nursing and medical staff is deciding when to impose and reduce special observations (Nielson and Brennan, 2001, p. 155)

It is possible to note that there is still some misinterpretation of the terms and little standardisation, as was also confirmed by the Department of Health (2001), which stated that where observation policies exist, there is a great deal of inconsistency in their interpretation. The confusion around the language to be used, coupled with possible resistance of staff to full implementation of new policies, can provoke confusion, lack of clarity and reduced patient safety (Bowers *et al*, 2000).

Another important issue is related to the prescription of close observations. The most common reasons include aggression (either to self or others); violence (usually towards others); a risk of suicide or self-harm; a risk of absconding; and being acutely disturbed and difficult to manage (Bowers *et al*, 2000; Ward and Jones, 2007). According to Barker and Cutcliffe (1999), the practice of observation was developed as a means to inform medical staff of the status of the patient and it served the function of assuring the 'absent' doctor of the physical safety of the patient. Powers (1996) even argues that close observations are construed as a mechanism for perpetuating power inequalities that compel nurses to perform specific work practices under the guise of medically prescribed treatment. However, if the doctor decides that the patient is 'at risk' for suicide via some inferential processes, then the issue that remains unsettled is how successful is each doctor at making such an assessment (Horsfall and Cleary, 2000).

On the other hand, we know that in relation to those who are considered to be at higher or lower risk of suicide, the consistency of judgments (between physicians and nurses) is low because clinicians use cues that have been associated with suicide in traditional predictive models based on epidemiological studies and short-term factors that may be particularly relevant to acute psychiatric settings

(Paterson *et al*, 2008). Despite that, when increased levels of patient support are needed (whether it be observation or containment), as the SNMAC guidelines (Department of Health, 1999) suggest, nurses should be involved in the decision to implement them (Bowles *et al*, 2002), which can be seen in some situations in England (Bowers *et al*, 2000). However, this cannot be generalised. Ward and Jones (2007) mention that close observations assignments are often decided by other members of the multidisciplinary team, who are guided by the hospital policies and the need to reduce the possibilities of 'untoward events'. This idea seems to be congruent with Cutcliffe and Barker (2002), who argue that close observations are a system that was designed originally to inform medics and now, at least in part, is concerned with meeting the needs of the organisation.

According to Bowers *et al* (2000), observations aim to reduce the risk for self-harm or completed suicide and to prevent aggressive behaviour or absconding. For some authors, nursing observation is a key component of psychiatric inpatient nursing care (Jones *et al*, 2000). The view that close observation should be seen as having a therapeutic purpose is shared by some authors (Fletcher, 1999). Ward and Jones (2007) argue that the therapeutic intention of close observations can be seen under four ideas: care-based; management based; care team-based; and patient–personal. They also criticise those who reduce close observations to a controlling process. But observations have been more about prevention than about cure – suggesting that nurses know that they are keeping the patient safe, but that it is not necessarily treatment in the sense of changing the patients' presentation (Rooney, 2009).

For patients, the experience of being observed is often less than therapeutic and, in some cases, counterproductive (Bowles *et al*, 2002). Intrusive observation to stop suicidal thoughts seems to contradict views on western humankind's willfulness (Horsfall and Cleary, 2000), and the imposition of controlling actions without consent is likely to confirm to the patient that they have failed and are worth nothing (Fletcher, 1999) It is a crude, 'custodial'-orientated form of intervention to meet the highly complex, convoluted and sophisticated care needs of this client group (Cutcliffe and Barker, 2002).

Being under close observation is associated with negative feelings of anger, rebelliousness, punishment, discouragement, anxiety, unhelpfulness, failure, worthlessness, impotence and hopelessness in patients (Briggs, 1974; Fletcher, 1999; Cardel and Pitula, 1999; Horsfall and Cleary, 2000; Cutcliffe and Barker, 2002) and staff express feelings of anger, inadequacy, anxiety, fear of precipitating suicide attempts, stress and burden (Briggs, 1974; Fletcher, 1999; Wilstrand *et al*, 2007; Rooney, 2009). Duffy (1995) reported nurses' discomfort with being identified (by some disciplines) as custodians rather than therapeutic practitioners. If formal observations were introduced for defensive reasons, then they also created a voyeuristic mentality – an intrusive, disengaged gaze on human suffering – and something was lost when nursing observations became the norm in inpatient units (Bowers *et al*, 2000).

These data can perhaps explain the fact identified by Whittington and McLaughlin (2000) that around 80% of the time spent during constant observation has been identified as 'non-interactional'. This idea can be questioned, as observations without conversation are mere surveillance (Hamilton and Manias, 2007).

Sometimes staff members were considered hostile and punitive by patients (Duffy, 1995; Fletcher, 1999) and, whilst being 'under observation', users felt neither safe nor supported (Barker and Walker 1999). Therefore the practice of formal observation might both be ineffective and contribute to the maintenance of ritualised, impersonal care (Dodds and Bowles, 2001).

Special attention should be given to the person carrying out the close observation, as patients' experiences of being observed are strongly influenced by the attitudes and behaviours of the observing nurses (Jones *et al*, 2000), and a wide range of messages are communicated by the nurse's attitude, demeanour and approach. If the suicidal person senses that a nurse is uninterested, uncaring, condemning or judgmental, then the effect on the person's feelings of self-worth is likely to be negative (Cutcliffe and Barker, 2002).

Despite the fact that Ward and Jones (2007) consider close observations to be an advance procedure that requires many years of supervised practice to perfect, in most cases nurses have received no official training or clinical education for special observation (Duffy, 1995; Barker and Cutcliffe, 1999; Fletcher, 1999; O'Brien and Cole, 2003; Westhead *et al*, 2003; Rooney, 2009). The majority of the observation is not carried out by trained nurses. Consequently, observation is invariably regarded as a low skill activity, often carried out by support staff (rather than registered nurses), or by bank or agency nurses who, due to their transient nature, have only limited knowledge of the person (Cutcliffe and Barker, 2002). Even so, patients prefer to be observed by nurses they know and who talk to them (Jones *et al*, 2000). In one Canadian hospital, security guards rather than P/MH nurses sometimes carry out the observations of the suicidal person (Cutcliffe, 2003). This can be partly explained by the reported worldwide shortage of qualified P/MH nurses and the effects this has had on the variety of care offered, as has been noted in several reviews. Particularly in the UK, these shortages appear to have dramatically reduced the amount of therapeutic activity being undertaken by nurses (Ward and Jones, 2007). The fact that these observations imply major costs should also be taken into account (Sullivan *et al*, 2005).

The effectiveness of close observations is still to be confirmed. There is no real 'evidence base' for the effective practice of close observations, and the written guidance that exists is highly variable across different settings and localities (Ward and Jones, 2007). However, between 20 and 33% of inpatient suicides were completed while the clients were under levels of observation (Department of Health, 2001) and the number of deaths under observation has not fallen significantly since 1997, which means that they have increased as a proportion of inpatient suicides (National Institute for Mental Health in England, 2007).

This ineffectiveness can be partly explained by the difficulties in observing patients because of ward design and nursing shortages, which were both reported in around a quarter of inpatient suicides (Appleby *et al*, 1999). In a large-scale study carried out in England by Bowers *et al* (2008), involving 128 acute National Health Service units and including 16,420 admissions, of which 4,112 had valid inclusions for the study, it was concluded that no relation was found between constant special observation and rates of self-harm, but the use of intermittent observation may act to reduce rates of self-harm (Bowers *et al*, 2008).

Some form of observation is sometimes necessary, but this occasional necessity should not obscure the mind-numbing ritualisation of nursing practice that formal observation often degenerates into (Bowles *et al*, 2002), which can undermine the potential for nurses to develop satisfying, supportive relationships with the entire inpatient group (Dodds and Bowles, 2001). Nursing needs to reintroduce a therapeutic approach to practice in close observation areas that will define its role and contribution to the multidisciplinary team approach to patient care (O'Brien and Cole, 2003), because P/MH nurses potentially have a major input into the everyday lives of suicidal inpatients. Despite this vital responsibility for safeguarding people at risk of harm and the potential to offer therapeutic intervention, exactly how P/MH nurses should go about providing this care to suicidal clients is not well understood (Cutcliffe and Barker, 2002). One thing seems almost certain: it is not through close observations.

Dodds and Bowles (2001) have led a project to reduce formal observations and replace 'control' oriented interventions with 'care' interventions. They believe that formal observation of 'at risk' patients is ineffective, possibly counter-therapeutic and contradicts humanistic nursing values, principles of individualised care and meaningful nurse–patient engagement. The following findings were established: incidents of deliberate self-harm reduced by two-thirds, violence and aggression reduced by over a third, staff sickness fell by two-thirds, absconding declined by half, and there was no increase in suicides during the corresponding period (18 months). Importantly, they state: 'the effect on patient care has been striking: patients are more engaged with their named nurses, better informed and more involved with their care and the financial savings have been significant' (Dodds and Bowles, 2001).

Seclusion and containment/coercion. For what purpose? For whom?

Both seclusion and coercion are forms of defensive procedures in nursing practice. Despite being controversial matters, these practices still exist today. The reduction of its use in psychiatric services is a priority health political issue in Western countries (WHO, 2005). Will nurses be able to respond to this challenge? In this chapter, we use the term *seclusion* to mean the confinement of a patient in a single room or in a separate unit or area inside the ward accompanied by staff, and the term *restraint* to mean strapping a patient to a bed with mechanical devices (Husum *et al*, 2010) such as belts or handcuffs which restrict the patient's movement. In our opinion, seclusion and restraint are different forms of coercion which can be defined as the use of force that limits a person's choices and/or which can involve physical or psychological distress (Wynn, 2006).

Coercion and seclusion are used purposefully to help/protect the patient, thus preventing suicidal behaviour, and they are also supposed to help the patient regain control over her/his psychiatric symptoms, such as anxiety, restlessness, paranoia, hallucinations or aggression. As a measure of control, seclusion and restraint are used when a patient threatens the safety of others – in other words, is violent or threatens to become violent (Kaltiala-Heino *et al*, 2003).

Prevention of self-harm is a usual justified motivation for seclusion and/or containment (Gutheil, 1987; Fisher, 1994; Kaltiala-Heino *et al*, 2003). In a study carried out in Finland, threatening self-harm was the reason for seclusion/restraint at first hand in the treatment of voluntarily admitted patients suffering from affective disorders (Kaltiala-Heino *et al*, 2003). So as to understand the worldwide dimension of the phenomenon, Steinert *et al* (2010) compared data from 12 countries and found a huge variety in the type, frequency and duration of coercive measures used. Most of all, they concluded that western European mental health services are broadly similar in terms of resources and populations at risk, and the data obtained suggest that the use of coercive measures may be based much more on culture, traditions and policies than on medical or safety requirements. Kaltiala-Heino *et al* (2003) had already confirmed a gap between theory and practice when they analysed the Finnish situation. Even if theoretically seclusion/restraint is in the first instance justified by the need for treating violent patients in emergencies, this is not the most important application in practice.

What are the reasons mentioned by nurses for using coercion?

In order to better understand nurses' attitudes and how they can be changed, Happell and Harrow (2010) conducted a literature review and identified six main reasons for using coercion: a necessary intervention; workplace culture; staff composition and experience; conflict; ethical considerations; and consumer characteristics. Despite the fact that nurses are aware of uncomfortable ethical questions related to seclusion, these alone have not been enough to change practice. Seclusion is seen as one of the few options open to staff to manage violent or aggressive patients. Wynn (2006), in an attempt to tackle the ethical issue, analysed the reality in different countries and concluded that while some see all use of coercion as unethical, most seem to agree that the use of coercion is ethically acceptable when the benefits with regard to protection or treatment outweigh the negative effects on patients' autonomy, integrity and comfort. However, this is both an ethical and a technical issue. Frequent use of seclusion or restraint can increase stress on the ward, harm therapeutic relations, decrease the effect of medicines, and harm the recovery (Putkonen, 2007), although little evidence exists about the clinical outcomes of coercion (Wynn, 2006). There are reports on the consequences of restraint that estimate that 50–150 deaths occur every year in one single nation because of restraint or seclusion (McCue *et al*, 2004).

So as to determine the impact of coercion on Norwegian patients, Iversen *et al* (2007) interviewed patients subject to seclusion during hospitalisation. The authors concluded that coercion had a significant negative effect on overall satisfaction, and it was even considered as a punishment (Brown and Tooke, 1992).

Despite the data available on this matter, while seclusion is still regarded favourably amongst nurses and other health professionals who are actively involved with its use (Happell and Harrow, 2010), it is often believed to be practitioners who are more removed from the clinical setting who can see the benefit of finding an alternative practice (Doeselaar *et al*, 2008).

McCue *et al* (2004), so as to reduce restraint use, have organised an intervention programme at a psychiatric hospital based on six interventions: better identification of restraint-prone patients; a stress/anger management group for patients; staff training on crisis intervention; development of a crisis response team; daily review of all restraints; and an incentive system for staff. Two years after the beginning of this intervention, the rate of restraint use had already decreased. This can be used as a good example. However, to ensure the success of seclusion reduction techniques, further research is needed to investigate the factors that might influence attitudes, in order to develop and implement interventions to effectively reduce its use (Happell and Harrow, 2010).

A close look at no-suicide contracts

The first study on no-suicide contracts was published in 1973 by Robert Drye, Robert Goulding and Mary Goulding. The authors asked their patients to make verbal decisions not to hurt themselves. This was one of the first approaches to this type of commitment between technicians and patients. In the nursing area, Farrow *et al* (2002) mention that it was Twimane, in 1981, who extended the boundaries of the usage of no-suicide contracts when she introduced the concept to nursing literature. Twimane (1981) argues that this tool was appropriate for use by nurses both in hospitals and with persons who called crisis hotlines.

Drye *et al* (1973) considered that the theoretical foundations of no-suicide contracts were enmeshed in psychoanalysis, transactional analysis and gestalt therapy. Transactional analysis is based on the theory that there are three ego states: child, adult and parent. Suicidal feelings belong to the child ego state, and the role of the therapist is to help the service user move from this state to the mature adult state. However, Lester (1994) argues that asking a service user to 'promise' not to kill themselves merely reinforces the executive role of the child's ego state. Farrow (2003) agrees with him in that no-suicide contracts reinforce the 'child' role of the service user, who is forced to agree to an action by the 'parent' (clinician) for fear of retribution. Egan (1997) has also criticised transactional analysis foundations. Despite these concerns, the users of no-suicide contracts seem to accept this connection between these contracts and transactional analysis (Farrow, 2003). However, some authors, such as Range (2005) and Rudd *et al* (2006) see clear links between no-suicide contracting and cognitive behavioural therapy approaches to treatment.

Despite the lack of consensus on this conceptual framework, the perspective of the transactional analysis seems to be the most prevalent. Nonetheless, analysis of the use of transactional analysis as the theoretical underpinning of the use of no-suicide contracts in community crisis situations suggests that the concept is flawed, indicating that consideration needs to be given to abandonment of this tool in such a context (Farrow, 2003).

There are multiple terms in literature: no-suicide contracts, no-harm contracts, no-suicide agreements, contracting for safety, contracting to stay alive, suicide-prevention contracts, safety agreement, no-kill contract and no-suicide decisions

(Farrow, 2002; Lewis, 2007). We will use the most common term in this chapter: no-suicide contracts. According to Rudd *et al* (2006), common elements in no-suicide contracts include the following: an explicit statement agreeing not to harm or kill oneself; specific details about the duration of the agreement; a contingency plan if a crisis that would jeopardise the patient's ability to honour the agreement emerges; and the specific responsibilities of both patient and clinician.

In the clinical setting, no-suicide contracts are verbal (or verbal and written) decisions between a practitioner and suicidal patient to undertake pre-defined tasks to keep the suicidal patient safe, usually until the next scheduled follow-up appointment (Edwards and Harries, 2007). According to Edwards and Harries (2007), the dissemination of the use of no-suicide contracts was developed in five stages:

1. The emergence of volunteer suicide crisis centres, essentially reducing the technique from being part of an extended therapeutic process to operating within the context of brief crisis relationships
2. The adoption of no-suicide contracts and no-suicide agreements by the nursing profession
3. Occurrence when practitioners saw congruence in the ability of the technique to support behavioural and cognitive approaches to managing suicidality (treatment)
4. Occurrence when practitioners began to use these clinical interventions for self-protection – attempting to mitigate the demands of an over-stretched service environment while being mindful of litigation (administrative matters) in the event of adverse clinical outcomes
5. Contemporary stage, in which no-suicide contracts appear to have become almost routine (Edwards and Harries, 2007).

What are the existing reports on the use of no-suicide contracts in nursing?

In a study conducted in New Zealand with nurses, Farrow (2002) found that the most prevalent theme in the interviews was one of no-suicide contracts being used as a means of self-protection for nurses; no nurse could recall any formal training in the use of no-suicide contracts. It was apparent that the concept had been either learned through observation of peers or taught informally by colleagues; finally, some nurse participants indicated that a lack of available resources is one reason why NSCs are used so frequently. Specifically mentioned were a dearth of inpatient or respite facilities for suicidal patients, and difficulties in allocating time to spend with people because of the demands of other concurrent crises. Besides the lack of reasons confirming the clinical effectiveness of no-suicide contracts, arguments for its use include nurses' self-protection and the lack of resources. The lack of specific training on this matter is also evident.

It is, therefore, important to clarify that no-suicide contracts do not afford any legal protection (Simon, 1999); nor do they have legal authority, and the perception of *confining*, *restraining*, and *restricting* patients' behaviours at a time when they are struggling for control can prove disastrous (Rudd *et al*, 2006). As for the lack of training, Miller *et al* (1998) had already mentioned that the use of these contracts is based upon subjective belief rather than on objective data or formal training.

In another study conducted at a community crisis clinic, Farrow *et al* (2002) interviewed nurses and, shockingly, they discovered situations where a management decision which was inconsistent with the high level of suicide risk had occurred because the patient had agreed to a no-suicide contract and managers had not hospitalised some patients. However, most of the nurses believed that no-suicide contracts were an important tool in assessing overall risk of suicide, formulating a therapeutic relationship, and encouraging patient empowerment. In addition, Potter *et al* (2005) found positive aspects mentioned by nurses in relation to the use of no-suicide contracts. These RNs perceived increased patient responsibility, nurse contact, safety guidance, safety discussions and time guidelines with the use of safety agreement, even though the implementation of the safety agreement tool did not result in statistically significant decreased levels of self-harm.

What is the users' opinion?

Farrow *et al* (2002) reported that, rather than finding no-suicide contracts empowering, several patients described no-suicide contracts as being disempowering. They felt that they were expected to be responsible for initiating further contact if the suicidal urges increased, meaning that they were solely responsible for their safety.

With the same objective, ie. to identify inpatients' opinions about no-suicide contracts, Davis *et al* (2002) acknowledged three factors underpinning a service user's commitment to safety when no-suicide contracts were used: the therapeutic features of the no-suicide contracts, its coercive features and its detached features. It can be concluded that, in this study, no-suicide contracts were considered therapeutic but also coercive (when service users felt manipulated to sign a no-suicide contract aimed at protecting the staff), and their use by the service users led to secondary gains, namely early discharge. Weiss (2001) had previously argued that the suggestion of no-suicide contracts could imply to the service user that the clinician was more concerned with protecting themselves from legal or professional consequences than with the wellbeing of the service user.

What is the evidence being produced to confirm their effectiveness?

This is one of the weakest factors of no-suicide contracts. Indeed, most authors do not identify any clinical effectiveness of no-suicide contracts. No other empirical evidence supports the effectiveness of no-suicide contracts in preventing suicide. Such contracts should be used only as an adjunct to full assessment with patients who are at high risk of self-harm (Kelly and Knudson, 2000).

Edwards and Harries (2007), in an analysis of multiple guidelines, concluded that there is a current lack of any rigorous scientific data attesting to the efficacy or effectiveness of such techniques, and the technique may be routinely used and overly relied upon at the expense of a thorough assessment, treatment or management process.

Farrow (2003) also concluded that there is no empirical evidence that no-suicide contracts are efficient at either preventing suicide or in having suicidal persons fulfil the 'promise' to contact mental health services if they are suicidal in the future. Rudd *et al* (2006) affirm that a common definition should remove the term *contract* and provide a broader construct and that the conceptual model needs to view such agreements as clinical interventions, part of the broader treatment that fits within the full range of theoretical orientations.

Despite the lack of evidence on their clinical effectiveness, how can we justify the use of no-suicide contracts?

Some authors mention positive aspects in using no-suicide contracts. These contracts appear to offer patients opportunities for self-respect and control over their life (Assey, 1985; Edwards and Harries, 2007) and they may serve several useful purposes, including fostering a therapeutic alliance between the clinician and patient and assisting in suicide assessment (Kelly and Knudson, 2000). In a literature review, Lewis (2007) found advantages in using them both as assessment tools and interventions. The author also mentioned that, although contracts cannot protect a clinician from malpractice in the event of a suicide, contracts can be part of the documentation demonstrating clinician's efforts to manage suicidal impulses.

Rudd *et al* (2006) recommend the use of a commitment to treatment statement in which the patient agrees to make a commitment to the treatment process and living by identifying the roles, obligations and expectations of both the clinician and the patient in treatment; communicating openly and honestly about all aspects of treatment including suicide; and accessing identified emergency services during periods of crisis that might threaten the patient's ability to honour the agreement.

Which conclusions can be drawn from the use of no-suicide contracts?

According to Edwards and Sachmann (2010), no-suicide contracts have proved to be poorly understood and remain a questionable clinical practice intervention. Education initiatives are required that will alert mental health practitioners to the dangers of no-suicide contracts for patients and practitioners alike, and to present alternative interventions presenting less risk. Moreover, there are some risks resulting from the use of no-suicide contracts. According to Drew (2001), negotiation of a contract is a reflection of staff assessment that the patient was at high risk for suicide. These ideas confirm the need for thorough, ongoing assessment of suicidal risk, whether or not a patient has agreed to a no-suicide contract.

Some authors also support their specific use under the following circumstances: as part of a comprehensive assessment and plan of treatment; as part of an existing therapeutic relationship, with understanding that risk still remains; and with clear documentation that data and clinical judgment were both used in making a decision not to hospitalise, while avoiding the shorthand of 'contracted for safety' (Miller, 1999).

Lewis (2007) sums up the discussion about no-suicide contracts: perhaps the most compelling argument against the use of no-suicide contracts is that there is no empirical evidence that they are effective; it is unwise and potentially harmful to use interventions that one has little training in using; another argument against NHCs is that patients are not actually competent to agree to any treatment contract while actively suicidal; contracts can be harmful if clinicians use the contract as a standalone tool or believe that a contract eliminates suicide risk.

We agree with Farrow (2003) when he states that, rather than using an empirically unproven and conceptually flawed concept, the focus should be on assessing and managing suicidal crises using existing nursing and multidisciplinary expertise, and that there is a firm consensus within the literature that its use should only occur as an adjunct to, and never as a replacement for, comprehensive suicide risk assessments for suicidal people (Cutcliffe and Stevenson, 2008).

Alternatives to defensive practices

Even a cursory examination of the relevant theoretical and empirical literature demonstrates that the priority for some nurses is providing a physically safe environment and preventing self-harm by using methods such as removing service users' day clothes, threatening negative consequences to self-harm, 'special observations', no-harm contracts and distraction techniques (O'Donovan, 2007). However, despite their prevalence and the (for some) continued, unquestioning

Table 5.1 Alternatives to the use of more defensive practices.

Assessment: use of valid, systematic clinical assessment tools
Nurse autonomy: policies that facilitate nurses assuming the responsibility for commencing and reducing observation levels
Supervision, staff team reviews and staff support meetings: ward management initiatives that commit to clinical supervision, staff team reviews and staff support meetings
Engagement, collaboration and structured weekly activity programmes: working structures and practices that champion 'the gift of time' to patients and facilitate engagement and collaboration between staff and patients, structured weekly activity programmes for patients and regular patient community meetings
A 'team' approach: greater 'team' approach towards decision making within the multidisciplinary team and overall service development

adherence to defensive practices as the *modus operandi* for 'caring' for suicidal people, it needs to be noted that there are alternatives to these practices.

The view of the authors is that there remains an urgent need to move away from defensive strategies and risk management-oriented (or driven) positions (Cutcliffe and Stevenson, 2008). As to the use of distraction strategies with people who self-harm, it is contraindicated by Gallop and Tully (2003), who reported that people who self-harm believe that distraction techniques cover up the real problem and demonstrate a lack of understanding on the part of the practitioner.

According to Cox *et al* (2010), the following interventions (in Table 5.1) can be considered alternatives to the use of more defensive practices.

References

Appleby L, Shaw J, Amos T, McDonnell R, Kiernan K, Davies S, Harris C, McCann K, Bickley H, Parsons R (1999) Suicide within 12 months of contact with mental health services: national clinical survey. *British Medical Journal* **318**: 1235–9.

Assey J (1985) The suicide prevention contract. *Perspectives in Psychiatric Care* **23**(3): 99–103.

Barker P, Cutcliffe J (1999) Clinical risk: a need for engagement not observation *Mental Health Practice* **2**: 8–12.

Barker P, Walker L (1999) *A Survey of Care Practices in Acute Admission Wards*. Reports submitted to the Northern and Yorkshire Regional Research and Development Committee, University of Newcastle.

Bowers L, Gournay K, Duffy D (2000) Suicide and self-harm in inpatient psychiatric units: a national survey of observation policies. *Journal of Advanced Nursing* **32**(2): 437–44.

Bowers L, Whittington R, Nolan P, Parkin D, Curtis S, Bhui K, Hackney D, Allan T, Simpson A (2008) Relationship between service ecology, special observation and self-harm during acute in-patient care: City-128 study. *British Journal of Psychiatry* **193**: 395–401.

Bowles N, Dodds P, Hackney D, Sunderland C, Thomas P (2002) Formal observations and engagement: a discussion paper. *Journal of Psychiatric and Mental Health Nursing* **9**: 255–60.

Briggs P (1974) Specialing in psychiatry; therapeutic or custodial? *Nursing Outlook* **22**: 632–5.

Brown J, Tooke S (1992) On the seclusion of psychiatric patients. *Social Sciences and Medicine* **35**: 711–21.

Cardell R, Pitula CR (1999) Suicidal inpatients' perceptions of therapeutic and non-therapeutic aspects of constant observation. *Psychiatric Services*, **20**(8): 1066–70.

Cox A, Hayter M, Ruane J (2010) Alternative approaches to 'enhanced observations' in acute inpatient mental healthcare: a review of the literature. *Journal of Psychiatric and Mental Health Nursing* **17**: 162–71.

Cutcliffe J (2003) The differences and commonalities between United Kingdom and Canada psychiatric/mental health nursing: a personal reflection. *Journal of Psychiatric and Mental Health Nursing* **10**: 255–7.

Cutcliffe J, Barker P (2002) Considering the care of the suicidal client and the case for 'engagement and inspiring hope' or 'observations'. *Journal of Psychiatric and Mental Health Nursing* **9**: 611–21.

Cutcliffe J, Stevenson C (2008) Feeling our way in the dark: the psychiatric nursing care of suicidal people – a literature review. *International Journal of Nursing Studies* **45**: 942–53.

Davis S, Williams I, Hays L (2002) Psychiatric inpatients' perceptions of written no-suicide agreements: an exploratory study. *Suicide and Life Threatening Behavior* **32**: 51–66.

Department of Health (1999) *Practice Guidance: Safe and Supportive Observation of Patients at Risk.* Standing Nursing and Midwifery Advisory Committee, Department of Health, London.

Department of Health (2001) *Safety First: Five Year Report of the National Confidential Inquiry Into Suicides and Homicide by People with Mental Health Problems.* HMSO, London.

Dodds P, Bowles N (2001) Dismantling formal observation and refocusing nursing activity in acute inpatient psychiatry: a case study. *Journal of Psychiatric and Mental Health Nursing* **8**: 183–8.

Doeselaar M, Sleegers P, Hutschemaekers G (2008) Professionals' attitudes towards reducing restraint: the case of seclusion in the Netherlands. *Psychiatric Quarterly* **79**: 97–109.

Drew BL (2001) Self-harm behavior and no-suicide contracting in psychiatric inpatient settings. *Archives of Psychiatric Nursing* **15**: 99–106.

Drye RC, Goulding RL, Goulding ME (1973) No-suicide decisions: patient monitoring of suicidal risk. *American Journal of Psychiatry* **130** (2): 171–4.

Duffy D (1995) Out of the shadows: a study of the special observation of suicidal psychiatric in-patients. *Journal of Advanced Nursing*, **21**: 944–50.

Edwards S, Harries M (2007) No-suicide contracts and no-suicide agreements: a controversial life. *Australasian Psychiatry*, **5**(6): 484–9.

Edwards S, Sachmann M (2010) No-suicide contracts, no-suicide agreements, and no-suicide assurances: a study of their nature, utilization, perceived effectiveness, and potential to cause harm. *Crisis* **31**(6): 290–302.

Egan MP (1997) Contracting for safety: a conceptual analysis *Crisis* **18**(1): 17–23.

Farrow, T (2002) Owning their own expertise: why nurses use 'no suicide contracts' rather than their own assessments. *International Journal of Mental Health Nursing* **11**: 214–19.

Farrow T (2003) 'No-suicide contracts' in community crisis situations: a conceptual analysis. *Journal of Psychiatric and Mental Health Nursing* **10**: 199–202.

Farrow T, Simpson A, Warren H (2002) The effects of the use of 'no-suicide contracts' in community crisis situations: the experience of clinicians and consumers. *Brief Treatment and Crisis Intervention* **2**: 241–6.

Fisher W (1994) Restraint and seclusion: a review of the literature. *American Journal of Psychiatry* **151**(11): 1584–91.

Fletcher RF (1999) The process of constant observation: perspectives of staff and suicidal patients. *Journal of Psychiatric and Mental Health Nursing* **6**(1): 9–14.

Gallop R, Tully T (2003) The person who self-harms. In: Barker P (ed.) *Psychiatric and Mental Health Nursing The Craft of Caring*. Arnold, London, pp. 236–43.

Gutheil TG (1987) Observations on the theoretical bases for seclusion of the psychiatric inpatient. *American Journal of Psychiatry*, **135**(3): 325–8.

Happell B, Harrow A (2010) Nurses' attitudes to the use of seclusion: a review of the literature. *International Journal of Mental Health Nursing* **19**: 162–8.

Hamilton B, Manias E (2007) Rethinking nurses' observations: psychiatric nursing skills and invisibility in an acute inpatient setting. *Social Science and Medicine* **65**: 331–43.

Horsfall J, Cleary M (2000) Discourse analysis of an 'observation levels' nursing policy. *Journal of Advanced Nursing* **32**(5): 1291–7.

Husum T, Bjørngaard J, Finset A, Ruud T (2010) A cross-sectional prospective study of seclusion, restraint and involuntary medication in acute psychiatric wards: patient, staff and ward characteristics. *BMC Health Services Research* **10**: 89.

Iversen K, Høyer G, Sexton H (2007) Coercion and patient satisfaction on psychiatric acute wards International. *Journal of Law and Psychiatry* **30**: 504–11.

Jones J, Ward M, Wellman N, Hall J, Lowe T (2000) Psychiatric inpatients' experience of nursing observation: a United Kingdom perspective. *Journal of Psychosocial Nursing and Mental Health Services* **38**(12): 10–20.

Kaltiala-Heino R, Tuohima C, Korkeila J, Lehtinen V (2003) Reasons for using seclusion and restraint in psychiatric inpatient care. *International Journal of Law and Psychiatry* **26**, 139–49.

Kelly K, Knudson M (2000) Are no-suicide contracts effective in preventing suicide in suicidal patients seen by primary care physicians? *Archives of Family Medicine* **9**: 1119–21.

Lester D (1994) Psychotherapy for suicidal clients. *Death Studies* **18**: 361–74.

Lewis L (2007) No-harm contracts: a review of what we know. *Suicide and Life-Threatening Behavior* **37**(1): 50–7.

McCue R, Urcuyo L, lilu Y, Tobias T, Chambers M (2004) Reducing restraint use in a public psychiatric inpatient service. *Journal of Behavioral Health Sciences and Research* **32**: 217–24.

Miller M, Jacobs D, Gutheil T (1998) Talisman or taboo: the controversy of the suicide prevention contract. *Harvard Review of Psychiatry* **6**: 78–87.

National Institute for Mental Health in England (2007) *National Suicide Prevention Strategy for England: Annual Report on Progress 2006*. HMSO, London.

Nielson P, Brennan W (2001) The use of special observations: an audit within a psychiatric unit. *Journal of Psychiatric and Mental Health Nursing* **8**, 147–55.

O'Brien L, Cole R (2003) Close-observation areas in acute psychiatric units: a literature review. *International Journal of Mental Health Nursing* **12**: 165–76.

O'Donovan (2007) Pragmatism rules: the intervention and prevention strategies used by psychiatric nurses working with non-suicidal self-harming individuals. *Journal of Psychiatric and Mental Health Nursing* **14**: 64–71.

Paterson B, Cassels C, Dowding D, Morrison D, Niven C (2008) Managing the risk of suicide in acute psychiatric inpatients: a clinical judgement analysis of staff predictions of imminent suicide risk. *Journal of Mental Health*, **17**(4): 410–23.

Potter M, Vitale-Nolen R, Dawson A (2005) Implementation of safety agreements in an acute psychiatric facility. *Journal of the American Psychiatric Nurses Association* **11**: 144–55.

Powers, P (1996) Discourse analysis as a methodology for nursing inquiry. *Nursing Inquiry* **3**: 207–17.

Putkonen A (2007) The need to develop alternative measures to seclusion and restraint. *BMC Psychiatry* **7**(suppl 1): S63.

Range L (2005) No-suicide contracts. In: Lester D, Yufit R (eds.) *Assessment, Treatment and Prevention of Suicidal Behavior*. Wiley and Sons, New York.

Rooney C (2009) The meaning of mental health nurses experience of providing one-to-one observations: a phenomenological study. *Journal of Psychiatric and Mental Health Nursing* **16**: 76–86.

Rudd M, Mandrusiak M, Joiner T (2006) The case against no-suicide contracts: the commitment to treatment statement as a practice alternative. *Journal of Clinical Psychology* **62**: 243–51.

Shneidman E (1996) *The Suicidal Mind*. Oxford University Press, New York.

Simon RI (1999) The suicide prevention contract: clinical, legal, and risk management issues. *Journal of the American Academy of Psychiatry and the Law* **27**: 445–50.

Standing Nursing and Midwifery Advisory Committee (1999) *Practice Guidance: Safe and Supportive Observation of Patients at Risk: Mental Health Nursing – Addressing Acute Concerns*. Department of Health, London.

Steiner, T, Lepping P, Bernhardsgrütter R, Conca A, Hatling T, Janssen W, Keski-Valkama A, Mayoral F, Whittington R (2010) Incidence of seclusion and restraint in psychiatric hospitals: a literature review and survey of international trends. *Social and Psychiatric Epidemiology* **45**: 889–97.

Sullivan A, Barron C, Bezmen J, Rivera J, Zapata-Vega M (2005) The safe treatment of the suicidal patient in an adult inpatient setting: a proactive preventive approach. *Psychiatric Quarterly* **76**(1): 67–83.

Twimane B (1981) No-suicide contracts for nurses. *Journal of Psychiatric Nursing and Mental Health Services* **19**: 11–12.

Ward M, Jones J (2007) Close observations: the scapegoat of mental healthcare? In: Cutcliffe J, Ward M (eds.) *Key Debates in Psychiatric/Mental Health Nursing*. Churchill Livingstone/Elsevier, Edinburgh, pp. 257–271.

Weiss A (2001) The no-suicide contract: possibilities and pitfalls. *American Journal of Psychotherapy* **55**: 414–19.

Westhead J, Cobb S, Boath E, Bradley E (2003) Feedback on constant observations. *Mental Health Nursing* **23**: 4.

Whittington D, McLaughlin C (2000) Finding time for patients: an exploration of nurses' time allocation in acute psychiatric settings. *Journal of Psychiatric and Mental Health Nursing* **7**: 259–68.

Wilstrand C, Lindgren B, Gilje F, Gilje F, Olofsson B (2007) Being burdened and balancing boundaries: a qualitative study of nurses' experiences caring for patients who self-harm. *Journal of Psychiatric and Mental Health Nursing* **14**: 72–8.

World Health Organization (2005) *WHO Resource Book on Mental Health, Human Rights and Legislation Stop Exclusion, Dare to Care* World Health Organization.

Wynn R (2006) Coercion in psychiatric care: clinical, legal, and ethical controversies. *International Journal of Psychiatry in Clinical Practice* **10**: 247–51.

CHAPTER 6

Pharmacological interventions

> Psychopharmacotherapy does not target suicide *per se*. There simply is no anti-suicide pill. (Maris *et al*, 2000, p. 525)

Introduction

Rather than discussing the issue of prescription of medication by nurses *per se*, or exploring/arguing/identifying the most appropriate pharmacological treatment for the prevention of suicidal behaviours, this chapter aims to explore the existing evidence-based practice related to pharmacological 'treatment' for suicidal people. At the outset, it should be taken into account that medication is only one measure, among many others, to 'treat' or help suicidal people and it may or may not be a priority. However, in certain parts of the world, even despite the evidence pertaining to the questionable efficacy of pharmacological interventions for treating suicide (see van Praag, 2004), pharmacological 'treatment' or interventions is the 'mainstay' of 'care' offered to suicidal people, and in some places, the only 'care' that suicidal people receive. So while the chapter does indeed consider the wider evidentiary context of pharmacology, we do also review and explore some of the more common pharmacological 'treatments' provided to suicidal people. In this way, this chapter is expected to contribute to a more profound discussion about pharmacological interventions for suicidal people among nurses (and other formal caregivers).

A close look at the need for psychotropic medication

Some epidemiological studies have reported the presence of so-called psychiatric disorders in suicidal people, namely: mood disorders, substance use disorders, psychoses and personality disorders (Henriksson *et al*, 1993; Bertolote *et al*, 2004; Lönnqvist, 2009). However, some authors draw attention to the limited contact between suicidal people and the health services, as well as to the difficulty in distinguishing between 'real'/clinical depression and sadness/distress/mourning. The problem is not so much defining a 'case', as defining the 'non-case', and indicating where distress and worrying end and 'case' depression begins (Van

Praag, 2004), as most people who have completed suicide are sad, but not necessarily clinically depressed (Maris *et al*, 2000).

Is it the case then that, after deconstructing the issue of psychiatric diagnosis, psychotropic medication for suicidal people stops making sense? To paraphrase, if the diagnostic constructs which underpin the case for a pharmacological response to suicide are de-legitimised (or/and de-constructed), does the argument for psychotropic medication to 'treat' suicidal people (especially when medication is the *modus operandi*) stop making sense? This requires a thoughtful response; however, the use of psychopharmacology as a strategy for nursing's professional affirmation (and how this can influence the debate) cannot be ignored (Cutcliffe and Wieck, 2008). According to Harrison *et al* (2011), psychopharmacology is a core, prominent attribute for psychiatrists and prescribing a medicine is the most significant action they will undertake in patient care (see also the Royal College of Physicians, 2009). In this sense, neurobiological manipulation is the main objective of psychotropic drugs. In this context, the theorised[1] role of serotonin in anxiety, aggression, appetite and pain perception; of noradrenalin in attention, activation, memory and data processing; and of dopamine in cognition, reward and sexual behaviour (Saraiva, 2006) should be acknowledged. Despite being bedevilled by issues of conceptual and clinical definition, close attention should still be given to studies on the use of medication to treat/prevent suicide.

A close look at the 'construction of evidence'

The issue of efficacy, and the case for a particular treatment in the epoch of evidence-informed practice, is inevitably linked to discussions and debates around the very nature of evidence itself. At the outset, it should be noted that it is difficult to design a study aimed to assess the effectiveness of a certain drug on the prevention of suicidal behaviours. Some of these reasons have to do with the complexity of suicidal behaviours, the different terminologies associated with these behaviours, the different variables involved in these behaviours, the low base rate and the multidimensional level of interventions. Thus it is difficult to identify which action or component produces the desired outcome. More specifically, difficulty in establishing causality in the use of psychotropic medication to 'treat' suicide can be related to the following factors:

(a) Short duration of most trials: these are important in the evaluation of causal relationships since the conclusions differ depending upon the estimates of their length (Möller, 2006a; Baldessarini and Toldo, 2011)

---

1 And there is some – though inconclusive, empirical evidence to support this theory (see Stoff and Mann, 1997)

(b) In some trials, patients with serious suicidal ideation are often excluded (Verkes and Cowen, 2002)
(c) Naturalistic course of the depressive episode: worsening of a depressive syndrome or suicidality in temporal association with the administration of an antidepressant does not mean that the antidepressant can be accused of being the only cause. It has to be clarified whether the depressive syndrome or suicidality has increased as a part of the natural course of depression (Möller, 2006a)
(d) Non-response to antidepressants/chronicity: if the depression has been present for a longer time these factors can result in increased hopelessness and subsequent suicidality (Möller, 2006a)
(e) Setting factors: the organisational setting can also increase depression and/or suicidality (Möller, 2006a), hospitalisation period, and access to clinical services or social supports (Baldessarini and Toldo, 2011)
(f) Psychosocial factors: the fact that situational stress factors can intensify an existing depression corresponds to general life experience
(g) Failure to administer a sedating drug: the psychopathological picture may change under treatment with antidepressants, either independent of the medication or not, for example in the sense of increased psychomotor agitation and anxiety (Möller, 2006a)
(h) Unwanted drug interactions and issues related to polypharmacy: benzodiazepines, for example, can induce or increase suicidality in rare cases as part of a paradox reaction, or if pharmacological effects not directly but indirectly related to suicidal behaviour were included, for example via effects on impulsivity or aggressiveness (Möller, 1992, 2006a)
(i) Risk factors: irrespective of the type of medication used, certain patients have an increased risk of suicidality for reasons of their family or own medical history, personality traits and comorbidity (Möller, 2003, 2006a; Verkes and Cowen, 2002)
(j) Control for confounding variables: given the difficulty in isolating the dependent (suicide risk/suicide attempts) and independent variable (use of psychotropic medication) – ie. there is very little or no realistic way to control all the potentially confounding variables in such a drug trial – establishing direct causality is unrealistic.

Common and robust research designs?

For the reasons highlighted above, it is necessary to take a more careful look at research designs, method and methodology in order to understand how these mattes can affect the accuracy, validity and ultimately, utility of the findings. The most common designs used in such studies are ecological studies; cohort and case-control studies; and randomised controlled trials. Here we examine the principal features of each of these.

Ecological studies include data from correlative or 'ecological' pharmacoepidemiological studies that compare suicide rates by regions or years with concurrent rates of prescriptions for antidepressant drugs. There are some limitations to these designs which become primarily apparent in studies which seek to determine an association between a treatment and an outcome when the outcome itself is strongly associated with the condition being treated (Möller, 2006a).

Cohort and case-control studies include large cohorts of 'depressed' patients from general practice or health-maintenance organisation data sources, and relatively large, case-control comparisons of subgroups varying in exposure to antidepressants. Clinical cohort studies try to assess the risk of suicidality/ suicidal behaviour in cross-sectional analyses of clinical samples, calculating risk figures based on prescription rates of individual antidepressants. Unfortunately, the risk differences found in these studies are often not statistically controlled for confounding factors and can therefore generate misleading results (Möller, 2006a). Generally, the results of control group studies have to be evaluated critically under consideration of the methodological pitfalls inherent in the design of such trials. For example, most studies do not include patients with high suicidality and therefore do not provide data for the most relevant risk groups. The opposite is true: special risk conditions such as comorbidity, including comorbidity with accentuated personality traits, or even personality disorders, are mostly exclusion criteria in such trials (Möller *et al*, 2008).

Randomised controlled trials, it has been argued by some, can be regarded as the 'best' source of data about the effects of pharmacological agents (most commonly antidepressants), on suicidal behaviours[2] (Goldney, 2007; Olfson *et al*, 2003). Considering the low base rate of suicide attempts and especially of completed suicide, one might argue that the database for one individual antidepressant is still too small to have enough statistical power to give an indication of its effects. Following this line of argumentation, meta-analyses based on the huge data

2 Goldney (2007) argues, even while 'tipping his hat' to the need to use all the evidence, and admitting that certain questions cannot be answered by such trials, and offering a timely reminder of the potential limitations of relying solely on randomised clinical trials (RCTs) in making decisions about the use of medications, that the RCT is the 'gold standard'.

sets available to drug authorities might represent a better approach to test the hypothesis of an increased suicide risk or/and therapeutic value associated with Selective Serotonin Reuptake Inhibitors (SSRIs) or antidepressants in general (Möller, 2006b; Kahn, 2001).

Pharmacoepidemiological studies collect aggregate, not individual data; for example, national suicide rates are compared with national antidepressant prescription rates. It is of great importance that these data are analysed by multivariate statistical procedures taking into account as many of the most relevant confounders (such as the type of antidepressants, gender, age, unemployment rate, alcohol consumption) as possible in the calculation. Such studies are also limited to the extent that they can normally only analyse data on suicides, but not on suicide attempts (Möller *et al*, 2008).

The negative effects of antidepressants on suicidality are difficult to investigate in empirical studies due to several methodological limitations. A broad scientific approach therefore has to use complementary methods to obtain the most comprehensive evidence (Möller, 2006a; Goldney, 2007). This is similarly applicable when investigating both negative and positive effects. In the light of the scientific evidence, can we prove the efficacy of pharmacology in reducing suicidal behaviours? It remains the case that this issue is still a matter of debate (at times, passionate debate) and thus, at the very least, some caution may be required when making any assertions about the efficacy or potential dangers of SSRIs and other antidepressants for suicidal people.

A close look at placebo-controlled studies

The placebo effect exists and it should neither be underestimated nor considered innocuous. Placebo responses are general phenomena in medicine, and they seem to be particularly powerful in depression (Rief *et al*, 2009). It should be kept in mind that, in clinical practice, the placebo response in the treatment of depression is substantial; therefore, clinicians should attempt to retain and optimise the non-specific effects (Rief *et al*, 2009). Interestingly, in terms of analgesics, Waber *et al* (2008) were able to show that the analgesic placebo effect is higher if people expect the drug to be expensive and valuable. This is a possible consequence of the biomedical and deeply medicalised culture which is still predominant in our society(s). The effect can be maximised with placebo-induced positive expectations (Benedetti *et al*, 2006). However, when talking about studies on suicidal behaviours, there is another aspect which may confound the results: 'overdose' might sometimes not be detected as such in the placebo group because it has no medical consequences. This may result in an apparently lower rate of suicidal behaviour in the placebo group, at least as far as cases are concerned in which the medication in the respective trial arm is used as the method of deliberate self-harm (Möller *et al*, 2008).

A close look at 'cases of success'

Despite the many difficulties already mentioned during the construction of evidence, a significant proportion of the existing evidence indicates that clozapine, lithium and antidepressants are effective in preventing suicidal behaviours. However, they can contribute to an increase in the number of suicidal behaviours; for instance, there is also some evidence to suggest that the use of SSRIs as a 'treatment' for suicidal people, particularly children and adolescents (Baldessarini and Tondo, 2011). The majority of studies have focused on some of the drugs which are most commonly used for 'treating' suicide, such as lithium, antidepressants (SSRIs) and clozapine.

Lithium

Cipriani *et al* (2005) reported a meta-analysis of the few available randomised controlled trials (RCTs), in which they found a four- to five-fold superiority for lithium treatment versus alternatives (placebo, anticonvulsants or antidepressants) with regard to risk of suicide, suicide plus self-harm, and/or mortality. Baldessarini *et al* (2006) in a meta-analysis of different studies, concluded that the risks of completed and attempted suicide were consistently lower, by approximately 80%, during treatment of so-called bipolar and other major affective disorder patients with lithium for an average of 18 months. These benefits were sustained in randomised as well as open clinical trials and in the fewer available randomised trials that included a lithium arm, even against other active mood stabilising treatments. Following this meta-analysis, the authors stated that these findings provided strong support for major reductions in the risk of completed and attempted suicides among bipolar disorder and other major affective disorder patients during long-term treatment with lithium, and suggested that the lethality of suicidal acts may also be reduced, perhaps by limiting impulsivity and aggressiveness (Baldessarini *et al*, 2006).

However, in another analysis to assess polypharmacy and adherence, in a sample of 7,406 patients with bipolar disorder (bipolar I (55%), bipolar II (15%), or bipolar disorder not otherwise specified (30%)), it was concluded that the use of antidepressants was highly prevalent and sustained, despite limited evidence of their efficacy or safety in bipolar depression (Baldessarini *et al*, 2008). And more curiously, a remarkable new finding was that at one year the proportion of patients not receiving psychotropic treatment was about as prevalent as the proportions receiving mood-stabilising monotherapy or polytherapy (Baldessarini *et al*, 2008). How can this be explained? This is indeed an issue worth exploring with caution!

Despite a few preliminary studies with different ideas, the findings strongly and consistently support the proposal that lithium has substantial suicide risk-reducing effects . There is also suggestive evidence that it may be more effective for this indication in comparison to other mood stabilising treatments, including carbamazepine, divalproex and lamotrigine (Baldessarini *et al*, 2006; Baldessarini and Tondo, 2011).

It should also be pointed out that clinical use of lithium with the hope of reducing suicidal risk may seem paradoxical, in that lithium has a very limited therapeutic index or margin of safety, can be lethal in acute overdoses (Baldessarini and Tarazi, 2005), and can be used deliberately for suicidal purposes (ie. some suicidal clients take lithium as their over-dose drug of choice). However, the choice of lithium as a toxin for suicide attempts appears to be uncommon, an observation that, itself, may reflect an anti-suicidal effect of lithium (Waddington and McKensie, 1994). Accordingly, where a person's increased risk of suicide appears to be closely linked to/influenced by his/her so-called bipolar disorder, there appears to be a cogent and empirically robust case for the use of lithium as a means to reduce the person's risk of suicide.

Antidepressants

The use of antidepressants in suicide prevention has been widely discussed, but as yet there is no consensus. According to Möller (2008), the American Food and Drug Administration (FDA, 2004, 2007), the British Medicines and Healthcare Products Regulatory Agency (MHRA, 2003), and the European Medicines Evaluation Agency (EMEA, 2005) claim that induction of suicidality should be regarded as a serious potential side-effect of the SSRIs and some other antidepressants in children and adolescents, and that the use of antidepressants in these groups should be highly restricted (Licinio and Wong, 2005). Although the concerns primarily focused on the SSRIs, they later spread to include the tricyclic antidepressants. On the basis of several re-analyses, not only children and adolescents, but also younger adult patients were seen to be an at-risk group (Möller *et al*, 2008).

Despite the fact that the Task Force by the American College of Neuropsychopharmacology recommends continued use of fluoxetine as an effective and readily available treatment for major depression in youth, they also believe that other SSRIs need further testing to establish efficacy by use of RCTs, preferably including fluoxetine as a reference compound (Mann *et al*, 2006). This issue will be analysed by comparing the SSRIs and the tricyclic antidepressants and following the analysis of age and antidepressants. There is strong evidence for a higher fatal toxicity of tricyclic antidepressants compared to SSRIs and some other modern antidepressants in most of the studies (Möller, 2006a, 2008). However, when one analyses the effects of both in suicidal behaviours, Fergusson *et al* (2005) concluded that there is no difference between them. Despite that, after a systematic review of randomised controlled trials, they documented a more than twofold increase in the rate of suicide attempts in patients receiving SSRIs compared with placebo or therapeutic interventions other than tricyclic antidepressants (Fergusson *et al*, 2005). These data seem to confirm the results of Wong *et al* (2004), who argued that despite repeated reports of associations of increased harm-related events and SSRIs, there is insufficient safety information from the RCTs to draw any conclusions about a possible association between SSRIs and suicide, but there may be an association with harm-related behaviours (Wong *et al*, 2004).

Barbui *et al* (2009) found with data from observational studies that the relation between exposure to SSRIs and the risk of suicide is influenced by age. Exposure to SSRIs decreased the risk of suicide by over 40% among adults and decreased the risk by over 50% among elderly people. However, among adolescents, exposure to SSRIs almost doubled the risk of suicide.

According to Wong *et al* (2004), SSRIs should not be considered for use as first-line treatment in mild or moderate depression of childhood, where psychological interventions such as cognitive behavioural therapy or interpersonal therapy are the mainstay. SSRIs should be considered when there is severe depression that does not respond to psychological interventions; when the child is suicidal and is admitted as an inpatient, is severely depressed or has bipolar depression despite adequate doses of mood-stabilisation agents; or when the child or family prefers pharmacotherapy to psychological interventions and gives informed consent (Wong *et al*, 2004). However, the most important aspect is that psychological interventions remain the first choice.

Most psychiatrists were prepared to accept the possibility that SSRIs had occasional adverse effects like agitation, even if such effects intensified subjective distress (Möller *et al*, 2008). But the hypothesis that SSRIs may induce suicidal thoughts, attempted or completed suicide and even homicide has reacquired active support (Healy *et al*, 2006). However, Möller *et al* (2008) concluded that ADs, including SSRIs, carry a small risk of inducing suicidal thoughts and suicide attempts in age groups below 25 years, the risk reducing further at the age of about 30–40 years.

Paroxetine and venlafaxine may be better avoided, based on the increasing evidence from randomised and observational studies that the risks might outweigh the benefits for most adolescents (Barbui *et al*, 2009).

Sondergard *et al* (2006) were not able to identify an association between treatment with SSRIs and completed suicide among children and adolescents. Nevertheless, psychopharmacological antidepressant treatment of depressed children and adolescents remains controversial (Sondergard *et al*, 2006). However, the risk has to be balanced against the documented beneficial effects of antidepressants on depressive and other symptoms (anxiety, panic, obsessive-compulsive symptoms), including suicidality and suicidal behaviour. According to the principles of good clinical practice, decision-making should consider carefully the beneficial effects of antidepressant treatment as well as potentially harmful effects and attempt to keep the potential risks of antidepressant treatment to a minimum (Möller *et al*, 2008).

Fluoxetine is more effective than placebo in the treatment of severe depression in children; however, a strong placebo effect was observed. Fluoxetine in combination with cognitive behavioural therapy (CBT) appears to be superior to fluoxetine or CBT alone. SSRIs should not be considered for use as first-line treatments in mild to moderate depression of childhood, where psychological interventions such as CBT or interpersonal therapy are the mainstay (Wong *et al*, 2004).

Clozapine

Clozapine is an anti-psychotic drug. However, the American FDA approved clozapine as a treatment with an antisuicide indication (Baldessarini and Tondo, 2011). This conclusion was based mainly on a randomised trial named InterSePT which compared clozapine and olanzapine in schizophrenic patients with high suicidal risk (Meltzer *et al*, 2003). The authors concluded that clozapine therapy demonstrated superiority to olanzapine therapy in preventing suicide attempts in patients with schizophrenia and schizoaffective disorder at high risk for suicide. Use of clozapine in this population should lead to a significant reduction in suicidal behaviour (Meltzer *et al*, 2003). One year later, Glick *et al* (2004) supported the conclusion that the effects of clozapine in reducing the risk of suicidal behaviour derive from its intrinsic pharmacology and not from the influence of concomitant psychotropic medications.

Conclusion

The pharmacological component in the prevention of suicidal behaviours brings about issues related to its effectiveness and there is far from being a consensus about it. There are, for example, opposite views about the role of antidepressants. On one hand, increasing use of antidepressants did not reduce suicide rates (Van

Praag, 2003), while on the other hand Möller *et al* (2008) argued that it is evident that an increased use of antidepressants, especially SSRIs, was accompanied by a relevant decline of national suicide rates in several countries, particularly in those where the suicide rates were previously very high. It can be seen as a very robust finding due to the fact that it could be replicated in several countries under different psychosocial and care conditions (Möller, 2006b).

According to the same author, pharmacoepidemiological studies that investigate the association between the prescription risks for TCAs/SSRIs and suicide rates by applying multivariate statistical methods show no increased risk of suicide in association with antidepressants, and especially no increase of suicide risk in conjunction with SSRIs (Möller, 2006b). Antidepressants remain first-choice therapy for most patients because of their good tolerance, despite the strongly discussed problematic in the last years regarding the possible induction of suicidality by antidepressants, especially through SSRIs. Extensive meta-analyses have shown that the risk of induction of suicidality, initially attributed to SSRIs, is a problem related to all antidepressants, which applies especially to adolescents and younger patients but is generally only of a minor size (Möller, 2009). Nevertheless, they should be used when psychological interventions are not efficient (Wong *et al*, 2004).

Despite the focus of the discussion on suicide prevention using medication being on antidepressants, Baldessarini and Tondo (2011, p. 256) mention that

> antidepressant treatment appears to reduce suicidal ideation in depressed adults patients, whereas only clozapine and lithium have secure evidence of reducing risk of suicide attempts or suicides, suggesting that 'suicidality' is not usefully considered as a unitary clinical phenomenon or therapeutic target. Instead, there may be a differential pharmacology of particular aspects of suicidality. These probably include a need to limit rage, aggression, and impulsivity to reduce risks of attempts and suicides. Such properties are more to be expected of antipsychotic or mood-stabilising agents than of antidepressants.

Verkes and Cowen (2002) concluded that there is reasonable evidence that drug treatment can lower suicidal behaviours in patients with major mood disorders.

Antidepressants are only a part of the complex therapeutic process in the treatment of depressed patients. The efficacy of antidepressants is increased by sequential and combinatory therapies in the daily clinical practice. Psychosocial as well as psychotherapeutic factors add to a positive therapeutic result additionally. Therefore, it is important not to regard therapy with antidepressants as the only solution, but to embed the antidepressant therapy into the complex therapeutical approach (Möller, 2009).

Health economic analyses also play an increasingly important role in times of scarcity of resources in the healthcare sector and they can bring additional aspects into clinical decision-making processes, especially if in future the resource allocation in the healthcare system is not primarily carried out according to the medical results of therapy trials, but results from health economic differentiations between different therapies by respective institutions (Möller, 2009).

To sum up, the use of psychoactive drugs in suicidal ideation only makes sense when aimed at treating an underlying disorder (Kishi and Kathol, 2002) and when integrated into a broader and more encompassing therapeutic intervention which is more than a simple prescription (Gil, 2006). Nurses are expected to use their critical judgment to manage the pharmacological treatment, and to have a broad knowledge of the different variables and consequences by analysing both the risks and the benefits.

References

Baldessarini R, Tondo L (2011) Psychopharmacology for suicide prevention. In: Pompili M, Tatarelli R (eds.) *Evidence-Based Practice in Suicidology*. Hogrefe Publishing, Cambridge, MA, pp. 243–64.

Baldessarini R, Henk H, Sklar A, Chang J, Leahy L (2008) Psychotropic medications for patients with bipolar disorder in the United States: polytherapy and adherence. *Psychiatric Services* **59**(10): 1175–83.

Baldessarini RJ, Tarazi FI (2005) Pharmacotherapy of psychosis and mania. In: Brunton LL, Lazo JS, Parker KL (eds.) *Goodman and Gilman's The Pharmacological Basis of Therapeutics*, 11th edn. McGraw-Hill, New York, pp. 461–500.

Baldessarini RJ, Tondo L, Davis P, Pompili M, Goodwin FK, Hennen J (2006) Decreased risk of suicides and attempts during long-term lithium treatment: a meta-analytic review. *Bipolar Disorder* **8**: 625–39.

Barbui C, Esposito E, Cipriani A (2009) Selective serotonin reuptake inhibitors and risk of suicide: a systematic review of observational studies. *Canadian Medical Association Journal* **180**(3): 291–7.

Benedetti F, Arduino C, Costa S, Vighetti S, Tarenzi L, Rainero I, Asteggiano G (2006) Loss of expectation-related mechanisms in Alzheimer's disease makes analgesic therapies less effective. *Pain* **121**: 133–44.

Bertolote J, Fleischmann A, De Leo D, Wasserman D (2004) Psychiatric diagnoses and suicide: revisiting the evidence. *Crisis* **25**(4): 147–55.

Cipriani A, Pretty H, Hawton K, Geddes J (2005) Lithium in the prevention of suicidal behaviour and all-cause mortality in patients with mood disorders: a systematic review of randomized trials. *American Journal of Psychiatry* **162**: 1805–19.

Cutcliffe J, Wieck L (2008) Salvation or damnation: deconstructing nursing's aspirations to professional status. *Journal of Nursing Management*, **16**: 499–507.

EMEA (2005) *European Medicines Agency finalises review of antidepressants in children and adolescents.* http://www.ema.europa.eu/ema/index.jsp?curl=pages/news_and_events/news/2009/12/news_detail_000882.jsp&mid=WC0b01ac058004d5c1 (accessed 10 July 2012).

FDA (2004) *Public Health Advisory: Suicidality in Children and Adolescents Being Treated with Antidepressant Medications.* http://www.fda.gov/Drugs/DrugSafety/PostmarketDrugSafetyInformationforPatientsandProviders/DrugSafetyInformationforHeathcareProfessionals/PublicHealthAdvisories/ucm161679.htm (accessed 10 July 2012).

FDA (2007) *Public Health Advisory: Suicidality in Adults Being Treated with Antidepressant Medications.* http://www.fda.gov/Drugs/DrugSafety/PostmarketDrugSafetyInformationforPatientsandProviders/DrugSafetyInformationforHeathcareProfessionals/PublicHealthAdvisories/ucm053169.htm (accessed 10 July 2012).

Fergusson D, Doucette S, Glass KC, Shapiro S, Healy D, Hebert P, Hutton B (2005) Association between suicide attempts and selective serotonin reuptake inhibitors: systematic review of randomised controlled trials. *British Medical Journal* **330**: 396.

Gil N (2006) Abordagem psicofarmacológica da ideação suicida In: Peixoto B, Saraiva B, Sampaio D (eds.) *Comportamentos Suicidários.* Sociedade Portuguesa de Suicidologia, pp. 377–422.

Glick I, Zaninelli R, Hsu C, Young F, Weiss L, Gunay I, Kumar V (2004) Patterns of concomitant psychotropic medication use during a 2-year study comparing clozapine and olanzapine for the prevention of suicidal behavior. *Journal of Clinical Psychiatry* **65**: 679–85.

Goldney RD (2007) Antidepressants and suicide in young people. *Medical Journal of Australia* **187**(10): 586–7.

Harrison P, Baldwin D, Barnes T, Burns T, Ebmeier K, Ferrier I, Nutt D (2011) No psychiatry without psychopharmacology. *British Journal of Psychiatry* **199**: 263–5.

Healy D, Herxheimer A, Menkes DB (2006) Antidepressants and violence: problems at the interface of medicine and law. *PLoS Medicine* **3**: e372.

Henriksson M, Aro H, Marttunen M, Heikkinen M, Isometsä E, Kuoppasalmi K, Lönnqvist J (1993) Mental disorders and comorbidity in suicide. *American Journal of Psychiatry* **150**(6): 935–40.

Kahn A, Kahn SR, Leventhal RM, Brown WA (2001) Symptom reduction and suicide risk in patients treated with placebo in antidepressant clinical trials: and analysis of the Food and Drug Administration Database. *International Journal of Neuropsychopharmacology* **4**: 113–18.

Kishi A, Kathol R (2002) Assessment of patients who attempt suicide. *Journal of Clinical Psychiatry* **4**(4): 132–6.

Licinio J, Wong M (2005) Depression, antidepressants and suicidality: a critical appraisal. *Nature Reviews Drug Discovery* **4**: 165–71.

Lönnqvist J (2009) Major psychiatric disorders in suicide and suicide attempters in Wasserman D, Wasserman C (eds.) *Oxford Textbook of Suicidology and Suicide Prevention: A Global Perspective*. Oxford University Press, Oxford, pp. 275–86.

Mann J, Emslie G, Baldessarini R, Beardslee W, Fawcett J, Goodwin F, Leon A, Meltzer H, Ryan N, Shaffer D. Wagner K (2006) ACNP Task Force report on SSRIs and suicidal behavior in youth. *Neuropsychopharmacology*: **31**: 473–92.

Maris RW, Berman AL, Silverman MM (2000) *Comprehensive Textbook of Suicidology*. Guilford Press, New York.

Meltzer HY, Alphs L, Green AI *et al* (2003) Clozapine treatment for suicidality in schizophrenia: International Suicide Prevention Trial (InterSePT). *Archives of General Psychiatry* **60**: 82–91.

MHRA (2003) *Selective Serotonin Reuptake Inhibitors (SSRIs): Overview of Regulatory Status and CSM Advice Relating to Major Depressive Disorder (MDD) in Children and Adolescents Including A Summary of Available Safety and Efficacy Data*. http://www.mhra.gov.uk/Safetyinformation/Safetywarningsalertsandrecalls/Safetywarningsandmessagesformedicines/CON019494 (accessed 10 July 2012).

Möller HJ (1992) Antidepressants – do they decrease or increase suicidality? *Pharmacopsychiatry* **25**: 249–53.

Möller HJ (2003) Suicide, suicidality and suicide prevention in affective disorders. *Acta Psychiatrica Scandinavica* Supplementum: 73–80.

Möller H (2006a) Is there evidence for negative effects of antidepressants on suicidality in depressive patients: a systematic review. *European Archives of Psychiatry and Clinical Neuroscience* **256**: 476–96.

Möller H (2006b) Evidence for beneficial effects of antidepressants on suicidality in depressive patients: a systematic review. *European Archives of Psychiatry and Clinical Neuroscience* **256**: 329–43.

Möller H (2009) Antidepressants: controversies about their efficacy in depression, their effect on suicidality and their place in a complex psychiatric treatment approach. *World Journal of Biological Psychiatry* **10**(3): 180–95.

Möller H, Baldwin D, Goodwin G, Kasper S, Okasha A, Stein D, Tandon R, Versiani M (2008) Do SSRIs or antidepressants in general increase suicidality? WPA Section on Pharmacopsychiatry: consensus statement. *European Archives of Psychiatry and Clinical Neuroscience* **258**(suppl 3): 3–23.

Olfson M, Shaffer D, Marcus SC, Greenberg T (2003) Relationship between antidepressant medication treatment and suicide in adolescents. *Archives of General Psychiatry* **60**: 978–82.

Rief W, Nestoriuc Y, Weiss S, Welzel E, Barsky A, Hofmann S(2009) Meta-analysis of the placebo response in antidepressant trials. *Journal of Affective Disorders* **118**: 1–8.

Royal College of Physicians (2009) *Innovating for Health: Patients, Physicians, the Pharmaceutical Industry and the NHS. Report of a Working Party*. Royal College of Physicians, London.

Saraiva C (2006) *Estudos sobre o para-suicídio O que leva os jovens a espreitar a morte*. Coimbra Edição do Autor.

Sondergard L, Kvist K, Andersen P, Kessing L (2006) Do antidepressants prevent suicide? *International Clinical Psychopharmacology* **21**: 211–18.

Stoff DM, Mann JL (eds.) (1997) *The Neurobiology of Suicide: From the Bench to the Clinic*. New York Academy of Science, New York.

Van Praag HM (2003) A stubborn behaviour: the failure of antidepressants to reduce suicide rates. *World Journal of Biological Psychiatry* **4**: 184–91.

Van Praag HM (2004) Stress and suicide: are we well equipped to study this issue? *Crisis* **25**(2): 8–85.

Verkes R, Cowen P (2002) Pharmacotherapy of suicidal ideation and behavior. In: Hawton K, Heeringer K (eds.) *The International Handbook of Suicide and Attempted Suicide*. Wiley, Chichester, pp. 487–502.
Waber RL, Shiv B, Carmon Z, Ariely D (2008) Commercial features of placebo and therapeutic efficacy. *Journal of the American Medical Association* **299**: 1016–17.
Waddington D, McKensie IP (1994) Overdose rates in lithium-treated versus antidepressant-treated outpatients. *Acta Psychiatrica Scandinavica* **90**: 50–2.
Wong I, Besag F, Santosh P, Murray M (2004) Use of selective serotonin reuptake inhibitors in children and adolescents. *Drug Safety* **27**(13) 991–1000.

CHAPTER 7

Talking therapies: cognitive behavioural therapy and dialectical behaviour therapy

> What are we to make of these findings? Five psychosocial treatments and one pharmacotherapy regime showed significant reductions in subsequent parasuicide acts, and the simple act of making non-demanding phone calls and sending a letter produced a trend towards lower suicide rates over time. (Linehan, 2000, p. 104)

Introduction

Shneidman (1996) posited that we can reduce the lethality of suicidal people if we lessen the suicidal person's anguish – their perturbation – but key questions remain around how this can be accomplished. For some authors, caring for suicidal people must be an interpersonal endeavour, one personified by talking and listening (Cutcliffe and Stevenson, 2007)[1]. This position is even more difficult to refute if one accepts the axiomatic complexity and multi-dimensionality of suicide, and at the same time, if one accepts the undeniable fact that suicide is a human drama, played out in the everyday lives, minds, brains and interactions of people (Cutcliffe and Stevenson, 2008).

The utility of, for want of a better, more capacious, expression 'talk therapy', in helping suicidal people, is the focus of this chapter. It begins by reviewing common elements and aspects of psychotherapeutic attempts to help suicidal people. Given the existing evidence (such as it is) pertaining to the efficacy of cognitive therapy (or approaches) for suicidal people, we examine such approaches in some detail. Similarly, the chapter then focuses on dialectical behaviour therapy as a means for working with certain groups of suicidal people. We draw the chapter to a

1 This does not mean that the only intervention(s) offered to suicidal people is, for want of a better expression, 'talk therapy', but it does mean that 'talk therapy' should be included in the range of interventions offered.

close by reviewing the empirical evidence pertaining to these psychotherapeutic approaches.

Talk therapy, interpersonal approaches and psychotherapeutic approaches for suicidal people

Unfortunately, the contemporary P/MH nursing literature is clear in highlighting that, all too often, what suicidal people receive in the way of interpersonal care is second rate, ineffective and impersonal (Cutcliffe and Stevenson, 2008). Let us try to understand this. Both parties (clinician and suicidal patient) may feel vulnerable, powerful, scared, angry, worried and wary (Michel and Jobes, 2011), and the working alliance between a patient and a clinician may be influenced by the therapist's sensitivity (Michel *et al*, 2004). Clinicians and therapists play a very active and direct role in helping patients to change, as well as understand, their behaviour (Heard, 2000).

According to Linehan *et al* (in press), of all of the undesired outcomes in clinical practice, a client's suicide is perhaps both the most stressful and the most feared. To avoid this, many clinicians either refuse to accept suicidal clients or they refer clients who become suicidal. In contrast to a medical model approach, in which patient and technician join forces together to battle a disease such as cancer, within mental health the prospect of suicide can pit patient and professional against each other (Michel and Jobes, 2011). However, a warm, supportive therapeutic relationship, although perhaps not always sufficient, is necessary and a key ingredient (Leenaars, 2011b).

According to Michel and Jones (2011), it is important that suicidal patients are given the opportunity to tell their complete story; that really listening to the patient's story with empathy, support, no judgment and no shame is critical for success; and that finding a way to work collaboratively is essential to clinically-based suicide prevention (Michel and Jones, 2011). Leenaars (2011a) also stresses the importance of the narrative and argues that, to establish an effective therapeutic relationship, a shared understanding of the patient's suicidality is needed. Thus the key concept may be engagement.

Engagement[2] appears to comprise several processes: forming a relationship (a human–human connection), conveying acceptance and tolerance, and hearing and understanding. Engaging with suicidal clients is clearly concerned with forming a relationship – a human–human connection between the client and the nurse

2 See the next two chapters for a more detailed explanation of the nature and utility of engagement.

(Cutcliffe and Barker, 2002) – and this is crucial to make an effective approach in this field.

Mindful of the purported elements of engagement, it is interesting to note Shneidman's (1985) list of some practical measures for helping highly suicidal persons:

- stimulus (unbearable pain): reduce the pain
- stressor (frustrated needs): fill the frustrated needs
- purpose (to seek a solution): provide a different answer
- goal (cessation of consciousness): indicate alternatives
- emotion (hopelessness–helplessness): give transfusion of hope
- internal attitude (ambivalence): play for time
- cognitive state (constriction): increase the options
- interpersonal act (communication of intention): listen to the cry, involve others
- action (egression): block the exit
- consistency (with lifelong patterns): invoke previous positive pattern of successful coping.

Questions do remain, however, as to how we can identify the best or most effective psychotherapy(ies). According to Leenaars (2011b) there is no 'the best' psychotherapy, but the most important aspect is quality care (Leenaars, 2011a). We need to shift the paradigm from a simplistic, linear drug metaphor model to a contextual or process model (Wampold, 1997; Saunders, 2003; Orlinsky *et al*, 2004; Leenaars, 2011b).

There are commonalities in psychotherapy that arguably make psychotherapies effective (Leenaars, 2011b).

1. Treatment developers develop treatment operations to be consistent with theory and research and believe that the actions prescribed by the treatment lead to therapeutic change
2. When that treatment is shown to be efficacious, the proponents believe that these specific operations were responsible for the positive outcomes and typically will argue to that end
3. The very essence of looking for a set of empirically validated treatments supposes a belief that some treatments are not efficacious and consequently operations common to therapies cannot be responsible for treatment effects
4. Knowledge of factors related to outcome leads to redefining treatments and increased potency (Wampold, 1997; Leenaars, 2011b).

Rudd *et al* (2009) identified eight commonalities:

1. Being theoretically based and containing a language that is easy to understand
2. High-risk cases with broad inclusion criteria
3. Training clinicians well using manualised treatment and providing them with adequate supervision
4. Treatment focus being specific to suicide rather than other associated symptoms or diagnoses
5. Plan for compliance and continuity of care
6. Interventions incorporating education on skill sets such as emotion regulation and problem solving
7. Emphasis on internal locus of control and personal responsibility
8. An element of crisis management (Rudd *et al*, 2009).

Two of the most commonly accepted ways of working with people are problem-solving therapy and cognitive behavioural psychotherapy (Heard, 2000; Collins and Cutcliffe, 2003). Problem-solving therapy is recognised as holding some clinical efficacy. These psychotherapeutic approaches may well be offered by nurses in addition to providing outreach and intensive interventions (Heard, 2000).

Generally increased problem-solving capacity, more intensive outreach activities, an invitation to the patient to participate more actively in the analysis of their own problems and efforts to ameliorate the feelings of shame and guilt are all efforts to deal with painful interpersonal problems (Beskow *et al*, 2009). However, one approach which, up to now, has received limited attention within the psychiatric/mental health nursing literature, is that of using a cognitive behavioural approach to help address the client's sense of hopelessness (Cutcliffe and Collins, 2003).

What is cognitive therapy?

Cognitive therapy is a short-term, active, directive, structured, collaborative, psychoeducational and dynamic model of psychotherapy. Developed by Dr Aaron Beck, it is one of several models of therapy (Freeman and Reinecke, 1993). Following the lead of Beck and others, the empirical and clinical testing of cognitive therapy has undoubtedly brought about alterations and modifications to the basic model for the treatment of suicidal behaviour, recognising that often the therapist may be the only person between the patient's life and death. Cognitive psychotherapy involves supporting the patient with new concepts, new knowledge and new techniques, adapted to their actual personal needs, and immediately useful in their efforts to change their behaviour (Beskow *et al*, 2009).

The major therapeutic focus in the cognitive behavioural models for suicidal people is to help the patient examine the manner in which he or she construes and understands the world (cognitions) and to experiment with new ways of responding (behavioural). The purposes of the first phase are to:

- obtain informed consent and socialise patients into the structure and process of this treatment
- engage patients in treatment
- conduct a psychological and suicide risk assessment and, especially, obtain a narrative of the most recent suicidal crisis
- develop a safety plan
- instill a sense of hope (Brown *et al*, 2011).

There are basic premises to this model and these are briefly summarised in Box 7.1 .

The authors also refer to the cognitive triad (negative view of the self, the world and the future) and the need to work with patients' cognitive distortions (all or nothing thinking; catastrophising; overgeneralisation; selective abstraction; arbitrary interference; magnification and minimisation; emotional reasoning; should, must, ought to statements; labelling and mislabelling; personalisation; control fallacies; comparative thinking; disqualifying the positive; fallacy of fairness) and schema assumptions (Freeman and Reinecke, 1993).

The use of cognitive psychotherapy is increasing. One of the prime reasons for the rapid progress and excellent treatment results in cognitive psychotherapy is the use of the normalcy theory of emotion and emotional problems, rather than a theory of pathology (Beskow *et al*, 2009). This idea is central to understanding the interventions and evaluating the results.

During the development of cognitive psychotherapy, the way in which we understand suicidality has changed profoundly from primarily being a symptom of

Box 7.1 Based on Freeman and Reinecke (1993)

- The way individuals construe or interpret events and situations mediates how they subsequently feel and behave.
- This process of interpretation is active and ongoing.
- Individuals develop idiosyncratic belief systems that guide behaviour.
- These stressors consequently contribute to a functional impairment of the individual's cognitive processing and activate maladaptive, overlearned coping responses.
- Clinical syndromes can be distinguished by the specific content of the belief system and the cognitive processes that are activated.

depression (a pathological perspective) to being the result of a complex interaction of many cognitive, emotional and behavioural structures (a normal and systemic perspective). The suicidal process may be seen as a cognitive process of its own, separated from, but interacting with, depressive processes (Beskow *et al*, 2009). The nature and efficacy of cognitive therapy will continue to be empirically tested by clinical researchers worldwide. One challenge is to solve the internal drop-out from the therapy, which remains high (Beskow *et al*, 2009).

What is dialectical behaviour therapy?

Dialectical behaviour therapy (DBT) is an outpatient, cognitive behavioural treatment shown to reduce self-injury and suicidal behaviour in individuals with so-called borderline personality disorder (BPD) (Stanley and Brodsky, 2009). It was developed by Marsha Linehan (1993), who has provided empirical evidence of its effectiveness in reducing self-injurious and suicidal behaviours in individuals with BPD (Stanley and Brodsky, 2009). DBT combines standard cognitive behavioural therapy with Eastern philosophy and meditation practices and shares elements with psychodynamic, client-centred, gestalt, paradoxical and strategic approaches (Koerner *et al*, 1998). It is considered a principle-driven therapy, as opposed to a protocol-driven treatment (Wagner *et al*, 2007).

The focus of DBT intervention is emotion regulation and behavioural changes. Cognitions are also targeted in DBT, but they are not the main focus of treatment, as they are in Beck's cognitive therapy for BPD (Stanley and Brodsky, 2009). The DBT strategy aims to introduce acceptance of whatever is valid about the individual's current behaviours, viewing these behaviours as the patient's best efforts to cope with unbearable pain, balanced with change strategies (Stanley and Brodsky, 2009). Change is achieved through standard CBT techniques such as functional analyses, contingency management, cognitive restructuring, exposure and skills training (Rizvi, 2011).

DBT emphasises mindfulness, validation, targeting, dialectics and chain analyses as mechanisms of change that reduce ineffective action tendencies linked with dysregulated emotions in individuals with BPD (Lynch *et al*, 2006). Mindfulness is the core skill enhancing self-acceptance and behavioural and emotional regulation (Stanley and Brodsky, 2009). According to Luoma and Villatte (in press), supporting mindfulness and psychological acceptance is a means to target experiential avoidance in suicidal clients, thereby reducing the risk of suicide.

In contrast to more traditional suicide treatment models that see suicidality as a symptom of a diagnosis and assume that it will resolve if the diagnostic condition is treated (Jobes, 2006), these authors believe that it is important to address suicidality directly as a primary target of concern and to identify trans-diagnostic processes that cut across the many different diagnostic conditions associated with suicidal behaviour (Luoma and Villatte, in press). The individual therapist plays the role of a skills coach, both within and between sessions (Stanley and Brodsky, 2009).

According to Linehan *et al* (1993), DBT had significantly larger decreases in parasuicidal behaviours, fewer inpatient hospitalisations, and a lower drop-out rate than those in the 'treatment as usual' condition at the completion of one year of treatment.

The DBT treatment is guided by several assumptions (Linehan, 1993):

- clients are doing the best that they can
- clients want to improve
- clients need to do better, try harder, and be more motivated to change
- clients may not have caused all of their own problems, but they have to solve them anyway
- the lives of suicidal, borderline personality disorder individuals are unbearable as they are currently being lived
- clients must learn new behaviours in all relevant contexts
- clients cannot fail in therapy
- Therapists treating individuals with borderline personality disorder need support.

Following the analysis of these assumptions, the functions of DBT have to be considered, and these are listed in Table 7.1

What is the evidence?

Rudd *et al* (2009) provided a critical review of the literature on suicidality and psychosocial treatments and highlighted the paucity of RCTs and the limited methodological practices of the available RCTs as being a major obstacle to advancing treatment effectiveness. They were concerned about the exclusion of high-risk participants (ie. multiple attempts of suicide and individuals who have recently attempted suicide) from many studies and the limited follow-up periods.

Crawford *et al* (2007) developed a meta-analysis of psychosocial interventions which provided no evidence that addition to psychosocial interventions following self-harm has a marked impact on the likelihood of subsequent suicide. However, they also concluded that they had insufficient power to detect smaller – but still clinically significant – reductions in the level of suicide (Crawford *et al*, 2007).

Table 7.1 Functions of DBT for outpatients with BPD (based on Linehan, 1993; Koerner *et al*, 1998; Katz *et al*, 2002).

Functions	Strategies
Enhancing the patient's capabilities	The patient makes a commitment to one year of treatment consisting of a weekly psychoeducational skills training group
Improving motivation to change	Weekly sessions with an individual therapist to identify and reduce factors that interfere with the ability to use skills
Ensuring that new capabilities are generalised from therapy to the patient's everyday life	Telephone contacts with the therapist on an as-needed basis when crises arise, thus facilitating generalisation through these *in vivo* interactions
Enhancing the therapist's capabilities and motivation to treat patients effectively	The therapist in turn agrees to provide one year of treatment during which he or she participates in a weekly therapist consultation group that offers both technical help and emotional support
Structuring the environment to support the patient's and therapist's capabilities	If necessary, the environment may be restructured to ensure that the patient does not have to get worse in order to obtain additional help and that therapists have reasonable time demands to prevent burnout

The conclusions by Crawford *et al* (2007) confirm the difficulty to develop evidence on a rather rare phenomenon such as suicide. Nevertheless, we can identify some indicators which help us understand the value of psychosocial interventions. The Task Force on Empirically Supported Therapy Relationships (2001) had previously identified the following common elements of effective therapy relationships: therapeutic alliance (or rapport), therapist empathy, and patient–therapist goal consensus and collaboration.

Two critical studies were conducted with adults: one by Brown *et al* (2005) with cognitive therapy interventions and the other one by Linehan *et al* (2006) with DBT interventions. The study led by Brown *et al* (2005) was conducted with adults who attempted suicide with a diversity of diagnoses. Two groups were compared: one with usual care and another one with cognitive therapy interventions. Participants in the cognitive therapy intervention group were scheduled to receive 10 outpatient cognitive therapy sessions specifically developed for preventing suicide attempts. The cognitive therapy sessions were provided on a weekly or biweekly basis or as needed. The central feature of this psychotherapy was the identification of proximal thoughts, images and core beliefs that were activated prior to the suicide attempt. Cognitive and behavioural strategies were applied to address the identified thoughts and beliefs and participants were helped to develop adaptive ways of coping with stressors. Specific vulnerability factors that were addressed included hopelessness, poor problem solving, impaired impulse control, treatment noncompliance and social isolation (Brown *et al*, 2005). The results of this RCT indicated that a relatively brief cognitive therapy intervention was effective in preventing suicide attempts for adults who had recently attempted suicide.

The cognitive therapy group reported significantly less hopelessness than the usual care group at six months and, specifically, participants in the cognitive therapy group were approximately 50% less likely to attempt suicide during the follow-up period than participants in the usual care group (Brown *et al*, 2005). The strengths of this study are that it targeted the suicidal mode as it expressed itself immediately before the act; included patients with different psychiatric disorders, including substance use disorders; had special study case managers following the patients and making contact when necessary; and involved the creation of action plans for avoiding further suicide attempts at the end of the therapy (Beskow *et al*, 2009).

In the study of Linehan *et al* (2006), the participants were women aged 18–45 years who met criteria for BPD and for current and past suicidal behaviour as defined by at least two suicide attempts or self-injuries in the previous five years, with at least one in the past eight weeks. The intervention is one year of DBT or one year of community treatment by experts (developed to maximise internal validity by controlling for therapist sex, availability, expertise, allegiance, training and experience, consultation availability and institutional prestige). Standard DBT addresses the following functions: increasing behavioural capabilities; improving motivation for skilful behaviour (through contingency management and reduction of interfering emotions and cognitions); assuring generalisation of gains to the natural environment; structuring the treatment environment so that it reinforces functional rather than dysfunctional behaviours; and enhancing therapist capabilities and motivation to treat patients effectively. These functions are divided among the following four modes of service delivery:

1. Weekly individual psychotherapy (1 hour/week)
2. Group skills training (2½ hours/week)
3. Telephone consultation (as needed within the therapist's limits to ensure generalisation)

4. Weekly therapist consultation team meetings (to enhance therapists' motivation and skills and to provide therapy for the therapists).

In the end, DBT was associated with better outcomes in the intent-to-treat analysis than community treatment by experts in most target areas during the two-year treatment and follow-up period. Subjects receiving DBT were half as likely to make a suicide attempt, required less hospitalisation for suicide ideation, and had lower medical risk across all suicide attempts and self-injurious acts combined. Subjects receiving DBT were less likely to drop out of treatment and had fewer psychiatric hospitalisations and psychiatric emergency department visits. They concluded that the effectiveness of DBT cannot reasonably be attributed to general factors associated with expert psychotherapy, but appears to be uniquely effective in reducing suicide attempts (Linehan *et al*, 2006).

From a methodological point of view, this study seems to be well-designed, allowing for a better assessment of DBT's effectiveness. Nevertheless, some of its limitations include a sample only composed of women and the fact that the number of participants who completed the programme in the control group were about half of those who completed the programme in the intervention group with DBT. Young people require special attention, given the high occurrence of behaviours and self-harm in this age group. However, there are insufficient data available from controlled trials to recommend one intervention over another for the treatment of suicidal youth. Despite this, interventions that are sensitive to the multiple developmental contexts have potential for greater effectiveness in reducing adolescent suicidal behaviour (Daniel and Goldston, 2009).

In a systematic review, these authors concluded that interventions for suicidal youth have in general been more successful at affecting aspects of service utilisation and delivery (eg. compliance with medical recommendations, aftercare utilisation, reduced hospitalisation, decreased time to outpatient appointments) than in reducing rates of suicide attempts *per se* (Daniel and Goldston, 2009). They also found a high drop-out rate, which can be explained by a variety of reasons for why suicidal adolescents drop out of therapy prematurely (Daniel and Goldston, 2009).

Concluding remarks

It can be concluded that there is some empirical evidence on the effectiveness of psychotherapeutic interventions for suicidal people, though this currently remains far from being a robust and extensive body of work. This can be explained by four main reasons: one, undoubtedly an important factor, is the lack of rigorous clinical trials for suicidal individuals, while exclusion of suicidal individuals from clinical trials is a second factor that has arguably crippled the field of suicide intervention research. A third factor that impedes effective interventions for suicidal individuals is the unwillingness of many mental healthcare providers to treat suicidal individuals (Linehan *et al*, in press), and the final reason is that of limited follow-up periods (Rudd *et al*, 2009).

However, the limited evidence that does exist seems to suggest that suicidality can be resolved (or alleviated) when clinicians focus on addressing the suicidal intent and/or behaviours, rather than seeking 'cure': resolution of an associated diagnostic condition (eg. depression). Mindfulness of ensuring 'talk therapy' for suicidal people as a key aspect of such care perhaps reduces the chance of clinicians offering suboptimal treatment or increased risk of re-emergence of suicidality (Luoma and Villatte, in press). It is thus important to address suicidality directly as a primary target of concern.

For the time being it is important to refine studies from both theoretical and methodological perspectives in ways that will allow researchers to make strong and empirically supported recommendations related to the identification of evidence-based interventions for suicidal individuals (Rogers *et al*, 2011).

Lambert (2004) stresses the fact that the success of treatment appears to be largely dependent on the patient and the therapist, not on the use of 'proven' empirically based treatments. According to the Evidence-Based Medicine Working Group (1992), the evidence-based effectiveness in psychotherapy with suicidal people depends on individually tailored evidence-based therapy to the unique characteristics/qualities of each patient.

In fact, therapists must understand that there are no universal formulations regarding talk therapy for suicidal people, and that the search for a singular universal response is also a foolish and unrealistic fancy. We have to be person-centred or person-oriented, and the relationship that the therapist develops is, in fact, central in effective psychotherapy with suicidal people (Leenaars, 2011a). This may constitute an opportunity for P/MH nurses, and both interpersonal relationship and engagement may be the key concepts. According to Rudd and Brown (2011), at the heart of this issue is the need to develop, facilitate and maintain hope with patients who are suicidal. This will be covered in the following chapters.

References

Beskow J, Salkovskis P, Beskow A (2009) Cognitive treatment of suicidal adults. In: Wasserman D, Wasserman C (eds.) *Oxford Textbook of Suicidology and Suicide Prevention: A Global Perspective*. Oxford University Press, Oxford, pp. 413–20.

Brown G, Ten Have T, Henriques G, Xie S, Hollander J, Beck A (2005) Cognitive therapy for the prevention of suicide attempts: a randomized controlled trial. *Journal of the American Medical Association*, **294**: 563–70.

Brown G, Wenzel A, Rudd D (2011) Cognitive therapy for suicidal patients. In: Michel K, Jobes, D (2011) Building a therapeutic alliance with the suicidal patient American Psychological Association, Washington, DC, pp. 273–91.

Collins S, Cutcliffe JR (2003) Addressing hopelessness in people with suicidal ideation: building upon the therapeutic relationship utilizing a cognitive behavioural approach. *Journal of Psychiatric and Mental Health Nursing* **10**: 175–85.

Crawford MJ, Thomas O, Khan N, Kulinskaya E (2007) Psychosocial interventions following self-harm: systematic review of their efficacy in preventing suicide. *British Journal of Psychiatry*, **190**: 11–17.

Cutcliffe JR, Barker P (2002) Considering the care of the suicidal client and the case for 'engagement and inspiring hope' or observations. *Journal of Psychiatric and Mental Health Nursing*, **9**(5): 611–21.

Cutcliffe J, Stevenson C (2008) Feeling our way in the dark: the psychiatric nursing care of suicidal people – a literature review. *International Journal of Nursing Studies*, **45**: 942–53.

Daniel S, Goldston D (2009) Interventions for suicidal youth: a review of the literature and developmental considerations. *Suicide and Life-Threatening Behavior*, **39**: 252–68.

Evidence-Based Medicine Working Group (1992) Evidence-based medicine: a new approach to teaching the practice of medicine. *Journal of the American Medical Association*, **268**(17): 2420–5.

Freeman A, Reinecke M (1993) *Cognitive Therapy of Suicidal Behavior: A Manual for Treatment*. Spring Publishing Company, Inc.

Heard H (2000) Psychotherapeutic approaches to suicidal ideation and behaviour. In: Hawton K, van Heeringen K (eds.) *The International Book of Suicide and Attempted Suicide*, John Wiley & Sons, Surrey, pp. 503–18.

Katz LY, Gunasekara S, Miller AL (2002) Dialectical behavior therapy for inpatient and outpatient parasuicidal adolescents. *Adolescent Psychiatry*, **26**: 161–78.

Koerner K, Miller A, Wagner A (1998) Dialectical behavior therapy, Part I: Principle-based intervention for patients with multiple problems. *Journal of Practical Psychiatry & Behavioral Health*, **4**: 28–36.

Jobes D (2006) *Managing Suicidal Risk: A Collaborative Approach*. Guilford Press, New York.

Lambert M (ed.) (2004) *Bergin and Garfield's Handbook of Psychotherapy and Behavior Change*, 5th edn. Wiley, New York.

Leenaars A (2011a) Psychotherapy with suicidal people: some common implications for response. In: Michel K, Jobes D (eds.) *Building a Therapeutic Alliance with the Suicidal Patient*. American Psychological Association, Washington, DC, pp. 231–54.

Leenaars A (2011b) Evidence-based psychotherapy with suicidal people: a systematic review. In: Pompili M, Tatarelli R (eds.) *Evidence-based Practice in Suicidology*. Hogrefe Publishing, Cambridge, MA, pp. 89–123.

Linehan MM (1993) *Cognitive-Behavioral Therapy of Borderline Personality Disorder*. Guilford Press, New York.

Linehan M (2000) Behavioral treatments of suicidal behaviors: definitional obfuscation and treatment outcomes. In Maris RW, Canetto SS, McIntosh J, Silverman MM (eds.) *Review of Suicidology 2000*. Guilford Press, New York, pp. 84–111.

Linehan M, Heard H, Armstrong H (1993) Naturalistic follow-up of a behavioral treatment for chronically parasuicidal borderline patients. *Archives of General Psychiatry*, **50**, 971–4.

Linehan M, Comtois K, Murray A, Brown M, Gallop R, Heard H, Korslund K, Tutek D, Reynolds S, Lindenboim N (2006) Two-year randomized controlled trial and follow-up of dialectical behavior therapy vs therapy by experts for suicidal behaviors and borderline personality disorder. *Archives of General Psychiatry*, **63**: 757–66.

Linehan M, Comtois K, Ward-Ciesielski E (in press) Assessing and managing risk with suicidal individuals. *Cognitive and Behavioral Practice*.

Luoma J, Villatte J (in press) Mindfulness in the treatment of suicidal individuals. *Cognitive and Behavioral Practice*.

Lynch T, Chapman A, Rosenthal M, Kuo J, Linehan M (2006) Mechanisms of change in dialectical behavior therapy: theoretical and empirical observations. *Journal of Clinical Psychology*, **62**(4): 459–80.

Michel K, Jobes D (2011) *Building a Therapeutic Alliance with the Suicidal Patient*. American Psychological Association, Washington, DC.

Michel K, Dey P, Stadler K, Valach L (2004) Therapist sensitivity towards emotional life-career issues and the working alliance with suicide attempters. *Archives of Suicide Research* **8**: 203–13.

Orlinsky D, Ronnestad M, Willutzki U (2004) Fifty years of psychotherapy process–outcome research: continuity and change. In: Lambert M (ed.) *Bergin and Garfield's Handbook of Psychotherapy and Behavior Change*, 5th edn. Wiley, New York, pp. 307–89.

Rogers J, Madura T, Hardy J (2011) Evidence-based psychosocial interventions and suicidal behavior. What is the evidence? In: Pompili M, Tatarelli, R (eds.) *Evidence-based Practice in Suicidology*. Hogrefe Publications, Cambridge, MA, pp. 125–38.

Rizvi S (2011) The therapeutic relationship in dialectical behavioral therapy for suicidal individuals. In: Michel K, Jobes D (eds.) *Building a Therapeutic Alliance with the Suicidal Patient*. American Psychological Association, Washington, DC, pp. 255–71.

Rudd D, Brown G (2011) A cognitive theory of suicide: building hope in treatment and strengthening the therapeutic relationship. In: Michel K, Jobes D (eds.) *Building a Therapeutic Alliance with the Suicidal Patient*. American Psychological Association, Washington, DC, pp. 169–181.

Rudd M, Joinier T, Trotter D, Williams B, Cordero L (2009) The psychosocial treatment of suicidal behavior: a critique of what we know (and don't know). In: Kleespies PM (ed.) *Behavioral Emergencies*. American Psychological Association, Washington, DC, pp. 339–50.

Shneidman E (1985) *Definition of Suicide*. Aronson, Northvale.

Shneidman E (1996) *The Suicidal Mind*. Oxford University Press, New York.

Stanley B, Brodsky B (2009) Dialectical behavior therapy for suicidal individuals. In: Wasserman D, Wasserman C (eds.) *Oxford Textbook of Suicidology and Suicide Prevention. A Global Perspective*. Oxford University Press, Oxford, pp. 413–20.

Task Force on Empirically Supported Therapy Relationships (2001) *Empirically Supported Therapy Relationships: Conclusions and Recommendations of Division 29 Task Force*. http://www.scranton.edu/faculty/norcross/ConcsRecomms.doc (accessed 16 July 2012).

Wagner A, Rizvi S, Harned M (2007) Applications of dialectical behavior therapy to the treatment of complex trauma-related problems: when one case formulation does not fit all. *Journal of Traumatic Stress*, **20**: 391–400.

Wampold B (1997) Methodological problems in identifying efficacious psychotherapies. *Psychotherapy Research*, **7**: 21–43.

CHAPTER 8

Engagement and inspiring hope: reconnecting the person with humanity – an introduction to the nursing care of the suicidal person

> There is no way that you can come up with one or two simple techniques that can solve all problems... however, it is helpful to understand and appreciate the importance of compassion in human relationships and empathy. (Dalai Lama, 1998, p. 91)

> But then there's another level of spirituality. This is what I call basic spirituality, basic human qualities of goodness, kindness, compassion and caring.... But as long as we are human beings, as long as we are all members of the human family, all of us need these basic human values. Without these, human existence becomes very hard, very dry. (Dalai Lama and Cutler, 1998, p. 307)

Introduction

As we have pointed out in previous chapters, even a cursory survey of mental health facilities in most parts of the so-called 'developed' world will show that the current standard 'modus operandi' for the nursing care of suicidal people is to place the person 'under observation'[1]. Interestingly, our previous chapters have also shown how woefully inadequate such practices often are: how they do little or nothing to help alleviate the suicidal person's psychache and/or genesis of his or her suicidal ideation. Further evidence previously provided also shows how

1 Or whatever vernacular term is used to connote keeping the suicidal person under some form of surveillance.

they (observations) often fail in even their most basic function: keeping the person physically safe.

Yet it would be remiss of the authors of this book to point out the serious and significant limitations of this current practice without, at the same time, offering an alternative. Accordingly, this chapter focuses on such an alternative – one that has been termed the 'engagement/inspiring hope – reconnecting the person with humanity' approach (see for example Cutcliffe and Barker, 2002; Cutcliffe and Stevenson, 2007). This chapter begins by drawing the reader's attention to the literature which has repeatedly shown how suicidal people feel a sense of disconnection. We then go on to underscore this experience with reference to the literature linking suicide with isolation/loneliness and then highlight the links between a sense of disconnection and Shneidman's psychache. Following this, we draw on the findings of a recent federally funded study that explored how P/MH nurses work with suicidal people (Cutcliffe *et al*, 2006; Cutcliffe and Stevenson, 2007). It provides a summary of the three stage process and explains how P/MH nurses work day-by-day, hour-by-hour and minute-by-minute with suicidal people.

The suicidal person: evidence of 'disconnection' – what does the literature say?

Suicide and social integration

Since the beginning of the formal study of suicide, the relationship between the individual person's sense of connection (and associated synonyms) and the resultant increase in suicidality has been posited and discovered with conspicuous regularity. Furthermore, it is interesting to note, especially in light of Maris' (1997) comments regarding the requirement to adopt a biopsychosocial perspective for studying suicide[2], that this sense or experience of 'disconnection' is manifest in a variety of ways; it is a multi-dimensional, multi-faceted existential experience.

For some, the formal study of suicide began with Emile Durkheim's classic work *Le Suicide* (1897/1951). Durkheim's central claim was, perhaps counter-intuitively, that the apparent highly personal and individual act of suicide was in fact driven or even determined by social, external (and constraining) forces. Moreover, he was clear in predicating the causal relationship between the individual person's sense of social isolation (what he termed *egoism*) and the eventual suicide. For Durkheim, the suicide rate had an inverse (though variable)

2 It is worthy of note that Maris's views are echoed throughout the international academe of suicidologists, wherein a multidimensional and multidisciplinary approach to the study of suicide is now, for many, regarded as *de rigeur*.

relationship with the person's sense of social integration. He posited three 'types' of suicide: egoistic, altruistic and anomic. Highlighting the then differences in rates of suicide of people who claimed to be Protestant, Catholic or Jewish[3] (with rates recorded as highest in the Protestant population and lowest in the Jewish population), Durkheim asserted that these differences in rate occurred as a result of the different degrees of 'unity, solidarity and integration' that existed within these groups. He argued that, for example, in response to the external hostility directed towards people who held the Jewish faith, this helped establish and maintain strong community ties of thought and action and also discouraged divergence. To use contemporary suicidology parlance, these community ties thus acted as very powerful 'protective factors'.

A further interesting proposition from Durkheim was that there was a relationship between the degree of free thought or free inquiry and the rate of suicide. To paraphrase, the more a group 'permits' or encourages free thought, the more the result will be increased knowledge and, Durkheim argued, a corresponding increase in suicide rates (since free inquiry can result in as much sorrow and despair as it can happiness). It is worthy of note that in Durkheim's view, the protective influence of religion and religious beliefs do not arise as a result of the particular theological view of suicide (eg. suicide as a sin against God), but occurred rather because religion is a society[4]: it enhanced the person's sense of integration, belonging and connectedness. Thus we find Durkheim's famous reference to a 'coefficient of preservation', and his conclusion that the stronger the integration of the religious community, the greater its preservative value.

Interestingly, Durkheim's views of the preservative value of societies were not comprehensively supported by the rates of suicide in other societies, though there was some supporting evidence reported. For example, Durkheim produced evidence to show that marriage acted as a preservative factor for men *but not for women*; also, when the marriage partner died, the loss of the preservative influence of this 'society' was marked.

While we wish to include a caveat here that Durkheim did not define what he meant by his use of the term 'social integration', the authors of this book argue that there is an apparent, noticeable and palpable relationship between the terms 'social integration' and a 'sense of connectedness'. Synonyms for the word 'integration' include inclusion, incorporation, combination, assimilation, merging and merger, whereas antonyms include separate, exclude and reject. Similarly, the synonyms

3 These differences continue to be reported in some studies.

4 And arguably reduces the opportunity for the 'free thought', preferring instead adherence to the particular religious doctrine.

for connection include bond, relationship, link, association, union, tie, network and bring together. Thus it is clear that integration and (re)connection appear, at the very least, to share an etymological connection[5]. For the authors of this book, the relationship between this connectedness and integration transcends the uni-dimensional view of 'social' connectedness/integration[6].

Interestingly, while one has to recognise and acknowledge the 'vintage' of Durkheim's work, contemporary findings lend much support to the notion of social integration and the resultant sense of connection as a distinctive protective factor against suicide. Perhaps a robust contemporary example of this phenomenon can be seen when one examines suicide rates within Northern Ireland and the context of political instability and associated acts of terrorism, known or referred to colloquially as 'the troubles' (McGowan *et al*, 2005, p. 400). McGowan *et al* (2005) accessed official suicide statistics in Northern Ireland for the period 1966–1999 and found that nearly 7,000 people had died prematurely during these years. A highly significant inverse correlation ($p < 0.01$) was found between the annual number of suicides and deaths associated with/linked to terrorist activity. This correlation was found to exist across both genders. McGowan *et al* (2005) conclude that the strengthening social bonds that occur as a result of experiencing 'the troubles'; or to paraphrase the increased sense of being connected to one's social community arising from the sense of being persecuted or being under attack, acted as a significant protective factor against the risk of suicide.

Social isolation, loneliness and suicide

A further experience(s) that is perhaps synonymous with a sense of disconnection is that of social isolation and loneliness. A sizeable literature exists that indicates a positive correlation between a person's sense of isolation and/or loneliness and increased risk of suicide; furthermore, this isolation is manifest in a variety of forms. While noting its vintage, a seminal paper on the role of social isolation and suicide was written by Trout (1980). Trout's conclusions, if subsequent studies (see below) are anything to go by, still have meaning and significance in the 21st century. Trout's systematic review of the literature concluded that social isolation seems to be related to suicidal behaviours in a direct and fundamental way.

More recent work, and work with specific populations who can and do experience a high degree of social isolation, reiterates and supports Trout's findings. One such population is the elderly and more especially, the widowed. A well-established

5 We will return to and develop this connection throughout this chapter.

6 Again this is further explored below.

literature purports that the risk of suicide is increased in the widowed (see for example Wenz, 1977; Motto *et al*, 1985; Fawcett *et al*, 1987; Goldstein *et al*, 1991; Powell *et al*, 2000; Luoma and Pearson, 2002; Erlangsen *et al*, 2004). Indeed, again accepting the vintage of the study, Wenz concluded that in addition to the social psychological factor of anomie, it was the *actual social isolation* and the concerns about *future social isolation* (our emphasis) that were the key factors that increased the suicide risk of widows who lived in suburban areas.

Loneliness, which clearly has an association with social isolation, has often been identified as having a correlation with suicide and increased suicide risk; furthermore these associations are not limited to one group or population. In the Western World the elderly population[7] continues to have an alarmingly high of rate of suicide, and it similarly reports high levels of social isolation and loneliness (due to a wide range of variables). Not surprisingly, the association between loneliness in the elderly and suicidal ideation/behaviour has been reported (Osgood, 1991; Osgood and Brant, 1990; Tatai and Tatai, 1991). While it would be rash or hasty to suggest a direct causal link between social isolation, the resultant loneliness and all suicides in this population, it is evident that a link exists.

A larger number of studies and, as a result, a more developed body of knowledge, refers to loneliness in young people: most often in high (senior) school and college (university) students. At first glance, such findings might seem counter-intuitive, given the close physical proximity of people in such places to one another. Yet the findings are consistent over time and place: they repeatedly show a significant link between loneliness and suicide in these populations (Bonner and Rich, 1987; Garnefski *et al*, 1992; Rich and Bonner, 1987; Rich *et al*, 1992). More recent evidence indicates that during a cluster of suicides at New York University in 2003 students reported the sense of isolation and stated that there wasn't a social atmosphere. Interestingly, this mix of academic pressure and social isolation has been reported in other schools and universities and is clearly a high-risk mix.

Loneliness has been discovered to feature as one of the principal factors that contribute to suicide in several other studies, for a variety of nationalities (Lavigne-Pley, 1983; Stravynski and Boyer, 2001). In a recent study, Stravynski and Boyer (2001) found strong associations, in a population-wide survey, between suicide ideation and different ways of being lonely and alone. They further noted that the prevalence of suicide ideation increased correspondingly with the degree

7 We are mindful of both (a) the sometimes pejorative nature of the term 'elderly', although this is the term used commonly in the literature and (b) that it would be simplistic to refer to one homogeneous group called 'the elderly'.

of loneliness. These associations were found to almost the same degree in males and females.

Further evidence points to the association between social isolation and increased suicide risk. Suicide rates are frequently found to be higher in rural and remote regions than they are in densely populated regions. Drawing on the example of British Columbia, Canada, when compared to their urban counterparts who live in the south of the province, health outcomes, including rates of suicide, are markedly worse (BCVSA, 2001, 2002). The epidemiological picture is further complicated across Northern British Columbia, wherein some geographical areas have very low (almost non-existent) suicide rates and others have suicide rates well above the national or provincial average. Annually collected data indicate that there were 192 completed suicides in 2001 within the geographical area covered by the Northern Health Authority. Moreover, of this number 136 (71%) occurred within the North West Health Authority region area; a region with the significant majority of the population living in remote and rural areas. Similar findings have been reported in other countries – see for example, recent epidemiological data from Australia, Wales and the USA. While acknowledging the social isolation that can occur with remote and rural populations, the authors urge a degree of caution here; it may well be that there are other variables that contribute to or 'cause' the high rate of suicide in these regions. Nevertheless, it is worthy of note.

Another population group that is perhaps synonymous with experiencing isolation is the homeless. While accepting that homeless people may (or may not) belong to a social group of their 'peers', it similarly needs to be accepted that the homeless person is likely to be isolated from his or her family, friends and various support systems. Eynan *et al* (2002) undertook a study to examine the association between homelessness and suicidal ideation and behaviours; their findings were disturbing. Out of their sample of 330 homeless people, 61% reported suicidal ideation and 34% had made an actual attempt. Of particular support for the relationship between isolation (as experienced through homelessness) and suicidal ideation was that their study also found that childhood experiences of homelessness were found to be associated with suicidal ideation.

Accordingly, one can conclude with a degree of empirical confidence that social isolation/loneliness, in a variety of forms and individualised experiences, has been clearly identified as having a correlation with suicide and increased suicide risk. Furthermore, this link has been observed across several specific population groups as well as different nationalities.

Suicide, psychache and (dis)connectedness

Edwin Shneidman is often regarded to be the pre-eminent suicidologist of his generation and is credited with fashioning the contemporary formal study of suicide and thus creating, the scientific field of 'Suicidology'. Shneidman's central premise appears to be that suicide is inextricably linked to the term he coined '*psychache*' [original emphasis]:

> Stripped down to its bones, my argument goes like this: In almost every case, suicide is caused by pain, a certain kind of pain – *psychological pain* or 'psychache'. Further this psychache stems from thwarted or distorted psychological *needs* [original emphasis] (Shneidman, 1997, p. 23).

While Shneidman qualifies his remarks and acknowledges that there are certainly exceptions and that the topic is a very complicated business and thus *ipso facto* is unlikely to be explained by a straightforward single causative relationship, he makes a compelling case for considering the relationship between the presence and influence of pervasive and pernicious individualised psychache and suicide. He continues:

> even though I know that each suicidal death is multi-faceted event; that biological, biochemical, cultural, sociological, interpersonal, intra-psychic, logical, philosophical, conscious, and unconscious elements are always present – I retain the belief that, in the proper distillation of the event, it's essential nature is *psychological*. That is, each suicidal drama occurs in the *mind* of a unique individual [original emphasis] (Shneidman, 1997, p. 23).

Accepting the cogency of this premise, it is then worth considering how psychache might affect a person's sense of disconnection. Furthermore, if we invert this conceptual relationship – if we accept the possibility of an existential state of disconnection – it is worth considering how this might affect a person's psychache.

It is now accepted as axiomatic that the experience of pain has an emotional as well as a physical component. This multi-dimensionality of pain is encountered not only in the nature of the pain experience itself, but also in *the effects* of experiencing pain. Furthermore, while a range of pain-relieving interventions can alleviate the physical sensation of pain (Schofield 2005; Carr and Mann, 2000), there is a large and well-established body of extant literature that indicates how pain can wear the person down: make him/her feel emotionally exhausted, anxious, depressed, and/or overwhelmed. Indeed, there is a growing body of work that refers to the 'depressant' effects that chronic pain can have on people (Turk *et al*,

Box 8.1 The psychological and social effects of pain

- Being less able to function
- Feel tired and lethargic
- Loss of appetite and/or nausea
- Not being able to sleep, or have one's sleep interrupted by pain
- Experiencing less enjoyment and more anxiety
- Becoming depressed, anxious, or unable to concentrate on anything except pain
- Feeling a loss of control
- Having less interaction with friends
- Being less able to enjoy sex or affection
- Feeling that one is more of a burden on family or other caregivers

1995; Mossey and Gallagher, 2004; Tesch *et al*, 2004). Additional psychological and social effects of pain have been reported and these are summarised in Box 8.1.

Also, there are narrative-based accounts that people experiencing pain may well be afraid to tell anyone about their pain. The concern most often reported is that such individuals worry that they will be labelled a 'complainer'; it is the person's lot to endure or suffer in silence. This is despite the copious and convincing evidence that refers to the subjectivity of pain. Indeed, the often cited maxim in nursing is that pain is what the person says it is and when the person says it is! The extant 'pain'-related literature has also illustrated how that the experience of pain can feel all-encompassing: the individual can at times be unable to look beyond his/her current experience of pain (Mossey and Gallagher, 2004); it starts to define and colour all other experiences (Turk *et al*, 1995).

Accordingly, the extant literature is clear in demonstrating the psychological and 'social' effects that pain can (and does) have on the individual. Moreover, each of the effects of pain listed above in Box 8.1, to a greater or lesser extent, will either directly or indirectly lead to a greater sense of disconnection from humanity. An 'indirect' example is where the individual's lethargy and inability to function inevitably lead to less inclusion in social functions and interpersonal relationships and thus a greater sense of disconnection; whereas a 'direct' example would be having less interaction with one's friends. Thus it becomes apparent that pain, be it physical or psychological in origin[8], has another effect on the person and

8 It may even be unhelpful to posit such simplistic 'Aristotelian' either/or depictions of pain as it is most likely to be 'and/both'.

that it creates or enhances the person's experiential sense of disconnection from humanity.

So, to return to the notion of the cyclic nature of this relationship, in addition to pain leading to disconnection, we posit that the experiential sense of disconnection will, for some (if not many) be, in and of itself, a source of psychological pain for the suicidal person. Theoretical evidence of this relationship already exists across a number of linked disciplines, such as sociology, psychology, philosophy and nursing. We have already drawn attention to Durkheim's views on how pain (and ultimately suicide) can result from this sense of disconnection (lack of integration, alienation). The contemporary philosopher Sartre (1943) made similar remarks on the pain associated with an individual's sense of aloneness. Frankl (1959), Shneidman (1997) and Maris *et al* (2000) have drawn attention to the often difficult nature of life; under the best of conditions, life is often lonely and anxiety provoking and consequently, often a source of psychological pain for the person (Maris, 1981).

Similarly, a large body of work exists within the domain of P/MH nursing which alludes to the need to be interpersonally connected. Regarded affectionately as 'the founding mother of psychiatric nursing', Peplau (1952, 1988) has repeatedly purported both the necessity of locating P/MH nursing in an 'interpersonal' context and similarly, the therapeutic value of experiencing interpersonal connection; an empirical finding found repeatedly in studies that look at what people want and need from their mental health services. For example, in Rogers *et al*'s (1993) study of mental health service users' appreciation of psychiatric services in the UK[9], it was found that the preferred model of practice centred on involved personal contact. Related evidence from studies undertaken in numerous centres around the world affirms this interpersonal (and thus 'connected') form of P/MH nursing (see for example, Gordon *et al*, 1979; McIntyre *et al*, 1989; Elbeck and Fecteau, 1990; Avis *et al*, 1994; Beech and Norman, 1995; Rudman, 1996; Cutcliffe *et al*, 1997). More latterly, compelling findings reported in the Mental Health Foundation (2000) report *Strategies for Living* once more reiterated the centrality of 'accepting relationships' and the value that mental health service users place on such relationships.

Interestingly, there is another body of related work which speaks to disconnection and increased suicidality as it is experienced (and manifest) through the very basic human need of physical touch. Orbach's undeniable contributions in this area offer some illuminating evidence. Orbach (2003) summarises his

9 To this day this remains the largest UK study of its kind.

findings and reports results that point to suicidal youngsters having lower tactile sensitivity and responsiveness and lower emotional investment in the body. These suicidal youngsters were found to be disconnecting from the normal, required, basic human need of connection through touch and touching (see also Harlow and Soumi, 1970). Related findings have been uncovered in associated areas, such as the empirical correlation reported between increased use of touch and physical comforting and survival rates in low birth weight infants (Sloan *et al*, 1994; Feldman *et al*, 2002).

Additionally, the French contemporary philosopher Gabriel Marcel (1948) constructed a persuasive and convincing argument about the nature of human existence and what he referred to as the '*ontological* exigence'. According to Marcel, exigence refers to the person's need/demand for some level of coherence in the cosmos and more importantly (in terms of the issue of connectedness) for some understanding of one's place and role within this coherence. For Marcel, *ontological* exigence is not simply a wish or desire; it is not reducible to some psychological state, mood or attitude. It is more central to existence than that; it is a movement of the human spirit that is inseparable from being human. To paraphrase, there is an alienable element of the human condition that is concerned with experiencing a sense of knowing one's place in the world; feeling connected to the world and others in it; feeling that one has a place and purpose. To live in the existential state then of feeling disconnected – to live with a pervasive sense of alienation, separateness and isolation – must be a dreadful source of psychological pain; of psychache.

How to care for suicidal people: reconnecting the person with humanity

Overview

The key psychosocial process synonymous with care of the suicidal person is reconnecting the person with humanity. In order to move the suicidal person from a 'death orientated' to a 'life orientated' position, it is necessary for the P/MH nurse to facilitate this reconnection with humanity. This occurs over a three-stage process of healing (see Figure 8.1): each stage has its own conceptual heading, comprised of a number of conceptually dense, developed categories[10] and these are described and explained in more detail below.

10 Each category in turn is comprised of a number of preliminary categories – see Cutcliffe and Stevenson, 2007).

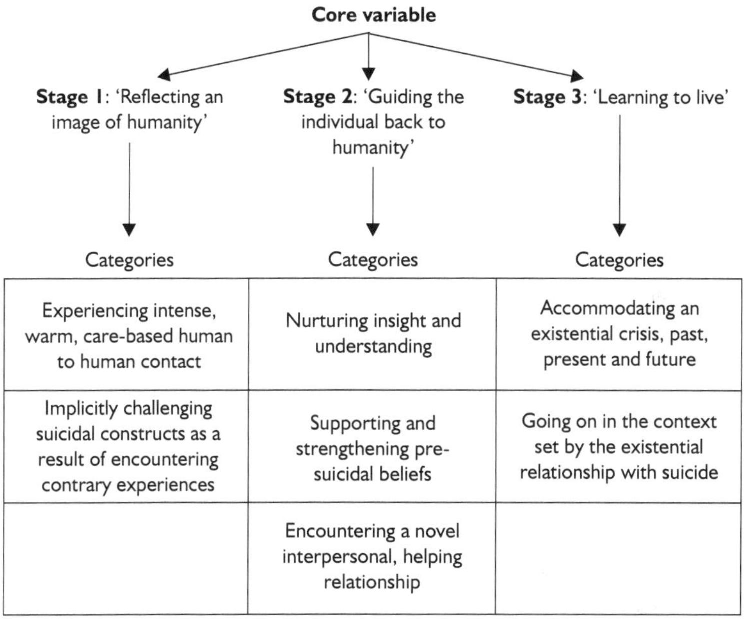

Figure 8.1 Reconnecting the person with humanity.

Table 8.1 Sub-core variables category composition.

'Reflecting an image of humanity' (Stage 1)
Experiencing intense, warm, care-based human to human contact
Implicitly challenging suicidal constructs as a result of encountering contrary experiences
'Guiding the individual back to humanity' (Stage 2)
Nurturing insight and understanding
Supporting and strengthening pre-suicidal beliefs
Encountering a novel interpersonal, helping relationship
'Learning to live' (Stage 3)
Accommodating an existential crisis, past, present and future
Going on in the context set by the existential relationship with suicide

The first stage is concerned with reflecting an image of humanity, and this appears to begin with a recognition that the person has indeed disconnected from humanity. This recognition can then set the 'tone' and the 'direction' of the intra- and interpersonal work that needs to be done, namely finding ways to reconnect the person with humanity and/or help the person gain a sense that he or she is indeed connected. The contact with the suicidal person at this stage needs to be intensive; the intensive contact which occurs in or at many levels serves several purposes; not least it offers a direct contradiction to any experiences of lack of integration, social isolation and/or loneliness. The intensive contact is, in and of itself, both a tentative connection and a medium in which further connection can occur. It is important to point out that this intensive contact is purposeful, necessary and deliberate. Furthermore, this should in no way be confused with the type of close physical proximity synonymous with defensive and custodial approaches to care of the suicidal person, most often expressed as 'close observations' or some synonym[11]. This intensive contact also makes possible the increased use of physical comforting and touch. Again, acknowledging as stated above that suicidal people can even disconnect from this other form of basic human connection – touch – the healing potential of this was not lost on the P/MH nurses.

As the authors have noted earlier, suicidal ideation does not happen in a vacuum; fortunately, the same can be said of care of the suicidal person. Indeed, the environment, both internal and external to the person, is used deliberately in a way to help facilitate the person's reconnection. As noted previously, suicide is often considered as a means to end one's psychache; a way of achieving peace from the sense of constant and pervasive pain. Thus, part of the facilitation of reconnecting the person with humanity involves helping the suicidal person find peace in other ways or through other means. Correspondingly, the increased sense of peace with the world and within oneself can then help the person feel more connected to the world and other people in it.

Further, the sense of reconnecting with humanity is brought about in these early stages through re-establishing the person's trust in humanity. Through gaining trust in the nurse, the participant is then reconnecting with a person, taking the first tentative steps towards reconnecting with the wider community of 'humanity'. This is achieved through listening to and understanding the person. Participants in the original study (Cutcliffe *et al*, 2006; Cutcliffe and Stevenson, 2007) were very clear about how they often just needed someone to talk to during their 'recovery' from their suicide attempt and/or ideation. These interpersonal transactions and processes were not personified by erudite sentences, cleverly constructed deep analytical insights into the clients' psyche. The transactions were personified by

11 Where the practitioner engages only in close observations and follows the suicidal person around like some form of 'magnetic zombie'; often saying nothing if anything to the person and having minimal interaction with the person.

the 'normalness' of the interactions and were most commonly described as 'just chatting'.

The key processes of communicating – being heard and understood – are some of the most basic, necessary and powerful interpersonal experiences; and yet simultaneously they are eminently *human experiences*, perhaps some of the experiences that define what it is to be human, to belong to the 'brother/sisterhood' of humankind[12]. In beginning or recommencing these communication processes, the participant can be seen to be entering into reconnecting with humanity. In the first instance, the person is reconnecting first with the nurse, who acts as a 'representative' of humanity. As stated above, the increasing sense of peace that arose from speaking and being listened to helped reduce the suicidal person's sense of psychache. The cathartic effect of talking through the situations and perceptions that had ushered the person towards suicide, and the 'novel' experience of finding someone who is willing to listen without prejudice, are all immensely valuable processes in countering a person's sense of hopelessness and combatting the person's desire to take their own life.

In addition, this reconnecting with humanity, brought about in this early stage by connecting first with the P/MH nurse, is realised by the suicidal person increasingly feeling cared about and cared for, experiencing this sense and process of 'co-presencing'. Through demonstrating caring, compassion, and concern the P/MH nurse becomes the first 'point' of reconnection with humanity. The suicidal person connects with the nurse and thus begins to reconnect with humanity. This sense of being valued – feeling that they matter – helps the suicidal person realise that they are not alone; that their death would matter; that there are people around them who are invested in them as a human being. Further, there is immense therapeutic healing power in feeling cared about; it is a direct counter-action to the experiencing of 'psychache'.

As the process moves into its second stage, the reconnection with humanity is brought about by experiencing the additional sense of security offered within the novel relationship, which allows feelings, previously kept internalised by the person, to be discussed freely. It allows the P/MH nurse to ask, 'Where does it hurt?' and allows the suicidal person to respond without 'internal censorship' or 'editing'. This externalisation and subsequent rationalisation of these thoughts permits the suicidal person to seek understanding of his or her feelings. There is appreciation that they do indeed need help. A connection is made between the internal turmoil and the fact that through talking with the P/MH nurse these

12 See Marcel's (1948) comments earlier in this chapter.

feelings can be managed; that they can indeed discuss these thoughts and feelings without harming the P/MH nurse and therein would do no harm to their tenuous connection with humanity. Having previously felt controlled (to a greater or lesser extent) by the suicidal thoughts, the suicidal person is able to take more responsibility over controlling *them*. The suicidal person also begins to reconnect with his or her pre-suicidal beliefs. During times of high suicidality, the person's pre-suicidal beliefs unfortunately do not serve as strong enough protective factors; yet the original beliefs can still have some protective value. Further, such beliefs were almost inevitably associated with feeling more connected with humanity. Building on the progress that the suicidal person has begun to make in connecting with humanity through connecting with the P/MH nurse, this connection is further strengthened by getting back in touch with these pre-suicidal beliefs. Now, with the additional support of their connection with the P/MH nurse, the suicidal person can once again draw on the protective elements contained within these beliefs.

Interestingly, despite being the *modus operandi* for some (many) practitioners and the primary treatment option, the use of medication has only a limited part to play in this transformative process of recovery. The facilitative aspects were concerned with providing respite, albeit temporary, from the psychological pain and stress. More notably, the restrictive elements of the use of medication centred on increasing the person's sense of disconnection, most often as a result of the person feeling 'numbed, slowed down' and experiencing an altered level of mental functioning. This was especially the case if taking medication meant that the suicidal person was unable to resume their normal activities. It was also apparent when the suicidal person asked for and expected something more than medication and what they actually received was pharmacologically based 'help'[13].

Additionally, part of the process at this stage involves attempts to re-frame constricted constructs through gentle challenge, offering alternative explanations and providing information. The constructs relating to a sense of disconnection, being different and worthless/hopeless, are addressed and re-framed into experiences that are essentially the epitome of what it is to be human. Suicidal people are introduced to the constructs that what they are experiencing can very much be part of what it means to belong to the 'human community'; that their experiences are actually in keeping with others rather than being different. Further, they can be shown that feeling disconnected is common and, moreover, can be remedied.

---

13 Interestingly, the suicidal people in this study were adamant that they wanted the 'human touch' rather than 'more drugs'.

This reconnection with humanity is also brought about as a result of the novel relationship between themselves and the nurse, and a product of this is that hope starts to emerge. While more work on promoting the re-emergence of hope appears to occur in Stage 2, the beginnings of this re-emergence are evident in Stage 1. The person starts to look towards the future to see what it might hold for them. He or she moves from questions of 'What happened to me?' to 'What *will* happen to me?'. There is an increasing need to take control over their situation, whereas in the early stage of the process control of the situation was perhaps predominantly with the P/MH nurse in their 'co-presencing' and guiding of the individual.

As the process moves into the third stage, this reconnection with humanity is brought about by the participant gaining understanding of, and beginning to make sense of his/her suicidality. In Stage 1, the P/MH nurse has offered a co-presence that has served to keep the suicidal person anchored to life, partly by reflecting an image of humanity. In Stage 2 the P/MH nurse provides information when asked, supporting the person emotionally and re-framing the suicidal person's negative constructs. In Stage 3 the continued presence of the P/MH nurse, albeit in different guises, represents a longitudinal reconnection; a thread that pulls the person back to the land of the living from the land of the dead, and offers a handhold on the path to the future. In other words, the P/MH nurse is the bridge that helps the suicidal person reconnect with humanity. The continuing professional presence of the P/MH nurse acts as a safety net, in case the process of reconnecting overwhelms the person and suicidality gains a foothold. The journey from death to life is an uphill struggle and the suicidal person needs emotional sustenance on the way. The support does not have to be physical, but may be virtual; knowing that there is a P/MH nurse who is a phone call away is sustaining in and of itself. However, this connectivity must be carefully managed. Its abrupt withdrawal can make the suicidal person feel that the P/MH nurse has lost interest in her or him and that attachment to the world of people and objects is not worthwhile.

This reconnection with humanity was also brought about by the suicidal person becoming more confident about the meaning of the suicide attempt and how it 'fits' into her/his past, present and future life trajectory. This understanding helps to give the suicidal person power over the suicidality, whereas before the suicidal person's sense of being and the suicidality were collapsed together. Putting the suicide 'in its place' allows more space for reconnection. Consequently, it becomes possible to begin to make plans and set goals, which serve to help the suicidal person feel reconnected and hopeful. Without hope, the person simply cannot be bothered to stay connected to her or his world. At this point, the P/MH nurse is continuing to be a resource, not undertaking the work for the suicidal person, but helping the person to project a positive future and encouraging the generation of ideas and possibilities.

This reconnection with humanity was also brought about by revisiting the decision to commit suicide, considering whether life was, is and will be worth living. There is an acceptance by the suicidal person that she or he would have been missed (significant others may have expressed this directly) and this fuels the reconnection process. Further, by engaging in small but significant practical everyday activities the suicidal person begins to feel normal again: more a part of the human race; more connected. Success breeds success: as small changes occur, larger ones follow. Thus it can be seen and argued that competency in the practical world is a barometer of increased hope in the person.

Overview: concluding remarks

A well-constructed grounded theory will fit the realities under study in the eyes of subjects, practitioners and researchers in the area and it will have 'conceptual grab' (Glaser, 1978; 1992, 2001; Glaser and Strauss, 1967). Additionally, given that these are findings from a qualitative study, any attempt to infer nomothetic generalisable findings would be inappropriate and epistemologically flawed. The findings should, however, have idiographic (or naturalistic) generalisability; a generalisability about and based on the 'cases' (Sandelowski, 1997). In this instance, the 'cases' were concerned with suicidal people who had received formal mental healthcare, principally from P/MH nurses. Thus the findings should (can) have generalisability to other 'cases' involving formal care for suicidal people; irrespective of the similarities between different demographic groups (Denzin and Lincoln, 1994). Research cases involving or focusing on the P/MH nursing care of the suicidal person should therefore bear a resemblance to care of the suicidal person as a 'whole' (Morse, 1999). A process of caring identified in one setting, group or population can then be similarly experienced by another group (and have fit and grab for them too) or population in another setting.

With these thoughts in mind, the authors would like to draw attention to a recent view emanating from the WHO. In 2005, a consulting a group of suicidology experts, including anthropologists, psychiatrists, sociologists and epidemiologists were brought together by the WHO and

> They were unanimous in identifying a common denominator (in completed suicide cases) – a lack of connectedness. And this lack of connectedness permeates modern life, impacting society at three distinct levels – the family, the community, the workplace.

The WHO's (2005) unequivocal response was to assert that,

> We have to revitalize our communities so that the connectedness people once felt in their communities, their workplaces and their families can be restored.

The authors believe that the findings and theory described in this and the next three chapters contribute one part of the multi-dimensional and multi-professional theory that explains these much-needed processes of reconnection in suicidal people.

Acknowledgement

Parts of this chapter were originally published in, and adapted from:

Cutcliffe JR, Stevenson C (2007) *Care of the Suicidal Person.* Elsevier/Churchill Livingstone.

We not only wish to extend our most profound thanks to Elsevier for permission to use this material, but for more a more detailed explanation of these findings and much more, please do access and refer to the Cutcliffe and Stevenson (2007) text.

References

Avis M, Bond M, Arthur A (1994) *Patient Satisfaction and the Management of Outpatient Consultation.* Unpublished Report, University of Nottingham, Nottingham.

Beech P, Norman IJ (1995) Patients' perceptions of the quality of psychiatric nursing care: findings from a small-scale descriptive study. *Journal of Clinical Nursing* **4**: 117–23.

Bonner RL, Rich AR (1987) High consequences of loneliness: a review of the literature. *Journal of American College Health*, **37**: 162–7.

British Columbia Vital Statistics Agency (2001) *Selected Vital Statistics and Health Status Indicators: One Hundred and Thirtieth Annual Report of the BCVSA.* BCVSA, Victoria.

British Columbia Vital Statistics Agency (2002) *Selected Vital Statistics and Health Status Indicators: One Hundred and Thirty First Annual Report of the BCVSA.* BCVSA, Victoria.

Carr E, Mann E (2000) *Pain: Creative Approaches to Effective Pain Management.* Palgrave Macmillan, Basingstoke.

Cutcliffe JR, Barker P (2002) Considering the care of the suicidal client and the case for 'engagement and inspiring hope' or observations. *Journal of Psychiatric and Mental Health Nursing*, **9**(5): 611–21.

Cutcliffe JR, Stevenson C (2007) *Care of the Suicidal Person*, Elsevier, London.

Cutcliffe JR, Dukintis J, Carberry J, Tilley C, Turner S, Anderson-Moll D, Cooper W (1997) Users' Views of their continuing care community psychiatric services. *International Journal of Psychiatric Nursing Research*, **3**(3): 382–94.

Cutcliffe JR, Stevenson C, Jackson S, Smith P (2006) A modified grounded theory study of how psychiatric nurses work with suicidal people. *International Journal of Nursing Studies*, **43**(7): 791–802.

Dalai Lama, Cutler HC (1998) *The Art of Happiness: A Handbook for Living*, Hodder, Sydney.

Denzin N, Lincoln YS (1994) Introduction: entering the field of qualitative enquiry. In: Denzin N, Lincoln YS (eds.) *Handbook of Qualitative Research.* Sage, London, pp. 1–14.

Durkheim E (1951) *Suicide: a Study in Sociology*. Free Press, Glencoe, IL (original work published 1897).

Elbeck M, Fecteau G (1990) Improving the validity of measures of patient satisfaction with psychiatric care and treatment. *Hospital and Community Psychiatry*, **41**(9): 998–1001.

Erlangsen A, Jeune B, Bille-Brahe U, Vaupel JW (2004) Loss of partner and suicide risks among oldest old: a population-based register study. *Age and Aging*, **33**(4): 378–83.

Eynan R, Langley J, Tolomiczenko G, Rhodes A, Links P, Goering P (2002) The association between homelessness and suicidal ideation and behaviours: results of a cross-sectional survey. *Suicide and Life-Threatening Behavior*, **32**(4): 418–27.

Fawcett J, Scheftner W, Clark D, Hedeker D, Gibbons R, Coryell W (1987) Clinical predictors of suicide in patients with major affective disorders: a controlled prospective study. *American Journal of Psychiatry*, **144**(1): 35–40.

Feldman R, Eidelman AI, Sirota L, Weller A (2002) Effects of skin-to-skin contact (Kangaroo care) on parenting and infant development in premature infants. *Paediatrics*, **110**: 16–26.

Frankl V (1959) *Man's search for meaning*. Hodder & Stoughton, London.

Garnefski N, Diekstra RF, DeHeus P (1992) A population-based survey of the characteristics of high-school studens with and without a history of suicidal behaviour. *Acta Psychiatrica Scandinavia*, **86**: 189–96.

Glaser, BG (1978) *Theoretical Sensitivity: Advances in the Methodology of Grounded Theory*. Sociology Press, Mill Valley, CA.

Glaser BG (1992) *Basics of Grounded Theory Analysis: Emerging Versus Forcing*. Sociology Press, Mill Valley, CA.

Glaser BG (2001) *The Grounded Theory Perspective*: *Conceptualisation Contrasted with Description*. Sociology Press, Mill Valley, CA.

Glaser BG, Strauss AL (1967) *The Discovery of Grounded Theory: Strategies for Qualitative Research.* Aldine, Chicago.

Goldstein RB, Black DW, Nasrallah A, Winokur G (1991) The prediction of suicide: sensitivity, specificity and predictive value of a multivariative model applied to suicide among 1906 patients with an affective disorder. *Archives of General Psychiatry*, **48**: 418–22.

Gordon D, Alexander DA, Dieztan J (1979) The psychiatric patient: a voice to be heard. *British Journal of Psychiatry*, **135**: 115–21.

Harlow HF, Suomi SJ (1970) The nature of love simplified. *American Psychologist*, **25**: 161–8.

Lavigne-Pley C (1987) Le suicide chez les personnes agees (Suicide among the elderly). *Canadian Journal of Community Mental Health*, **6**: 55–77.

Luoma JB, Pearson J (2002) Suicide and marital status in the United States, 1991–1996: Is widowhood a risk factor? *American Journal of Public Health*, **92**(9): 1518–22.

McGowan IW, Hamilton S, Miller P, Kernohan G (2005) Contrasting terrorist related deaths with suicide trends over 34 years. *Journal of Mental Health*, **14**(4): 399–405.

McIntyre K, Farrell M, David A (1989) In-patient psychiatric care: the patient's view. *British Journal of Medical Psychology*, **62**: 249–55.

Marcel GG (1948) in Blackham HJ (1986) *Six Existentialist Thinkers*. Routledge, London, pp. 140–59.

Maris RW (1981) *Pathways to Suicide*. Johns Hopkins University Press, Baltimore.

Maris RW (1997) Social forces in suicide: a life review, 1965–1995. In: Maris RW, Silverman MM, Canetto SS (eds.) *Review of Suicidology 1997*. Guilford Press, New York, pp. 42–60.

Maris RW, Berman AL, Silverman MM (2000) *Comprehensive Textbook of Suicidology*. Guilford Press, New York.

Mental Health Foundation (2000) *Strategies for Living*. Mental Health Foundation, London.

Morse JM (1999) Qualitative generalisabilty. *Qualitative Health Research*, **9**(3): 5–6.

Mossey JM, Gallagher RM (2004) The longitudinal occurrence and impact of co-morbid chronic pain and chronic depression over two years in continuing care retirement community residents. *Pain Medicine*, **5**(4): 335–48.

Motto JA, Heilbron DC, Juster RP (1985) Development of a clinical instrument to estimate suicide risk. *American Journal of Psychiatry*, **142**: 680–6.

Orbach I (2003) Suicide and the suicidal body. *Suicide and Life-Threatening Behavior*, **33**(1): 1–8.

Osgood NJ (1991) Psychological factors in late-life suicide. *Crisis*, **12**: 18–24.

Osgood NJ, Brant BA (1990) Suicidal behavior in long-term care facilities. *Suicide and Life-Threatening Behavior*, **20**: 113–22.

Peplau H (1952) *Interpersonal Relations in Nursing*. Macmillan Press, New York.

Peplau H (1988) *Interpersonal Relations in Nursing*, 2nd edn. Macmillan Press, New York.

Powell J, Geddes J, Hawton K (2000) Suicide in psychiatric hospital in-patients. *British Journal of Psychiatry*, **176**(3): 266–72.

Rich AR, Bonner RL (1987) Concurrent validity of a stress–vulnerability model of suicidal ideation and behavior: a follow up study. *Suicide and Life-Threatening Behavior*, **17**: 265–70.

Rich AR, Kirkpatrick-Smith J, Bonner RL, Jans F (1992) Gender differences in the psychosocial correlates of suicide ideation among adolescents. *Suicide and Life-Threatening Behavior*, **22**: 364–73.

Rogers A, Pilgrim D, Lacey R (1993) *Experiencing Psychiatry: Users' Views of Services*. Macmillan/MIND, London.

Rudman, MJ (1996) User involvement in the nursing curriculum: seeking users' views. *Journal of Psychiatric and Mental Health Nursing*, **3**: 195–200.

Sandelowski M (1997) 'To be of use': enhancing the utility of qualitative research. *Nursing Outlook*, **45**(3): 125–32.

Sartre JP (1943) in Blackham HJ (1986) *Six Existentialist Thinkers*. Routledge, London, pp. 58–79.

Schofield P (2005) Effects of chronic pain. In: Schofield P (ed.) *Beyond Pain*. Whurr Publishers, London.

Shneidman ES (1997) The suicidal mind. In: Maris RW, Silverman MM, Canetto SS (eds.) *Review of Suicidology*. Guilford Press, New York, pp. 22–41.

Sloan N, Leon-Camacho WL, Rojas PE, Stern C *et al* (1994) Kangaroo mother method: randomized control trial of an alternative method of care for stabilizing low birth weight infants. *Lancet*, **344**: 782–5.

Stravynski A, Boyer R (2001) Loneliness in relation to suicide ideation and parasuicide: a population-wide study. *Suicide and Life-Threatening Behavior*, **31**(1): 32–40.

Tatai K, Tatai K (1991) Suicide in the elderly: a report from Japan. *Crisis*, **12**: 40–3.

Tesch RS, Denardin OVP, Baptista CA, Dias FL (2004) Depression levels in chronic orofacial pain patients: a pilot study. *Journal of Oral Rehabilitation*, **31**: 926–32 .

Trout DL (1980) The role of social isolation in suicide. *Suicide and Life-Threatening Behaviour*, **10**(1): 10–23.

Turk DC, Okifuji A, Scharff L (1995) Chronic pain and depression: role of perceived impact and perceived control in different age groups. *Pain*, **61**: 93–101.

Wenz FV (1977) Marital status, anomie, and forms of social isolation: a case of high suicide rate among the widowed in an urban sub-area. *Diseases of the Nervous System*, **38**(11): 891–5.

World Health Organization (2005) The Regional Director for the Western Pacific, WHO, Suicide Prevention in the Western Pacific Region. http://www.who.int/regional_director/speeches.

CHAPTER 9

Engagement – reconnecting the person with humanity: the three stages

> There were these two women sat on the edge of the bed dragging me back, mentally, intellectually and emotionally by making me engage with them. (Interview N3)

Introduction

The previous chapter introduced the reader to and provided an overview of the 'engagement – reconnecting the person with humanity' approach to caring for suicidal people. These are the principal findings from the federally funded study that explored how P/MH nurses work with suicidal people (Cutcliffe *et al*, 2006; Cutcliffe and Stevenson, 2007). This chapter provides a more comprehensive and detailed account of this approach and in so-doing, explains how P/MH nurses work day-by-day, hour-by-hour and minute-by-minute with suicidal people. The chapter provides a detailed account of each of the three stages and illustrates the key psychosocial care practices and processes therein by drawing on participant quotes (provided by formerly suicidal clients) which were procured during our study.

Stage 1: 'Reflecting an image of humanity'

Overview

This first stage of this process of engagement and reconnection is concerned with communicating a sense of care: communicating that the individual matters. It is very important for suicidal people to have a sense that they matter – to feel that someone else is concerned about and interested in them. This perception or sense has a distinct countering effect on their suicidal ideation and perspectives. Feeling cared about helps create the perspective for the suicidal person that he or she is no longer alone. The therapeutic value of such a perspective in the context of providing care for the suicidal person should not be underestimated. The sense of being disconnected from humanity is directly countered by this connecting with the P/MH nurse. Participants in the original study (Cutcliffe *et al*, 2006; Cutcliffe and Stevenson, 2007) made clear references to the feelings that were stimulated when they experienced another person demonstrating an interest in their wellbeing. The participants were aware that they needed to feel that they mattered; they needed to feel that someone cared about them, and they were also very clear that they received such confirmation and validation from the P/MH nurses. These 'fresh' and therapeutic experiences of feeling cared about, feeling that they mattered, and feeling connected all occurred in a very specific interpersonal atmosphere, one that was exemplified by the presence and influence of human warmth. Further, these experiences were directly opposite to their suicidal 'felt sense', namely that they did not matter, that nobody did care about them, that it would not make a difference whether they lived or died. Additionally, it is important (though perhaps somewhat obvious) to point out that the presence of these qualities and feelings in the P/MH nurse (eg. care and concern for the client's wellbeing, compassion, understanding) was not enough. The qualities and feelings also had to be communicated.

This first stage of engagement and reconnection is also concerned with facilitating the person's reconnection with humanity, and this is achieved in the first instance by connecting with the P/MH nurse. This reconnection with humanity is brought about by feeling cared about and cared for: experiencing this sense and process of 'co-presencing'. Through demonstrating caring, compassion and concern the P/MH nurse becomes the first point of reconnection with humanity. The person connects with the P/MH nurse and thus begins to reconnect with humanity. In essence, this process shows how the P/MH nurse becomes a 'representative' or 'emissary' for humanity. When the person experiences this sense of being cared for by the P/MH nurse, they are at the same time communicating that at least one 'part' of humanity still cares about the person. Engaging with the P/MH nurse in this way allows the participant to begin to internalise that they can still engage with humanity. The P/MH nurse's attitudes, demeanour and behaviour provide an 'in road' or if you will, an opportunity to reconnect.

Suicidal people often need to have their basic psychological/spiritual needs met, including (if not especially) their fundamental need to feel connected to or engaged with other people. These basic needs can be met by the P/MH nurse possessing (or adopting) and communicating a sense of warmth for the person; care for the person; compassion for the person's situation and experience; a sense of hope and hopefulness for the person's future; unconditional acceptance and tolerance; empathy; understanding; and positive regard. Further, in order to feel connected or reconnected with humanity, the person(s) needs to feel they can trust 'humanity'. Through developing a sense of trust in the P/MH nurse, the person is then reconnecting with another person; taking the first tentative steps towards reconnecting with the wider community of 'humanity'.

In addition, another key psychosocial process occurs in the first stage, and that is the subtle, implicit challenge of the person's suicide constructs. Suicidal people experience and interpret the world in a very constricted and particular way and consequently form these distinctive suicide constructs. P/MH nurses can challenge these constructs essentially by means of what they are and what they do, and less by means of what they say. This subtle and gentle reflection provides the opportunity for suicidal people to consider some of their negative assumptions and challenge some of their restrictive beliefs. When suicidal people can begin to internalise that many of their beliefs about past failures, present limitations and future restrictions are based on unrealistic constructs and inaccurate self-perceptions, and furthermore when they can begin to recognise that these constructs are perpetuated by their current state of hopelessness, then they can begin to challenge these for themselves. As a result, suicidal people can begin to deconstruct some of their suicide constructs and hopelessness and began to construct a more hopeful future. This was captured and described in the following ways:

> It is important that the nurses spent time with me; demonstrated that I was important; showed that I matter. (Int. S2)

> They were a lovely mixture of professional but human. (Int. N5)

> There were these two women sat on the edge of the bed dragging me back, mentally, intellectually and emotionally by making me engage with them. (Int. N3)

> They are really good people and I like that. They were interested in me. I felt like I was in good hands. (Int. N5)

> And then finally I had someone who understood how I was feeling. (Int. S3)

> I was getting a lot of human warmth. (Int. N5)

> I talked about what mattered in my life and he listened. (Int. S3)

It helped me not commit suicide, even though I was thinking about it, because I now knew there were people (the CAT) who were bothered about me and didn't want me to. (Int. N7)

They (the C.P.N.s) would ask how I was feeling; he wanted to understand how I was feeling. (Int. S3)

The hour with the C.P.N. was a different experience to my usual experience of being completely locked into my own spiral of horror and death. (Int. N3)

I wanted someone to just talk to. (Int. S2)

I felt like the CAT team did care for me. They kept making sure that if I ever needed to speak to them I could just ring. (Int. N7)

It can only be good for people with an illness like mine to have someone come out and sit with them for an hour at a time; listening to my fears and just talking in general about whatever problems they may have. (Int. S1)

I felt that she was bothered about me; that I mattered to her. (Int. N8)

It was the regularity of them coming out and feeling like I was a priority. (Int. S8)

I could connect with Val because she came across as both a mum and a mate. (Int. N8)

It is marvelous when someone cares; to know that someone in that field (mental healthcare) knows what you are feeling. (Int. S3)

After talking to my nurse, instead of thinking 'Oh my God, I might as well kill myself', I was thinking, 'Right, what can I do to put this right?' (Int. N2)

I didn't like talking to the Psychiatrist who made notes as I was talking. (With the nurse) it was more open, more human, more natural, and more friendly. (Int. S8)

I was able to talk about the things that had been making me feel so low. (Int. N2)

My improvement had to do with the people and the talking. (Int. S8)

The nurses didn't come in with lectures and instructions, they came in to listen to me and that created trust. (Int. N9)

You just need the nurses to listen because you want them to be there to help you. They (the clients) might blurt out everything that is on their mind or they might sit for half and hour before they say anything because they don't have the strength to speak about it. So put everything in their control and say, 'Right, this is your floor, you take over and tell me, or if you don't want to speak I will just sit here with you, if you just want the company.' Just be there for them (the clients), be compassionate. (Int. N5)

The developed categories

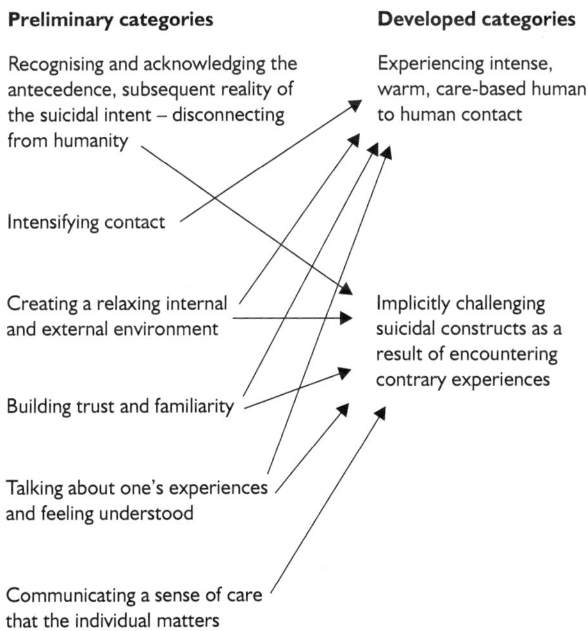

Figure 9.1 Development of the Stage 1 categories.

Table 9.1 'Reflecting an image of humanity' (Stage 1).

Developed categories
Experiencing intense, warm, care-based human to human contact.
Implicitly challenging suicidal constructs as a result of encountering contrary experiences.

Experiencing intense, warm, care-based human to human contact

Connection with the P/MH nurse occurs as a result of the nurse's demeanour and attitude, the nurse's warmth towards the participant, and the nurse's care and concern for the participant. In other words, the P/MH nurse unconditionally provides for very basic and yet essential interpersonal needs. This process has two properties: one that is concerned with starting the process of reconnecting with humanity through connecting with the P/MH nurse and the other with the attitudes, qualities and interventions that the P/MH nurse makes use of in order to facilitate this reconnection; it is a property that Cutcliffe and Stevenson (2007) refer to as 'co-presencing'.

Participants in the original study (Cutcliffe *et al*, 2006; Cutcliffe and Stevenson, 2007) made reference to how they would begin to connect and thus feel comfortable with their P/MH nurse. These connections, at least in the beginning, occurred at the most fundamental human level, gaining the existential experience that one is not alone – by talking, sometimes referred to as 'just chatting'; by laughing together; and by being there when the suicidal person experiences (and releases) any pent up pain. It may sound rather simplistic that the beginnings of recovery from their suicidal 'crisis' for these people in the original study were rooted in connecting with their P/MH nurse. On first consideration, it may appear too easy, in that 'all' the P/MH nurse needs to focus on is demonstrating care, understanding and compassion. After all, that doesn't sound overly sophisticated or complex. However, there is firm support for this approach within the theoretical and empirical suicide literature. Suicidal people, probably as a result of a number of related factors, often feel disconnected from humanity, and often from themselves (see Orbach, 2003, for example). The need to feel connected to humanity and to have a sense of belonging is a basic need (Marcel, 1948; Maslow, 1962; Alderfer, 1972). Whether this is feeling connected to the *macro level* of humanity or the *micro level* (eg. family, friends, colleagues) with the participants in this study, this basic need was not being met. Given the basic nature of thc needs that are not being met, it should not be altogether surprising that 'basic' interpersonal 'interventions' are called for at this point in the process rather than anything more sophisticated.

This property explains the process of the P/MH nurse 'representing' or becoming an emissary for humanity. When the suicidal person experiences being cared for by a P/MH nurse, the nurse is communicating (perhaps implicitly) that humanity still cares about the person. Engaging with the P/MH nurse in this way allows the suicidal person to begin to internalise that they can still engage with humanity. The P/MH nurse's attitudes, demeanour and behaviour provides an 'in road': an opportunity to reconnect. Given the sense of disconnection from their loved ones that the participants described, it was unlikely that they would suddenly encounter a spontaneous reconnection with such people. Indeed, no such spontaneous reconnections were reported in the original study (Cutcliffe *et al*, 2006; Cutcliffe and Stevenson, 2007). They needed P/MH nurses to facilitate this reconnection by being envoys, enabling the suicidal person to internalise that they can engage and connect with humanity in the form of the nurse. This serves as the bedrock for future reconnection with the micro and macro levels of humanity. The process was described and captured in the following ways:

> I wanted to be with people who I knew cared about/loved me. I knew my nurse cared about me. (Int. S1)
>
> I just needed someone to talk to as I had no support from anyone. (Int. N2)
>
> I felt as though there was someone 'in there' with me; somebody caring for me. (Int. S3)
>
> The nurse came on the Sunday and we just talked. (Int. N3)
>
> It was easy to talk to my nurse because he respects me and I respect him, and that's why I like him so much. (Int. S4)
>
> We would laugh together; if something was funny we laughed. (Int. N5)
>
> Just to see a face, to tell them (the nurses) about my problem and feel that they understood it, was brilliant. (Int. S4)
>
> I had been needing someone to talk to for a long time and couldn't get that from anywhere. So it was really good to finally have someone to talk to. (Int. N2)
>
> It helped me so much to know that people (in this case the nurse) was thinking about me. (Int. S8)

> I just wanted and needed someone to talk to as I felt so alone. (Int. N5)

> I felt a bit better that someone had talked to me and realised that I needed help. (Int. N7)

> It is very important that you have a cup of tea or something so that it isn't too professional. (Int. N5)

> I don't know exactly what kind of help I do need, but I do know that I don't need someone patronizing me. (Int. N8)

Implicitly challenging suicidal constructs as a result of encountering contrary experiences

Suicidal people often possess a number of 'suicidal constructs'. The presence and influence of these constructs in the suicidal person is well documented in the associated literature. According to Beck *et al* (1990, p. 190) a suicidal person can

> systematically misconstrue his or her experience in a negative way and anticipate dire outcomes to his or her problems.

According to Schotte and Clum (1987), this constriction has also been described as cognitive rigidity and has been defined as a rigid style of perceiving and reacting to the environment that renders it difficult for a suicidal individual to formulate alternative approaches to problems. The suicidal person therefore experiences the world and interprets the world in a very constricted and particular way. Some of the origin of this constriction may be based in 'real' events and/or circumstances, eg. experiencing stressful life events, living in poverty or living with unmet needs. Furthermore, these constructs may have been reinforced by certain life experiences and/or interactions with various people around the suicidal person (including some formal healthcare workers). For example, one participant in the original study (Cutcliffe *et al*, 2006; Cutcliffe and Stevenson, 2007) spoke of how his feelings of worthlessness and disconnection from humanity were further exacerbated and 'reinforced' by the way he was 'treated' and dismissed by some formal healthcare individuals[1]. Nevertheless, these constructs are still only that; constructs. They are interpretations of one's experiences; interpretations of one's place and value in the world; they are not necessarily 'truth'. Accordingly, part

1 This finding has been discovered repeatedly in related studies; see for example, Aish *et al*, 2002; Ouzouni and Konstantinos, 2009; Scheerder, 2009; Cutcliffe *et al*, 2012a,b).

of the role of the P/MH nurse is to acknowledge the reality of these thoughts and feelings for the suicidal person, yet at the same time recognise them for what they are – interpretations of experience and, subsequently, constructs.

In this way the P/MH nurse communicates to the suicidal person that they are being heard, listened to and understood. The suicidal person begins to gain a sense that someone (finally) is listening and acknowledging the reality of the problem(s) as they are encountered and experienced by the person. The value and power of such actions on the part of the nurse was abundantly clear throughout the data in the original study and clearly should not be underestimated. This was captured and described by the participants in the following ways:

> I felt like my feelings were trivial (Int. S3)

> I felt as if everyone was against me. I couldn't trust my own family. (Int. N1)

> When my mother died I felt like there was nothing what-so-ever. No point in going on. (Int. N1)

> I felt like nobody wanted me so I might as well be dead. (Int. N2)

Perhaps the most important element of this category is that P/MH nurses *challenge these constructs essentially by means of what they are and what they do, and less by means of what they said.* As a means to counteract the suicidal person's constructs (and subsequent experiences) the P/MH nurses communicate and engage in a way that provides an 'opposite' sense of the experience(s) and construct(s). Similarly, other interventions, such as they were, indicated that all interactions and engagements were personified by the atmosphere of warmth, care, compassion, unconditional acceptance and tolerance, empathy and positive regard for the suicidal person. The therapeutic and healing power of these qualities has been shown repeatedly in the relevant empirical literature (see Adam *et al*, 2003 for a further recent example). Consequently, it is not entirely surprising that the participants who had experienced a lack of these qualities gained such a beneficial, therapeutic effect from experiencing these qualities manifest in the P/MH nurse. Support for the therapeutic value of these qualities and attitudes can be found within the empirical suicide literature. The value of these qualities as demonstrated and communicated by a mother or father to a child has been highlighted in the literature. The argument in essence is that children identify with their mother and father's love for them; they internalise this for themselves; they learn to love and protect themselves. Similarly Anna Freud's (1949) theory posits that a warm, gentle, caring mother may tone down any (untamed) aggressive behaviours. There are clear parallels here with a P/MH nurse who can 'tone down' the suicidal person's self-focused aggressive behaviour, and can help the person to internalise their love and care for themselves (and thus give rise to self-protective rather than self-destructive behaviours) in response to the P/MH nurse's care, warmth, compassion, and 'love' for the suicidal person.

Subtle and gentle reflection provides the opportunity for suicidal people to consider some of their negative assumptions and challenge some of their restrictive beliefs. When suicidal people can begin to internalise that many of their beliefs about past failures, present limitations and future restrictions are based on unrealistic constructs and inaccurate self-perceptions and are perpetuated by their current state of hopelessness, then they begin to challenge these for themselves. The suicidal people begin to deconstruct some of their suicide constructs and hopelessness and begin to construct a more hopeful future. For example, as participants in the original study (Cutcliffe *et al*, 2006; Cutcliffe and Stevenson, 2007) spoke of their feelings and sense of hopelessness, the P/MH nurse would project hope and hopefulness into the atmosphere by remaining hopeful themselves. They brought hope with them into the interaction and this permeated the 'emotional atmosphere' and was 'transplanted' into the participant by means of the close interpersonal connection (Cutcliffe, 2004). The P/MH nurses would begin to introduce and articulate the possibility of hopeful outcomes. As the participants described how lonely they felt, the P/MH nurses would ensure that the suicidal people in this study were not alone – not only in a physical sense, but they would communicate a sense that there was someone alongside them in their struggle. They would ensure that there were messages of support, and make sure there was always someone available for the suicidal person. The intensive, regular, warm and compassionate contact began to challenge, implicitly, the participants' construct of being alone. As the participants described how they felt that nobody cared about or loved them, the P/MH nurses would communicate how they cared very much about the total wellbeing of the participant, how the participant's health, wellbeing and future mattered very much to the P/MH nurse. They would demonstrate that they were vested in the ongoing life of the participant.

Participants in the original study (Cutcliffe *et al*, 2006; Cutcliffe and Stevenson, 2007) also referred to the construct of having no-one to talk to. Here the P/MH nurses could provide a straightforward yet valuable intervention by offering themselves as someone willing to listen. Having had the experience of there being no-one with whom they could share their thoughts, feelings, fears and concerns, there was an immense sense of relief at finally being able to talk someone. Further, this experience served to challenge the construct that there is no-one to talk to. Bound up with this was the experience to counteract the construct of feeling that one's feelings are trivial. The fact that the P/MH nurses are more than willing to spend concentrated amounts of time focusing entirely on the participant, his or her thoughts/feelings and his or her experience provides a powerful challenge to the construct of 'my feelings are trivial'. They are direct and relevant responses to the expression of these feelings.

When the suicidal people in the original study (Cutcliffe *et al*, 2006; Cutcliffe and Stevenson, 2007) described feeling ashamed, again the P/MH nurses counteracted this construct by demonstrating genuine acceptance, tolerance and communicate a sense of being non-judgmental and non-condemning. Again, messages of support were common in response to such expressions and the P/MH nurses engaged in a lot of 'permission giving': informing the participants that thinking about or making an attempt on one's life need not be regarded as anything to be ashamed of and that such acts can be thought of as an expression of need. This was described and captured in the following ways:

> I was able to get some of that need for companionship met by the PET. (Int. S1)

> You feel that you are not alone because they (the nurses) are caring for you. (Int. S3)

> It felt as though there were other people thinking about me and other people helping me. (Int. S8)

> The CPN took an interest in what I was doing, what I did with my time, how I filled my days. (Int. S3)

> They just changed my life, in just three days, because they were so loving and kind. (Int. S7)

> I got a sense of being understood first of all by the person being there for me. (Int. S3)

> The company, the presence of another who demonstrated care and concern, was crucial. (Int. S4)

The PAT helped me by the support they gave, just support. (Int. S4)

The nurses communicated their care for me by means of – their sympathy, the expression on their faces, by means of the frequent phone calls. (Int. S8)

I was feeling that when they said that, they meant that. It wasn't just a trained response. (Int. N5)

What I got from the nurses was a bit of compassion; somebody to listen to me; a bit of understanding and somebody trying to help – and it did help. (Int. N9)

I had come to the conclusion that nobody cared. Thus what I needed was someone to convey that they did. (Int. S1)

My nurse was easy to communicate with. He could be quite funny (witty) at times, without laughing at me or my situation. (Int. N2)

The human warmth was crucial. They didn't just come in and get their stuff out. They looked me in the eye; they listened. Just chatting, even if it was going off at a tangent – was valuable. You know, when I said something, they didn't just move onto the next question. (Int. N5)

Q: What did the PET do? A: They listened. (Int. S1)

I remember having such freedom to talk. (Int. N3)

I got to release all my pent up emotion and grief over my granddaughter, with the C.P.N. (Int. S3)

He (C.P.N.) was a brilliant guy. He talked to me for an hour. The absolutely brilliant thing about it is there is no looking at clocks; no thinking you have only got ten minutes. (Int. N5)

I felt better for knowing that somebody could understand how I was feeling. (Int. S3)

I wanted and needed that 'human thing'. (Int. N5)

> They sat down and listened to me; showed me understanding when I cut my wrists. (Int. S4)

> In terms of being the recipient of nursing, I would want a quick acceptance that what I am going through is a bit horrible. (Int. N5)

> I felt understood and being understood was important. (Int. S4)

> The difference with the nurses that helped me was the WAY they spoke to me. (Int. N8)

> Frankie (nurse) was brilliant; she listened to everything I said. (Int. S4)

Stage 2: guiding the individual back towards humanity

> Putting my life into a different perspective – seeing things in a different, more positive way, really made a difference and it was my time with my nurse and the CAT team that did that. (Int. N2)

Overview

Guiding the individual back towards humanity signals the arrival of a new stage in the person's ability to make a connection with the world about them. In Stage 1, the person gains a sense of reconnection with humanity through the act of being cared about and 'co-presencing'. This relationship, built up between the P/MH nurse and the suicidal person, now takes on a different pace. During this stage there is a more active focus to this process of reconnection, whereas previously in Stage 1 the clear focus for the P/MH nurse was on 'being' rather than 'doing'. Concerned as they were with guiding the person back to humanity, in this second stage the P/MH nurses attempt to nurture insight and understanding: particularly a renewed insight and understanding *vis-à-vis* control. The participants in the original study (Cutcliffe *et al*, 2006; Cutcliffe and Stevenson, 2007) were very clear that an increased sense of control *over* their suicidal thoughts and feelings rather than the suicidal thoughts and feelings having control *over them*, was not only extremely important, but further, it was indicative of reconnecting with humanity. In gaining or regaining insight into and understanding of their experiences and situation (not least in part by reconstructing or reframing certain constricted personal constructs), the suicidal people begin to see that they are not as irremediably disconnected from humanity as they once thought; there is still a way back. Furthermore, the increased insight and understanding was concerned with a new awareness of the suicidal person's increased need for help; in some cases a recognition that they needed to reach out to humanity, and reach out to the P/MH nurse as a means of helping the person overcome their suicidal ideation.

The data provided by the participants in the original study (Cutcliffe *et al*, 2006; Cutcliffe and Stevenson, 2007) indicated that suicidal people often feel they are a burden to those family and friends who are close to them. It is not until the P/MH nurse has a strong bond that suicidal people are able to express their emotions to their nurse. The unburdening of problems with the P/MH nurse indicates that a reconnection with humanity is present, given that prior to this stage, withdrawal and disconnection had interfered with and inhibited communication. The seeds of hope and hopefulness projected by the P/MH nurse in Stage 1 are then nurtured by the nurse in this stage and start to re-surface in the individual. This hope is drawn out and strengthened by the P/MH nurse's attention to the suicidal person's positive attributes and the nurse's complete faith in the person's ability to deal with their problems, given the appropriate help and support.

P/MH nurses can encourage suicidal people to use their own belief systems to enhance this process and, as a result, the people started to move towards a 'life position' rather than opting for suicide. By opening up the communication between the P/MH nurse and the suicidal person, a more active, therapeutic basis for the relationship is encouraged and suicidal people can become more accepting of the tools offered to them by the P/MH nurse. Although apparently making forward progress, suicidal people remain uncomfortable being left without support. Support comes from human contact: from the P/MH nurse and/or the suicidal person's significant others. This was captured and described in the following ways.

> The nurses gave me a positive attitude as I hadn't always felt positive. (Int. S3)

> They let me come out of myself and talk more frankly than I would to other people. (Int. N3)

> The changed the way I was viewing the world has made a big difference. It made me stop and start to think again – more positively. (Int. S1)

> I could say what I wanted to my nurse, even things about my feelings and I have difficulty with that, even with my wife. (Int. N1)

> I thought to myself – I'm going to fight this. (Int. S3)

The more I talked, the more understanding of my conflict I gained and the less likely I was to get into my downward, deep spiral. (Int. N3)

It was so helpful in being able to recognise that I had an internal conflict going, and through talking about it I could identify what was going on for me. (Int. N3)

They gave me handouts/information on the signs and symptoms of anxiety. (Int. S3)

...coping strategies, some tools; I think that was important. When I first went to the services what I needed from people were tools. (Int. N5)

It was important and helpful to be able to talk about my problems with my nurse, and feel that they understood me, because I don't get this anywhere else, not even from my family. (Int. S4)

It was encouraging to know that the CAT team thought I was strong enough to get through this. (Int. N7)

We talked about what I thought were the positive things in my life. It was good not to just focus on the bad. (Int. N7)

The developed categories

Nurturing insight and understanding

This key process is concerned with facilitating the rise in the suicidal person's personal awareness and having the ability to subsequently externalise these moments of awareness. A connection is made between the internal turmoil and the fact that, through talking with the P/MH nurse, these feelings can be managed. Having previously felt controlled by their suicidal thoughts the suicidal person is able to take more responsibility over controlling *them*. Furthermore, it is important

Table 9.2 'Guiding the individual back to humanity' (Stage 2).

Developed categories
Nurturing insight and understanding
Supporting and strengthening pre-suicidal beliefs
Encountering a novel interpersonal, helping relationship

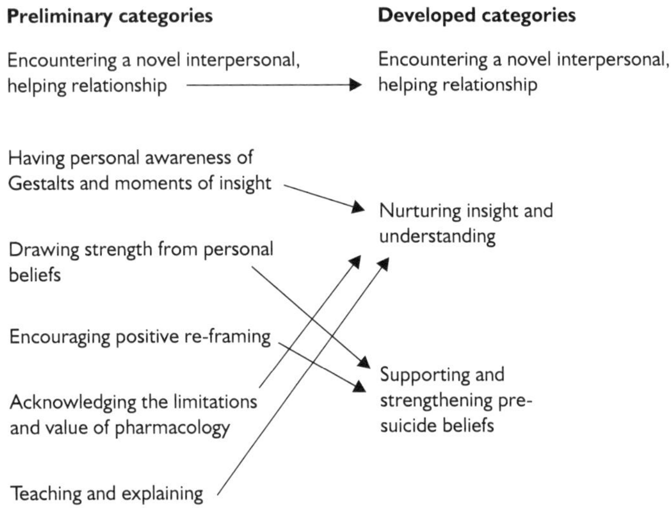

Figure 9.2 Development of the Stage 2 categories.

to note another important shift from Stage 1 to Stage 2. Each of the developed categories in this core variable indicate a more active focus to this processes, whereas in Stage 1 the clear focus was on 'being' rather than 'doing'.

'Nurturing insight and understanding' contains at least three properties. The first of these relates to the suicidal person's ability to make a link between internal feelings and the subsequent actions. It relates to a growth in awareness that the suicidal person *can* have power over these thoughts and feelings; that they do not necessarily have to expect a dire future; there is an awareness that a hopeful future is a possibility. The second property relates to a rise in the suicidal person's awareness of what type(s) of help he or she needed, and perhaps more importantly, what they found to be helpful and unhelpful. A further aspect of this property refers to the suicidal person's increasing willingness and ability to articulate what they need from their P/MH nurse and from the formal mental healthcare system. It is noteworthy that the suicidal people were adamant and vociferous about articulating what they did not want. Of special importance, particularly in terms of the current *modus operandi* for care of the suicidal person, and the current emphasis within this approach, are the suicidal people's remarks about the limitations and value of pharmacological intervention. The third property relates to the suicidal person's readiness to accept the help offered to them by the P/MH nurse.

The authors have already pointed out, in Chapter 7, that suicidal people can systematically misconstrue their experience(s), and invariably anticipate dire outcomes to their problems, including the outcome of their own future (Beck *et al*, 1990; Weisharr, 2000). One such constricted construct that suicidal people often possess is a sense of inevitable doom; a lack of control related to a hopeless future. There is an established, though relatively underdeveloped literature that refers to, what is sometimes termed 'dysfunctional assumptions' (Ellis and Ratliff, 1986; Bonner and Rich, 1987; Ranieri *et al*, 1987; Weishaar, 2000.) Ellis and Ratliff (1986) reported how suicidal psychiatric inpatients scored higher than non-suicidal patients in terms of various dysfunctional assumptions. Very similar findings are reported by Bonner and Rich (1987), who discovered that these dysfunctional assumptions are a key indicator in predicting suicidal ideation in college students. Ranieri *et al* (1987) also found a positive correlation between severity of dysfunctional assumptions and suicidal ideation in psychiatric inpatients. As a result, if we accept these consistently reported findings as credible, it seems that one possible method of, at least in part, combating a person's risk of suicide is to attempt to address these dysfunctional assumptions. This was captured and described in the following ways.

> It was so helpful in being able to recognise that I had an internal conflict going on, and through talking about it I could identify what was going on for me. (Int. N3)

> It was the encouragement and the reminder that I had some control, some responsibility – that I could help myself. (Int. S8)

> I intended to get better and realised that I had an opportunity – what with the kindness and people similar to me. (Int. S3)

> I was ready to accept help when it was offered. (Int. N2)

> Talking about my son and what I could have done to him had a big effect on me not taking my life. (Int. N1)

> The more I talked the more understanding of my conflict I gained and the less likely I was to get into my downward, deep spiral. (Int. N3)

> They gave me handouts on the signs and symptoms of anxiety. (Int. S3)

> They explained things to me. (Int. S4)

> ...what I wanted from people were some tools. (Int. N5)

> I saw the doctor and he put me on some anti-depressants, but I said to him that I really needed some counselling. (Int. N2)

> I felt more in control after my medication. (Int. S4)

> They changed my medication and I felt brilliant. (Int. S1)

> I would not have got better if all I had received was more tablets. (Int. S3)

> The tablets did me some good in that they calmed me down. (Int. S1)

> The doctors prescribe me some paroxetine, and I started to take those, but the side-effects kick in bad enough for me not to be able to go to work. (Int. N5)

Supporting and strengthening pre-suicidal beliefs

This key process is concerned with suicidal people becoming increasingly able to assimilate information provided by the P/MH nurse and then contemplate this in relation to their own belief systems. As stated previously, suicidal people experience and interpret the world in a particular way (Shneidman, 2004) and inevitably, this 'constricted' way of thinking/experiencing was different from the person's pre-suicidal patterns of thinking, feeling and behaving. Suicidal people describe how their pre-suicidal beliefs are inevitably more hopeful, indicative of the fact that they felt life was worth living and, importantly, indicative of the person's sense of feeling connected to, or part of, humanity. Accordingly, this category is concerned with the P/MH nurse's attempts to help guide the person back to these more hopeful, more connected, beliefs; supporting and encouraging the person in re-framing his or her constricted thoughts. It is concerned with helping the suicidal person reconstruct a more connected and hopeful construct of the world and his or her place in it. There are at least two properties to this category. The first of these is concerned with helping suicidal people regain the support, comfort and 'strength' of their personal belief system (whatever it may be)[2]. The second property relates to the P/MH nurse's ability to ensure that the suicidal person's beliefs are kept strong through positive re-framing.

2 It is worthy of note that, on their own, such belief systems had not prevented the suicidal person from making an attempt on their life.

It needs to be recognised that as a community of suicidologists and mental health practitioners we can as yet answer only a few of the most fundamental questions raised with regard to the treatment of suicide (Rudd, 2000). Nevertheless, an emerging trend is distinctly noticeable among the reported empirical work that focuses on short-term treatment (less than six months). For those studies that contain positive findings, each employed some form or version or element of cognitive behavioural therapy, and each included some form of problem-solving component as a core feature (Rudd, 2000). Rudd (2000, p. 54) continues:

> This is not particularly surprising given that CBT is perhaps the approach most amenable to a brief format.

Similarly, the work being led by Professor Paul Links, who held the 'Arthur Somnerberg Chair in Suicidology', University of Toronto, and Dr Shelley McMain, from the Centre for Addictions and Mental Health, is producing similar findings. This work is producing clear positive correlations between providing care, including brief dialectic therapy as a core component, and a reduction in subsequent suicide attempts and suicidal intent. Interestingly, while not a deductive study *per se*, and thus not concerned with producing correlations, the findings from the original study (Cutcliffe and Stevenson, 2007) perhaps indicate why and how these types of cognitive re-framing are of particular value for suicidal people. This was described and captured in the following ways.

> The PET helped change my thoughts, helped me see that people were not against me. (Int. S1)

> They tried to help me think differently about myself and my circumstances. (Int. S4)

> Because my nurse stirred up different feelings, helped me change my perspective and I found this so helpful. (Int. N2)

> I used to draw on my Christian beliefs, but even that left me when I got ill. (Int. S1)

> I felt more powerful, felt I had got some power back at the end of the process. (Int. N3)

> I have to focus at the moment, something tangible for the future, something to build on. That's what's driving me at the moment, giving me positive thoughts. (Int. N1)

> I thought to myself, I'm going to fight this. (Int. S3)

> We talked about what I thought were the positive things in my life – as well as the bad things. It was good to not just focus on the bad. (Int. N7)

> Putting my life into a different perspective – seeing things in a different more positive way, really made a big difference. (Int. N2)

> At first I would ridicule what I had achieved and then the PET would say, 'You should be proud of that.' (Int. S1)

> It was encouraging to know that the CAT team thought I was strong enough to get through this. (Int. N7)

Encountering a novel interpersonal, helping relationship

This key process is concerned with suicidal people encountering a novel interpersonal, helping relationship. Participants in the original study (Cutcliffe *et al*, 2006; Cutcliffe and Stevenson, 2007) were clear that they gained a sense of increased hope and relief by being able to talk about their feelings, thoughts and experiences. Interestingly though, there was something qualitatively different about the relationship with the P/MH nurse, as opposed to the person's relationship with his or her family and friends, that allowed for this freedom to express and to talk frankly. As a result, the suicidal people in this study experienced a sense of emancipation. This freedom to reflect and talk with an experienced 'professional', in a non-judgmental atmosphere, can give an increased sense of feeling secure, given that P/MH nurses have faced such situations before, know what to do and have helped resolve similar situations previously. The participants in the original study (Cutcliffe *et al*, 2006; Cutcliffe and Stevenson, 2007) were also abundantly clear that, at times, they were extremely reluctant to share any of their thoughts and feelings with family or friends, as they feared that this would somehow harm their significant other. Feelings are expressed sparingly within the family for fear of causing pain or risking alienation. Accordingly, the novel relationship with the P/MH nurse enabled the suicidal people to express feelings and thoughts without risking damage to their human contacts: because the P/MH nurses have been through similar before and survived, they would not be harmed (and thus neither would the person's connection with humanity).

A number of noted suicidologists including Shneidman, Maltsberger, Maris and Leenaars for example, have noted that the relationship (and attachment) that the therapist develops is central in effective psychotherapy. This axiom is similarly applicable to working with suicidal people. Further, we have already predicated the importance of the nurse-suicidal person relationship in Stage 1. However, in their excellent text, *Comprehensive Textbook of Suicidology*, Maris and colleagues (2000) draw attention to common errors of suicide interventionists.

> Professionalism: ...caregivers might insulate or protect themselves from the exhausting task of empathic pairing by seeking refuge in the boundaries afforded by their role. This may overly distance and detach the caregiver and convey disinterest. Most important, it does not build upon the relationship (Maris *et al*, 2000, p. 521).

Accordingly, while an over-reliance on or perhaps retreating within the boundaries of professionalism can clearly be counter-productive when working with suicidal people, it is worth noting that the suicidal people in this study drew strength from the knowledge that they were working with a mental health professional. The suicidal people placed a great deal of faith in the P/MH nurses' ability to be able to hear and deal with whatever they brought up – a dynamic that wasn't available to them with their family relationships. When the authors considered what were the key psychosocial processes in Stage 1, it became clear that part of this faith, and thus part of the sense of encountering a novel relationship, was bound up with *first* establishing the human–human contact in Stage 1 (and thus avoiding the damaging dynamics described by Maris *et al*, 2000). Then the suicidal people were able to gain the sense of the 'novelty' of the helping relationship and found this to be emancipatory.

'Encouraging a novel interpersonal, helping relationship' has at least three properties. The first is concerned with the suicidal person's need to talk through his or her problems and feelings. The second property is concerned with the ability of the P/MH nurse to receive the suicidal person's story in a manner that will not jeopardise their relationship. The third property is the P/MH nurse's ability to provide security for the suicidal person by showing experience and skill in working alongside people who feel vulnerable. This was described and captured in the following ways.

Q: Why does listening make a difference?

A: It clears your mind if you can talk it over with someone else – but somebody who is not family. Family are too close. (Int. S1)

You can't talk to friends about some things because you want to keep them private. (Int. N2)

I can't talk to my wife because she doesn't really understand what I am going through. (Int. S4)

When you try to talk to family, or friends, there is always a kickback, so you need a professional. (Int. N3)

You can't explain everything to your family, you need the professional. (Int. S3)

I can tell the nurse things without him getting all emotional and I couldn't do that with my family and yet I needed that. (int. S1)

I needed something different from 'Pull yourself together!', which is what I was getting from my family. (Int. N2)

You need trained people when you are in this mess. You need input from people who know what they are doing. (Int. S3)

I knew I had confused things in my head – and I couldn't talk to my friends about these things. (Int. N2)

As a result of the input from the team, they made me feel secure, and I felt as though I didn't have to rely on my family. (Int. S3)

It was nice just to be able to sit and chat, as I find it easier to talk to someone who doesn't know me. (Int. N7)

Stage 3: Learning to live

Every minute I was there, they were bringing me back to the land of the living – not the land of the dead. (Int. S3)

Overview

This is the third stage of 'Reconnecting the person with humanity' and is concerned with how suicidal people begin to pick up the threads of their life, and how the professional (P/MH nurse) response continues to have a place, although this is somewhat different to that of earlier stages. In Stage 2, the P/MH nurse is 'walking with' the suicidal person, setting the scene for reconnecting with humanity through positive re-framing, teaching and explaining, capitalising on personal awareness moments etc. In Stage 3 the P/MH nurse adopts the role of 'wise consultant'. However, the P/MH nurse must also be prepared to let the suicidal people engage with their own 'sense making' in relation to their suicidality, as this remains an existential crisis. The importance of sense making in relation to suicide was recognised by Albert Camus (1945):

> There is but one serious philosophical problem, and that is suicide. Judging whether life is or is not worth living amounts to answering the fundamental question of philosophy.

The suicidal people in the original study (Cutcliffe *et al*, 2006; Cutcliffe and Stevenson, 2007) were undertaking momentous work, so it is not surprising that, at times, they become overwhelmed and need to turn to the P/MH nurse for help. At this stage, however, the P/MH nurse is a source of expert advice and not simply a co-presence. The P/MH nurses recognised that they cannot impose their meaning on the suicidality for it is deeply personal and individual. The P/MH nurse's counsel was offered, but would not always be accepted as the suicidal people fitted together a story that accounts for the way in which their suicidality came into their life, its place in the here and now and its trajectory into the future – hard and demanding and long term work.

Understanding their own suicidality can help suicidal people feel more in control. Personal understanding allows the suicidal people to re-engage more fully with people other than the professionals. The suicidal people in the original study (Cutcliffe *et al*, 2006; Cutcliffe and Stevenson, 2007) were often reluctant to discuss their thoughts and actions with significant others; there are varied reasons for this. Sometimes, it is because their suicidality seems like a 'private function'. Alternatively, there was evidence of a belief that other people could not appreciate or understand something that the suicidal people themselves could not account for. In Stage 3 the suicidal people in this study revisited their decision to engage with suicidality. The reappraisal took place in relation to whether life was, is and will be worth living, and involved revisiting many factors, for example their degree of connectedness with others. A re-working of previous assessments occurred, for example in relation to whether or not the suicidal person would be missed, and the effect that suicide would have had and would have if executed in the here and now. At this stage, there is a focus on how a worthwhile life can be re-established.

An important process in this phase, and one concerned with re-establishing the suicidal person's reinvestment in life, is 'doing' as well as 'talking'. Sometimes, the P/MH nurses would encourage the suicidal people to engage in practical activity. Small successes can also help suicidal people to gain power over their suicidality, because even very basic everyday activities will at times have seemed impossible to achieve. The 'doing' helps suicidal people to feel more hopeful. It offers a counterpoint to the difficult, thoughtful work that they were undertaking in relation to their suicide attempt. While it is tempting for all concerned to think of suicidality as an entirely negative phenomenon, for some of the suicidal people in this study, it was more complex than that. Some of the participants in this study referred to how their suicidality could have a place as 'friend' and 'foe' for them. While the P/MH nurse may hope for the suicidality to depart from the suicidal person's life, there are at times, according to the some of the suicidal people in the original study (Cutcliffe *et al*, 2006; Cutcliffe and Stevenson, 2007) good reasons for them to maintain a relationship with it. However, the suicidal people in this study were clear that their relationship with their suicidality needed to be one in which they had a sense of power and control over it if it was to have a positive as well as potentially negative function for them. This was captured and expressed in the following ways:

> It feels fabulous to be doing these normal, everyday things again, because I had stopped doing them. (Int. S3)

> I couldn't handle more challenge early on. It would have been too much. I needed people to be nice to me. I needed everything from the cotton wool world (Int. N3)

> So there is a time for challenging constructions of hopelessness and negative, limiting constructs and there is a time for leaving well alone and providing another way of help (Int. N1)

> Talking to my C.P.N. helped me gain a different perspective on the significant events. Instead of seeing the bad and feeling disconnected from my family, I was able to see the good, feel compassion, and feel more connected with her (daughter) (Int. S3)

He suggested things like imagining the top of my head was open and I could put my hand in and pull out my problems and pull out the tension and put it on the table just things like that. But there was also lots of praise, 'well done, you went in and you tried it, well done'. Lots of praise. 'You are top man'. A lot of what the nurses are doing you can see why they are doing it. It is overt help, but it doesn't feel false. It is genuine. It is trained. It is their job, they are saying things they are trained to say, but, what the hell, it feels fine. (Int. N5)

[The feeling less suicidal] is not clear-cut or the kind of process that makes you suddenly think 'I want to live'. It is extremely difficult to work out what they did or said. But they did stop me wanting to die, stopped me doing anything about it. (Int. N3)

He [nurse] encouraged me, said positive things to me; encouraged me to attend to the small things, like washing, shaving. (Int. S4)

It was four or five weeks when I came back a bit (Int. N3)

Six weeks ago, I could not have gone out with the kids – but now it has shifted (Int. N3)

My thread was not wanting my kids to end up traumatised by my suicide (Int. N3)

It was like feeling a bit more in line with society again. I felt a bit more in line with the usual. This made me feel a bit better. (Int. S8)

[I think of my possible suicide as] an enemy, because you are doing something to yourself which is going to cause so much heartache to other people (my son and parents). But I couldn't live with the way my life was going at the time; I couldn't handle it any more.... That side was a good side of it, if there was one, because it was a way out of my problems (Int. N7)

The feeling [suicidal feelings] never goes away – it is there at the back of my head all the time. (Int. N8)

The developed categories

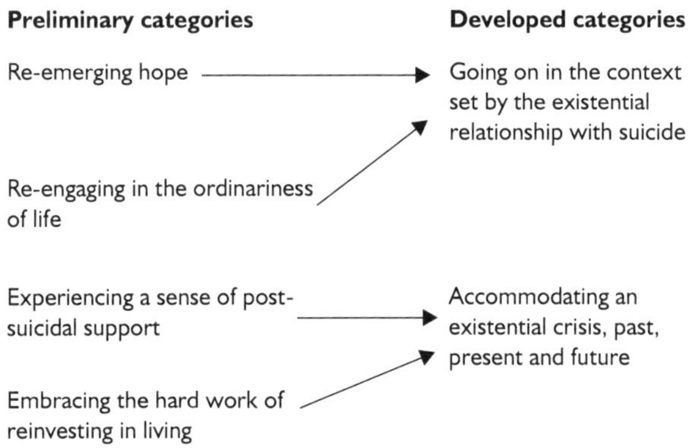

Figure 9.3 Development of the Stage 3 categories.

Table 9.3 'Learning to live' (Stage 3).

Developed categories
Accommodating an existential crisis, past, present and future
Going on in the context set by the existential relationship with suicide

Accommodating an existential crisis, past, present and future

This key process is concerned with making sense of the suicidality in a complex way, rather than dismissing it. Further, this 'sense making' is achieved through an array of interpersonal processes, including supportive involvement from professionals (mainly P/MH nurses in this study), family and fellow travellers on the suicidality path. These processes indicated at least two properties of the category. First, there is a property concerned with dealing with existential angst. Existential crises concern facing up to the realities of living and dying in the context of the inevitability of dying. The suicidal person has somehow, 'short-circuited' the normal trajectory and come to face his or her own mortality in a dramatic way. Nothing can ever be the same again, and it is naïve of P/MH nurses to look for a return to the person's pre-suicide state. Consequently, the process of sense making is still relevant and less academic than for many other people. Important 'self-searching' questions that the suicidal people in this study asked themselves (directly or indirectly) included:

- 'How could I have reached such a place?'
- 'Why did I feel so far away from those I love?'

- 'How do I explain to them what I tried to do?'
- 'How do I go on living the rest of my life knowing I tried to commit suicide?'
- 'How can I use this experience so that I don't end up here again?'
- 'Maybe some good will come of this? Maybe there will come a time when I won't have to do this again?'

Thus, if suicidal people can arrive at a satisfactory account – if they can consider these questions (and their own individual set of sense making questions) – then it is possible to have some power over their relationship with suicidality. In some ways, for the suicidal people in this study, their relationship with death was, in a somewhat counter-intuitive or paradoxical way, more empowering than that afforded to many other people, provided that it could be kept in its place. Their attempt at suicide became a reminder of what could happen when life became difficult. Their attempt served as an *aide-mémoire* of a course of action that had been 'tried out' and found to be lacking; as a result it helped the suicidal people opt for 'life choices' rather than 'death choices' and it helped them engage in more rational and informed choices.

The second property is concerned with how the individual resolution of the existential crisis is moderated by significant others, both professional and family. There is a rhythm of support established between the suicidal person, family and P/MH nurses. Of course, dealing with an existential crisis is hard, tiring and lengthy work. It necessarily has to be undertaken by the suicidal person in a 'private space'. However, the P/MH nurse's co-presence and experience serves to keep the suicidal person anchored, even if this presence is virtual rather than physical, and the suicidal people in this study used this 'sense of being anchored' as the platform from which to begin their reconnection with humanity. Without protracted contact and support from the P/MH nurse, the suicidal people were in danger of feeling that nothing is real except their own thought processes, leading to what Sartre would describe as 'Nothingness': the antithesis of 'Being'. As the suicidal people acknowledged the effects of their suicidal act on others, they were starting (already) to move forward from their existential crisis, in that there was an acknowledgement of their attachment to the world; a growing acknowledgment that they were (and are) connected to others in the world. The drastic and dramatic effects of their suicidality in the past, present and future can thus act as a deterrent against future suicide attempts.

Being at least partially reconnected with humanity brings with it a peril. The P/MH nurse's withdrawal can be experienced as a rejection. Accordingly, and as with many other therapeutic relationships (Peplau, 1988), the end of the relationship may need to be gradual, delayed, protracted and managed, so that the suicidal people feel that they are letting go; so that they don't feel that the P/MH nurse has simply lost interest in them or is ignorant of the ongoing management of life post-suicidality. In this context, it is not surprising that the suicidal people in this study were open to contact with others who have been or are addressing the place of suicidality in their lives. These properties are expressed and captured in the participants' own words.

> [The feeling less suicidal] is not clear-cut, or the kind of process that makes you suddenly think, 'I want to live'. It is extremely difficult to work out what they did or said. But they did stop me wanting to die, stopped me doing anything about it (Int. N3)
>
> Every minute I was there, they were bringing me back to the land of the living – not the land of the dead. (Int. S3)
>
> Talking to my C.P.N. helped me gain a different perspective on the significant events. (Int. N2)
>
> The feeling [suicidal feelings] never goes away – it is there, at the back of my head all the time (Int. N8)
>
> If I get suicidal thoughts now I try to push them out. I also think about the repercussions on those I leave behind and this helps stop me do it (Int. N7)
>
> I wanted the contact with my nurse to go on longer. (Int. S8)
>
> I had to re-establish a connection with my daughter and her family after talking with my nurse (Int. N2)
>
> It is hard to explain to your family why you have done what you have; they don't understand. (Int. N4)
>
> Instead of seeing the bad and feeling disconnected from my family, I was able to see the good, feel compassion and feel more connected with her [daughter]. (Int. N2)
>
> By the time those two women [C.P.N.s] left, I was looking less miserable, less desperate. (Int. N3)

> The only support I was getting was from my nurse and the CAT team and I was scared about not seeing him any longer; no longer having this support. (Int. S2)

> It was easy to give up, so reconnecting was scary. (Int. N3)

> I felt there was a thread keeping me on this planet. (Int. N3)

> I now view or describe my suicidal feelings as an option that I have closed the lid on, something like closing a box... I keep this box in the back of my head, right at the back in the attic. (Int. N8)

> It is the fact that I am not the only one. I am not on my own – that there are other people like me. (Int. N4)

> It is scary picking up the pieces, but I needed to. I wanted to make sure I wouldn't reach this place again. (Int. S3)

> You have to deal with what had gone on. (Int. S8)

Going on in the context set by the existential relationship with suicidality

This process is concerned with how life, for (formerly) suicidal people gradually can become more balanced between extremes. Possible extremes were: life and death, physical and emotional care, co-presence and direction, professional support and family support, and hopelessness and hopefulness. For the suicidal people in this study who were attempting to make sense of their suicidality, it was important to have the hard emotional work balanced by the practical. To a great extent, practically living life seemed to be helpful in accommodating the existential crisis; this practical, 'day to day' living also provided a context for the 'sense making' work. This 'day to day' life was, after all, the life that the suicidal person would need to go on living. This was the context into which the experience of suicide would now have to be woven. The engagement in the practical reinvests life with a sense of normality and this helps the suicidal person to feel reconnected with humanity.

In tandem, the P/MH nurse needed to offer different types of support. In relation to emotional support, s/he needed to offer both co-presence and some more challenging input. In relation to practical support, the P/MH nurse is an 'encourager', helping the suicidal person to do very basic things and also to engage in displacement activity, eg. swimming. The combination of extremes helps the suicidal people 'go on' with their life.

Similarly, the role of significant others becomes balanced. In the period before the suicide attempt and aftermath, the suicidal people in this study had been reluctant to speak with their family members. This seems to be so that the family's feelings are spared and because there is a sense of disbelief that anyone can understand what the suicidal people cannot understand themselves. To some extent, this accounts for why the P/MH nurses, with their special experience of people in suicidality, were more welcome co-respondents. However, as the suicidal people undertook the work associated with their existential crisis, their own understanding of past, present and future life appeared to increase. With the increased understanding, the suicidal people gained more capacity to hold the lack of understanding of others. Being able to be absorb the needs of significant others allows more sense of connection and the opportunity to connect with humanity.

In tandem with the increased everyday activity, and the reconnection with family, the suicidal people in this study experienced a resurgence of hope. In particular, as the suicidal people began to resolve some of their existential crisis there was an increased feeling of hopefulness. However, hope was related also to the more mundane aspects of living. As the suicidality had interrupted the flow of everyday living so dramatically, the re-institution of even very basic life skills became a barometer of hope. Thus the role of the P/MH nurse in helping suicidal people re-establish 'the basics' and recognise the small changes that are occurring should not be underestimated. Competence in the 'here and now' also helps with a re-evaluation of the past and present. Hope develops in an upward spiral that itself helps to control the suicidality. These properties are expressed and captured in the following ways.

> I could do with someone to help me get going, like going swimming, help me with my weights, do stuff together, maybe even help me get a job. (Int. S2)

> Just progress in the small things, like putting some smart clothes on, boosted me up. (Int. S4)

> The good ones (nurses) will take you out, take you for a drive, go for a coffee. (Int. S2)

> I was scared when I cooked again for the first time, so I cried. I was pleased but I was still scared. (Int. S1)

I started to take some positive steps, tried to reconnect, like sending a letter. (Int. N2)

My connection was, and is, the kids. (Int. N3)

Now, as I start to feel better, I would like to see what the next 50 years hold. (Int. N3)

I am more hopeful that I have a future and maybe that everything is not as bad as I think it is. (Int. N7)

Acknowledgement

Parts of this chapter were originally published in, and adapted from:

Cutcliffe JR, Stevenson C (2007) *Care of the Suicidal Person*. Elsevier/Churchill Livingstone.

We not only wish to extend our most profound thanks to Elsevier for permission to use this material, but for more a more detailed explanation of these findings and much more, please do access and refer to the Cutcliffe and Stevenson (2007) text.

References

Adam R, Tilley S, Pollock L (2003) Person first: what people with enduring mental disorders value about Community Psychiatric Nurses and CPN services. *Journal of Psychiatric and Mental Health Nursing*, **10**: 203–12.

Aish A-M, Ramberg I-L, Wasserman D (2002) Measuring attitudes of mental healthcare staff toward suicidal patients. *Archives of Suicide Research*, **6**: 309–23.

Alderfer B (1972) *Existence, Relatedness, and Human Growth: Human Needs in Organisational Settings*. Free Press, Oxford.

Beck A, Brown G, Berchick R, Stewart B, Steer B (1990) Relationship between hopelessness and ultimate suicide: a replication with psychiatric outpatients. *American Journal of Psychiatry*, **147**(2): 190–5.

Bonner RL, Rich AR (1987) High consequences of loneliness: a review of the literature. *Journal of American College Health*, **37**: 162–7.

Camus A (1945) *The Myth of Sisyphus* (transl. O'Brien J). Harris Hamilton, London.

Cutcliffe JR (2004) *The Inspiration of Hope in Bereavement Counselling*. Jessica Kingsley, London.

Cutcliffe JR, Stevenson S (2007) *Care of the Suicidal Person*. Churchill Livingstone/Elsevier, Edinburgh.

Cutcliffe JR, Stevenson C, Jackson S, Smith P (2006) A modified grounded theory study of how Psychiatric Nurses work with suicidal people. *International Journal of Nursing Studies*, **43**: 791–802.

Cutcliffe JR, Links PS, Ahern R, Ambreen M, Balderson K, Bergmans Y, Harder H, Nisenbaum R (2012a) Understanding the risks of recent discharge: the phenomenological lived-experiences – 'Existential angst at the prospect of discharge'. *Crisis*, **33**(1): 21–9.

Cutcliffe JR, Links PS, Ahern R, Ambreen M, Balderson K, Bergmans Y, Harder H, Nisenbaum R (2012b) Understanding the risks of recent discharge: the phenomenological lived-experiences – 'Trying to survive while living under the proverbial "Sword of Damocles"'. *Crisis*. Available online – DOI: 10.1027/0227-5910/a000132.

Ellis TE, Ratliff KG (1986) Cognitive characteristics of suicidal and non-suicidal psychiatric inpatients. *Cognitive Therapy and Research*, **10**(6): 625–34.

Freud A (1949) Introduction to the technique of child analysis. Nervous and mental diseases: notes on aggression. *Bulletin, Menninger Clinic*, **13**: 143–51.

Marcel GG (1948) In: Blackham HJ (1986) *Six Existentialist Thinkers*. Routledge, London, pp. 140–59.

Maris RW, Berman AL, Silverman MM (2000) *Comprehensive textbook of suicidology*. Guilford Press, New York.

Maslow A (1962) *Toward a Psychology of Being*. D van Nostrand, Princeton.

Orbach I (2003) Suicide and the suicidal body. *Suicide and Life-Threatening Behavior*, **33**(1): 1–8.

Ouzouni C, Konstantinos N (2009) Attitudes towards attempted suicide: the development of a measurement tool. *Health Science Journal*, **3**(4): 222–31.

Ranieri WF, Steer RA, Lavrence TI, Rissmiller DJ, Piper GE, Beck AT (1987) Relationship of depression, hopelessness and dysfunctional attitudes to suicide in psychiatric patients. *Psychological Reports*, **61**: 967–75.

Rudd DM (2000) The suicidal mode: a cognitive-behavioral mode of suicidality. *Suicide and Life-Threatening Behavior*, **30**(1): 18–33.

Schotte DE, Clum, G (1987) Problem-solving skills in suicidal psychiatric patients. *Journal of Consulting and Clinical Psychology*, **55**(1): 49-54

Scheerder G (2009) The care of depression and suicide: attitudes, skills, and current practices of community and health professionals. *Doctoral Dissertation*, submitted to Katholieke Universiteit Leuven. http://www.kuleuven.be/lucas/pub/publi_upload/2009_6_GS_The%20care%20of%20depression.pdf.

Shneidman, ES (2004) *Autopsy of a Suicidal Mind*. Oxford University Press, Oxford.

Weishaar ME (2000) Cognitive risk factors in suicide. In: Maris R, Canetto SS, McIntosh JL, Silverman MM (eds.) *Review of Suicidology*. Guilford Press, New York, pp. 112–39.

CHAPTER 10

Suicide following discharge – managing the transition from inpatient to community

Now this is not the end. It is not even the beginning of the end. But it is, perhaps, the end of the beginning.

Sir Winston Churchill

Introduction

Much of this book thus far has focused on the assessment, care and management of suicidal people during their 'acute' period of increased risk of suicide, often (but not always) involving some form of hospitalisation. There is a compelling body of evidence which indicates that people whose mental health problems lead them to require psychiatric hospitalisation are at a significantly increased risk for suicide (Appleby *et al*, 1999; Pirkola *et al*, 2005; Troister *et al*, 2008). However, hospitalisation for people at risk of suicide is only 'part of the bigger picture'; the period of time immediately following discharge after such hospitalisations appears to be a particularly high-risk time (see Goldacre *et al*, 1993; Geddes and Juszczak, 1995; Geddes *et al*, 1997; Lawrence *et al*, 2001; Ho, 2003; Yim *et al*, 2004; Troister *et al*, 2008).

A number of variables have been shown to be significantly related to suicide after recent discharge, such as previous suicide attempts (Fernando and Storm, 1984; King *et al*, 2001; McKenzie and Wurr, 2001; Yim *et al*, 2004); presence of affective disorder/depressive symptoms (King *et al*, 1995); unplanned discharge (Ho, 2006); and experience of negative life events following discharge (Pokorny and Kaplan, 1976). Conflicting findings exist regarding the link between duration of hospitalisation and increased risk (Qin and Nordentoft, 2005; Ho, 2006). While there is consensus within the limited literature concerning the existence of this increased period of risk, our understanding of the particular experience(s) that contribute to this risk is far from complete. Further, the authors could locate no qualitative studies that have systematically examined the post-discharge experiences of former hospitalised suicidal patients. Accordingly, this chapter reports on findings from a federally funded, mixed-methods study which sought to better understand the observed increased risk for suicide following discharge from an inpatient psychiatric service. Ultimately, the theoretical understanding of this specific high-risk period will lead to the development of selective prevention strategies that will decrease the risk for suicide and suicidal behaviour (Knox *et al*, 2004).

Research design and method: qualitative component

The study described in this chapter utilised a mixed-methods research design. The rationale or case for mixed-method research designs can be advanced on several methodological and epistemological grounds. The central premise of such designs, it has been argued (Cresswell and Plano Clark, 2011), is that the combination of quantitative and qualitative approaches provides a more comprehensive and complete understanding of problems than either approach can alone. Several authors have highlighted how mixed-methods research designs provide advantages/strengths that offset the limitations/weaknesses of both quantitative and qualitative research (eg. Goering and Streiber, 1996; Lester, 2002; Goldney, 2002; Leenaars, 2002; Cutcliffe and Harder, 2009). Green (2007) highlights how mixed-methods research designs enable questions to be answered that cannot be answered by qualitative or quantitative approaches alone. Mixed methods, according to Cresswell and Plano Clark (2003), enable researchers to use all of the tools of data collection available rather than being restricted to the types of data collection typically associated with qualitative or quantitative research. Further, mixed-methods designs encourage the use of multiple worldviews or paradigms rather than the typical association of certain paradigms for quantitative researchers and others for qualitative researchers (Cresswell and Plano Clark, 2003). This methodological consilience (Wilson, 1998) and the resultant unification of ways of knowing (and associated ways of conducting research) are highly congruent with complex, multi-dimensional healthcare problems. Professor of Psychiatry Goldney (2002, p. 70) makes this point most clearly:

> it is increasingly more difficult for even the most partisan of researchers to ignore the nexus between the qualitative and quantitative approaches.

Despite these methodological and epistemological exhortations, mental health/care and suicidology, it has been argued (see for example, Cutcliffe, 2003; White, 2003; Whitley, 2010; Bassett, 2010), are still somewhat lagging behind other disciplinary/academic groups when it comes to embracing qualitative and mixed-methods research designs. Mixed-methods research is inherently 'pragmatic'; researchers are unrestricted in selecting all methods possible to address a particular research problem. Further, the methodological pragmatism extends to enabling researchers to solve problems using data in the form(s) of numbers and words, and to combine inductive and deductive thinking. Accordingly, our study used a mixed-methods research design combining quantitative and qualitative methods. It combined a pre-test, post-test design ('before and after' design) with an intervention group and a control group, with a hermeneutic, phenomenological design, using van Manen's (1997, 2002) internationally established approach to phenomenology.

For the qualitative, phenomenological component, the research team was concerned with asking: what is the nature of this phenomenon (this experience of being discharged after being at risk for suicide) as an essentially human, lived-experience? How does it contribute to a person's ongoing risk of suicide? Accordingly, Van Manen's (1997) interpretation of hermeneutic phenomenology was used for this component of the study. The researchers obtained a purposive sample of 20 former inpatients, each of whom met the inclusion criteria (Box 10.1). For inpatients who consented to participate, a mutually convenient time for the interview to take place was arranged, at (or close to) the end of the first month following their discharge from the inpatient psychiatric service. Demographic details of the sample are displayed in Table 10.1.

In keeping with van Manen's (1997) interpretation of phenomenology, data were collected from the participants as a result of 'hermeneutic interviews, lasting between 1 and 2 hours; these occurred in a quiet, peaceful environment of the participants' choosing. At the beginning of the interview, the research team was concerned only with attempting to build rapport and help the participant feel at ease. While adopting a reflexive technique to qualitative interviewing (Kvale, 1996), the research team were seeking to elicit specific descriptions of the lived-moments of the experience of discharge; therefore certain types of questions

Box 10.1 Participant inclusion criteria

1. Had to be willing to participate and talk about their experiences
2. Aged 18 years or over
3. Must have been admitted to hospital with suicidal ideation or/and a lifetime history of suicidal behaviour
4. Must have subsequently stabilised based on the inpatient psychiatrist's assessment

Table 10.1 Sample socio-demographics.

Socio-demographics	
Age mean (SD)	36.3 (10.7)
Gender (*n*, %)	
Males	10 (50.0)
Females	10 (50.0)
Race/ethnicity	
Caucasian	13 (65.0)
Black 1	1 (5.0)
Asian 0	0
Other 6	6 (30.0)
Marital status (*n*, %)	
Single	14 (70.0)
Married/common-law	2 (10.0)
Divorced/separated/widowed	4 (20.0)
Diagnoses	
Affective disorder	= 7 (35%)
Affective disorder and borderline personality disorder	= 8 (40%)
Affective disorder and schizophrenic disorder	= 1 (5%)
Neither borderline personality disorder nor affective disorder nor schizophrenic disorder	= 4 (20%)
Definitions	
Affective disorder = bipolar or major depression	
Schizophrenic disorder = schizophrenia or schizoaffective	
Education (*n*, %)	
Less than high school	1 (5.0)
High school	5 (25.0)
College/University/Graduate school*	14 (70.0)
Current place of residence (*n*, %)	
Shelter	2 (10.0)
Living with parents/family	1 (5.0)
Rent	14 (70.0)
Own	3 (15.0)
Source of income in the past year (*n*, %)	
Disability pension	9 (45.0)
Other	11 (55.0)

Table 10.1 *(continued)*

Current employment status (*n*, %)	
Full time	6 (30.0)
Part time	6 (30.0)
Unemployed	2 (10.0)
Disabled**	6 (30.0)

* It might be noteworthy that this is a high percentage of participants who have a higher education background. While this may be a nuance or idiosyncrasy of this particular sample, it is also possible that this high number reflects the greater degree of comfort that higher educated individuals feel when participating in research interviews. That is to say that individuals with a higher education background are more likely to be familiar with the research process per se and arguably, less intimated by this.

** It might be noteworthy that these figures represent higher percentages than are typically associated with the adult population. While sampling for phenomenological studies seek informants who can provide the richest, deepest understanding into the phenomenon and thus deliberate eschew random (representative) samples, it remains possible that different findings may have been discovered from a sample that was representative of the adult population.

needed to be asked to assist the participant in accessing the moment as lived were asked. For example: 'If you could focus on an example of your post-discharge suicidal experience which stands out for its vividness, can you describe your experience of being discharged following your admission for suicidal ideation, as you live(d) through it?' 'Can you try to describe the experience from the inside as it were; what were your feelings, your mood, your emotions, your thoughts?' And 'Could you describe how your body felt at that time, how things smelled, how they sounded?' Furthermore, given the reflexive nature of hermeneutic interviews, some questions were asked in order to provide clarity in response to initial questions and in response to potential key moments described by the participants. Interviews ceased when the participants felt they had said all they had to say about the experience and when prompts from the interviewer do not elicit any new information.

Phenomenological data analysis

Too often, phenomenological thematic analysis is posited as an unambiguous and mechanical application of some frequency count or coding selected terms in transcriptions of text (Morse, 1995; Kvale, 1996; van Manen, 1997). However, more accurately, making something of a text or of a lived experience by interpreting its meaning is a process of insightful invention, discovery or disclosure. Accordingly, our approach to data analysis followed, with a high degree of fidelity, van Manen's (1997) methodological interpretation of phenomenology (see also Kleiman, 2004).

For hermeneutic phenomenology, the act of writing is not something that occurs *ex post facto*; writing is closely fused into the research activity. However, for ease of understanding, here we describe the approach to data analysis adopted by the research team in a linear rather than cyclic (or iterative) fashion.

Following verbatim transcription of the interview(s), the whole research team read the entire transcript. This process has been described as giving the researcher(s) a global sense of the whole (Kleiman, 2004) and/or a feeling for the subject's inherent meanings (see Colaizzi, 1978). The first author then undertook a second reading of the transcript and asked questions of the text, such as: What is going on here? What is this an example of? This enabled the first author to divide the data into meaningful sections and then integrate those that had a similar focus or content.

The first author then took each of these sections and formulated meaning in the context of the subject's own words/terms. This was achieved by asking questions of these collated sections, such as: What does this passage of text, or more accurately, the collections of passages, say about the essence of the experience of being discharged after receiving inpatient mental healthcare for the risk of suicide? These meanings, drawn from a number of interviews, were then grouped or clustered (or even reduced) together, as a result of individual meaning units having shared and/or common patterns, content, or trends, into themes. Further, in the repeated examination of the transcripts, themes were supported or exemplified by highlighting and 'lifting' appropriate phrases or capturing singular key statements (thematic statements).

Following this, the themes texts were shared with all members of the research team, who were encouraged to rewrite them as a means to enhance the richness and depth of the text. The team then revisited the interview transcripts once more as a means to ensure that their interpretations could be substantiated by reference to the raw data (see direct quotes from the interviews that substantiate the induced themes). Thus, themes captured the phenomenon; they are a means to access the meaning of the experience; they provide shape to the shapeless; form to the formless and content to the core or essence of the experience (van Manen, 1997).

Consequently, this process of writing and rewriting was used to make aspects of the lived experience reflectively understandable and was guided by van Manen's (2002) recent text on phenomenological writing ('Writing in the dark'). Furthermore, the interdisciplinary nature of the research team[1] meant that

1 Our research team was comprised of a psychiatric/mental health nurse (with a predominantly person-centred orientation), three psychiatrists (each with a supportive psychodynamic orientation), a psychologist (rehabilitation specialist with an eclectic

each member was able to bring his or her particular disciplinary experience and expertise to the data analysis and to the rewriting of the phenomenological text.

Ethical concerns

Given the 'vulnerable' nature of the population and the potentially sensitive nature of the phenomenon of interest, particular attention was devoted to considered ethical issues before commencing the study. Though the research team recognises that qualitative research interviews do *ipso facto* re-traumatise interviewees (see Ramcharan and Cutcliffe, 2001; Cutcliffe and Ramcharan, 2002), they were cognisant of the potential risks and so provided a number of 'safety measures' for the participants. All the information collected was treated confidentially and any information provided that could compromise the confidentiality of the person or the programs was disguised. All electronic data files were protected by a password system and the study computer remained within a locked office.

Research design and method: quantitative component

Study groups and recruitment

This study was carried out in a large urban general hospital with an active inpatient psychiatric service between May 2007 and December 2009. High-risk patients admitted to the inpatient psychiatric service and a short-stay crisis stabilisation unit with a lifetime history of suicidal behaviour accompanied by some level of intent to die and current suicidal ideation, based on self-report or chart documentation, were eligible to participate in the study. After receiving permission to approach patients from their treatment team, newly admitted patients were asked for their consent to participate in the investigation. After providing signed informed consent, patients participated in the baseline assessment during their hospital admission. The study received research ethics approval from the hospital Research Ethics Board.

Exposure: risk of lack of continuity of care

The research team defined inpatients who were at risk for a lack of continuity of care on discharge because they had no customary mental health/healthcare provider available on admission to hospital as being 'Exposed' and at higher risk of suicide. The 'Unexposed' cohort was defined by individuals who had a customary mental health/healthcare provider available on admission and were not at risk for a lack of continuity of care on discharge.

---

orientation), a social worker (person-centred orientation), a research coordinator (no specific theoretical orientation) and a biostatistician (no specific clinical orientation).

Baseline measures

While in hospital, the participants were assessed for baseline suicidal ideation measured with the clinician-administered version of the Scale for Suicide Ideation (SSI) (Beck *et al*, 1979) a 21-item, interviewer-administered rating scale that measures the current intensity of the participants' specific attitudes, behaviours and plans to die by suicide on the day of the interview and during the preceding week. This scale has demonstrated internal consistency, inter-rater reliability and concurrent validity (Beck *et al*, 1979) and adequate predictive validity significantly predicting eventual suicide (Brown *et al*, 1994).

To assess major current and lifetime psychiatric disorders (Axis I) and personality disorder diagnoses (Axis II) the Structured Clinical Interview for DSM-IV (SCID I and II) (First *et al*, 1997) was used. The SCID I is a semi-structured interview for making the major DSM-IV Axis I diagnoses. The output of the SCID is a record of the presence or absence of each of the disorders being considered, for current episode (past month) and for lifetime occurrence. SCID II is a semi-structured diagnostic interview for assessing the 12 DSM IV Axis II personality disorders. It closely follows the language of the DSM-IV Axis II Personality Disorders criteria. The interviews were administered by a clinician with psychiatric training and experience. Participants were also assessed during their index hospital admission for a history of suicidal behaviour; severity of depression, hopelessness, and impulsivity; and deficits in emotional regulation, problem solving skills, supports, life stress, symptom intensity and health outcomes using the following standard questionnaires.

The self-administered questionnaires included the Beck Depression Inventory (BDI-II) (Beck *et al*, 1961, 1996), which is a 21-question multiple-choice self-report inventory, one of the most widely used instruments for measuring the severity of depression. The BDI-II has demonstrated internal consistency (Cronbach's alpha for psychiatric populations' ranges from 0.76 to 0.95), convergent validity with hopelessness and suicidal ideation, and a strong positive association with an earlier version of the measure (Beck *et al*, 1961, 1996). To assess hopelessness, Beck Hopelessness Scale (BHS) (Beck *et al*, 1974), a 20-item self-report inventory was used. This questionnaire was designed to measure three major aspects of hopelessness: feelings about the future, loss of motivation and expectations (Beck *et al*, 1974). The BHS has demonstrated internal consistency (Cronbach's alpha ranges from 0.82 to 0.93), and convergence with clinician ratings of hopelessness (correlation coefficients ranges from $r = 0.62$ for inpatients to $r = 0.74$ for medical patients), and with measures of depression and suicide intent ($r = 0.68$) (Beck *et al*, 1974, 1985).

Impulsivity was recorded using Barratt's Impulsivity Scale (BIS-11) (Barratt *et al*, 1997), a 30-item self-report questionnaire that is a widely used measure of impulsive traits. The BIS-11 has demonstrated internal consistency (Cronbach's alpha ranging from 0.89 to 0.92 for all the three subscales), clinical utility and trait specificity (Barratt *et al*, 1997). Toronto Alexithymia Scale (TAS-20) (Taylor and Taylor, 1997) is a 20-item instrument which is one of the most commonly used measures of alexithymia. The TAS-20 has been used in a variety of populations, including psychiatric outpatients and previous evidence supports the convergent, discriminate and concurrent validity of the TAS-20 (Bagby *et al*, 1994; Taylor and Taylor, 1997; Taylor, 2000).

Problem-solving skills were assessed using Problem-Solving Inventory (PSI) (Heppner, 1988; Heppner and Peterson, 1982), a widely used self-report measure of applied problem-solving. Based on previous research, the PSI has demonstrated adequate reliability and validity (Heppner, 1988; Dixon *et al*, 1993). The People in Your Life (Marziali, 1987) inventory assesses psychiatric patients' perceptions of the quality and quantity of supportive relationships. The scale has shown good subscale alpha coefficients, test–retest reliability and face and construct validity (Marziali, 1987). Subjective Response to Events Scale (SRES) (Marziali and Pilkonis, 1986) was used to assess patients' perceptions of the events one month preceding their admission to the hospital. The SRES has demonstrated acceptable psychometric properties (Marziali and Pilkonis, 1986).

Follow-up measures

The SSI was administered at 1, 3 and 6 months after hospital discharge. At the sixth month follow-up appointment, participants were asked to report on any self-injury events without intent to die or suicide.

Outcomes

For suicidal ideation we considered two outcomes: (1) Change in SSI scores from baseline to 1 month post-discharge; and (2) SSI scores at 1, 3 and 6 months post-discharge dichotomised as ≥ 3 (indicating that the patient is positive for suicide ideation) and < 3 (negative for suicide ideation). We used these SSI categories due to the high proportion of zero scores at follow-up. For suicide behaviour we used the composite of the indicator of self-injury or suicide attempts within 6 months of hospital discharge or death by suicide after discharge.

Statistical analyses

Descriptive statistics (mean, standard deviation, quartiles) were calculated to characterise the participants with respect to suicidal history (ie. hospital admission due to suicide attempt or suicide ideation, number of past suicide attempts before hospital admission) and the predictive variables from the three thematic areas: socio-demographics at admission (age, gender, marital status, current place of residence, employment status, receiving disability), psychopathologic risk factors at/during admission (BDI-II, BHS, BIS, TAS-20, PSI) presence of affective disorders, schizoaffective disorders, substance use disorders, number of Axis-II disorders, Borderline Personality Disorder, and care variables (exposure status at admission, length of hospital admission).

Predictors associated with change in SSI scores from baseline to one month were identified using linear regression models. We fitted logistic generalised estimating equations (GEE) models with exchangeable correlation structure to determine predictors of risk of being positive for suicide ideation post-discharge while accounting for the correlations between repeated SSI measures at 1, 3 and 6 months. Suicide behaviour at 6 months after hospital discharge was analysed using logistic regression analysis. Univariate models assessed associations between factors in each of three thematic areas and suicide ideation and behaviour. A sequence of multivariate models was fitted, starting by including all factors with univariate p-values < 0.20 and the indicator of lack of a customary mental health/healthcare provider upon hospital admission (Exposure). Next, factors were dropped from the model if p-values were greater than 0.20 and they had missing data. A new model was fitted with the remaining variables and the process was repeated. The final multivariate model included statistically significant (p-value $<$ 0.05) and clinically relevant variables, adjusting for exposure status. All analyses were performed using SAS v9.2 (SAS Institute Inc., Cary, NC, USA).

Phenomenological findings: key theme one

Existential angst at the prospect of discharge

The first key theme of the lived experiences of being discharged following inpatient care for a suicidal crisis posits the essence of this experience as existential angst, dread or anguish at the prospect of discharge – of no longer being an inpatient 'recovering' from one's suicidality (a temporary yet significant 'pillar' of self and/or identity), and transitioning back to a meta-physical situation where the person has (little or) no option but to experience the 'freedom' and responsibility to care of oneself (once more), despite not feeling up to the task.

The experience is embodied by feeling scared, fearful, anxious and stressed; as concerned with being un- or ill-prepared, not feeling ready and fully informed. The essence of the experience includes disbelief, shock and surprise; leaving the place where they feel safe, looked after and cared for to venture to a place where the person has to become personally responsible again; it is an experience rife with a sense of disconnection and distance from (significant) others.

Such individuals experienced a multitude of concerns and questions: How will I survive? Do I have the tools? Am I equipped to make it? Am I prepared? How will I cope? How do I face my family? Will I make another attempt on my life? Will I be safe? It is a time of existential angst and uncertainty at the most base level: Will I continue to exist as meta-physical being? What is to stop me from making another attempt on my life? The participants in this study were acutely aware that they had made an attempt on their lives and had (some) expectations, rightly or wrongly, that the hospitalisation would make things better. In many cases, these expectations were unrealistic or not in keeping with what the formal mental health services could offer: a one week inpatient stay will not fix or solve all of life's problems. As a result, the experience is often one of feeling ill-prepared for discharge: that one is not ready, that there is more work to be done and ultimately, that discharge could bring about a further suicide attempt.

To use a metaphor to try to convey the lived-moments, the experience of discharge following care for a suicidal crisis can be likened to that of a raw recruit in the infantry (military) facing the prospect of a fierce and very life-threatening battle for the first time. Though trained or prepared to some extent in 'basic

Figure 10.1 Key theme one composition.

training' (the place of safety and preparation), the raw recruit is acutely aware of the potentially life-threatening circumstances that face him or her once he or she steps out onto the battlefield. Familiar to a degree with the threat and challenge that awaits him or her, questions of preparedness and/or readiness abound. The sense of shock, surprise and disbelief that is experienced when one is finally told that one is going into a combat situation accompany the sense of having to be responsible for oneself (again). Further, the rapidly approaching combat situation, and with it, the very real prospect or possibility of one's death, not surprisingly produces a viscerally and psychologically experienced sense of fear and anxiety. The key theme contains five themes, each of which is described below and is exemplified through 'thematic statements' (van Manen, 1997) extracted from the interviews (see Figures 10.1 and 10.2).

Phenomenological findings: key theme two:

Trying to survive while living under the proverbial 'sword of Damocles'

The second key theme of the lived experiences of being discharged following inpatient care for a suicidal crisis posits the essence of this experience as trying to survive while living under the proverbial 'Sword of Damocles'. There is a sense of people trying to re-engage with and pick up the pieces of their lives; reconnect with the world and with others in it, yet all the while all of these efforts occur under the ever-present shadow of a further (future) serious suicide attempt. There is a sense of wanting to make their situation work; a willingness to survive and even thrive yet being aware that they are unsure where to begin or how to make it work without help.

The experience is embodied by feeling that one needs help and can't cope alone, and not knowing where (or to whom) to go for help (though inversely feeling tremendously reassured when help is available). The essence of the experience also includes a sense of feeling lost, uncertain, disorientated, insecure and in a daze; the experience is rife with a sense of isolation and disconnection from the world and from others. The experience has a distinct sense of being incomplete, unfinished and unresolved; that there remains much work to be done and thus still the potential for suicide. As a result the experience also includes the self-soothing, coping and self-comforting that accompanies the moment-by-moment, day-to-day living that enables such people to endure the sense of foreboding that comes from living in the precarious situation of a further suicide attempt. There is (consciously and sub-consciously) an ever-present threat of further attempts on one's life when it seems like there is so little preventing this action; when life feels to hang so delicately in the balance.

As pointed out in the first key theme, any sense of unfulfilled (maybe unrealistic) expectations of the formal health service that the participants had left them feeling un- or ill-prepared for discharge. The sense of unfinished or unresolved issues contributed to the participants' awareness that their suicidality had not been 'settled' or worked out'; that suicide still remained an option. Such individuals experienced a multitude of concerns and (unanswered) questions: Who (where) can I turn to? What am I going to do? Where do I go for help? How do I face the 'real world' again? Will I be OK (safe) on my own? What do I do with my life from here on in? What can I do to help me endure/survive/get through this? While basic questions of existential being are still around (eg. will I continue to exist as meta-physical being?) other meaning-making questions are evident, most especially: How does one re-engage in life (in all of its dimensions) when one has tried to end that life?

To continue the metaphor from the first key theme, the experience of discharge following care for a suicidal crisis can be likened to that of a previously severely injured infantry (military) person facing the prospect of returning to fierce and very life-threatening battle having been hospitalised for a self-inflicted injury. Though strengthened, healed and helped (to a greater or lesser extent) by the hospitalisation, the recruit feels out of touch with his or her fellow soldiers; disconnected and unsupported yet wanting to survive, contribute (and even thrive). Unsure of how to proceed, and acutely aware that there is a very real life-threat looming, the recruit finds his or her own ways to make the lived-moments bearable; in some cases engaging in coping methods that his or her officers perhaps wouldn't approve of. The key theme contains five themes, each of which is described below and is exemplified through 'thematic statements' (van Manen, 1997) extracted from the interviews.

Phenomenological findings: themes

Theme 1: Feeling scared, anxious, fearful and/or stressed – 'Back into the lion's den'

This theme describes the sense of fear, being scared, feeling terrified, anxious, and/or nervous at the prospect and reality of impending discharge. This fear was experienced viscerally and somatically as well as cognitively/psychologically. Participants described how they experienced this fear physically in their chests: as a tightness or heavy feeling and/or feeling their hearts racing. Others experienced it in their stomach and others in their musculature. The fear of impending discharge was experienced as an overall sense of tension: a 'pressure cooker that was

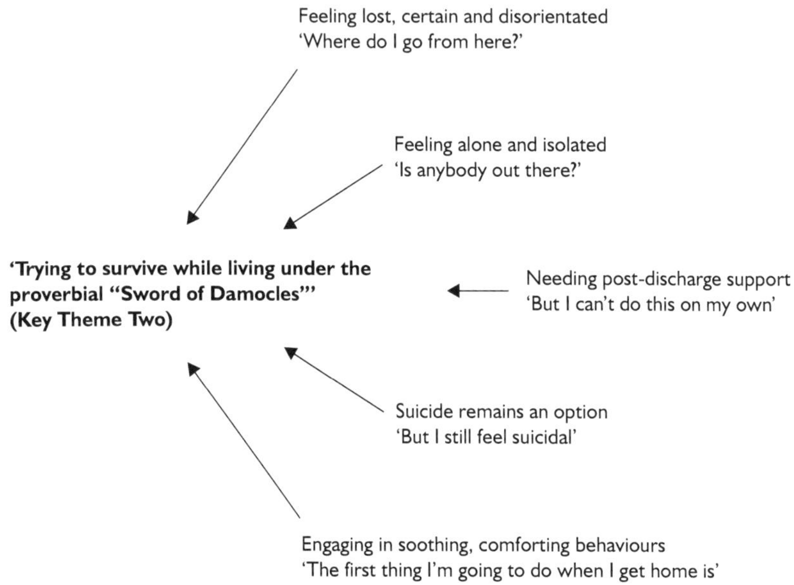

Figure 10.2 Key theme two composition.

about to explode'. Further participants described experiencing a change in body temperature: some feeling hotter, others a distinct chilling or sense of coldness. Others had both hot and cold 'spells'.

> But I was scared, I was scared, I was leaving (Int. 1)

> It's, I can feel it physically, see I can feel it in my chest, my chest feels tight. It's a heavy feeling and it's a, I don't know if you want to call it sadness or an emptiness, but it's very painful. (Int. 2)

The feeling of fear of impending discharge was also experienced in the participants' sense of lived relations, with a greater sense of distance between themselves and others being described. The sense of disconnection was evident, as were 'aloneness' and distance. Participants described eschewing social, interpersonal situations, experiencing at times a sense of being looked/stared at, of being surrounded by other people physically while simultaneously feeling alone. The feeling of fear was also experienced in the participants' sense of lived time, with various 'distortions' being reported. For some, their sense of time slowed down, while for others it seemed to speed up. Others lost their perspective on time, and thus when the moment came for actually leaving the hospital it was a surprise and produced a sense of shock.

> Well I was probably, my heart rate was probably going a mile a minute and my blood pressure was probably through the roof. I was also very cold and um I distanced myself from everyone really. (Int. 12)

> Oh my God, this is my last night here. (Int. 7)

The essence of this sub-theme is perhaps captured with the metaphor 'Back into the lion's den'. For the most part, the participants' 'home' was not experienced as a place of safety, comfort, healing and/or tranquillity; 'home' was experienced as a very dangerous metaphysical place. It was regarded as a place of uncertainty, of unknown, potential threat and overwhelming fear. For some participants, the metaphysical 'home' was experienced physically, interpersonally, psychologically, economically and spiritually as being the same or very similar to the 'place' that had given rise to (or contributed to) their suicide attempt/increased suicide ideation in the first place. To be discharged back to the same 'metaphysical' place that gave rise to or contributed to their previous suicide attempt/increased suicidal ideation was, not surprisingly, a very scary experience.

> No, no, no just really I feel it in the pit of my stomach and my heart like you have that fear, it's a, like you know it's going to happen again... and yeah like you don't trust yourself. (Int. 11)

> I was like, Oh my God, I'm going back to the same thing where nothing has really changed. (Int. 18)

Theme 2: Preparedness – 'But I'm not ready'

This theme describes the sense of feeling under- or unprepared for the reality of impending discharge; of not being ready, though some participants did describe themselves as ready or prepared for discharge. Those participants whom described their experiences as not being ready or adequately prepared for discharge also spoke of their sense of fear. Such experiences were exacerbated by the sense of decisions about discharge being imposed upon them by the healthcare team. Participants also referred to this sense of not being ready because they felt they had not spent enough time dealing with their issues; that there were still unresolved matters that required more time (in a place of safety). Some participants reported that they felt they did not have the 'tools' or skills for coping/survival post-discharge. That nothing substantive had changed in their circumstances, and they had no or limited safety plans in place.

For some participants there was a sense of not being informed about discharge dates; of having no (or minimal) input into the decision making process; of having important decisions made about their very existence (potentially) made without the healthcare team listening to the participant's point of view. Further, participants described the distinct sense of surprise and/or shock that some experienced when the 'news' of their discharge was 'sprung upon them' at such short notice.

> Yeah the psychiatrist I had in there wasn't listening to me anyways and she had her own protocols and she said I was being discharged and it's like all the time I was there treatment wise you know I was telling her that I was still not feeling well and you know you don't know say that with suicide. (Int. 9)

> The word discharge wasn't actually said until the end of the sentence on the last day, the second last day, like the night, the day before, the word. So it was like you're going to be leaving... you're going to be discharged tomorrow, okay. (Int. 10)

This sense of unpreparedness was also experienced bodily; participants described a sense of breathlessness, of having to monitor and control their reaction to prevent themselves from crying. Others used the metaphor of jumping into 'icy' water in the middle of winter.

> Yeah a big shock. It was like you know like those people that jump into Lake Ontario in the middle of winter, it would be like that. You know it was just sort of every single raw emotion was sort of came at me at once when I started talking about it and the biggest one being fear. (Int. 12)

Interestingly, in those cases where there was sufficient notice of discharge date (usually a longer period of notice), where the participant had some input into the decision-making process, where the participant's views of readiness (or otherwise) for discharge were listened to and taken into account, then the reported lived experiences of discharge were different. In these cases, participants felt prepared, felt less scared, and described themselves as being better able to cope once they were discharged home. Interestingly, the experience of discharge was still not free of fear and anxiety, even in the instances when participants felt prepared, but these feelings were lessened.

> Being prepared and having that kind of knowing the course of treatment and having that foreknowledge helps when you actually are discharged. I mean it doesn't it doesn't take away all the things you experience after you're discharged but it does give you some um I don't know the right word but um it is good to have kind of the knowledge of what's going to happen next cause um you can you can prepare yourself a bit more and um just be kind of ready for when you are discharged. (Int. 4)

Theme 3: Leaving the place of safety – 'But I feel safe in my cave!'

This theme describes the great deal of difficulty that some participants had in leaving the hospital, as they experienced it as a place of safety and comfort. Hospital for some participants had become very comfortable: a 'safe haven' where they were free from imminent threat of suicide. Participants described how they often felt cared for in hospital, in the sense of having one's daily needs met and in that they were free from or spared the vagaries of 'the outside world', experienced less suicidal ideation and had a very clear sense of feeling protected.

> I felt very safe here and I really didn't want to just dig that hole again, and I thought it was fine, that's why I really didn't want to leave. (Int. 1)

> It was nice, 'cause you're stuck in a room, and you have a nice air-conditioned building, you had three meals a day, and some people might say 'Well hey you know you've got it, you know you had it clean, you had three meals a day'. (Int. 3)

However, despite feeling safe and comfortable, some participants described how they were then told or instructed that they would have to leave. For some this produced a profound sense of nervousness and for others, a sense of anger/resentment. The 'cocoon' or 'bubble' that they experienced while in hospital was going to be removed, and this meant that the participants would once more need to experience life outside of the hospital, with all its challenges and stressors. The experience was also described in terms of how discharge from the 'place of safety' would result in the termination of the social, interpersonal connections that the participants had made while in hospital. Such connections were described, especially in terms of the 'lived-relations' of the experience, as valuable, rewarding and therapeutic, particularly since some participants described how it was often the case that these therapeutic relationships and connections were not made available to them once they had been discharged.

> I felt like I was going to miss a lot of the people like I was going to miss you know the nurses and [nurse's name] and you know Dr [Dr's name] and so forth because I felt like they were just like really nice warm people and I really enjoyed talking to them. (Int. 6)

Participants described this element of their lived experiences also in terms of the meanings and symbolism that they attached to hospital itself; and what it meant to them when the meanings/symbolism were to be lost (or removed from them). Hospitals were described in very Freudian ways; they were described as or given meaning as 'authority' (parental) figures. The authority figures had everything in control and organised; they kept them safe. Hence to be discharged from hospital was experienced as being discharged (sent away) from the symbolic parental figure; the participants were going to have to cope without the 'overshadowing protective blanket' of the hospital and the safety that this represented. As a result, some participants described themselves as not being sure of their ability to be in control of themselves.

> I guess the hospital represents something to me, it represents authorities being in charge, or someone else being in charge besides myself, and I think I needed that, I know I needed that at the time but I wasn't sure that I was going to be able to be in control of myself once I was out. (Int. 7)

Theme 4: Duality and ambivalence – 'I like it here, but I can't stay forever'

This theme describes how for some participants there were mixed feelings about being discharged, which can be divided, somewhat simplistically, into positive and negative feelings. Further, such duality was present across comparisons between different participants and also sometimes within an individual (singular) participant. Participants described their sense and realisation that, at some point, they were going to have to leave the hospital (as they could not stay forever), yet at the same time, the idea of leaving the hospital was both scary and frightening.

> It's kind of a mixture of um apprehension and relief um knowing that you're on your own again.... I was so happy to get out of hospital um and the relief of not being a patient but also the apprehension of being back on your own and having to deal with all the uncertainty of what's going to happen next. (Int. 4)

The participants also described a sense of looking forward to having the restrictions and rules that were sometimes imposed upon while in hospital, removed. The associated sense of increased freedom that accompanied the lifting of these restrictions was simultaneously experienced as both liberating and emancipatory and yet risky and potentially unsafe.

> I was worried because, yeah, I was like well I could do it again, but there was freedom now and I smoke, it's like I had one every hour like I could you know and I'd have my own bathroom again. I have a one-bedroom apartment and I'd have my own bed like you know it's just you go back home. (Int. 11)

The duality of the experience was also described in terms of the meaning(s) attached to being discharged. For some participants this was experienced as evidence of progress, of recovery, of not being a patient any longer. But simultaneously, it also meant that not being a patient equated with not receiving the support and that, as a result, one was responsible for oneself again; one was back alone with the corresponding 'freedom' (existentially) and corresponding uncertainty of the future to deal with.

Theme 5: Feel like a burden – 'I don't want to be any trouble'

This theme describes how some of the participants spoke of not wanting to be a burden to their family, to their friends, to their partner and even in some cases, to the mental health professionals involved in their care. Participants described how they did not feel they were worthy of such involvement and support, and/or how they felt a profound sense of guilt regarding what they felt they had already put their significant others through, and thus to have them further involved in their ongoing care would be to (in effect) cause more grief and pain to these people. Some participants spoke of wishing to spare their family members from any worry or stress that they felt they would feel if they got involved in the care of the participant; thus some described how after discharged they isolated themselves further. Participants spoke of how they would deliberately not say much to their significant others; how they edited and truncated their story when recounting it to others. There was a sense of shame and guilt and thus a recalcitrance; their lived-relations aspect of their experience then was one exemplified by holistic withdrawal and further disconnection.

> It gets me worried about what's going to happen to the whole family because apparently this is going to affect the whole family. (Int. 5)

> I've always felt that my problems would be a burden on them if I talked to them. So I don't really talk to anyone. (Int. 12)

Participants' descriptions of their experiences also indicated that there was a sense (or extension of) the participants' lack of self-esteem and self-worth (ie. I am not worthy of another's concern/attention). Without wishing to pathologise or 'medicalise' these experiences, the participants' views and expressions of self are suggestive that their suicidality was far from resolved.

> I don't like being a burden to anybody, and that includes my family, my friends, and even the physicians that treat me. I um I just you know I just feel like I'm wasting their time or you know taking up too much of their. (Int. 4)

Further, some participants described how they deliberately don't share or talk about their problems with their significant others because they experience a profound sense of shame. They spoke of how they viewed their actions as shameful and thus 'confessing' or 'disclosing' these acts to their significant others was not an easy act, since their family and friends were unable to offer any absolution to the participants.

Theme 6: Needing post-discharge support – 'But I can't do this on my own'

This theme describes the sense of feeling the need for post-discharge support, in various guises, and from a variety of different people. It also describes the growing sense of discomfort and dis-ease experienced when participants felt the level or extent of post-discharge, interpersonal support was insufficient. For those participants who described having some form(s) of post-discharge support in place, this interpersonal contact was experienced as a form of security. While the experiences of post-discharge support referred to contact with various individuals/groups, it is notable that the participants highlighted the particular value and utility of post-discharge support provided by formal mental health professionals.

> I'm going back home and so there's some concern about feelings coming back again, that was a concern but because like they'd be having mental health professionals come to the house, that was alleviated. (Int. 3)

Inversely, when the post-discharge support was absent from such individuals and services, this had a profound effect of the experience.

> My feelings were getting worse. I remember thinking OK, my father is working or something, my mother is doing what or she was away, my psychiatrist must have been away and then I was like 'Oh my God, there's nowhere to turn to. There's nothing I can do' and I was like that shouldn't be the case. (Int. 16)

The phenomenological lived relations of this theme were clearly evident: participants described their increased sense of safety, wellbeing and hope as a result of the closeness of others, both physically and interpersonally. Participants also described how the post-discharge support they experienced (and felt they needed) took various forms: face-to-face support, virtual support (eg. emails) and formal support groups. Also, several different forms of support were accessed/utilised at the same time. Being involved (to a greater or lesser extent) in the decision making regarding post-discharge support was also described as highly beneficial. There was a great deal of reassurance and comfort in knowing that these support systems and people were being arranged in advance of discharge – that they would be there 'waiting for the participant' upon discharge.

> I know there are lots of times where I feel so overwhelmed from the discharge especially if I'm being discharged before I feel ready so it would be really helpful to have someone else there with me um while they're going over the discharge planning and to leave with me um just so that there's someone who is hearing it who can help me remember. (Int. 21)

Theme 7: Feeling lost, uncertain and disorientated – 'Where do I go from here?'

This theme describes the sense of 'feeling lost' (metaphorically) and disorientated. Participants spoke of how, when they arrived home, they did not know what to do next. For some, there was a sense of being aware that they needed to pick up the threads of their lives and yet they did not know where (or how) to begin. For others there was an experience of feeling lost with regard to where (and/or to whom) they could go to seek help, especially if the experience of hospitalisation had not sufficiently or comprehensively helped with their suicidal ideation and increased risk of suicide. Others still had a more 'existential' sense of feeling lost in terms of their 'place' in the world.

> I had my old feeling, which was anxious, worrying again about what am I going to do?... Just having to live again, you know get back on top of my bills, find a home, just face the real world again I think is what I was afraid of. (Int. 8)

> All those factors were complete unknowns to me now because I was so used to being in the hospital, I felt safe and now the next step was now again was going to be completely unsafe... it was very different, you know very foreign again. (Int. 12)

> I literally felt like I was *carrying all of these emotions with me as* well and *I didn't feel grounded.* I didn't feel like I knew exactly where I was going except that I was going home.... Nothing really felt ready. It was kind of like baking a cake without a recipe. (Int. 10)

Participants were also very uncertain about the future, both in terms of whether or not they would be able to survive (not succumb to suicide) but also uncertain about what they should do with their lives now. This led to a distinct experience of uncertainty, insecurity and disorientation. Some experienced this disorientation to such an extent that they were in a 'daze'; they didn't realise where they were, didn't notice other people, and existed in their own world. Others referred to the sense of disorientation impacting on their experience of lived-time. Participants described how time seemed to pass slowly: how the whole day of the day they were discharged seemed to take longer, with hours feeling like they were days.

> I didn't notice anyone. I usually don't look at other people. I'm in my own world like... like I daze like, I disassociate. I don't know maybe it was because I felt I wasn't ready to leave the hospital and it took me three days to realize well you're home now so get used to it. (Int. 11)

> (At discharge) I just felt so very disorientated... that isn't the right word... it was more my sense of spatial connectivity was out of synch. The gradually, the next day, it was a little bit better and then I went outside again and it got better. I remember thinking that I was glad I wasn't driving. (Int. 17)

Theme 8: Feeling alone and isolated – 'Is anybody out there?'

This theme of the lived-experience describes the sense of feeling alone, isolated and disconnected. Participants described themselves as feeling disconnected from the world and from humanity. The phenomenological experience of the their lived-relations was one where they witnessed other people getting on with their lives, and this only served to reinforce how they were different to these people.

> They are just carrying on. They're getting what they need. I can see them just, you know, like it just, they're going through life and they want it. They want, it's precious to them like worse then gold and I can't connect with that. (Int. 9)

> Actually it was hard at times because even if I was around them I would still feel very lonely and isolated from them so it didn't always help. (Int. 7)

Further, the experience of isolation and disconnection was described in terms of missing the interaction with people within the hospital: the clients and clinicians. Even in such somewhat artificial circumstances the participants reported having some sense of comfort and therapeutic value in these interpersonal encounters and connections. When the participant was discharged, this precipitated a further severing of their tentative connections with humanity; a further and more pronounced sense of isolation and 'aloneness'.

> When in hospital, you have people around and then you, you're in your apartment alone. Yeah there's a definitely um that's definitely probably the hardest part about coming out of the hospital is because even though you only get like a minimal amount of support from the staff while you're there. At least the option of going to talk to staff and then there's your peers and um generally speaking I can connect at least with one other person there. (Int. 21)

Perhaps counter-intuitively, even though the experience of aloneness and disconnection was profound, some participants described how they actively pushed people away from themselves; even (or perhaps especially) those people who are close to the participant. There was a sense and experience of shame related to having made an attempt on their life, and as a result of having to explain these behaviours to family/friends.

> I'm ashamed, I'm very ashamed of you know my past, you know being admitted into hospital multiple times um attempting suicide multiple times, you know I just I'm very ashamed of you know the things I've done and you know try not to let anyone else know... I'm alone, um, you know my family does try you know to connect and I um I tend to push them away. (Int. 4)

Theme 9: Suicide remains an option – 'But I still feel suicidal'

This theme of the lived-experience describes how for some of the participants in this study suicide remained (very much) as an option after they were discharged. Thoughts of ending their lives occurred to some participants on the very day that they were discharged; for others, thoughts of suicide and/or suicide remaining in their consciousness as a viable solution to their problems persisted for many months after discharge and in some cases, years after.

> I'm probably still going to be depressed and you know suicide will be on the table um you know kind of as one of the options. (Int. 4)

> What was going through your head on the day of discharge? I'm going to end my life. (Int. 13)

Participants described, again perhaps somewhat paradoxically, that having suicide as an option for them post-discharge actually served as a 'security blanket'. There was a sense of participants being willing to try to resolve their issues but if they couldn't, if they couldn't cope then they still had a way out in the form of suicide.

> [upon discharge] Like I immediately want my safety blanket of suicide and for me that's a safety blanket, that's where I want to be. (Int. 9)

Participants were very clear that, for the most part, the act and experience of being discharged in no way prevented them from still feeling suicidal. Just because the formal mental healthcare system (services) had decided that it would be safe to discharge them, that did not necessarily mean that the person's suicidality had been resolved or the suicidal 'episode' was now concluded. It may well have been the case that the crisis point or highest point of risk had elapsed, but participants were adamant that they left the hospital still feeling suicidal. Some participants described their experiences as the system letting them down; the described not getting their issues resolved or that their 'recovery' was incomplete. Some participants' experiences appeared to indicate that it takes a great deal longer to resolve these complex issues and that at times, their experience of the healthcare system was one characterised as a 'Band-Aid' approach.

> There was no communication and just because you put me there it doesn't change the internal workings so I still was suicidal. (Int. 9)

> I was still suicidal when they let me go but they did what they were supposed to do. They upped my drugs, they gave me some sleeping medication and they were all kosher like everything was aesthetic and it doesn't matter where you're at and so I'm still struggling with it. (Int. 9)

For some the experience of being discharged before they felt that they had resolved their suicidal issues actually served to potentially increase their risk. Some participants referred to the increased sense of hopelessness that resulted from going to a place/organisation where they were expecting things to improve, and yet they didn't improve. There was a sense of, 'Where can I get help? If I can't get help from the formal mental health services, then where can I get help?'.

Theme 10: Engaging in soothing, comforting behaviours – 'The first thing I'm going to do when I get home is...'

This theme describes the wide range of behaviours that participants engaged in as a form(s) of self-soothing, comforting and/or coping when they arrived back 'home'. There was great diversity in the behaviours described including: hiding, staying busy, self-medicating, starting to try to pick up the threads and activities of one's pre-hospitalised life, putting structure in place, and finding comfort. Further, while the nature of the activity varied in form from person-to-person, in each case one of the goals was easing the transition from inpatient to being discharged. Some of the participants described how they engaged in self-medicating as a means to obtain relief from the psychological pain/stress. Powerful metaphors of oblivion and, to a lesser extent, nothingness were used and clearly communicated a sense that for some participants, these metaphysical states anaesthetised them from their 'psychache'. Others used more socially acceptable means to relieve the psychological pain, such as listening to music, relaxing and/or watching a lot of TV.

> Well I've gotten home and the first thing I do is self-medicate. You know a little bit of alcohol, try to plan for some marijuana, just try to shutdown. If I can shutdown that's almost like ah being dead because I'm not aware. It's sort of like a black out for an alcoholic. So if I can shutdown, then I don't feel. I don't feel the hopelessness and I don't feel like I'm disconnected because I'm not aware and if I can be not aware at least I'm not in pain. (Int. 9)

> I'm going to get out of here and I'm going to go drinking right and so it, it was sort of a rush so that I could get to the alcohol and the drugs and stuff. It was like let me go, let me go, I got to get you know I got to get to the liquor store. (Int. 20)

Some of the participants described how they engaged in 'hiding', 'cocooning' and/or sleeping. They described a sense of wishing to not have to face the world; wanting to avoid contact with too many significant others and would thus barricade themselves in and hide. To a lesser extent, some participants described how these actions were motivated towards providing a time and space for healing.

> I didn't want to see a bunch of people, totally hyper arouses, like just very self-conscious so being around a lot of people so, just sort of anxious.... I didn't want to be looked at, I just wanted to kind of go and cocoon at home. (Int. 10)

> I just didn't feel comfortable being out, I didn't want to be around people, I didn't want to socialize, I was still unsure of myself, my judgment, and I didn't want to deal with other people's emotions.... I would spend the rest of the evening at home. (Int. 7)

Some of the participants described how they searched for and tried to (re) create structure and routine. This provided a sense of purpose and direction: it provided an increased sense of safety (as the familiar is often experienced as non-threatening) and prevented them from spending too much time ruminating. Other participants described how they merely attempted to keep busy. Others still described how they 'dived straight in' and attempted to pick up the threads of their life once more.

Quantitative results

Sample description

A total of 152 inpatients were eligible and 120 (78.9%) consented to participate in the study. By the end of the study, 10 (8.3%) participants had withdrawn and 8 (6.7%) were lost to follow-up. Table 10.1 shows the description of the baseline sample. There were similar numbers of male (52.5%) and female (47.5%) participants, and the mean age was 37.5 years (SD = 11.1). Most participants were admitted because of a current suicide attempt, but 22 (18.3%) were admitted because of suicide ideation. Only 27 (22.5%) participants were first time suicide attempters, ie. had no suicide attempts in the past, while 93 (78.5%) had a median number of two previous attempts (interquartile range = 2) over their lifetime. Twenty-four (20%) participants did not have any form of outpatient mental healthcare in the community and therefore were at risk (Exposed) for lack of continuity of care upon discharge. Ninety-six (80%) were Unexposed. Affective disorders were by far the most common current psychiatric diagnoses experienced by these participants with a history of suicidal behaviour, and a current diagnosis of major depression or bipolar disorder according to DSM-IV criteria was present in 99 (90%) of the participants. Table 10.2 lists the other common current psychiatric diagnoses in these participants. Borderline personality disorder was diagnosed in 31.9% of the participants. The mean BDI score was 39.1 (SD = 11.6). The median length of hospital admission was 3 days (interquartile range = 14) and 38.4% remained hospitalised for 11 days or more.

Suicide ideation and behaviour

At baseline (n = 119), SSI scores ranged from 10 to 31, with a mean of 23.6 and standard deviation of 3.8. Mean (SD) scores post-discharge were 7.9 (9.0), 6.6

(7.8) and 5.7 (7.8) at 1 month ($n = 100$), 3 months ($n = 96$) and 6 months ($n = 98$), respectively. Of note, a high proportion of risk factors for suicide ideation and behaviour participants reported no suicide ideation (SSI = 0): 40.0%, 44.8% and 48.0% at 1, 3 and 6 months, respectively.

The incidence of death by suicide during the study period was 3.3% (95% confidence interval [CI] = 0.9–8.3%); 1 participant died (0.8% or 1 in 120) while hospitalised and 3 participants (2.5% or 3 in 120) within 1 month of hospital discharge. Forty-one of 104 (39.4%; 95% CI = 30.0–49.5%) participants reported self-injury or suicide attempts within 6 months of hospital discharge.

Change in SSI scores from baseline to 1 month

Because of attrition, 100 participants had both baseline and 1 month SSI measurements. Overall, SSI scores significantly decreased from baseline to 1 month with a mean change of –15.7 (SD = 8.9, range = –31 to 7, p-value < 0.0001). From univariate analysis, the following variables were selected for the multivariate linear regression model ($p < 0.20$): more than one past suicide attempt, hospital admission for a current suicide attempt, being female, being currently unemployed, BDI, BHS, BIS, substance use disorder, more than one Axis-II disorder and length of admission (Table 10.3). Negative regression coefficients indicate lower SSI scores at 1 month while positive coefficients imply higher scores. In the final multivariate model (Table 10.3, $N = 98$), history of more than one past suicide attempt and BHS scores were significantly associated with higher SSI scores at 1 month post-discharge (coefficient = 5.41, SE = 1.67, p = 0.0017 and coefficient = 0.36, SE = 0.16, p = 0.0256, respectively). However, more than one Axis-II disorder was significantly associated with reduced SSI at 1 month after discharge (coefficient = –4.97, SE = 1.93, p = 0.0115). Exposure and female gender were not statistically significant but were kept in the model because they were deemed clinically relevant for change in SSI scores. The R^2 for the final model was 0.26.

Positive (SSI ≥ 3) and negative (SSI < 3) for suicide ideation at 1, 3 and 6 months

A total of 102 participants had at least one SSI measurement after hospital discharge. The prevalence of participants positive for suicide ideation was 59.0% ($n = 100$), 54.2% ($n = 96$) and 51.0% ($n = 98$) at 1, 3 and 6 months respectively, but this trend was not statistically significant ($p = 0.1487$, Table 10.3). In multivariate analyses (Table 10.4, $N = 96$, 279 measures), current suicide attempt compared with suicide ideation was significantly associated with positive suicide ideation

Table 10.2 Predictors of change in suicide ideation from baseline to 1 month in univariate and multivariate linear regression analyses.

	Univariate linear regression		Multivariate linear regression**	
	Estimate (SE)	***p*-value**	**Estimate (SE)**	***p*-value**
Intercept			–23.69 (2.38)	<0.0001
Suicidality factors				
First suicide attempt	–2.01 (2.19)	0.3617		
Number of past suicide attempts before current admission, >1 vs ≤1	6.31 (1.71)	0.0004	5.41 (1.67)	0.0017
Reason for admission, suicide attempt vs suicide ideation	3.16 (2.26)	0.1660		
Socio-demographics factors				
Age, 1 year increase	0.02 (0.08)	0.8232		
Female	3.27 (1.77)	0.0670	2.73 (1.59)	0.0894
Single	–0.33 (1.98)	0.8667		
Living in a shelter	–1.64 (2.17)	0.4534		
Disability pension in the past year	0.02 (1.79)	0.9911		
Currently unemployed	–2.81 (2.15)	0.1958		
Psychopathological factors				
Depression – BDI-II	0.11 (0.08)	0.1604		
Hopelessness – BHS	0.46 (0.17)	0.0093	0.36 (0.16)	0.0256
Impulsivity – BIS	0.17 (0.09)	0.0722		
Alexythymia –TAS–20	0.12 (0.10)	0.2267		
PSI – Problem solving confidence	0.11 (0.09)	0.2430		
PSI – Approach avoidance style	0.08 (0.09)	0.4227		
PSI – Personal control	0.04 (0.22)	0.8356		
Substance use disorder	3.02 (1.79)	0.0948		
Affective disorders (bipolar or major depression)	0.09 (3.05)	0.9754		
Schizophrenic disorders (schizophrenia or schizoaffective)	2.48 (3.04)	0.4156		

Table 10.2 *(continued)*

	Univariate linear regression		Multivariate linear regression**	
	Estimate (SE)	*p*-value	Estimate (SE)	*p*-value
Borderline personality disorder	1.98 (1.88)	0.2964		
Number of Axis–II disorders*, \>1 vs [EQ]1	–4.34 (2.15)	0.0464	–4.97 (1.93)	0.0115
Patient care factors				
Mental health/health care provider not available on admission – "Exposed"	2.76 (2.15)	0.2025	2.78 (1.93)	0.1545
Length of admission in hospital (days)				
1–3 vs >11	–3.25 (1.92)	0.0938		
4–11 vs > 11	–1.52 (2.96)	0.6073		

*Number of Axis–II diagnoses includes avoidant or dependent or OCPD or passive-aggressive or depressive or paranoid or schizotypal or schizoid or histrionic or narcissistic or borderline or antisocial; **R2 = 0.26

Table 10.3 Predictors of positive suicide ideation (SSI Scores ?3) at 1, 3 and 6 months in univariate and multivariate GEE models.

	Univariate GEE Model		**Multivariate GEE Model**	
	Odds Ratio (95% CI)	***p*-value**	**Odds ratio (95% CI)**	***p*-value**
Month of follow-up, for every month post discharge	0.94 (0.86, 1.02)	0.1487	0.93 (0.83, 1.03)	0.1592
Suicidality factors				
First suicide attempt	0.82 (0.41, 1.66)	0.5897		
Number of past suicide attempts before current admission, >1 vs ≤ 1	2.11 (1.09, 4.05)	0.0259	1.80 (0.94, 3.44)	0.0743
Reason for admission, suicide attempt vs suicide ideation	3.25 (1.37, 7.72)	0.0076	3.60 (1.27, 10.76)	0.0165
Socio-demographics factors				
Age, 1 year increase	1.01 (0.98, 1.04)	0.4291		
Female	2.22 (1.17, 4.21)	0.0150	2.46 (1.20, 5.05)	0.0140
Single	0.88 (0.45, 1.72)	0.7038		
Living in a shelter	0.64 (0.30, 1.35)	0.2417		
Disability pension in the past year	1.20 (0.64, 2.25)	0.5598		
Currently unemployed	0.59 (0.29, 1.21)	0.1516		
Psychopathological factors				
Depression –BDI-II	1.04 (1.05, 1.07)	0.0029	1.04 (1.01, 1.07)	0.0145
Hopelessness –BHS	1.07 (1.01, 1.14)	0.0255		
Impulsivity –BIS	1.04 (1.00, 1.08)	0.0481		
Alexythymia –TAS-20	1.02 (0.99, 1.05)	0.1809		
PSI – Problem solving confidence	1.04 (1.01, 1.08)	0.0383		
PSI – Approach avoidance style	1.03 (1.00, 1.07)	0.0816		
PSI – Personal control	1.09 (1.01, 1.18)	0.0273		
Substance use disorder	1.13 (0.60, 2.16)	0.7043		
Affective disorders (bipolar or major depression)	0.61 (0.23, 1.61)	0.3217		
Schizophrenic disorders (schizophrenia or schizoaffective)	1.53 (0.48, 4.88)	0.4765		

Table 10.3 (*continued*)

	Univariate GEE Model		Multivariate GEE Model	
	Odds Ratio (95% CI)	***p*-value**	**Odds ratio (95% CI)**	***p*-value**
Borderline personality disorder	1.34 (0.69, 2.63)	0.3905		
Number of Axis-II disorders*, >1 vs ≤1	0.88 (0.40, 1.89)	0.7268		
Patient care factors				
Mental health/health care provider not available on admission–"Exposed"	1.57 (0.71, 3.50)	0.2673	1.86 (0.76, 5.52)	0.1731
Length of admission in hospital (days)				
1–3 vs >11	0.85 (0.42, 1.71)	0.6461		
4–11 vs > 11	0.93 (0.36, 2.41)	0.8787		

*Number of Axis-II diagnoses includes avoidant or dependent or OCPD or passive-aggressive or depressive or paranoid or schizotypal or schizoid or histrionic or narcissistic or borderline or antisocial

Table 10.4 Predictors of the composite of intentional harm or death by suicide within 6 months of hospital discharge, in univariate and multivariate logistic regression models ($N = 107$).

	Univariate logistic regression		Multivariate logistic regression	
	Odds ratio (95% CI)	*p*-value	Odds ratio (95% CI)	*p*-value
Suicidality factors				
First suicide attempt	0.88 (0.35, 2.25)	0.7955		
Number of past suicide attempts before current admission, >1 vs ≤1	1.45 (0.66, 3.18)	0.3538		
Reason for admission, suicide attempt vs suicide ideation	3.40 (1.05, 11.01)	0.0408	6.45 (1.29, 32.18)	0.0230
Socio-demographics factors				
Age, 1 year increase	0.98 (0.95, 1.02)	0.3626		
Female	1.37 (0.63, 2.96)	0.4255		
Single	1.40 (0.59, 3.31)	0.4500		
Living in a shelter	1.94 (0.78, 4.87)	0.1560		
Disability pension in the past year	1.50 (0.69, 3.25)	0.3045		
Currently unemployed	0.62 (0.24, 1.60)	0.3208		
Psychopathological factors				
Depression – BDI-II	1.02 (0.99, 1.06)	0.2117		
Hopelessness – BHS	1.07 (0.99, 1.17)	0.0881		
Impulsivity – BIS	1.06 (1.01, 1.11)	0.0150	1.07 (1.01, 1.12)	0.0140
Alexythymia – TAS-20	0.98 (0.94, 1.02)	0.3845		
PSI – Problem solving confidence	1.01 (0.97, 1.05)	0.7364		
PSI – Approach avoidance style	1.03 (0.99, 1.08)	0.1464		
PSI – Personal control	1.00 (0.91, 1.10)	0.9905		
Substance use disorder	2.12 (0.93, 4.84)	0.0757		
Affective disorders (bipolar or major depression)	0.37 (0.10, 1.43)	0.1498		
Schizophrenic disorders (schizophrenia or schizoaffective)	1.32 (0.33, 5.25)	0.6957		
Borderline personality disorder	1.31 (0.57, 3.01)	0.5258		

Table 10.4 *(continued)*

	Univariate logistic regression		Multivariate logistic regression	
	Odds ratio (95% CI)	***p*-value**	**Odds ratio (95% CI)**	***p*-value**
Number of Axis-II disorders*, > I vs ?I	1.58 (0.59, 4.20)	0.3627		
Patient care factors				
Mental health/health care provider not available on admission – "Exposed"	1.28 (0.51, 3.20)	0.5947	0.88 (0.31, 2.53)	0.8129
Length of admission in hospital (days)				
1–3 vs > 11	1.08 (0.47, 2.47)	0.8588		
4–11 vs > 11	0.72 (0.19, 2.80)	0.6340		

*Number of Axis-II diagnoses includes avoidant or dependent or OCPD or passive-aggressive or depressive or paranoid or schizotypal or schizoid or histrionic or narcissistic or borderline or antisocial (odds ratio [OR] = 3.60, 95% CI = 1.21 – 10.75, p-value = 0.0216), even after adjusting for more than one suicide attempt before admission. Being female and higher BDI score at admission were also significantly associated with higher likelihood of positive suicide ideation at follow-up (OR = 2.46, 95% CI = 1.20–5.05, p-value=0.0140 and OR = 1.04, 95% CI =1.01–1.07, p-value = 0.0145, respectively).

Intentional harm or death by suicide within 6 months of hospital discharge

In the final multivariate model, admission for suicide attempt (OR = 6.45, 95% CI = 1.29–32.18) and BIS scores (OR = 1.07, 95% CI = 1.01–1.12) were the only significant predictors of self-injury, suicide attempts or death within 6 months of hospital discharge (Table 10.5).

Discussion

The data in this study indicated that being/feeling prepared for discharge appeared to have a major influence on the subsequent discharge experience. The reported senses of fear, dread and anguish about being sent 'back into the lion's den' were lessened when the participant felt more prepared; that he/she had a degree of control over when and how this happened.

While mindful of the many factors that influence (if not drive) decisions regarding discharge, relatively slight alterations in current practice appear to have significant utility. Involving patients in the decision-making process, encouraging expression and 'ventilation' of fears/anxieties; acknowledging that such fear is to be expected; seeking and taking account of the patient's views *vis-à-vis* readiness for discharge; where possible addressing specific concerns and exploring what can be put in place to help patients feel more supported; and wherever possible not forcing the discharge on patients who don't feel ready and/or prepared, would appear not only to be indicative of good practice but simultaneously potentially reduce the risk of further attempts post-discharge. Similar calls for involving patients (and their family carers) in discharge decision making have been advocated in the United Kingdom (see Social Care Institute for Excellence Research Brief 12, accessed 2010) and are commonplace in policy documents (see for example, Department of Health, accessed 2010). However, the norm is that people are not usually consulted about the planning of their discharge or care (SCIE, accessed 2010). Indeed, the limited literature shows that a 'top-down' or 'paternalistic' approach is the norm for discharge planning (Bull *et al*, 2000; Cornes and Clough, 2001; Mountain and Pighills, 2003). And yet the empirical findings, such as they are, indicate that patients who perceived that the time of discharge was consistent with the stage of their illness experienced significantly higher recovery (Schröder *et al*, 2007).

Further practice implications arising out of these findings include the need to commence the discharge process as soon as possible after admission, and in this way being discharged can then be experienced as a gradual process, one where the patient has time to prepare and plan. If possible, and the authors are mindful of the possible logistical difficulties, it would be prudent to introduce the patient to his or her post-discharge support staff before the discharge occurs (and thus enhance the continuity of care). The findings also suggested that there was a major disconnect in the expectations of admitted patients and what realistically could be offered by the formal mental healthcare services. For example, some participants referred to the expectation of getting fixed or cured; they expected (analogous to their experiences of receiving care for physical/medical problems) that being admitted to inpatient care would result in the cure/solution to their problem.

The difficulties associated with misconceptions/unrealistic expectations about formal psychiatric care have been documented previously (see for example, Douglas *et al*, 1999). Such disconnections are linked with drop-out rates (Bunn *et al*, 1997) and levels of satisfaction (Balogh *et al*, 1995). Interventions to enhance the congruence between patient expectations and what the mental healthcare services can realistically offer have resulted in improved attendance/satisfaction and decreased anxiety (Webster, 1992). Accordingly, the authors of this paper suggest that early exploration of and reconciling patients' expectations regarding inpatient care for their suicidality might be intervention that could diminish the post-discharge risk for further suicide attempts; this hypothesised intervention requires further empirical testing.

Furthermore, the data in this study also indicated that the risk of suicide continues long after the client has been discharged. Clients can still have a willingness to survive and even thrive; however, they are unsure where to begin to pick up the pieces of their life without help. Given the data that captures the sense of isolation, aloneness and need for ongoing interpersonal connection, the need for a range of post-discharge support orientated 'interventions' is indicated, such as scheduled visits in the community from a mental health clinician, follow-up phone calls, text messages, emails and/or postcards. If the client is willing to give his or her consent, the discharge process might also be adapted to include notifications sent to family, friends and formal carers (eg. managers of the homeless centres). There is some support within the albeit limited (in terms of quantity and scope) empirical literature. Driscoll (2001) for example found that carers who were present with their patients when they received information concerning post-discharge care experienced a decrease in anxiety during their patients' convalescence at home and greater satisfaction with the information they received, and their patients experienced fewer medical problems post-discharge. More specific to follow-up care for suicidal people, the novel studies by Motto and Bostrom (2001) and Carter and colleagues (2005, 2007) show that simply utilising letters or postcards as an intervention following discharge suggests that social connectedness – feeling that somebody still cares – may be a crucial component of post-discharge support.

The data indicated that for the participants in this study there was a clear sense of feeling lost (metaphorically) and disorientated. Participants spoke of how, when they arrived home, they did not know what to do next; they were uncertain about so many aspects of their lives. Accordingly, there appears to be significant utility in creating a post-discharge plan, working in collaboration with the client, which can subsequently explore pragmatic issues such as: What to do now/next? What needs to be addressed first and what can wait? How to begin re-engaging in life? How to pick up the threads of one's life again? Where can the client go for additional help/support? How can information on post-suicide support groups, be they physical 'face-to-face' groups or 'virtual' online groups, be provided? This ongoing, post-discharge support can be offered from both the mental health services and voluntary sectors (including peer support) and should logically include some work on helping the client become more comfortable with this sense of uncertainty, helping the client understand that this sense of being 'dazed' is normal and to be expected, and that this too shall pass. Mental health services might similarly think about augmenting their discharge process by producing some post-discharge literature and/or pamphlets. Perhaps analogous to current best practice in some medical/surgical situations (for example, when about to be discharged following a new diagnosis for diabetes, or following a myocardial infarction), patients are inevitably provided with pamphlets and literature regarding their ongoing, post-discharge recovery and how to reduce the risk of post-discharge complications.

While there is little evidence in the extant suicidology literature regarding post-discharge interventions, valuable lessons can be learned by drawing on related practices in other areas of healthcare. For example, in their thorough meta-analysis, Phillips *et al* (2004) found that comprehensive discharge planning plus post-discharge support for older patients with congestive heart failure (CHF) significantly reduced readmission rates and may improve health outcomes, such as survival and Quality of Life, without increasing costs.

The ongoing suicide risk, particularly in recently discharged patients admitted for suicidal behaviour, with high levels of depression, hopelessness or impulsivity must be monitored at discharge and in the early weeks and months following discharge (Links *et al*, 2012). In conjunction with ongoing risk monitoring, clinicians should help clients to understand that, even after discharge, there remains much work to be done; that the recovery from suicide can take a considerable length of time; that the short inpatient stay for the suicidal crisis can be just the beginning of their holistic recovery. In conjunction with this is the need for the suicidology community to perhaps revisit what we consider to be an appropriate time frame for dealing with suicidality. There is a need to reflect how, for many suicidal patients (see for example, Maris, 1981; Beautrais, recovered 2007), a more useful and accurate perception of the formal mental healthcare response to high-risk suicidal clients would be to regard the inpatient care as the acute, crisis stabilisation necessary as a preface to a longer-term, community-based recovery period. In such a model, the suicidology community would then acknowledge that the majority of the recovery work is likely to be undertaken post-discharge.

Some support for such a conceptualisations can be found in the relevant theoretical and empirical literature. While acknowledging its vintage yet significant status, the work of Maris (1981), *Pathways to Suicide*, drew attention to the notion of suicidal careers. The central premise of his thesis was that individuals who took their own lives had long suicidal careers involving complex mixes of biological, social and psychological factors. More recently, Joiner's (2005) illuminating book contains three central premises: (1) That people who make a serious attempt to end their own lives feel real disconnection from others[2]; (2) They feel that they are a burden on others; and (3) *The ability to enact the lethal self-injury is acquired.* Relatedly, Beautrais' important work on looking at the trends and outcomes of all admissions for suicide attempts to a New Zealand hospital over ten years, reports similar findings. Beautrais (recovered 2007) argues that her results clearly show that suicidal behaviour, for many, is a chronic condition, not just a single, impulsive event, and rather worryingly, for many the situation doesn't change much following a suicide attempt, because people don't get the help they need. Beautrais concludes that suicide is a complex response by vulnerable people who need extensive long-term treatment, care and support.

Lastly, there would appear to be merit also in exploring and encouraging ways that recently discharged clients might engage in coping mechanisms and practices of self-soothing upon post-discharge. Overall, the post-discharge risk of suicide calls for a comprehensive preventative intervention to assist patients with the difficult and life-threatening transition back to life in their community.

---

2 Here the authors will not belabour the obvious parallels with the key finding in Cutcliffe and Stevenson's (2007) research: 'Reconnecting the person with humanity'.

Acknowledgements

Parts of this chapter were originally published in, and adapted from the following references:

Cutcliffe JR, Links PS, Harder HG, Balderson K, Bergmans Y, Eynan R, Ambreen M, Nisenbaum R, (2012) Understanding the risks of recent discharge. *Crisis*, **33**(1): 21–9.

Cutcliffe JR, Links PS, Ahern R, Ambreen M, Balderson K, Bergmans Y, Harder H, Nisenbaum R (2012) Understanding the risks of recent discharge: the phenomenological lived-experiences – "Trying to survive while living under the proverbial 'Sword of Damocles'". *Crisis.* Available on line = DOI: 10.1027/0227-5910/a000132

We wish to extend our most profound thanks to Hogrefe for permission to use this material.

Links PS, Nisenbaum M, Ambreen M, Balderson K, Bergmans Y, Eynan R, Harder H, Cutcliffe JR (2011) Prospective study of risk factors for increased suicide ideation and behavior following recent discharge. *General Hospital Psychiatry.* Available online doi:10.1016/j.physletb.2003.10.071

We not only wish to extend our most profound thanks to Elsevier for permission to use this material, but for more a more detailed explanation of these findings and much more, please do access and refer to this reference.

References

Appleby L, Shaw J, Amos T, *et al* (1999) Suicide within 12 months of contact with mental health services: national clinical survey. *British Medical Journal*, **318**: 1235–9.

Bagby RM, Parker JDA, Taylor GJ (1994) The twenty-item Toronto Alexithymia Scale – I: Item selection and cross-validation of the factor structure. *Journal of Psychosomatic Research*, **38**: 33–40.

Balogh R, Simpson A, Bond S (1995) Involving clients in clinical audits of mental health services. *International Journal of Quality in Healthcare*, **7**: 343–53.

Barratt ES, Stanford MS, Kent TA, Felthous, A (1997) Neuropsychological and cognitive psychophysiological substrates of impulsive aggression. *Biological Psychiatry*, **47**: 1045–61.

Bassett R (2010) Time to catch up: qualitative research in child and adolescent psychiatry. *Journal of the Canadian Academy of Child and Adolescent Psychiatry*, **19**(1): 2.

Beautrais A (recovered 2007) *Suicide Researcher Receives Top International Award.* http://www.chmeds.ac.nz/newsevents/articles/suicidetopaward.htm.

Beck AT, Ward CH, Mendelson M, Mock J, Erbaugh J (1961) An inventory for measuring depression. *Archives of General Psychiatry*, **4**: 561–71.

Beck AT, Weissman A, Lester D, Trexler L (1974) The measurement of pessimism: the hopelessness scale. *Journal of Consulting and Clinical Psychology*, **42**: 861–5.

Beck AT, Kovacs M, Weissman A (1979) Assessment of suicidal ideation: the scale for suicide ideation. *Journal of Consulting and Clinical Psychology*, **47**: 343–52.

Beck AT, Steer RA, Kovacs M, Garrison B (1985) Hopelessness and eventual suicide: a 10-year prospective study of patients hospitalized with suicidal ideation. *American Journal of Psychiatry*, **142**: 559–63.

Beck AT, Steer RA, Brown GK (1996) *Manual for the Beck Depression Inventory-II.* Psychological Corporation, San Antonio, TX.

Brown GK, Beck AT, Steer RA, Grisham JR (1994) Risk factors for suicide in psychiatric outpatients: a 20-year prospective study. *Journal of Consulting Clinical Psychology*, **68**(3): 371–7.

Bull MJ, Hanson HE, Gross CR (2000) A professional-patient partnership model of discharge planning with elders hospitalized with heart failure. *Applied Nursing Research*, **13**(1): 19–28.

Bunn MH, O'Connor AM, Tansey MS, *et al* (1997) Characteristics of clients with schizophrenia who express uncertainty about continuing treatment with depot neuroleptic medication. *Archives of Psychiatric Nursing*, **11**: 238–48.

Carter GL, Clover K, Whyte IM, Dawson AH, D'Este C (2005). Postcards from the Edge project: randomized controlled trial of an intervention using postcards to reduce repetition of hospital treated deliberate self poisoning. *British Medical Journal*, **331**: 805–10.

Carter GL, Clover K, Whyte IM., Dawson AH, D'Este C (2007) Postcards from the Edge: 24-month outcomes of a randomized controlled trial of hospital-treated self-poisoning. *British Journal of Psychiatry*, **191**: 548–53.

Colaizzi P (1978) Psychological research as the phenomenologist views it. In: Valle R, King M (eds.) *Existential Phenomenological Alternatives for Psychologists*. Oxford University Press, New York.

Cornes M, Clough R (2001) The Continuum of Care: older people's experiences of intermediate care. *Education and Ageing*, **16**(2): 179–202.

Cresswell JW, Plano Clark VL (2011) *Designing and Conducting Mixed Methods Research.* 2nd edn. Sage, Los Angeles.

Cutcliffe JR (2003) Research endeavours into suicide: a need to shift the emphasis. *British Journal of Nursing*, **12**(1): 92–99.

Cutcliffe JR, Harder H (2009) The perpetual search for parsimony: enhancing the epistemological and practical utility of qualitative research findings. *International Journal of Nursing Studies*, **46**: 1401–10 (doi:10.1016/jijnurstu200905005).

Cutcliffe JR, Ramcharan P (2002) Levelling the playing field: considering the 'ethics as process' approach for judging qualitative research proposals. *Qualitative Health Research*, **12**(7): 1000–10.

Cutcliffe JR, Stevenson C (2007) *Care of the Suicidal Person.* Churchill Livingstone/Elsevier, Edinburgh.

Cutcliffe JR, Links PS, Ahern R, Ambreen M, Balderson K, Bergmans Y, Harder H, Nisenbaum R (in press) Understanding the risks of recent discharge: the phenomenological lived-experiences – 'Existential angst at the prospect of discharge'. *Crisis* (accepted February 2011).

Department of Health (accessed 2010) *Intermediate Care and Integrated Discharge Planning/Care Pathways (LIN)* http://webarchive.nationalarchives.gov.uk/+/www.dh.gov.uk/en/Healthcare/IntegratedCare/ChangeAgentTeam/DH_4049393.

Dixon WA, Heppner PP, Burnett JW, Anderson WP (1993) Distinguishing among antecedents, concomitants and consequences of problem-solving appraisal and depressive symptoms. *Journal of Counseling Psychology*, **40**: 357–64.

Douglas BC, Noble LM, Newman SP (1999) Improving the accuracy of patients' expectations of the psychiatric out-patient consultation. *Psychiatric Bulletin*, **23**: 425–7.

Driscoll A (2001) Managing post-discharge care at home: an analysis of patients' and their carers' perceptions of information received during their stay in hospital. *Journal of Advanced Nursing*, **31**(5): 1165–73.

Fernando S, Storm V (1984) Suicide among psychiatric patients of a district hospital. *Psychological Medicine*, **14**: 661–72.

First MB, Spitzer RL, Gibbon M, Williams JBW (1997) *Structured Clinical Interview for DSMIV Axis-I Disorders: Patient Edition* (SCID-I/P, Version 20, 4/97 revision). Biometrics Research Department, New York State Psychiatric Institute, New York.

Geddes JR, Juszczak E (1995) Period trends in rate of suicide in first 28 days after discharge from psychiatric hospital in Scotland, 1968–92. *British Medical Journal*, **311**: 357–60.

Geddes JR, Juszczak E, O'Brien F, Kendrick S (1997) Suicide in the 12 months after discharge from psychiatric inpatient care, Scotland 1968–92. *Journal of Epidemiological Community Health*, **51**: 430–4.

Goldacre M, Seagrott V, Hawton K (1993) Suicide after discharge from psychiatric inpatient care. *Lancet*, **342**: 283–6.

Goldney RD (2002) Qualitative and quantitative approaches in suicidology: commentary. *Archives of Suicide Research*, **6**(1): 69–73.

Green J (2007) *Mixed Methods in Social Inquiry*. Wiley, San Francisco.

Heppner PP (1988) *The Problem Solving Inventory (PSI) – research manual*. Consulting Psychologists Press Inc., Palo Alto, CA.

Heppner PP, Peterson CH (1982) The development and implications of a personal problem solving inventory. *Journal of Counseling Psychology*, **29**(1): 66–75.

Ho TP (2003) The suicide risk of discharged psychiatric patients. *Journal of Clinical Psychiatry*, **64**: 702–7.

Ho TP (2006) Duration of hospitalization and post discharge suicide. *Suicide Life Threatening Behavior*, **36**(6): 682–8.

Joiner T (2005) *Why People Die by Suicide*. Harvard University Press, Cambridge, MA.

King CA, Segal H, Kaminski K, Naylor MW (1995) A prospective study of adolescent suicidal behavior following hospitalization. *Suicide and Life Threatening Behavior*, **25**(3): 327.

King EA, Baldwin DS, Sinclair JMA *et al* (2001) The Wessex recent in-patient suicide study, 1: Case-control study of 234 recently discharged psychiatric patient suicides. *British Journal of Psychiatry*, **178**: 531–6.

King EA, Baldwin DS, Sinclair JMA, Campbell MJ (2001) The Wessex recent in-patient suicide study, 2: Case-control study of 59 in-patient suicides. *British Journal of Psychiatry*, **17**: 537–42.

Kleiman S (2004) Phenomenology: to wonder and search for meanings. *Nurse Researcher*, **11**(4): 7–19.

Knox KL, Conwell Y, Caine ED (2004) If suicide is a public health problem, what are we doing to prevent it? *American Journal of Public Health*, **94**: 37–45.

Kvale S (1996) *Interviews: an Introduction to Qualitative Research Interviewing*. Sage, Thousand Oaks, CA.

Lawrence D, Holman CDJ, Jablensky AV *et al* (2001) Increasing rates of suicide in Western Australian psychiatric patients: a record linkage study. *Acta Psychiatrica Scandinavia*, **104**: 443–51.

Leenaars A (2002) Qualitative and quantitative approaches in suicidology: commentary. *Archives of Suicidology Research*, **6**(1): 69–73.

Lester D (2002) Qualitative versus quantitative studies in psychiatry: two examples of co-operation from suicidology. *Archives of Suicide Research*, **6**(1): 15–18.

Links P, Nisenbaum R, Ambreen M, Balderson K, Bergmans Y, Eynan R, Harder H, Cutcliffe JR (2012) Prospective study of risk factors for increased suicide ideation and behavior following recent discharge. *General Hospital Psychiatry*, **34**(1): 88–97.

McKenzie I, Wurr C (2001) Early suicide following discharge from psychiatric hospital. *Suicide and Life Threatening Behavior*, **31**(3): 358–63.

Maris RW (1981) *Pathways to Suicide*. Johns Hopkins University Press, Baltimore.

Marziali EA, Pilkonis PA (1986) The measurement of subjective response to stressful life events. *Journal of Human Stress*, **12**: 5–12.

Marziali EA (1987) People in your life: development of a social support measure for predicting psychotherapy outcome. *Journal of Nervous and Mental Disease*, **175**: 327–38.

Mountain G, Pighills A (2003) Pre-discharge home visits with older people: time to review practice. *Health and Social Care in the Community*, **11**(2): 146–54.

Morse JM (1995) The significance of saturation. *Qualitative Health Research*, **5**(2): 147–9.

Motto JA, Bostrom AG (2001) A randomized controlled trial of post-crisis suicide prevention. *Psychiatric Services*, **52**: 828–33.

Phillips CO, Wright SM, Kern DE, Singa RM, Shepperd S, Rubin HR (2004) Comprehensive discharge planning with post-discharge support for older patients with congestive heart failure: a meta-analysis. *Journal of the American Medical Association*, **291**(11): 1358–67.

Pirkola S, Sohlman B, Wahlbeck K (2005) The characteristics of suicides within a week of discharge after psychiatric hospitalization – a nationwide register study. *BMC Psychiatry*, **5**: 32.

Pokorny AD, Kaplan HB (1976) Suicide following psychiatric hospitalization. *Journal of Nervous and Mental Disease*, **162**(2): 119–25.

Qin P, Nordentoft M (2005) Suicide risk in relation to psychiatric hospitalization – evidence based on longitudinal registers. *Archives of General Psychiatry*, **62**: 427–32.

Ramcharan P, Cutcliffe JR (2001) Judging the ethics of qualitative research: considering the 'ethics as process' model. *Health and Social Care*, **9**(6): 358–67.

Schröder A, Larsson BW, Ahlström G (2007) Quality in psychiatric care: an instrument evaluating patients' expectations and experiences. *International Journal of Healthcare Quality Assurance*, **20**(2): 141–60.

Social Care Institute for Excellence (accessed 2010) SCIE Research Brief 12: *Involving Individual Older Patients and Their Carers in the Discharge Process From Acute to Community Care: Implications for Intermediate Care*. http://www.scie.org.uk/publications/briefings/briefing12/index.asp.

Taylor GJ (2000) Recent developments in alexithymia theory and research. *Canadian Journal of Psychiatry*, **45**: 134–42.

Taylor GJ, Bagby RM, Ryan DP, Parker JDA (1990) Validation of the alexithymia construct: a measurement-based approach. *Canadian Journal of Psychiatry*, **35**: 260–7.

Taylor GJ, Taylor HL (1997) Alexithymia. In: McCallum M, Piper W (eds.) *Psychological Mindedness: A Contemporary Understanding*. Lawrence Erlbaum, Mahwah, NJ.

Troister T, Links P, Cutcliffe JR (2008) Review of predictors of suicide within 1 year of discharge from a psychiatric hospital. *Current Psychiatry Reports*, **10**: 60–5.

Van Manen M (1997) *Researching Lived Experience: Human Science for Action Sensitive Pedagogy*. State University of New York Press, New York.

Van Manen M (2002) *Writing in the Dark: Phenomenological Studies in Interpretive Inquiry*. Althouse Press, London, Ontario.

Webster A (1992) The effect of pre-assessment information on clients' satisfaction, expectations and attendance at a mental health day centre. *British Journal of Medical Psychology*, **65**: 89–93.

Whitley R (2009) Introducing psychiatrists to qualitative research: a guide for instructors. *Academic Psychiatry*, **33**: 252–5.

Wilson EO (1998) *Consilience: The Unity of Knowledge*. Little, Brown &Co, London.

White J (2003) *Report on the Workshop on Suicide-related Research in Canada*. Health Canada/CIHR, Ottawa.

Yim PHW, Yip PSF, Li RHY *et al* (2004) Suicide after discharge from psychiatric inpatient care: a case-control study in Hong Kong. *Australian and New Zealand Journal of Psychiatry*, **38**(1–2): 65–72.

CHAPTER 11

Dealing with the aftermath of suicide – mental health practitioners as suicide survivors and exploring required support systems

The most authentic thing about us is our capacity to create, to overcome, to endure, to transform, to love and to be greater than our suffering. (Ben Okri, recovered 2012, http://thinkexist.com/quotations/suicide/)

Introduction

It is both interesting and disturbing to note that only a limited literature exists regarding practitioners' reactions to loss of a client due to suicide, very little of which focuses on Psychiatric/Mental Health nurses or general nurses. When one considers the worldwide prevalence of suicide and the estimates of how many people are affected by a single suicide (numbers ranging from 6 to 28), the under-developed nature of this associated literature is a puzzle. The 'immaturity' of this literature may be all the more counter-intuitive given the increasing attention since the 1980s to 'Suicide Survivors' *per se*. Conceptual and methodological limitations notwithstanding, the extant studies on mental health clinicians' exposure to suicidal behaviours indicates the following: Psychiatric/Mental Health nurses report rates of 58.3% (Itoh, 2006) and 32.4% (Itoh, 2005). For psychotherapists this exposure was found to be around 33% and for psychiatrists a figure of 51% was discovered (Valente, 1994). However, some authors have advanced the argument that these figures may be significant understatements (see for example Ruskin *et al*, 2004).

There exists a widely accepted and fairly well developed body of work that shows how a completed suicide can lead to a variety of mental health challenges for 'survivors' of a suicide – including increasing the survivor's own risk of suicide (Jobes *et al*, 2000). So when one considers how practitioners working in mental health settings (eg. P/MH nurses, psychiatrists, psychologists, theologians [ministers/priests etc.], general nurses etc.) can and do form close relationships with suicidal people, there is a logical intuitive position that the death by suicide of a person under one's care can have major effects on the (mental) health and wellbeing of the practitioner. Accordingly, this chapter begins by examining and problematising the definitions and conceptualisations of Suicide Survivors and goes on to make the case for considering that mental health practitioners who lose a client to suicide can be thought of as Suicide Survivors. The chapter then focuses on embracing (and ultimately implementing) Clinical Supervision as one means to help such practitioners deal and cope with their reactions to client suicide. The chapter closes by examining the case for regarding a client's suicide as a Critical Incident, and goes on to make the case for the potential utility in providing Critical Incident Debriefing in such instances.

Definitions and conceptualisations of suicide survivors: phenomenologically defined?

Examination of the extant literature will show that arriving at a precise, concise and widely accepted definition of 'suicide survivor' has proved to be difficult. Consequently, it should be noted that the international suicidology community is currently unable to provide answers to the question: who is (and inversely is not) a Suicide Survivor? Nevertheless, attempts have been made to answer this (and related) question(s). An early and important, though not empirically based, estimate/contribution to this body of knowledge, is that of McIntosh (1996)[1], who posited that there would be at least six people intimately affected by each suicide, and this figure continues to be cited by some senior suicidology scholars (see for example Hawton and Simkins, 2003). More recent research undertaken by a significant contributor to the Suicide Survivor literature (and so-called Suicide Survivor movement), Dr Frank Campbell, found that up to 28 people who had a relationship with the deceased have sought treatment at one crisis centre following a completed suicide (Campbell, 1997, Campbell and Cataldie, 2003). The American Foundation for Suicide Prevention/National Institute of Mental Health (NIMH) (recovered 2012) have argued that the 'early' estimates of 'survivors' impacted by a completed suicide are likely to be underestimates, and as a result they made an articulate case for the need to undertake well-designed epidemiological studies to determine how many survivors there are, what their characteristics are, and what they need.

1 For the authors of this book this is perhaps a conservative estimate.

In order to maximise the validity and utility of such epidemiological studies, it would be necessary to undertake some conceptual work in order to define the population. When one considers the remarks posed by Jobes *et al* (2000, p. 538), who state,

> In our view, no-one can externally or arbitrarily define who is a survivor and who is not a survivor; there can be no rigid or strict definition of the term,

this does not appear to be a straightforward task. In the 'early' estimations referenced above and some other estimates, it was common practice to require 'blood ties' or 'familial ties' in order to be counted as a Suicide Survivor. While these preliminary conceptualisations served as a useful starting point, more contemporary thinking on this issue has widened considerably the nature of the qualifiers required to be counted as a Suicide Survivor. It seems reasonable to posit that some form of connection, association, bond or relationship between the deceased and the survivor is necessary in order to 'qualify' as a Suicide Survivor. This raises the next problematic question: can we (and if so how) identify if and when such a connection, association, bond or relationship exists? Cutcliffe and Stevenson (2007) have proposed that it is likely, if not inevitable, that the presence and experience of such connections is likely to be a qualitative phenomenon; they are likely to be social constructs and thus not necessarily amenable to quantification.

By way of an example, we wish to draw upon a 'real world' example that, unfortunately, is all too commonly encountered, namely the death by suicide of a teenage high school student. Not only would one expect that the deceased's immediate family and close friends would be counted as Suicide Survivors, but school suicides often send waves or 'ripples' throughout the school. The suicide can and does impact on fellow students, teachers, coaches and teaching assistants (Society for the Prevention of Teen Suicide, recovered 2012). Similarly, support staff, secretaries and maintenance staff can be affected.

Broadening our thinking a little further, it can be seen that such a High School suicide can also affect parents of 'surviving' students, school boards, educational authorities, and members of the student's local community. It is also noteworthy that effects from the suicide can be experienced irrespective of whether or not there was a direct 'tie' or connection with the deceased. Interestingly, even models of Suicide Survivors that require some form of connection or tie between the deceased and the survivor have limitations given that these conceptualisations will not include the innocent bystander or first responder who may witness the suicide or discover the body of someone following the suicide of someone unknown to them (Cutcliffe *et al*, 2007). So whether one adopts views of Suicide Survivors such as those put forward by the American Foundation for Suicide Prevention (AFSP, 2003) and the National Institute of Mental Health (NIMH, 2003)[2], or adopts the more capacious, inclusive views espoused by Campbell (2003), Cutcliffe *et al* (2007) and others, it is abundantly clear that mental health practitioners who lose a client to suicide can be classified themselves as Suicide Survivors. This is even more the case when one considers that defining someone as a survivor of a suicide may actually be a phenomenologically defined 'state'; it is defined by the individual's own response (or indeed lack of response) to the suicide (Cutcliffe *et al*, 2007).

The impact of a suicide on practitioners: mental health clinicians as suicide survivors

The stress of working clinically with suicidal people has been well documented (Fothergill *et al*, 2004; Happell *et al*, 2003; Lauvrud *et al*, 2009; National Institute for Occupational Health and Safety [NIOHS], recovered 2011; Robinson *et al*, 2003; Spiegel, 1975) and the unfortunate truth depicted by the clinical evidence is that, despite our best efforts, some of the suicidal people under our care may well go on to complete suicide; either during their formal care episode or within the first year after discharge (Appleby *et al*, 1999; Geddes and Juszczak, 1995; Geddes *et al*, 1997; Goldacre *et al*, 1993; Ho, 2003; Lawrence, 2001; Pirkola *et al*, 2005; Troister *et al*, 2008; Yim *et al*, 2004). Such is the incidence that Jobes and Berman (1993) found that approximately one half of psychiatrists and one quarter of psychologists will lose at least one person to suicide during the course of their careers[3]. In addition to the stress of caring for suicidal people, the stress of losing a suicidal person is understandably worse given the sense of 'failure' that often occurs in such situations. Despite this documented evidence, healthcare organisations sometimes overlook the impact of a specific event on health professionals.

According to Sudak (2007), the effect of a patient's suicide will be quantitatively less than what the immediate family will undergo, but it will be qualitatively quite similar. A patient's suicide typically evokes a range of emotions and other symptoms in the practitioner, including denial, shock, disbelief, guilt,

2 The AFSP (20003) and the NIMH (2003) refer to identifying persons who have known someone who has died by suicide.

3 Interestingly, despite their high level of contact with suicidal people, the authors could find only limited data pertaining to P/MH nurses.

sense of failure, worthlessness, loss of confidence in oneself, sadness or insomnia (Valente and Saunders, 2002; Takahashi *et al*, 2011). These experiences can also lead to depression and post-traumatic stress disorder (PTSD).

Jobes *et al* (2000) provide a useful summary of the effects that have been reported in clinicians who have lost a suicidal client, including:

- high levels of intrusive thoughts relating to patient suicide
- avoidance of situations that might remind the clinician of suicide
- stress levels roughly equivalent to bereaved patients
- self-blame and guilt, particularly about their role in the suicidal person's care
- loss of confidence in their professional competence
- fear of losing face standing with professional colleagues
- fear of possible malpractice suits from relatives
- a refusal to 'treat' or work with other suicidal people.

Similar findings have been reported by Takahashi *et al* (2011) who refer to nurses becoming afraid of interacting in similar (future) situations, and Valente and Saunders (2002) who refer to developing fears of malpractice or lawsuit(s). 'Clinician Survivors' are also caught in a confusing set of rules and suggestions over how to respond to family questions following the suicide of a patient (Campbell, 2006)[4]. While in some healthcare organisations, little attention appears to be given to these effects, in a study conducted by Takahashi *et al* (2011) most of the nurses indicated the desire for mental healthcare programs targeted at healthcare workers who have experienced a shocking event in the hospital. Nurses also believed that the timely implementation of appropriate mental healthcare programs for nursing staff who have been through a patient suicide is a significant part of creating an effective healthcare environment. Unfortunately,

> contrary to supporting the bereaved clinicians, in some cases the corporate institutions reacted toward them with hostility, as if investigating a clinical wrongdoing. In the hands of personnel, even physician or nursing colleagues acting for the administration, a review might take on the characteristics of an inquisition (Ruskin *et al*, 2004, p. 109).

4 In the USA, several jurisdictions are developing 'Apology Laws' to allow the clinician to express a statement of condolence without that statement being used as a declaration of liability and then used against the physician in a wrongful death suit (Campbell, 2006). Although such a normal response to death of a patient and the offer to help the family in their grief is quite acceptable in most countries, it is often restricted in the USA by professional associations, and malpractice insurance carriers (Campbell, 2006).

Despite the fact that most nurses are aware of the need for staff-oriented mental healthcare services, systematic post-suicide mental healthcare programs for nurses are rarely available (Takahashi *et al*, 2011). In some cases, nurses withdrew at a time when they most needed assistance (Ruskin *et al*, 2004).

Some authors make recommendations for additional support and assessment and/or further specific skills training, namely Clinical Supervision, individual and group support or counselling, workshops on suicide prevention and post-suicide bereavement, formal assessment and policies for patients with suicide risk, emphasis on nurses' assessment of suicidal patients and standard suicide-risk evaluation procedures (Long and Reid, 1996). A milieu with individual and group support can help mental health staff share their fears, feelings and grief without fear or censure. Indeed, mental health practitioners need a support system to help them cope with their grief and reduce self-blame and excess responsibility (Valente and Saunders, 2002). The authors wholeheartedly concur with this view and posit that embracing and ultimately implementing Clinical Supervision would be just such a support system.

Mental health practitioners and completed suicide: the case for Clinical Supervision

According to the United States NIOHS (recovered 2011) occupational stress has been a longstanding concern of the healthcare sector. There is also a growing body of evidence highlighting how the particular challenges associated with mental healthcare contribute to practitioners having high rates of psychological distress, psychological burnout, absenteeism, employee intent to leave, lowered quality of life and increased incidence of diagnosis/treatment errors and reduced patient satisfaction (Spiegel, 1975; Happell *et al*, 2003; Fothergill *et al*, 2004; Lauvrud *et al*, 2009; Robinson *et al*, 2003). This evidence also shows that prolonged exposure to unrelenting and untreated stress has been linked with more severe negative outcomes in these variables. There is, however, a limited body of evidence[5] which shows that work-directed interventions can be effective in reducing burnout, stress and general symptoms in healthcare workers (see Marine *et al*, 2011). Moreover, the practice of providing high-quality and regular Clinical Supervision to mental health practitioners has been shown to help reduce practitioner stress levels, lower psychological burn out, reduce clinician absenteeism, increase

5 Limited in terms of the breadth of the body of work, the size of the individual studies and as a result of the methodological limitations evident in the individual studies.

job satisfaction and improve the quality of the care provided, resulting in better outcomes for patients/clients (Hallberg and Norberg, 1993; Berg *et al*, 1994; Butterworth *et al*, 1997; Cutcliffe and Epling, 1997; Holm *et al*, 1998, 2003; Berg and Hallberg, 1999; Cutcliffe and McFeely, 2001; Severinnson, 2001; Jones, 2003, 2009; Alleyne and Jumaa, 2007; Walker, 2009; White and Winstanley, 2010). Thus it can be seen that mental healthcare is a particularly high stress occupation and that there is an albeit limited body of evidence that shows how introducing formal Clinical Supervision is an intervention which can help address these related issues and improve outcomes for patients/clients (see Happell *et al*, 2003; Marine *et al*, 2011). As we have indicated previously in this chapter, a range of reactions to losing a client to suicide have been found in mental health practitioners (Collins, 2003; Hendin *et al*, 2000; Sudak, 2007; Darden and Rutter, 2011): shock, grief, guilt, fear of blame, self-doubt, shame, anger, betrayal and stress have all (not surprisingly) been reported. As a result, there appears to be obvious and logical utility in the highly therapeutic role that Clinical Supervision can play in helping mental health practitioners deal with their emotional challenges arising from losing a client to suicide.

What is Clinical Supervision? An overview

Given the very limited engagement with and participation in Clinical Supervision by nurses (and nursing) in US contemporary healthcare, it may be surprising to note that the USA is the birth place of Clinical Supervision (Wolf, 1941; Day, 1925; Schmidt, 1926; Freeman, 1952; Yegdich, 1999)[6]. Clinical Supervision is now much more of a genuine 'global phenomenon'; more countries (eg. Sweden, Finland, Norway, UK, New Zealand, Ireland, Australia, Canada) have embraced Clinical Supervision within various domains of practice and in a variety of clinical disciplines (eg. nursing, clinical psychology, social work, substance use/misuse counsellors, medicine). International interest in Clinical Supervision has grown significantly during the last three decades and several countries now have Clinical Supervision embedded formally in their healthcare systems (Lynch *et al*, 2011; Berggren and Severinsson, 2011; Gilbert and Cutcliffe, 2011; Arthur and Russell-Mayhew, 2011) where it is regarded as a strategy to decrease occupational stress, improve job satisfaction and simultaneously enhance the quality of care provided to consumers.

---

6 Some would argue that it still leads the rest of the world in certain areas of Clinical Supervision practice (eg. the USA Navy and Marine Corps Clinical Preceptorship Program, recovered May 2011).

The authors' position on Clinical Supervision

The first author has, together with colleagues (Cutcliffe *et al*, 2001, 2010) argued previously that there is no single correct or 'best' way to carry out Clinical Supervision and no single definition that captures all its features, nuances and elements. Both authors of this book regard these previous statements as accurate. While a universally applicable definition of Clinical Supervision remains both elusive and (arguably) unnecessary, here the authors draw upon Cutcliffe *et al*'s (2001) views of the necessary constituent elements required in Clinical Supervision. In essence, these elements then indicate what Clinical Supervision is and simultaneously what it is not. The authors' views of the constituent elements of Clinical Supervision are listed in Box 11.1.

The terminology of Clinical Supervision

The literature contains two principal, though broad, conceptualisations (categories) of Clinical Supervision. The term Clinical Supervision is used by some to refer to relationship(s) between an administrator, superior and/or more experienced clinician and a more junior 'other' (the supervisee). This conceptualisation implies that the supervisor has a 'supervisory responsibility' for the performance of the supervisee. This category also includes Clinical Supervision, whereby case conferences or caseload matters are the focus and practitioners receive support and guidance concerning how they are performing. Where Clinical Supervision follows this format it is similar to 'managerial or administrative supervision' for the purposes of satisfying the information needs of line managers. Where the approach to Clinical Supervision concentrates predominantly on case presentations and general caseload issues (Dudley and Butterworth, 1994; Swain, 1995; Scanlon and Weir 1997; Davidson, 1998) then the Clinical Supervision centres on patient treatment options, pathways and clinical decisions (eg. how care could be planned differently and what options are open to the practitioner.)

The second category conceptualises Clinical Supervision as that of a supportive, developmental and educative interpersonal process that focuses on supervisee-led issues (Johns, 1996, 1998; Cutcliffe and Epling, 1997; Cutcliffe and Burns, 1998; Scanlon and Weir, 1997). In addition to focusing on case specific matters, the range of issues to be considered is much broader (eg. conflict with colleagues and how this impacts on care, issues arising from interactions with clients and/or relatives, how to deal with the 'emotional baggage' (see Barker, 1999) that results from engaging in demanding interpersonal work. In such conceptualisations the Supervisor does not (necessarily) occupy a position of authority or seniority. Interestingly, this conceptualisation of Clinical Supervision is by far the closest in

Box 11.1 The constituent elements of Clinical Supervision

Clinical Supervision is necessarily:

- supportive
- safe, because of clear, negotiated agreements by all parties with regard to the extent and limits of confidentiality
- centred on developing best practice for service users
- brave, because practitioners are encouraged to talk about the realities of their practice
- a chance to talk about difficult areas of work in an environment where the person attempts to understand
- an opportunity to ventilate emotion without comeback
- an opportunity to deal with material and issues that practitioners may have been carrying for many years (the chance to talk about issues which cannot easily be talked about elsewhere and which may have been previously unexplored)
- not to be confused with or amalgamated with managerial supervision
- not to be confused with or amalgamated with personal therapy/counselling
- a regular, scheduled occurrence
- an activity that requires 'protected time and space'
- offered equally to all practitioners
- involves a committed relationship (from both parties)
- separate and distinct from preceptorship or mentorship
- a facilitative relationship
- challenging
- an invitation to be self-monitoring and self-accountable
- at times hard work and at others enjoyable
- involves learning to be reflective and becoming a reflective practitioner
- an activity that continues throughout one's working life

Reproduced from Cutcliffe *et al* (2011) with the kind permission from Routledge

form, theory and practice to the earliest conceptualisation of Clinical Supervision that originated in the USA during the first half of the 20th century. These seminal works and pioneering ideas were very clear about the nature, purpose and value of Clinical Supervision. For Wolf (1941), Clinical Supervision had to occur in a *wholesome atmosphere of informality* (emphasis added). For Day (1925) and Schmidt (1926), Clinical Supervision *had to be focused on professional growth and development* (emphasis added). And Freeman's (1952) position regarding Clinical Supervision *was that it must be geared towards permissiveness and support* (emphasis added). As a result, all these seminal contributions either alluded to or made specific reference to the important idea that clinical practitioners needed to take care of themselves, especially if they intended to provide effective care to the patients/clients. Furthermore, this necessity for taking care of oneself as a practitioner was necessary as a result of the cumulative emotional load that caring for people can and does create (Robinson *et al*, 2003).

Availability of Clinical Supervision

There is widespread variation in availability and organisation of Clinical Supervision. Availability of Clinical Supervision for practitioners varies from scenarios where no Clinical Supervision is offered to situations where practitioners engage in regular, protected Clinical Supervision (Kingsbury and Allsopp, 1994; Herriot *et al*, 1994; Panayitou and Fotherby, 1996). Surveys conducted tend to indicate that current Clinical Supervision delivery is inadequate. Surveys of physicians of various levels of seniority indicated that for each level, the Clinical Supervision provided was inadequate and insufficient (Davies and Campbell, 1995; Little, 1995; Panayiotou and Fotherby, 1996). Similar findings were discovered in a large postal, questionnaire-based survey of nurses; 29% of respondents reported working in a structure whereby they had an identified Clinical Supervision (Fowler and Chevannes, 1998). There is some evidence which indicates how access to Clinical Supervision varies significantly between different professional groups and in across/between different units/hospitals. Brocklehurst's (1997a,b,c) surveys, Redfern *et al*'s (1997) review and other literature (see for example, Watkins, 1995) each highlight how, for the most part, it is in mental health and learning disability units that Clinical Supervision appears to be more established. Clinicians who are based in or on what are characterised as 'innovative/progressive units' (eg. so-called 'Nursing Development Units') appear to have greater access to Clinical Supervision then other nursing units, perhaps because such units encourage and support innovation, progressive developments and attempt to focus on and promote contemporary, evidence-based practice (Redfern *et al*, 1997).

Barriers to the uptake of Clinical Supervision

A variety of factors have been reported as direct or/and indirect impediments to the successful implementation of Clinical Supervision into a healthcare organisation, including time constraints, views of Clinical Supervision as a low priority, lack of adequate numbers of (particularly adequately trained/skilled/experienced) supervisors, organisational changes and unrest, and shortage of suitable facilities/ accommodation for holding Clinical Supervision sessions. The barrier reported most commonly in the extant literature is that of time constraints, with requests for Clinical Supervision sessions having to be considered within the context of 'heavy' workloads, requests/demands for competing meetings and shortages of clinical staff (Johns, 1996; Scanlon and Weir, 1997; Bishop, 1998). Some resistance has been documented to protecting the time allocated to Clinical Supervision (Lilley, 1996; Johns, 1998; May *et al*, 1997; Nicklin, 1997; Sams, 1997; Bishop, 1998). Resistance to taking up and engaging in Clinical Supervision appears to arise from lack of knowledge of the purpose and nature of Clinical Supervision (Bishop, 1998; Cutcliffe and Proctor, 1998; May *et al*, 1997; Sams, 1997; Yegdich, 1999). In the absence of this clear conceptual understanding, administrators and managers are unsure of how it 'fits' with service priorities and question the time and cost needed for implementation (see also Bishop, 1998).

Practitioners' reasons for not attending Clinical Supervision include distrust of supervisor, not perceived as needed, not perceived as a high priority and staff shortages (Sams, 1997; Yegdich, 1999; Cutcliffe and Hyrkas, 2006). There is some evidence that supervisees feel guilty about 'taking the time out' for Clinical Supervision (Johns, 1997; Bishop, 1998). The literature also identified how insufficient supervisors are available, both in terms of the overall number and in terms of training/preparation, to meet the demand for Clinical Supervision. This problem of limited availability of adequately prepared/trained supervisors is exacerbated when organisations insist on hierarchical, 'pyramidal' or 'cascade' models of providing Clinical Supervision.

Lastly, in this section, the literature indicates the barrier(s) to successful Clinical Supervision that arise from inappropriate environmental conditions. Various authors have reported the lack of suitable accommodation to host Clinical Supervision sessions (Johns, 1996, 1998; Butterworth *et al*, 1997; Fyffe, 1997; May *et al*, 1997; Bishop, 1998; Dunn and Bishop, 1998).

The economic cost of Clinical Supervision

Unfortunately, the economic costs and benefits of Clinical Supervision have received only scant attention (Hyrkäs *et al*, 2001a,b; White and Winstanley, 2006). Dudley and Butterworth (1994) calculated the overall cost per session of team Clinical Supervision, in addition to the cost per participation/per session. Benefits were calculated in terms of patient cases examined. Methodological limitations notwithstanding, Dudley and Butterworth (1994) concluded that the cost of Clinical Supervision was not particularly high, especially when the reported benefits to nursing care were factored in. Supporting findings were discovered in the Finnish study to ascertain the costs and benefits of Clinical Supervision (see Kukkola, 1990) where the costs of team Clinical Supervision were found to be (regarded as) an efficient and 'sound' financial investment. Lastly, the attempt by Hyrkäs *et al* (2001a,b) to produce a cost–benefit algorithm for team supervision also found that team supervision was economical.

The quality of Clinical Supervision

A number of variables have been linked with influencing the quality of Clinical Supervision including: the preparation/training and overall quality of the supervisors; the quality of and degree of convergence within the supervisory relationship; and the degree to which a shared understanding of Clinical Supervision exists between supervisor and supervisee. Interestingly, there was unanimity in the literature regarding how the success (or otherwise) of the Clinical Supervision was dependent upon the degree of preparation/training and overall quality of the supervisors, although it is also accurate to point out that no consensus currently exists with regard to how much and what form/type of training/preparation is necessary to produce high-quality supervisors (Bishop, 1998; Butterworth *et al*, 1997; Cutcliffe and Fowler, 2011; Fyffe, 1997; Sloan, 2011).

There is some agreement in the literature concerning the relationship between the quality/duration of the Clinical Supervision preparation experience and the efficacy of Clinical Supervision subsequently offered by the practitioner. Similarly, preliminary arguments have been advanced that suggest short Clinical Supervision preparation courses are unlikely to produce well-prepared, highly effective supervisors – who in turn would not be able to deliver the quality of Clinical Supervision necessary to produce significant positive outcomes or improvements in practitioner wellbeing and client outcomes (Cutcliffe and Fowler, 2011; Sloan, 2011; Sloan and Fleming, 2011).

In order to deliver successful and effective supervision, supervisors need a range of specific skills and qualities (Bagnall *et al*, 2011; Johns, 1996, 1998, Cutcliffe and Fowler, 2011; Fyffe, 1997; Scanlon and Weir, 1997; Dunn and Bishop, 1998). These include the ability to form and maintain interpersonal relationships (Fyffe, 1997); treat the supervisee with respect (Watkins, 1997); promote personal responsibility and accountability in the supervisee (Challis *et al*, 1998); provide constructive feedback (Eaton *et al*, 1998); encourage the supervisee to engage in reflection (Bagnall *et al*, 2011); provide gentle confrontation skills (Cutcliffe and

Epling, 1997); maintain confidentiality (Johns, 1996, 1998; Fyffe, 1997; Scanlon and Weir 1997); and provide facilitation skills (Johns, 1996, 1998, Cutcliffe and Fowler, 2011; Fyffe, 1997). However, the same literature highlights how the presence of 'technical' skills in the supervisor does not appear to be sufficient on its own; the skills have to be accompanied (or embedded in) specific qualities such as empathy, (reciprocal) trust, support, compassion and flexibility. Rogerian or 'person-centered' core qualities are also frequently cited as necessary (but not sufficient) for effective supervision (see for example, Butterworth *et al*, 1997; Johns, 1998; Bagnall *et al*, 2011).

The degree of convergence within the Clinical Supervision relationship has been linked with the quality of the experience and the overall effectiveness of the Clinical Supervision, though it should be noted that there is currently no widespread consensus evident on this issue. One recurring theme in the literature is the value that arises when the supervisee and supervisor share a common set of beliefs and values; a common 'philosophy' so to speak (Fyffe, 1997; Scanlon and Weir, 1997).

The effectiveness of Clinical Supervision

The most developed body of work in this area is that of the qualitative, idiographic case study research and narrative accounts. The following issues/areas have a reasonably robust qualitative evidence-base: improved outcomes for clients as a result of the practitioner receiving effective and high-quality Clinical Supervision (Smith, 2001); practitioners feeling a much needed sense of support when they experience high-quality Clinical Supervision (Cutcliffe and McFeely, 2001; Jones, 2003, 2009); stress management (and reduction) (Alleyne and Jumaa, 2007); increases in self-awareness in practitioners (Cutcliffe and Epling, 1997; Marrow *et al*, 1997; Severinnson, 2001; Holm *et al*, 1998, 2003); relief of intra-personal angst such as feelings of guilt and inadequacy (Severinnson, 2001; Holm *et al*, 1998, 2003); and Clinical Supervision as a mechanism to improve an organisation's recruitment and retention of clinical staff (Akerjordet and Severinsson, 2004; Lynch and Happell, 2008; Walker, 2009; White and Winstanley, 2010).

There is a body of work that reports improvements in measurable phenomena as a result of engaging in Clinical Supervision, although most of these refer to 'improvements' in the practitioner rather than in the patients/clients cared for. A recent and comprehensive systematic review (Brunero and Stein-Parbury, 2008) indicates that benefits from receiving Clinical Supervision can be grouped under each area of Proctor's (2001) model of Clinical Supervision, namely 'normative' area (professional accountability and personal ethical), formative area (skills and

Box 11.2 Normative aspects of post-suicide Clinical Supervision

- Ethical issues/aspects – what ethical issues were relevant, considered and how were these resolved?
- Professional responsibilities:
  - (a) method, frequency and adequacy of suicide risk assessment
  - (b) suicide risk assessment using a formal instrument?
  - (c) were appropriate actions, interventions and safe guards 'put in place'
  - (d) familiarity with and adherence to local and national suicide prevention policies
- Examination and personal review of previous/prior training and/or education for suicide risk assessment, care of the suicidal person, and contemporary evidence-based and 'best practice' for suicidal people.
- Examination and personal review of the practitioner's moral response to the suicidal person and suicidal act.
- Juxtaposition of one's practice and responses to the suicidal person and the duties/responsibilities owed under one's professional code of conduct.

Box 11.3 Formative aspects of post-suicide Clinical Supervision

- Explore, review and critique (highlighting both strengths and limitations) of the interpersonal actions and interventions undertaken during one's care of the suicidal person.
- Consider and explore – what might you do differently next time (if anything) if this is to occur in a 'blame free' interpersonal environment.
- Consider and explore – what have you learned as a result of this experience?
- Consider and explore – what educational, personal/professional support needs has this experience identified for you?
- How and in what ways has this experience made you more/less confident in working with suicidal people? What can be done to assist you with this – increase your confidence?

- How would you suggest the healthcare organisation, hospital, ward, unit etc. evolve (if at all) as a way to improve the care provided to suicidal people?
- What 'new', 'original' or creative ideas for working with suicidal people has this experience highlighted for you?
- How, if at all, might you have enhanced your care of the suicidal person in terms of developing greater insight, enhanced therapeutic use of self and enhanced communication skills?

Box 11.4 Restorative aspects of post-suicide Clinical Supervision

- Ensure that as a Clinical Supervisor, one listens to the supervisee and demonstrates that one is attending and empathising.
- Ensure that the Clinical Supervisor offers support, compassion and understanding.
- Explore with the supervisee – what types of support/help the supervisee wants/needs – both within and outside of the organisation.
- Explore ways that the supervisee intends to cope with the experience.

knowledge acquisition) and restorative area (personal, collegial and professional support).

Normative area gains include outcomes such as increased understanding of professional issues and roles; increased moral sensitivity; and deeper understanding and more thorough application of professional codes.

Formative area gains include outcomes such as deeper/more thorough knowledge of problems/issues; increased self-confidence; enhanced engagement in the workplace; increased competence and creativity; greater insight into therapeutic use of self; and enhanced communication skills.

Restorative area gains include outcomes such as increased ability to listen and offer support; improved coping skills; better relationships amongst staff; lower perceived anxiety; increase in empathy; improved relationships with colleagues; reduced burn-out; reduced conflict; and reduced absence/'sick time' (absenteeism).

One area of the extant literature where there is a clear dearth of studies is that of research that attempts to measure improvements in patient/client care that occur from practitioners who receive and engage in Clinical Supervision, though it is accurate to note that a small number of studies do exist (see for example Kilminster and Jolly, 2000). This emerging evidence base indicates that clinical practice and patient/client outcomes, in a variety of clinical-focused disciplines (eg. physicians, nurses, psychotherapists) can suffer in the absence of Clinical Supervision (McKee and Black, 1992; Fallon *et al*, 1993; Gennis and Gennis, 1993; Little, 1996; Edberg *et al*, 1996, 1999; Sox *et al*, 1998), that 'healthy' mental health practitioners deliver care that results in increased patient satisfaction, and that practice outcomes for patients can improve when the clinicians receive and engage in Clinical Supervision (Butterworth *et al*, 1997; White and Roche, 2006; White and Winstanley, 2010). However, methodological limitations, relatively small effect sizes and the limited number of studies conducted mean that this is a substantive area that is in need of additional robust and rigorous evaluation studies.

Staying with Proctor's (2001) model, it is possible to explore and subsequently posit the likely areas, aspects or elements of post suicide Clinical Supervision. While these are tentative, the authors wish to posit a preliminary 'framework' which could serve as the basis for dealing with post-suicide issues in Clinical Supervision. This tentative framework is outlined in Boxes 11.2, 11.3 and 11.4.

Mental health practitioners and completed suicide: the case for critical incident debriefing

Few, if any, credible clinicians or academics would advance the argument that a client's death by suicide does not constitute a critical incident. Even though there does not appear to be a universally-accepted definitive list, examination of a broad range of critical incident definitions and policies clearly indicates a very broad consensus regarding suicide as such an incident. For example, broad conceptualisations (and definitions) refer to a critical incident (or acute stress response) as

> a powerful and overwhelming event that lies outside the range of usual human experience. (Antai-Otong, 2001, p. 127)

Soloman of the International Training Academy for Linguistics and Kinetics (recovered 2012) refers to a critical incident as situation(s) that fall outside of the person's range of usual experience, to the extent that the person feels overwhelmed and vulnerable and has a lack of control over the situation. Clinical Professor, Emergency Health Services, University of Maryland and President Emeritus, International Critical Incident Stress Foundation Dr Jeff Mitchell (National Center for Crisis Management, recovered 2012) describes critical incidents in first responders as

> Any situation faced by emergency service personnel that causes them to experience unusually strong emotional reactions which have the potential to interfere with their ability to function either at the scene or later.

Other descriptions refer to situations that might present a risk of significant bodily harm, property damage, or some form of legal (attorney) involvement. Some universities now have critical incident response policies which invariably include definitions or examples of critical incidents. According to the University of Washington (recovered 2012) policy, a critical incident is:

> ... any event that causes an unusually intense stress reaction. The distress people experience after a critical incident limits their ability to cope, impairs their ability to adjust, and negatively impacts the work environment. Examples of traumatic events that produce such reactions include:
>
> - A coworker's or student's death or serious illness,
> - Suicide,
> - A violent or threatening incident in the work setting,
> - Natural or man-made disaster that affects the workers' ability to function in the workplace.

Similarly, some police departments, fire departments, emergency paramedics and other so-called first responders have similar definitions and policies whereby critical incidents are regarded as dramatic events and/or events that result in a range of (stress-related) debilitating responses/conditions. For example, Australian (New South Wales) police departments now routinely use 'staff psychologists' to debrief the individual – most often within 72 hours of a critical incident (Leonard and Alison, 1999). Clearly, there appears to be significant consensus within the literature that such critical incidents have the potential to affect or seriously upset an individual in a variety of ways, to the extent that this leads to changes in the person's emotional, cognitive or behavioural functioning. For the authors of this book, Mitchell provides a parsimonious yet contextually accurate statement about the stress resulting from critical incidents when he refers to this being a normal reaction to an abnormal event. Indeed, one can find this phrase occurring with conspicuous regularity within the associated post-traumatic stress disorder literature. It is interesting to note that even for a discipline/profession that frequently encounters high stress-provoking situations such as the police force or our armed forces, in all of the literature the authors have located emanating from these disciplines regarding critical incident stress and debriefing, incidents of suicide (and suicide attempts) are commonly regarded as an example of a critical incident.

Given the frequency of client suicide during hospitalisation (or in the year immediately following discharge), and if one accepts a client's suicide as a critical incident for (mental) healthcare practitioners (as we do), then one could be forgiven for expecting there to be a significant and well-developed body of literature in this area. This is not the case. Several authors have pointed out[7] (see for Alexander *et al*, 2000; Akechi *et al*, 2003) most of the published literature on the aftermath of suicide in the hospital focuses on the emotional reactions of the survivors, such as family, friends, and to a lesser extent, healthcare providers. The work that has concentrated on (mental) healthcare providers has focused on medical staff, psychologists and psychotherapists (Akechi *et al*, 2003). A few notable exceptions can be found, such as Irving and Long (2001) and the aforementioned Akechi *et al* (2003). This remains surprising given that it is the (P/MH) nurse who has most contact with suicidal inpatients (Mishara, 2007).

In the absence of such literature, we must look to related disciplines and the extant literature produced by such disciplines. Perhaps in 'mining' said literature, we may be able to offer a tentative framework for P/MH nurse debriefing following the completed suicide of a client. The interesting study undertaken and reported by Alexander *et al* (2000) offers some potential helpful suggestions. Reviews[8] were found helpful by almost all of the 167 psychiatric consultants sampled. Some of the sample referred to the need for better training, repeating similar exhortations of student or trainee psychiatrists (Dewar *et al*, 1999). These findings also echo those which we reported in Chapter 4, whereby pre- and postgraduate training in and for suicide risk assessment (and care/management of suicidal people) is often – alas – severely lacking even in formal mental healthcare practitioners. An interesting slant in Alexander *et al*'s (2003) survey was the idea that the inevitability (rather than the risk) of suicide should be acknowledged in training in order that staff can be better prepared for such an event. A particularly interesting finding in the study was the reported need for a balance between (and having available) informal support and more formal methods of help (such as counselling and critical incident debriefing (Alexander *et al*, 2003).

Antai-Ontong (2001) advances a very useful seven stage framework for critical incident stress debriefing which clearly draws on cyclic (or iterative) models of reflection.

---

7 Our repeated searches of the extant literature seem to corroborate these statements.

8 While not specified in the paper, we take reviews to mean a clinical review of the case.

- Stage one involves setting the interpersonal climate, establishing boundaries and ground rules, providing immediate emotional support.
- Stage two is concerned with recalling and describing the event. Nurses are encouraged to describe what happened – the incident, the nurse's response/reaction, and the nurses' sensory perceptions during the event[9].
- Stage three is concerned with identifying, examining and affirming the nurses' thoughts – as they occurred during the event.
- Stage four is concerned with identifying, examining and exploring the emotional reaction to and during the event.
- Stage five is concerned with moving from an emotional to a more cognitive (reflective) stage.
- Stage six is concerned with affirming the participant's response as 'normal'; ergo a normal reaction to an abnormal event.
- Stage seven: is concerned with providing support and reassurance, drawing the debriefing to some appropriate closure and maybe even making appropriate referrals.

Conclusion

In summary, the unfortunate reality is that the chances of encountering a client who completes suicide, especially in mental healthcare practice contexts, are relatively high. There appears to be little or no argument that such experiences can (and do) qualify the practitioner as a Suicide Survivor. In so doing, it is important to be aware of the deleterious effects and affects that arise from encountering a client's completed suicide. As a result, the authors strongly recommend that practitioners who work with suicidal people must be given an opportunity to engage in regular Clinical Supervision. Furthermore, there may be additional utility for practitioners who do encounter a client suicide to also be offered the opportunity to engage in critical incident debriefing.

In this way, the authors would argue that practitioners will then have a robust chance to deal with the 'flotsam and jetsam' arising from the suicide and at the same time perhaps use the tragic experience as a learning opportunity. In so doing, the experience may actually help reduce the chances of having to deal with further client (or practitioner) completed suicide(s) sometime in the future.

---

9 Here we will not belabour the obvious similarity with obtaining phenomenological, hermeneutic accounts of people's lived experiences.

References

Akechi T, Sakuma K, Okamura M, Akizuki N, Oba A, Nakano T, Uchitomi Y (2003) Trauma in a nurse after patient suicide. *Psychosomatics*, **44**: 522–3.

Akerjordet K, Severinsson E (2004) Emotional intelligence in mental health nurses talking about practice. *International Journal of Mental Health Nursing*, **13**: 164–70.

Alexander DA, Klein S, Gray N, Dewar IG, Eagles JM (2000) Suicide by patients: questionnaire study of its effect on consultant psychiatrists. *British Medical Journal*, **320**(7249): 1571–4.

Alleyne J, Jumaa MO (2007) Building the capacity for evidence-based clinical nursing leadership: the role of executive co-coaching and group Clinical Supervision for quality patient services. *Journal Of Nursing Management*, **15**(2): 230–43.

Appleby L, Shaw J, Amos T *et al* (1999) Suicide within 12 months of contact with mental health services: national clinical survey. *British Medical Journal*, **318**: 1235–9.

American Foundation for Suicide Prevention/National Institute for Mental Health (recovered 2012) Survivor Research AFSP and NIMH Propose Research Agenda for Survivors of Suicide. http://www.afsp.org/index.cfm?fuseaction=home.viewpageandpage_id=2D9DF73E-BB25-0132-3AD7715D74BFF585.

Antai-Ontong D (2001) Critical incident stress debriefing: a health promotion model for workplace violence. *Perspectives in Psychiatric Care*, **37**(4): 125–39.

Arthur N, Russell-Mayhew S (2011) Clinical Supervision in Canada: bridging the education-to-practice gap through inter-professional supervision and lateral mentoring – a value-added approach to Clinical Supervision. In: Cutcliffe JR, Fowler J, Hyrkas K (eds.) *Routledge Handbook of Clinical Supervision: Fundamental International Themes*. Routledge, London, pp. 353–63.

Bagnall G, Sloan G, Platz S, Murphy S (2011) Generic supervision competencies for psychological therapies. *Mental Health Practice*, **14**(6): 18–23.

Barker P (1999) *The Philosophy and Practice of Psychiatric Nursing*. Churchill Livingstone/Elsevier, Edinburgh.

Berg A, Hallberg IR (1999) Effects of systematic clinical supervision on psychiatric nurses' sense of coherence, creativity, work related strain, job satisfaction and views of the effects of receiving clinical supervision: a pre-test, post design. *Journal of Psychiatric and Mental Health Nursing*, **6**(5): 371–81.

Berg A, Hansson UW, Hallberg IR (1994) Nurses' creativity and burn our during 1 year of clinical supervision and implementation of individually planned nursing care: comparisons between a ward for severely demented patients and a similar control ward. *Journal of Advanced Nursing*, **20**(4): 742–9.

Berggren I, Severinsson E (2011) The state of the science of Clinical Supervision in Europe. In: Cutcliffe JR, Fowler J, Hyrkas K (eds.) *Routledge Handbook of Clinical Supervision: Fundamental International Themes*. Routledge, London, pp. 327–37.

Bishop V (1998) What is going on? Results of a questionnaire. In: Bishop V (ed.) *Clinical Supervision in Practice, Some Questions, Answers and Guidelines*. Macmillan Press Ltd, London, Chapter 2.

Brocklehurst N (1997a) *Developing Clinical Supervision in Anglia and Oxford: a Regional Survey*. Report prepared for the NHS Executive, Anglia and Oxford Health Services Management Centre, University of Birmingham.

Brocklehurst N (1997b) Clinical supervision in nursing homes. *Nursing Times*, **93**(12): 48–9.

Brocklehurst N (1997c) *Clinical Supervision in Trent: a Survey of NHS Trusts*. Report prepared for the NHS Executive, Trent, Health Services Management Centre, University of Birmingham.

Brunero S, Stein-Parbury J (2008) The effectiveness of clinical supervision in nursing: an evidence based literature review. *Australian Journal of Advanced Nursing*, **25**(3): 86–94.

Butterworth T, Carson J, White E, Jeacock J, Clements A (1997) *Clinical Supervision and mentorship: It is Good to Talk: an Evaluation Study in England and Scotland*. University of Manchester, Manchester.

Campbell FR (1997) Changing the legacy of suicide: the telling and the knowing. *Suicide and Life Threatening Behavior*, **27**(4): 329–38.

Campbell FR (2006) The aftermath of suicide: the clinician's role. In Simon RI, Hales RE (eds.) *The American Psychiatric Publishing Textbook of Suicide Assessment and Management*. American Psychiatric Publishing, Washington DC, pp. 459–76.

Campbell FR, Cataldie L (2003) *Survivor Support Teams*. Paper presented at the Survivors of Suicide Research Workshop Program, NIMH/NIH Office of the Rare Diseases and the American Foundation for Suicide Prevention, Bethesda, MD.

Campbell FR, Cataldie L, McIntosh J, Millet K (2004) An active postvention program. *Crisis*, **25**(1): 30–2.

Challis M, Williams J, Bastone G (1998) Supporting pre-registration house officers: the needs of the educational supervisiors of the first phase of post-graduate medical education. *Medical Education*, **32**(2): 177–80.

Collins JM (2003) Impact of patient suicide on clinicians. *Journal of the American Psychiatric Nurses Association*, **9**(5): 159–62.

Cutcliffe J, Burns J (1998) Personal, professional and practice development: clinical supervision. *British Journal of Nursing*, **7**(21): 1318–22.

Cutcliffe J, Epling M (1997) An exploration of the use of John Heron's confronting interventions in clinical supervision; case studies from practice. *Psychiatric Care*, **4**(4): 178–80.

Cutcliffe JR, Fowler J (2010) Clinical supervision for the 21st century and beyond: successes, challenges and the road ahead. In: Cutcliffe JR, Fowler J, Hyrkas K (eds.) *Routledge Handbook of Clinical Supervision: Fundamental International Themes*. Routledge, London, pp. 374–94.

Cutcliffe JR, Proctor B (1998) An alternative training approach in clinical supervision: part one. *British Journal of Nursing*, **7**(5): 280–5.

Cutcliffe JR, McFeely S (2001) Practice nurses' 'lived experiences' of clinical supervision: a hermeneutic study. *British Journal of Nursing*, **10**(5): 312–23.

Cutcliffe JR, Hyrkas K (2006) Multidisciplinary attitudinal positions regarding clinical supervision: a cross-sectional study. *Journal of Nursing Management*, **14**: 617–27.

Cutcliffe JR, Stevenson C (2007) *Care of the Suicidal Person*. Elsevier, Edinburgh.

Cutcliffe JR, Butterworth T, Proctor B (2001) *Fundamental Themes in Clinical Supervision*. Routledge, London.

Cutcliffe JR, Stevenson C, Campbell F (2007) Suicide 'Survivors', reciprocity and recovery: issues around survivors as therapeutic agents in the care of suicidal people. In:

Cutcliffe JR, Stevenson C (2007) *Care of the Suicidal Person*. Elsevier, Edinburgh, pp. 179–96.

Cutcliffe JR, Fowler J, Hyrkas K (2010) *Routledge Handbook of Clinical Supervision: Fundamental International Themes*. Routledge, London.

Darden AJ, Rutter PA (2011) Psychologists' experiences of grief after client suicide: a qualitative study. *Omega: Journal of Death and Dying*, **63**(4): 317–42.

Davidson J (1998) Snapshots from Scotland. In: Bishop V (ed.) *Clinical Supervision in Practice, Some Questions, Answers and Guidelines*. Macmillan Press Ltd, London, Chapter 4.

Davies BW, Campbell WB (1995) Inguinal hernia repair: see one, do one, teach one? *Annals of The Royal College of Surgeons of England*, **77**(suppl. 6): 299–301.

Day GA (1925) Changing competencies of supervision. *The Modern Hospital*, **24**(5): 469–70.

Dewar I, Eagles JM, Klein S, Gray N, Alexander DA (1999) Psychiatric trainees' experience of, and reactions to, patient suicide. *Psychiatric Bulletin*, **24**: 20–23.

Dudley M, Butterworth T (1994) The costs and some benefits of clinical supervision: an initial exploration. *International Journal of Psychiatric Nursing Research*, **1**(2): 34–40.

Dunn C, Bishop B (1998) Clinical supervision: its implementation in one acute sector trust. In: Bishop V (ed.) *Clinical Supervision in Practice, Some Questions, Answers and Guidelines*. Macmillan Press Ltd, London, Chapter 5.

Eaton J, Coles C, Buckle L (1998) *Educational Supervision*. Department of Post Graduate Medical and Dental Education, Bristol.

Edberg AK, Hallberg IR, Gustafson L (1996) Effects of clinical supervision on nurse–patient cooperation quality: a controlled study in dementia care. *Clinical Nursing Research*, **5**(2): 127–46.

Edberg AK, Norberg A, Hallberg IR (1999) Mood and general behaviour of patients with severe dementia during one year of supervised, individualized planned care and systematic clinical supervision. *Aging Clinical Experimental Research*, **11**(6): 395–403.

Fallon WFJ, Wears RL, Tepas JJ (1993) Resident supervision in the operating room: does this impact on the outcome? *Journal Trauma*, **35**(4): 556–60.

Fothergill A, Edwards D, Burnard P (2004) Stress, burnout, coping and stress management in psychiatrists: findings from a systematic review. *International Journal of Social Psychiatry*, **50**: 54–65.

Fowler J, Chevannes M (1998) Evaluating the efficacy of reflective practice within the context of clinical supervision. *Journal of Advanced Nursing*, **27**(2): 379–82.

Freeman R (1952) Supervision in the improvement of nursing services. *Public Health Nursing*, **44**(7): 370–73.

Fyffe T (1997) *Clinical Supervision Exploratory Study of Staff Experiences and Perceptions*. Unpublished Masters in Medical Education thesis, University of Dundee.

Geddes JR, Juszczak E (1995) Period trends in rate of suicide in first 28 days after discharge from psychiatric hospital in Scotland, 1968–92. *British Medical Journal*, **311**: 357–60.

Geddes JR, Juszczak E, O'Brien F, Kendrick S (1997) Suicide in the 12 months after discharge from psychiatric inpatient care, Scotland 1968–92. *Journal of Epidemiological Community Health*, **51**: 430–4.

Gennis VM, Gennis MA (1993) Supervision in the putpatient clinic – effects on teaching and patient care. *Journal of General Internal Medicine*, **87**(7): 378–80.

Gilbert C, Cutcliffe JR (2011) The 'State of the Science' of Clinical Supervision in the United States: a social work and nursing focus. In Cutcliffe JR, Hyrkas K, Fowler J (eds.) *Routledge Handbook of Clinical Supervision: Fundamental International Themes*. Routledge, London, pp. 338–52.

Goldacre M, Seagrott V, Hawton K (1993) Suicide after discharge from psychiatric inpatient care. *Lancet*, **342**: 283–6.

Hallberg IR, Norberg A (1993) Strain among nurses and their emotional reactions during 1 year of systematic clinical supervision combined with the implementation of individualized care in dementia nursing. *Journal of Advanced Nursing*, **18**(12): 866–73.

Happell B, Pinikahana J, Martin T (2003) Stress and burnout in forensic psychiatric nursing. *Stress and Health*, **19**(2): 63–8.

Hawton K, Simkin S (2003) Helping people bereaved by suicide: their needs may require special attention. *Bereavement Care*, **22**(3): 41–2.

Hendin H, Lipschitz A, Maltsberger JT, Haas AP, Wynecoop S (2000) Therapists' reactions to patients' suicides. *American Journal of Psychiatry*, **157**(12): 2022–7.

Herriot P, Bhui K, Lelliot P (1994) Supervision of trainees. *Psychiatric Bulletin*, **18**: 474–6.

Ho TP (2003) The suicide risk of discharged psychiatric patients. *Journal of Clinical Psychiatry*, **64**: 702–7.

Holm AK, Lantz I, Severinsson E (1998) Nursing students' experiences of continual process-oriented group supervision. *Journal of Nursing Management*, **6**: 105–13.

Holm AK, Lantz I, Severinsson E (2003) A theoretical perspective of the core concepts of nursing supervision. *Norsk tidskrift for sykepleieforskning*, **5**: 71–82.

Hyrkäs K, Paunonen-Ilmonen M (2001a) The effects of clinical supervision on the quality of care – examining the results of team supervision and the conceptions of multiprofessional teams. *Journal of Advanced Nursing*, **33**: 492–502.

Hyrkäs K, Lehti K, Paunonen-Ilmonen M (2001b) Cost–benefit analysis of team supervision: the development of an innovative model and its application as a case study. *Journal of Nursing Management*, **9**: 1–15.

International Training Academy for Linguistics and Kinetics (recovered 2012) http://www.italkinc.com/.

Irving P, Long A (2001) Critical incident stress debriefing following traumatic life experiences. *Journal of Psychiatric and Mental Health Nursing*, **8**: 307–14.

Itoh O (2005) Suicide cases encountered by clinical psychiatric nurses – research and study for participants in the study meeting for registered nurses for psychiatric emergency units and acute patients. *Suicide Prevention and Crisis Intervention*, **26**(1): 32–9.

Itoh O (2006) Suicide incidents encountered by clinical psychiatric nurses (Part 2). *Suicide Prevention and Crisis Intervention*, **27**(1): 64–70.

Jobes DA, Berman AL (1993) Suicide and malpractice liability: assessing and revising policies, procedures and practices in outpatient settings. *Professional Psychology: Research and Practice*, **24**: 91–9.

Jobes DA, Luoma JB, Hustead LAY, Mann RA (2000) In the wake of suicide: survivorship and postvention. In: Maris RW, Berman AL, Silverman M (eds.) *Comprehensive Textbook of Suicidology*. Guilford Press, New York, pp. 536–60.

Johns C (1996) Visualising and realising caring in practice through guided reflection. *Journal of Advanced Nursing*, **24**: 1135–43.

Johns C (1998) Opening the doors of perception. In: Johns C, Freshwater D (eds.) *Transforming Nursing Through Reflective Practice*. Blackwell Science Ltd, Oxford, Chapter 1.

Jones A (2003) Clinical Supervision in promoting a balanced delivery of palliative nursing care. *Journal of Hospice and Palliative Nursing*, July/September, **5**(3): 168–75.

Jones A (2009) Fevered love. In: de Raeve L, Rafferty M, Paget M (eds.) *Nurses and their Patients: Informing Practice Through Psychodynamic Insights*. MandK Publishing, London.

Kilminster SM, Jolly BC (2000) Effective supervision in clinical practice settings: a literature review. *Medical Education*, **34**(10): 827–40.

Kingsbury S, Allsopp M (1994) Direct consultant supervision of higher trainees: child and adolescent psychiatry. *Psychiatric Bulletin*, **18**: 225–9.

Kukkola H (1990) *Clinical Supervision in Developing Teams – a Strategy for Nursing Homes' Development*. Vanhus – ja – lahimmaispalvelun litto rg, Helsinki.

Lauvrud C, Nonstad K, Palmstierna T (2009) Occurrence of post-traumatic stress symptoms and their relationship to professional quality of life (ProQoL) in nursing staff at a forensic psychiatric security unit: a cross-sectional study. *Health Quality Life Outcomes*, **7**: 31.

Lawrence D, Holman CDJ, Jablensky ,V *et al* (2001) Increasing rates of suicide in Western Australian psychiatric patients: a record linkage study. *Acta Psychiatrica Scandinavia*, **104**: 443–51.

Leonard R, Alison L (1999) Critical incident stress debriefing and its effects on coping strategies and anger in a sample of Australian police officers involved in shooting incidents. *Work and Stress*, **13**(2): 144–61.

Lilley L (1996) *Clinical Supervision: Progress Report*. Kettering General Hospital NHS Trust, Kettering.

Little P (1995) What do Wessex General Practitioners think about the structure of hospital vocational training? *British Medical Journal*, **308**(6940): 1337–9.

Long A, Reid W (1996) An exploration of nurses' attitudes to the nursing care of the suicidal patient in an acute psychiatric ward. *Journal of Psychiatric and Mental Health Nursing*, **3**(1): 29–37.

Lynch L, Happell B (2008) Implementing Clinical Supervision: part 1 laying the ground work. *International Journal of Mental Health Nursing*, **17**(10): 57–64.

Lynch L, Hancox K, Happell B (2011) The state of the science of Clinical Supervision in Australia and New Zealand. In: Cutcliffe JR, Fowler J, Hyrkas K (eds.) *Routledge Handbook of Clinical Supervision: Fundamental International Themes*. Routledge, London, pp. 317–26.

McIntosh JL (1996) Survivors of suicide: a comprehensive bibliography update, 1986–1995. *Omega*, **33**: 147–75.

McKee M, Black N (1992) Does the current use of junior doctors in the United Kingdom affect the quality of medical care? *Social Science & Medicine*, **34**(5): 549–58.

Marine A, Ruotsalainen JH, Serra C, Verbeek JH (recovered 16 May 2011) Preventing occupational stress in healthcare workers. *Cochrane Database of Systematic Reviews* 2006, Issue 4. Art. No.: CD002892. DOI: 10.1002/14651858.CD002892.pub2.

Marrow C, Macauley D, Crumbie A (1997) Promoting reflective practice through structured clinical supervision. *Journal of Nursing Management*, **5**: 77–82.

May L, Williams R, Gorman T (1997) *Clinical Supervision: Evaluation of a Pilot Study*. Edge Hill University College School of Health Studies, Liverpool.

Mishara BL (2007) Foreword. In: Cutcliffe JR, Stevenson C (eds.) *Care of the Suicidal Person*. Churchill Livingstone/Elsevier, Edinburgh, pp. xiii–xiv.

National Center for Crisis Management (recovered 2012) http://www.nc-cm.org/biojeffreymitchell.htm.

National Institute for Occupational Health and Safety (recovered 2011) *Exposure to Stress: Occupational Hazards in Hospitals* NIOSH Publication No. 2008-136: http://www.cdc.gov/niosh/docs/2008-136/.

Nicklin P (1997) *Clinical supervision – efficient and effective?* Paper presented at the British Educational Research Association Annual Conference, Department of Health Studies, University of York, September 1997.

Panayiotou BN, Fotherby MD (1996) Junior Hospital Doctors' views on their training in the UK. *Postgraduate Medical Journal*, **72**(851): 547–550.

Pirkola S, Sohlman B, Wahlbeck K (2005) The characteristics of suicides within a week of discharge after psychiatric hospitalization – a nationwide register study. *BMC Psychiatry*, **5**: 32.

Proctor BP (2001) Training for the supervision alliance – attitudes, skills and intention. In: Cutcliffe JR, Butterworth T, Proctor BP (eds.) *Fundamental Themes in Clinical Supervision*. Routledge, London, pp. 47–63.

Robinson R, Clements K, Land C (2003) Workplace stress among psychiatric nurses: prevalence, distribution, correlates, and predictors. *Journal of Psychosocial Nursing and Mental Health Services*, **4**(4): 32.

Redfern S, Norman I, Murrell T *et al* (1997*) External Review of the Department of Health – Funded Nursing Development Units*. Kings College, London.

Ruskin R, Sakinofsky I, Bably RM *et al* (2004) Impact of patient suicide on psychiatrists and psychiatric trainees. *Academic Psychiatry*, **28**: 104–10.

Sams D (1997) *Clinical Supervision: An Evaluation of the Implementation Process Within a Community Trust*. BHB Community Healthcare NHS Trust, Hornchurch.

Scanlon C, Weir WS (1997) Learning from practice? Mental health nurses' perceptions and experiences of clinical supervision. *Journal of Advanced Nursing*, **26**: 295–303.

Schmidt E (1926) Principles and practices of supervision. *American Journal of Nursing*, **27**(2): 119–20.

Severinsson E (2001) Confirmation, meaning and self-awareness as core concepts of the nursing supervision model. *Nursing Ethics*, **8**(1): 36–44.

Sloan G (2011) Clinical supervision in the United Kingdom – ten years on: a review of the United Kingdom clinical supervision literature. In: Cutcliffe JR, Fowler J, Hyrkas K (eds.) *Routledge Handbook of Clinical Supervision: Fundamental International Themes*. Routledge, London, pp. 136–47.

Sloan G, Fleming M (2011) Training requirements for clinical supervision in the United Kingdom. In: Cutcliffe JR, Fowler J, Hyrkas K (eds.) *Routledge Handbook of Clinical Supervision: Fundamental International Themes*. Routledge, London, pp. 79–92.

Smith, P (2001) Clinical Supervision: my path to clinical excellence. In: Cutcliffe JR, Butterworth T, Proctor BP (eds.) *Fundamental Themes in Clinical Supervision*. Routledge, London, pp. 159–69.

Society for the Prevention of Teen Suicide (recovered 2012) *Manasquan High School: Youth Suicide Contagion Containment: a Case History*. http://rems.ed.gov/docs/Training_FY09REMS_BOMA_YouthSuicide.pdf.

Sox CM, Burstin KR, Orar EJ, Conn A, Setnick G, Rucker DW Dasse P, Brenna TA (1998) The effect of supervision of residents on quality of care in five University-affiliated emergency departments. *Academic Medicine*, **73**(7): 776–82.

Spiegel JP (1975) Psychiatry: a high risk profession. *American Journal of Psychiatry*, **132**: 693–7.

Sudak D, Roy A, Sudak H, Lipschitz A, Maltsberger J, Hendin H (2007) Deficiencies in suicide training in primary care specialties: a survey of training directors. *Academic Psychiatry*, **31**(5): 345–9.

Swain G (1995) *Clinical Supervision: the Principles and Process*. Health Visitors Association, London.

Takahashi C, Chida F, Nakamura H, Akasaka H, Yagi J, Koeda A, Takusari E, Otsuka K, Sakai A (2011) The impact of inpatient suicide on psychiatric nurses and their need for support. *BMC Psychiatry*, **11**: 38.

Troister T, Links P, Cutcliffe, JR (2008) Review of predictors of suicide within 1 year of discharge from a psychiatric hospital. *Current Psychiatry Reports*, **10**: 60–5.

United States of America Navy and Marine Corps Clinical Preceptorship Program (recovered May 2011). http://www.clinicalpreceptor.com/index2.asp.

University of Washington Policy and Procedure on Workplace Violence – Critical Incident Debriefing (recovered 2012). http://www.washington.edu/admin/hr/polproc/work-violence/cid.html.

Valente SM (1994) Psychotherapist reactions to the suicide of a patient. *American Journal of Orthopsychiatry*, **64**: 614–21.

Valente SM, Saunders JM (2002) Nurses' grief reactions to a patient's suicide. *Perspectives in Psychiatric Care*, **38**(1): 5–14.

Walker J (2009) Examining the benefits of professional clinical supervision. *Kai Tiaki Nursing*, New Zealand **15**(5).

Watkins CE (1995) Psychotherapy supervision in the 1990s: some observations and accountability. *American Journal of Psychotherapy*, **49**(4): 568–81.

Watkins CE (1997) The ineffective psychotherapy supervisor: some reflections about bad behaviours, poor process and offensive outcomes. *Clinical Supervisor*, **16**(1): 163–80.

White E, Roche M (2006) A selective review of mental health nursing in New South Wales, Australia, in relation to clinical supervision. *International Journal of Mental Health Nursing*, **15**: 209–19.

White E, Winstanley J (2006) Cost and resource implications of clinical supervision in nursing: an Australian perspective. *Journal of Nursing Management*, **14**: 628–36.

White E, Winstanley J (2010) A randomized controlled trial of clinical supervision: selected findings from a novel Australian attempt to establish the evidence base for causal relationships with quality of care and patient outcomes, as an informed contribution to mental health nursing practice development. *Journal of Research in Nursing*, **15**(2): 151–67.

Wolf L (1941) Development of floor nursing and supervision. *Hospital*, March, 53–56.
Yegdich T (1999) Clinical supervision and managerial supervision: some historical and conceptual considerations. *Journal of Advanced Nursing*, **30**(5): 1195–204.
Yim PHW, Yip PSF, Li RHY *et al* (2004) Suicide after discharge from psychiatric inpatient care: a case-control study in Hong Kong. *Australian New Zealand Journal Medicine*, **38**(1–2): 65–72.

CHAPTER 12

The way ahead – practice, policy, education and research issues

> It is my belief that our best answers, as therapeutic suicidologists, cannot come from medicine or physiology, or group behavior or epidemiology or sociology, not from Kraeplin nor the *Diagnostic and Statistical Manual of Mental Disorders*, and certainly not from SmithKline Beecham. (Shneidman, 2001, p. 201)

Introduction – concerning (mis)conceptualisations of suicide

This book has been written purposefully to focus on clinical practice; for the authors, clinical practice is the *raison d'être* of our discipline. This axiom notwithstanding, the authors are also mindful that epistemologists have long purported that theory grows from practice and research, and in turn returns to inform practice. All credible disciplines, to a greater or lesser extent, value the contribution that theory has made to their development and for many the development of theory is inextricably linked to concepts and their analyses. As a result, it can be seen that to try to build, develop or use a theory without having a clear understanding of the conceptual 'building blocks' would be to lay faulty theoretical foundations for practice and ultimately for patient care (Cutcliffe and McKenna, 2005). To paraphrase: without being clear about how we understand, describe and define a concept (such as suicide), then any resultant theory or practice built upon these unclear concepts can at best be 'shaky', flawed and conceptually weak.

Thus it becomes clear that how a concept or issue is 'framed' has a huge impact (if not dominant influence) on how that concept is used, discussed and debated in any associated discourse – including a practice discourse. What this means in terms of suicide, then, is that how we define, conceptualise and problematise suicide has a huge influence on our resultant practice(s).

Conceptual confusion: suicide as a mental health problem?

One of the most common (though arguably inaccurate) 'frames' or conceptualisations of suicide as that of regarding suicide as a so-called 'mental illness'. While a well-developed body of literature exists which illustrates the link between suicide and certain mental health problems/diagnoses, evidence that contradicts the automatic association between these phenomena has been advanced by renowned international suicidologists (see, for example, Maris *et al*, 2000a; Shneidman, 2001; Silverman, 1997; Tanney, 2000; van Praag, 2004).

It is accurate to suggest that a statistically positive correlation has been established (and repeatedly re-established) between certain mental health problems (or diagnoses), most notably depression, and increased risk of suicide (see, for example, Barraclough *et al*, 1974; Powell *et al*, 2000; Arsenault-Lapierre *et al*, 2004). Nevertheless, it is also the case that a corresponding body of evidence exists which casts doubt on the view that *all* people who attempt suicide must *ipso facto* have a mental health problem. Furthermore, even proponents of these associations (such as the key text edited by Stoff and Mann, 1997) offer cautionary prefaces, and thus our views here should not be regarded as iconoclastic or heretical.

Evidence that contradicts the automatic association of depression and suicide is provided by many key international Suicidologists, including Maris *et al* (2000a), Shneidman (2001), Silverman (1997), Tanney (2000) and van Praag (2004), who contend that most people who complete suicide are sad, but they are not necessarily clinically depressed. To consider this in more detail, one needs to be aware of the process(es) of access to formal mental health services (particularly in the USA) and the resultant 'diagnostic classification'. Professor of Psychiatry Tanney (2000) highlights the striking phenomenon of gross under-reporting of suicide; he provides evidence to show that in actual fact, *the majority of suicides do not access formal mental healthcare services* (our emphasis). Luoma *et al* (2002) report similar findings whereby approximately (only) one-third of the suicide victims had contact with mental health services in the year prior to their suicide. Indeed, the data pertaining to suicidal individuals consulting their primary care physician in the month prior to suicide varies between 20% and 76%; with younger people (< 35 years old) having significantly lower rates of consultation and those aged > 60 years having higher rates.

Given the operational systems of both formal healthcare providers and insurance companies, anyone who does present to these services must be given (or receive) a formal psychiatric diagnosis in order to receive treatment. This is particularly clear in North America, where an insurance-driven healthcare system demands a diagnosis in order to make a claim. According to Tanney (2000), the requirements of these systems, then, must lead to over-estimates of the numbers of people with psychiatric diagnoses who have also engaged in suicidal acts. Additional well-documented methodological limitations have been recorded with suicide epidemiological studies, including sampling bias, problems of definition (eg. when does a so-called suicidal act become an actual suicidal act?), the exclusion of actively suicidal people from controlled trials (Mishara and Weistubb, 2005), and the various differing conceptualisations of suicide as an individual or societal issue.

In addition to access, clear imperfections are apparent in our systems and processes of diagnosis and classification. The esteemed international psychiatrist van Praag (2004), whose lifelong work has focused on the diagnosis and classification of mental health problems, draws attention to problems in distinguishing between 'real'/clinical depression and sadness/distress/mourning; the problem, he purports, is not so much defining a 'case' as defining the 'non-case', and indicating where distress and worrying end and 'case' depression begins. He states:

> The border then, between sadness/distress and depression is blurred

and

> Psychiatry so far, has failed to study this issue systematically... that border, if such a zone exists at all, is *phenomenologically defined* (original emphasis) and poorly studied. Mourning, for instance, may and often does, produce a mental state undistinguishable from major depression. (Van Praag, 2004, p. 83).

In addition to this diagnostic uncertainty concerning mental health problems, a parallel lack of conceptual clarity exists around defining suicide. According to Silverman (1997, p. 12),

> after more than 25 years of discussion and debate, there does not exist a universally accepted set of definitions and classifications of suicidal behaviours for the reliable labeling, counting and study of individuals who area at risk for self-destructive injuries.

As a result, if there is considerable doubt about what constitutes a genuine 'case' of depression, and what constitutes a genuine suicide, then it would be epistemologically imprudent to make the claim that depression is a necessary condition for suicide. Professor Ed Shneidman (arguably the most eminent Suicidologist of his generation) is equally critical of the automatic alleged isomorphic relationship between depression and suicide. Shneidman asserts (2001, p. 73),

> Converting suicide into depression is a kind of methodological sleight of hand. The central fact about depression is that one can lead a long happy life with depression... suicide and depression are not synonymous.

In addition to possibly misleading epidemiological data, and an ill-advised, over-pathologising of suicidal behaviours, perhaps the most important implication that arises from limiting our conceptualisation of suicide to that of a mental health problem is that *it serves to constrain or/and constrict our thinking on what can be changed/improved to help combat increasing rates of suicide* (our emphasis). Such a view is echoed in the findings of the recently published, federally supported study of suicidal young men in Northern Ireland (see Public Health Agency, recovered 2012). The data in this study indicated significant utility in reconfiguring mental health services to bring these more into line with what young men want/need[1]. Furthermore, the study also found that in order to maximise therapeutic effectiveness with this client group, effectively combating suicide in young men appears to need a broader approach; it needs a more comprehensive response than 'tinkering' with formal mental health services. The data and findings in this study indicated that reducing suicide rates in young men also appears to require consideration of social services, family dynamics/support, education and training for young men, and addressing societal-based stigma.

Further conceptual confusion? The continuing conflation of suicide with self-harm

As we have referred to earlier in this book, several papers continue to conflate suicide with self-harm (see for example Speckens and Hawton, 2005; Fortune and Hawton, 2005; Hawton and James, 2005; Anderson and Jenkins, 2006; James *et al*, 2012). Indeed, within some literature, there is a deliberate attempt to posit these two distinct phenomena as one and the same; as merely different points on a continuum of lethality. Anderson and Jenkins (2006, p. 645) for example suggest that given the methodological and ethical issues involved in research on 'treatments' for suicide, we should simply *substitute a population of people who self-harm for the 'missing' population of suicidal people* (emphasis added) given that:

> interventions following self-harm/suicidal behaviours are more amenable to evaluation.

1 In addition to certain qualities/skills that P/MH nurses need.

While it should be noted that distinctions between forms of self-harm and suicide are problematic, fundamental differences have been well documented and it is inaccurate and misleading to conflate the two. A thorough examination of the literature in this substantive area will indicate that, historically, many of the definitions constructed for suicide and self-harm did indeed overlap with one another. Furthermore, self-harm questions have been included in some suicide risk assessments. Undoubtedly, links between the two phenomena exist; sadly there is evidence to suggest that some people who self-harm do go on to take their own lives[2]. Nevertheless, there is a wealth of empirical evidence that shows that 95% or more of people who self-harm do not go on to take their own lives (Santa Mina and Gallop, 1998; Anderson, 2000). Indeed, even within some of the literature that appears to conflate suicide with self-harm (Zahl and Hawton, 2004), *it is made very clear that the vast majority of people who repeatedly engage in self-harm do not go on to take their own lives!*

> Although repetition of DSH may be one of the strongest risk factors for death by suicide (overall, it was confirmed in 59.9% of the suicides), it is also important to note that suicide occurred in a small minority of cases overall: 4.7% of those in the repeated DSH group died by suicide compared with 1.9% of those in the single-episode DSH group over 15 years.

Moreover, the large majority of more contemporary empirical work clearly distinguishes self-harm from suicide and suicidal ideation. There are well-documented significant differences between the act of suicide and the act(s) of self-harm, and not only a difference in the outcome. Perhaps these differences are most succinctly captured by Maris *et al* (2000b, p. 427) when they state

> As a starting point, we must distinguish indirect self-destructive behaviors from behaviors more directly suicidal.... In marked contrast, there are, however, a vast number of behaviors that are self-harmful, frequently injurious, self-negating, and self-defeating in which the individual engages but in which there may be no intention to die.

Similarly, Favazza (1996) clearly differentiates between self-harm and suicide, stating that self-mutilation is the deliberate alteration of body tissue *without conscious suicidal content or intent* (our emphasis). 'Boiled down' to perhaps their simplest (most fundamental) differences – self-harm is a life-orientated act and suicide is a death-orientated act. As a result, conflating the two and subsequently

2 Whether these are deliberate attempts to die or 'accidents' still remains unclear.

positing them as one phenomenon is a clear mistake, especially as it appears to be the case that these phenomena may very well require different approaches and responses from mental health practitioners and resultant treatment paradigms.

Moving practice forward: the key roles of psychiatric and mental health nurses in care of suicidal people

1. Talking as the centre piece

This book has attempted to draw together the most contemporary collection of evidence in order to inform the care of suicidal people. The existence of some evidence notwithstanding, the P/MH nursing care of the suicidal person is not an area that can claim to be grounded in an abundance of empirical literature. As a result, P/MH nurses have to 'feel their way in the dark' so to speak. As Maris *et al* (2000b) note, research on treatment effectiveness for suicidal people is both difficult and rare. Methodological limitations, problems with operational definitions, ethical concerns and the pervasive problem of a low base rate of suicide all to conspire to make such research, especially valid and reliable quantitative research, difficult to produce. While the nomothetic generalisations associated with this type of research may not be possible, idiographic *case-related* generalisable findings can be produced by means of well-designed qualitative studies, such as some of those described in this book. Together with the theoretical models purported (eg. Maris, 1997; Shneidman, 1997) these findings can lead to a deeper understanding of what appears to be effective for (some) suicidal people, and at the same time highlight what appears to be less effective.

Accepting the axiomatic complexity and multi-dimensionality of suicide, and at the same time, the undeniable fact that suicide is a *human drama*, played out in the everyday lives, minds, brains and interactions of people, it may not be entirely surprising that, for P/MH nurses at any rate, *caring for suicidal people must be an interpersonal endeavour; and one personified by talking and listening* (our emphasis). As he does so often, Shneidman eloquently captures the essence of this message when he states,

> There is a basic rule to keep in mind: We can reduce the lethality if we lessen the anguish, the perturbation. Suicidal individuals who are asked, 'Where do you hurt?' intuitively know that this is a question about their emotions and their lives, and they answer appropriately, not in biological terms but with some literary or humanistic sophistication, in psychological terms. What I mean by this is to ask about the person's feelings, worries and pain. (1997, p. 29)

Views highly congruent with Shneidman's are expressed by Maris *et al* when they assert,

> As important as the biological treatment of hopelessness is, any treatment of a suicidal patient that relies solely on impersonal therapies (eg. psychoactive medication, seclusion, restraint, and 15 minute checks (observations) may be second rate.... Many psychiatrists argue that the heart of the treatment of suicidal individuals is the relationship of the therapists and the patient. (Maris *et al*, 2000a, p. 13)

Sadly, the contemporary P/MH nursing literature is clear in highlighting that all too often, what suicidal people receive in the way of 'nursing care' is indeed second rate, ineffective and impersonal.

Findings from the recently completed study of suicidal young men in Northern Ireland (see Public Health Agency, recovered 2012; Jordan *et al*, 2012; Cutcliffe *et al*, 2012) and additional similar literature further illustrate the type(s), structures and emphasis in care that suicidal young men want/need. Jordan *et al* (2012) report findings that underscore the need for mental health practitioners (MHPs) to possess *and* convey therapeutic and supportive (non-judgemental) attitudes. As Jordan *et al* (2012) assert, such therapeutic attitudes included those which enable young men need to (re)connect with humanity. Participants recounted their deep sense of connection with, and concomitant therapeutic effectiveness of, particular MHPs. Their accounts focused on perceived 'human' qualities which they associated with the MHPs' ability to meaningfully engage with, and *thus* to help, them. The relevance of these 'human' qualities in effective care giving has been demonstrated in the small body of similar work conducted internationally (Cutcliffe *et al*, 2006; Sun *et al*, 2005; Talseth *et al*, 1999).

The findings of Cutcliffe *et al*'s (2006) study resonate particularly strongly with those of Jordan *et al* (in press) in terms of a joint identification of a phased *trajectory* of care delivered over the longer term, which responds to the changing circumstances and needs of suicidal individuals. MHPs are centrally involved, alongside care and support delivered by significant others, at both an individual and a societal level.

Participants in Jordan *et al* (2012) tended to make negative comparisons between themselves and others based on narrow perceptions of what it was to be a 'successful' man in 21st century. In essential ways, these perceptions can be seen to derive from hegemonic views of masculinity (Connell and Messerschmidt, 2005). Consequently, the present study lends important and original evidence that any programme of care for young suicidal men should include a focus on enabling them to appreciate that there are alternative, equally valid approaches to, and means of, achieving 'success' in life. Accordingly, one effective role of MHPs would be to gently challenge the limiting constructs and perceptions of young men and replace them with more helpful and realistic views of the wider possibilities open to them. As such, young men could be supported in a process of personal growth and development towards a much more inclusive appreciation of meaningful social participation. Consequently, the findings highlight the need for care to assume an explicitly future-orientated dimension so that young men are supported in the process of identifying (new) meaning in life and obtaining/refining necessary cognitive and other life skills. In the context of developing relevant cognitive resources, our findings highlight the importance of other therapies – for example, cognitive behavioural therapy (CBT) and dialectical behaviour therapy (DBT). The value of these types of therapeutic interventions in preventing (repeat) suicidal behaviour has been endorsed in a recent review of interventions to prevent suicide conducted by the Scottish government (Leitner *et al*, 2008), as well as other international research (Daniel and Goldston, 2009), including that relating specifically to young people (Nordentoft *et al*, 2005; Treatment of Adolescents with Depression Study Team, 2007).

And so, on the matter of talking as the centre piece of care of suicidal people, we leave the last words on the matter, fittingly, to Ed Shneidman, the founder of Suicidology as a discrete field of study, and equally fittingly to a mental healthcare survivor, Peter Campbell.

> When dealing with a highly suicidal person, it is simply not effective to address the lethality directly. We can address thoughts about suicide by working with this person and asking why mental turmoil is leading to feelings of lethality (Shneidman, 1997, p. 25).

> To understand suicide we must understand suffering and psychological pain and various thresholds for enduring it; to treat suicidal people (and prevent suicide) we must address and then soften and reduce the psych-ache that drives it (Shneidman, 1997, p. 29).

> Improving guidelines and training around procedures like close observation and seclusion can bring appreciable benefits, but positive change may not be sustained until underlying attitudes are addressed and consideration given to what P/MH nurses think they should best be doing and are capable of doing.... Denying the ability (to take one's own life) without

addressing the desire must be a major reason why service users find Close Observation unhelpful. Observation without interaction is a cold comfort (Campbell, 2006, p. 276).

2. Move away from defensive, surveillance and 'containment' orientated practices

In parallel with the introduction of an 'engagement' focused approach to care of the suicidal person, is the corresponding need for mental healthcare of the suicidal person to move away from defensive, surveillance and containment orientated practices. While we acknowledge that there is a lack of a shared nomenclature to describe the practices of 'observations', here we use the term 'surveillance' to capture all of those practices that are concerned with 'observation' of suicidal people. In order to understand this urgent requirement, it is perhaps necessary to remind ourselves of the well-documented limitations of observations as a means to care for suicidal people. We will achieve this by examining the evidence regarding surveillance/observations and a number of associated issues namely: who undertakes them; how expensive are they; what nurses' and clients' experiences of them are; and how efficacious close observations are.

Who undertakes close observations?

Some empirical and numerous anecdotal papers have been published and these are unswerving in showing that there is significant variation in who undertakes close observation, particularly when international data are examined. Close observations have been undertaken by the following groups: experienced, qualified psychiatric nurses (MacKay *et al*, 2005); inexperienced, qualified psychiatric nurses (Bowles *et al*, 2002; Dodds and Bowles, 2001); licensed practical nurses (Moore *et al*, 1995); nursing students/medical students (O'Brien and Cole, 2003); care aids (Fletcher, 1999); volunteers (Bowers *et al*, 2000); family members (Heyman and Lombardo, 1995); sitters (Cardell and Pitula, 1999; Pitula and Cardell, 1996); and security guards using closed circuit TV cameras (Cutcliffe, 2003; Holmes *et al*, 2004). There is also evidence of a strong degree of consensus within this literature that close observations are regarded as a 'low skill', unpleasant and unpopular activity (Buchanan-Barker and Barker, 2000, 2005; Stevenson and Cutcliffe, 2006). As a result, close observations are often delegated to junior and/or untrained staff. Training for such observations, if provided at all, is sporadic, lacking any theoretical underpinning and/or evidence base and inconsistent. There is no consensus, even among P/MH nursing educators, as to when and how much training/education for/on observations should occur, who should provide this or indeed how such training would be evaluated.

How expensive are close observations?

A number of papers have attempted to calculate the cost of providing close observations (see for example, Eastwood and Schechtman, 1996; Heyman and Lombardo, 1995; Moore *et al*, 1995), but these figures should with a degree of caution given that the calculations are based on estimations. Indeed, precise calculations of the cost of close observations are beset with conceptual and methodological problems: for example, the lack of conceptual and operational consistency of close observations (see Bowers *et al*, 2000). The cost of providing close observation is also going to vary across different clinical sites given the variation in how close observations are operationalised (Bowers and Park, 2001). Precise cost calculations would need to take account of the nature of the staff that actually undertake the observations; the frequency of close observations; and the duration of each occurrence of close observations. Notwithstanding the imprecision of the calculations, there is ample evidence that indicates that close observations are a staff-intensive activity: one that requires a high staff-to-client ration and therefore incurs a high cost (see for example O'Brien and Cole, 2003).

Nurses' and clients' experiences of close observations

A small number of studies have attempted to investigate both the clients' and P/MH nurses' experiences of observations and have similarly tried to extrapolate that the experience is either therapeutic or not therapeutic. These findings should be regarded with a degree of caution as a result of the methodological limitations found within the studies. *For example, tragically, the experiences of those people whom were under observations and still managed to complete their suicide will never be available to us. Even the most junior researcher would thus recognise that this will skew any sample of clients who have been under observation* (our emphasis) (Cutcliffe and Stevenson, 2007). However, critical examination and synthesis of this literature clearly indicates that the findings are equivocal.

A number of studies have identified and repeatedly reported how 'being under' close observations is experienced as non-therapeutic (Barker and Cutcliffe, 1999; Bowles *et al*, 2002; Cardell and Pitula, 1999; Cutcliffe and Barker, 2002; Dodds and Bowles, 2001; Fletcher, 1999; O'Brien and Cole, 2003; Pitula and Cardell, 1996). This body of work purports that non-therapeutic aspects of close observation include: lack of empathy, lack of acknowledgement, disinterested practitioners, lack of information provided, lack of privacy, invasion of personal space, observers reading newspapers/books/magazines while observing the client, and confinement.

Interestingly, some of these studies also report that clients have identified some therapeutic aspects to close observation (Cardell and Pitula, 1999; Fletcher, 1999; Jones *et al*, 2000; Pitula and Cardell, 1996). The therapeutic aspects have been described as observer intentions optimism, acknowledgement, distraction, emotional support, and protection. Further, this body of work has attempted to identify the characteristics and behavioural practices that are regarded as therapeutic. 'Therapeutic observers' are described as being caring, helpful and hopeful; acknowledging or recognising the client as unique; being known to the client (rather than being an unfamiliar face or stranger); and 'engaging' with the client.

This body of literature also alludes to the purported relationship(s) between the effectiveness of close observations and a number of related variables, including who undertakes the observations, how the observations are enacted, the extent of established familiarity between the observer and the client, and the overarching cultural perspective of the unit regarding the purpose/value of close observations (Buchanan-Barker and Barker, 2005; Cardell and Pitula, 1999; Fletcher, 1999; Pitula and Cardell, 1996; Stevenson and Cutcliffe, 2006).

How efficacious are close observations?

As with other issues associated with close observations, the literature in this area is under-developed and in a stage of relative 'infancy'. Indeed, perhaps the most important limitation of the extant literature is that no study has even tried to examine if 'being under' certain levels of observation actually reduces the number of suicide attempts, the person's suicide risk or extent of suicidal ideation; there is no randomised control trial that has attempted to compare psychiatric care units that use close observation against units without constant observation.

The data that does exist provides a highly disturbing picture of the abject failure of observations to prevent people taking their own lives. The United Kingdom Department of Health (2001) *Safety First* report highlighted that 18% of all completed mental health inpatient suicides occurred while people were under observation. More recently, the annual progress report on the National Suicide Prevention Strategy for England (Department of Health, 2005) reports that of the recorded cases of suicide as an inpatient of mental health services:

> Twenty two percent of the patients (185 cases) were under special (non-routine) observation, similar to the 23% in the previous inquiry report. Of

> those who died on the ward, 48% (117 cases) were under special observation.

It continues:

> In this sample, 18 cases (3%) were under one-to-one observations. The number of deaths under observation has not fallen since 1997, which means that they have increased as a proportion of inpatient suicides.

Similarly, Goh *et al*'s (1990) report indicated that 6 out of 57 completed suicides were under close or special observations. Gournay and Bowers (2000) report that, of the 31 cases of suicide or self-harm that they reviewed, 23 of these were under an observation 'level' greater than the minimum level of observations for all the clients on the unit. Furthermore, a disturbing finding from Cardell and Pitula's (1999) study was that 10% of the study participants informed researchers that they lied about their degree of suicidality in order to hasten the termination of constant observation.

These consistent findings are perhaps even less encouraging when one considers the very high number of people who go on to take their own lives once the close observations have been removed and/or they are discharged (Geddes and Juszczak, 1995; Geddes *et al*, 1997; Gournay and Bowers, 2000; Hawton *et al*, 2003; Ho, 2003; King *et al*, 2001; Pirkola *et al*, 2005). In the only published paper of practice development that was identified in the review, following the dismantling of observation and moving towards a more 'care' orientated system (Dodds and Bowles, 2001) there was no increase of suicides during the corresponding period (18 months). Furthermore, though not an empirical piece, in the discussion paper arising out of this 'study' a number of compelling testimonies are evident, as well as further confirmation that removing observations led to a reduction – not an increase in suicide rates (Bowles *et al*, 2002). As a result, one can conclude, with a degree of empirical confidence, that while close observation may have maintained the physical safety of some clients, in no way is this physical safety guaranteed. The existing empirical evidence is reasonable consistent in showing just what a woefully weak and ineffective 'intervention' surveillance (observations) can be (see for example the latest evidence reported by the National Institute for Mental Health, 2007).

More worryingly, close observation appears to lead some clients into deliberately misleading the clinician in order to have the observations 'lifted'.

To summarise, as a scientific and clinical community we really don't know whether or not placing a person 'under observation', or increasing the surveillance, reduces his or her suicidality; we don't know if placing a person under observation makes him or her feel less suicidal. What we do know is that placing a person under observation does not guarantee his or her physical safety. Indeed, if the UK referred data referred to are accurate, the efficacy of close observations as a means to prevent suicide has diminished since 2001. Furthermore, the findings pertaining to the experiences of 'being observed' are equivocal, with some data showing that clients as experience observations as non-therapeutic, while other data show that clients experience observations as therapeutic. Importantly, though, there is a growing body of evidence which indicates that even when observations are carried out 'well', it is certain 'micro-skills' or 'micro-interventions' that some P/MH nurses use (and these are captured and described in the literature pertaining to the P/MH nursing care of suicidal people: see Cutcliffe *et al*, 2006, Cutcliffe and Stevenson, 2007; Sun *et al*, 2005; Talseth *et al*, 1997, 1999) during the observations, and not the observations *per se*, that appear to have some therapeutic effectiveness for suicidal people.

While it would be epistemologically premature to posit a simple causative relationship between high rates of suicide and high rates of defensive practice, it is hard to ignore the empirical and anecdotal evidence which strongly suggests that defensive practices have, at best, a limited usefulness (and efficacy) in providing care to the suicidal person. Even if we were to invoke simplistic forms of logic, it would appear to be counter-intuitive (and an ill-advised choice) to 'treat' or 'care' for people with sophisticated, complex, multi-dimensional problems by preventing the physical means of attempting suicide, and hoping that the suicidal person spontaneously resolves whatever problems (and psychache) that ushered them towards suicide in the first instance. Clearly, more sophisticated and less defensive forms of practice are needed to care for suicidal people. Accordingly, the authors purport that such defensive, containment and surveillance orientated 'care' for suicidal people needs to be replaced as a matter of urgency by a more engagement, 'talking-centred' nursing approach.

3. The focus on risk assessment at the expense of what comes after

Few credible suicidologists or clinicians would dispute the importance of clinicians developing and maintaining their assessment skills. While the authors in no way wish to decry the value and necessity of suicide risk assessment, we do however wish to emphasise that *determining the degree of risk of suicide in a person is only the beginning.*

Numerous state and national suicide strategies are replete with recommendations on how to improve and enhance risk assessment. These exhortations are laudable.

There is a clear need to enhance the accuracy (and frequency of use) of suicide risk assessment, but on its own this will not be enough.

Thorough and accurate risk assessment that does not lead to intervention is not only inadequate but a pathway to frustration. In order to emphasise this point, we would like to draw on the analogy of coronary care and the risk of myocardial infarction. A significant and very well developed literature exists around the issue of risk factors in coronary care. Many of these are well known to members of the public; in no way are they restricted to the purview of medicine or healthcare. Several risk assessment tools have been developed and shown to be reliable and valid. But where coronary care risk assessment differs markedly for assessing risk of suicide is that the assessment actually leads somewhere. Having undertaken the risk assessment a variety of primary, secondary and tertiary interventions are enacted. The person's diet is changed, exercise regimens are put in place, a variety of efficacious medications are prescribed and administered, family histories are explored, educational packages are provided, gradual reintroductions to activities occur etc. We would like to suggest that the reader pause for a moment here and consider: what do you think would happen if after conducting a thorough risk assessment for myocardial infarction the practitioner did not then proceed to implement a variety of interventions? Or stopped at only preventing the physical means for the person to overstress themselves and administered medications? Yet all too often this is analogously the 'care' provided to suicidal people; assessment of risk, while imperfect, is little more than a beginning. Maris (2007, p. vi) eloquently sums up the issue when he states:

> I wrote a major book on suicide risk assessment in 1992 and I know full-well that risk assessment itself never saved anyone's life. We already knew and strongly suspected that most people we assessed were suicidal, otherwise we would not be doing it in the first place.

Accordingly, while the authors join with others in advocating for enhanced suicide risk assessment skills and practices[3], our greater concern is that practitioners must use these assessment data in a number of meaningful ways. Suicide risk assessment scores ought to be tied to the level of engagement provided (see Cutcliffe and Barker, 2004). Suicide risk assessment must be a repeated, ongoing endeavour, producing cumulative patterns of data that provide a more accurate assessment of changes in suicide risk over time. Further, suicide risk assessments ought to be used (at least in part) as an evaluator mechanism, as well as a predictive

3 And we are both engaged in research and practice development initiatives focused in this area.

mechanism. That is to say, reductions in suicide risk assessment scores can be evidence of diminishing suicide risk and *ipso facto* evidence that the prescribed interventions and care plan actions are working effectively.

4. The focus on initiatives to reduce access to lethal means

With apologies to the Nobel Laureate Dr John Nash, while the authors continue to understand that there is some merit in attempts to limit access to means, such an emphasis is not only 'incomplete'[4] but it also misses the key point. We explain this argument in more detail below.

Recently, a special supplement dedicated to exploring/controlling access to means of suicide was published with the journal *Crisis: The Journal of Crisis Intervention and Suicide Prevention*. According to the editor of this special edition (Beautrais, 2007a, p. 1),

> There is now a large body of research literature suggesting that restricting access to a particular method of suicide may successfully reduce suicides by that method. However, the extent to which reductions in rates of suicide by one method that is restricted are paralleled by reductions in *overall* [original emphasis] suicide rates is less clear; and this has led to debates about the extent to which restriction of one method may lead to substitution through an equally lethal method.

In the light of this compilation of evidence it is necessary to consider how this can and should affect mental healthcarer efforts to reduce means to access as a method of combating suicide. For some (see Hawton, 2007, for example), the utility of restricting access as a means to prevent suicide is beyond debate, though Hawton acknowledges that preventing access to means does not address the underlying cause(s) of suicide. The International Association of Suicide Prevention (2003) also contributes to the debate and purports that this method of suicide prevention has particular utility when such access can be readily controlled. Hawton (2007) rightly draws attention to the data that offer the most support for restricting access to means, namely changing from 'coal gas' to a non-toxic 'domestic gas' supply in the UK. He argues that there was little evidence of an immediate compensatory increase in the use of other methods of suicide following the reduction in suicides by carbon monoxide poisoning. Interestingly though, the data reported by Charlton *et al* (1994) also indicate that subsequent to the recorded reduction in the overall rate, the suicide rate for males later began to

4 As Nash might say.

increase again as other means were discovered or became more 'popular'. Further telling and more longitudinal evidence is reported in Gunnell *et al*'s (2000) study, where it was found that following the change in domestic gas, for males aged 15–34 the overall rate of suicide increased by 37% between 1973 and 1975. There was a 34% decrease in suicides by gas, but a 299% increase in suicide by drug overdose. Correspondingly, for females, there was a 54% increase overall, and 89% decrease in suicide by gas, but a 305% increase in suicide by drug overdose. Accordingly, while it is accurate for Hawton (2007) to highlight that there was little evidence of an *immediate compensatory (substitution) increase* (original emphasis) the longitudinal data tend to indicate that there does appear to have been a longer-term substitution effect occurring.

Similarly, a number of studies have illustrated the apparent effect on suicide rates by controlling access to firearms (see for example, Lester and Murrell, 1982; Loftin *et al*, 1991; Cantor and Slater, 1995). However, within the same body of work, there is evidence of the substitution effect: as access to means of one method of suicide is restricted or removed (usually), following a period of time the rate of suicide by alternative means rises dramatically. Recent evidence of this phenomenon can be found in the study undertaken by De Leo *et al* (2003), where these researchers examined the increase in the rate of suicide by hanging and an apparently simultaneous decrease in the rate of suicide by firearm as hypothetical evidence that Australian males have substituted one method of suicide for another.

In terms of reducing access to means for people admitted to psychiatric and/or mental healthcare facilities, some evidence indicates how the rate of suicide has reduced recently (National Institute for Mental Health in England, 2007). In the UK, the data indicate that the number of mental health inpatients dying by suicide dropped from 217 in 1997 to 154 in 2004[5]. One might speculate that this reduction occurred as a result of the range of 'interventions' and strategies identified in the original National Suicide Prevention Strategy (Department of Health, 2002); including reducing the person's access to means (eg. installing collapsible curtain rails as potential ligature points). However, no control group was used in these reports and thus there is no comparative data available.

There appears to be particular utility in restricting access to means as a suicide prevention strategy for those people who would be categorised as having high 'impulsivity'. In such instances, where the desire to die by suicide is an impulsive decision, being less able or unable to access the means during the period of high

5 Though the same reports shows that in the same time frame, the number of people in contact with the mental health services who die by suicide has increased; and it is perhaps notable that this finding is less prominent in the report.

impulsivity would seem like an intuitively logical prevention strategy. As a result, the authors would commend the logic of practitioners considering practices to reduce access as one component of (inpatient) care for suicidal people. However, there is also evidence that suicide as an impulsive act fails to account for many of the population that present to formal mental healthcare services (see Beautrais, 2007b); and that correspondingly, for a larger number of people, suicide is a chronic problem.

While acknowledging its vintage (and for some in international suicidology academe, highly significant) status, the work of Maris (1981), *Pathways to Suicide*, drew attention to the notion of suicidal careers. The central premise of his thesis was that individuals who took their own lives had long suicidal careers involving complex mixes of biological, social and psychological factors. More recently, Joiner's (2005) illuminating book contains three central premises: (1) that people who make a serious attempt to end their own lives feel real disconnection from others[6]; (2) they feel that they are a burden on others; and (3) *The ability to enact the lethal self-injury is acquired.* As a result of numerous studies Joiner (2005, p. 63) concludes that suicide

> occurs because one instance of suicidal behaviour lays the groundwork for later instances and it does so specifically through the accrual of fear-lessness and competence.

Relatedly, Beautrais' important work on looking at the trends and outcomes of all admissions for suicide attempts to a New Zealand hospital over 10 years reports similar findings. Beautrais (2007b) argues that her results clearly show that suicidal behaviour, for many, is a chronic condition, not just a single, impulsive event, and rather worryingly, for many the situation does not change much following a suicide attempt, because people do not get the help they need. Beautrais concludes that suicide it is a complex response by vulnerable people who need extensive long-term treatment, care and support.

In the context of all this evidence, one is left thinking what a P/MH nurse should make of the policy direction and any resultant practice emphasis concerned with limiting access to means. It would be difficult to disagree with the view that reducing access to means is likely to have a positive impact (reduce the numbers) of those 'impulsive' suicides, and consequently this should be included in care planning for inpatients who are at risk of suicide; however, this is an incomplete representation. In order to see the whole clinical picture, one needs to consider

6 Here we will not belabour the obvious parallels with the key finding in Cutcliffe and Stevenson's (2007) research: 'Reconnecting the person with humanity'.

the body of evidence that speaks to the possibility of a (*ex post facto)* substitution effect and the evidence that shows how one can learn or acquire the 'ability' to enact lethal self-injury. One also needs to be cognisant of how most people who present to mental healthcare services with a high risk of suicide are likely to have a 'chronic suicide' problem and associated suicidal career, rather than suicide as a 'spur of the moment', impulsive act. One also needs to be mindful of the not insignificant practical problems that exist with trying to create or ensure a 'means-free environment'. *With this important context established, while P/MH nurses should be mindful of the physical environment and its associated access to means, it seems that this should be an adjunct to the more central aspects of MH nursing care of suicidal people*. In the light of the limited long-term efficacy of limiting access to means for the majority of the types of suicidal people who present to formal mental healthcare services, there might be more valuable and effective interventions that P/MH nurses can engage in than managing the physical environment. The authors purport that such environmental management should be one of many 'interventions' that P/MH nurses have available to them, and moreover, that the same nurses should be painfully aware that while reducing access to one method/means in the 'here and now' might prevent an impulsive suicide, much more P/MH nursing interpersonal work is needed to help the (more common) person with a chronic suicide problem. As a speculative rather than empirically based finale to this section, the authors also wonder – does the P/MH nurse who becomes focused (pre-occupied?) with maintaining the elusive risk-free environment, simultaneously lose sight of the person?

Moving practice (and policy) forward: reconfiguring, re-thinking and developing mental healthcare service delivery

In line with some extant literature (see, for example: Barney *et al*, 2006; Renaud *et al*, 2006), we are mindful of the often reported under-utilisation of mental health services. However, discoveries reported in Jordan *et al* (2012) advance the findings and implications arising from previous epidemiologically informed studies in that these findings address the underlying reasons for this lack of engagement from the perspectives of young suicidal men in Northern Ireland. Mindful of idiographic generalisability[7] the authors argue that there may be case-

7 Qualitative researchers do not seek to generalise their findings in the same way that a quantitative researcher might. That is, they do not seek nomothetic generalisations relating to universal laws and absolute 'truths'. They do seek, however, to produce idiographic or naturalistic generalisations – generalisations about and drawn from cases (Sandelowski, 1998). These generalisations are drawn from purposeful samples who

related transferable findings here regarding the current under-utilisation of mental health services by suicidal people *per se*. In so doing, Jordan *et al* (2012) highlight a pervasive understanding (or more accurately perception) of current services as both stigmatised and stigmatising; as being inadequately available to young men in need and, where access is achieved, as lacking (at least, consistently) the necessary qualities to provide effective care.

The discoveries reported in Jordan *et al* (2012) also highlighted the need for suicide prevention programmes which reach out to young men *proactively*. In this regard, services that are embedded in the local community are of particular merit for a number of reasons. They are more likely to be informal in nature, based for example, on their association with social interaction *per se* (rather than interaction focused exclusively on clinical care). In addition, they are more easily and discreetly accessed, increasing the likelihood of contact at the time of need and in ways which are seen to protect confidentiality. These ideas and proposals are further supported by results from a range of internationally conducted research studies that have sought to understand (young) men's reluctance to engage with formal healthcare (Burke and McKeon, 2007; Centre for Suicide Prevention, 2007)[8]. Research undertaken specifically with young men who have experienced suicidal behaviour and/or thinking (see Jordan *et al*, 2012; Cutcliffe *et al*, 2012) endorses the appropriateness of embedding mental health related services in locations and venues in which young men are otherwise ordinarily present (Russell *et al*, 2004). These 'contexts' of engagement present as relatively familiar, informal and otherwise promote social interaction.

---

have experience of the 'case' and are thus applicable to similar 'cases', questions and problems, irrespective of the similarity between the demographic group (Morse, 1999). In nursing studies for example, each 'case' of nursing will bear a clear resemblance to nursing as a 'whole' and any related, similar 'cases'. Denzin and Lincoln (1994, p. 201) make this point most cogently when they state

> Every instance of a case or process bears the general class of phenomena it belongs to.

Thus, a process that is identified in one setting, group or population (ie. one case), can be similarly experienced by another related setting, group or population. For example, a Grounded Theory concerned with credentialising that was induced from a sample of nurses is likely to be generalisable to, and bear similarity with, any population that shares the process of credentialising.

8 As useful as such findings in such studies are, they are limited by the fact that they are based on research conducted amongst the general population of (young) men – not suicidal young men *per se*.

In addition, Jordan *et al* (2012) identify the value of suicide-related outreach work using more 'novel' forms of media to enhance therapeutic engagement. Such media include, but are not necessarily restricted to, social networking systems, the internet, text messaging and email. Not only do such means of contact/ communication reach out to those otherwise marginalised (van Spijker *et al*, 2010), but such efforts help simultaneously address concerns about stigma and confidentiality and reflect what is becoming increasingly common practice in terms of how (young) people communicate and interact.

Participants in the Jordan *et al* (2012) study gave powerful descriptions of the value of support they had received from a range of self-help groups or individuals who had experienced the same kind and/or degree of emotional distress. These study findings might be particularly innovative in suggesting the value of the principle of 'equivalence' to inform the development of community-based services. These services would enable young men to mix with and, in the process, learn from others with experience of suicidal behaviour. Jordan *et al* (2012) report that exposure of young people to suicidal behaviour among their peers can work to reduce the risk of their own suicidal behaviour, so long as the nature of this exposure is appropriate. Thus the accounts offered by participants suggest that being exposed 'close-up' to the devastating reality and aftermath of suicide (for example, personally encountering the effects of a peer's death on his family or hearing the testimonies of peers who had attempted suicide concerning these effects), it becomes understood as something to be avoided, irrespective of personal pressures and incentives. Consequently, direct 'first-hand' contact with suicidal behaviour among peers would seem to be a key property of relevant exposure in that it is more likely to foster a necessary emotional engagement with and learning from this behaviour.

Additionally, the discoveries reported in Jordan *et al* (2012) suggest that learning about the experiences of other young survivors may be particularly useful in helping young men to appreciate and see ways of personally coping with the realities of day-to-day living and prospering over the longer term. If young male suicide is mediated by a tendency in vulnerable individuals to make negative comparisons between themselves and other members of their peer groups (Russell *et al*, 2004), then promoting engagement between suicidal young men and their peers with the same or similar experiences is likely to reduce this general tendency. In keeping with this line of thinking, Harden *et al* (2002) highlighted the potential value of 'peer counselling' from their UK scoping exercise on the effectiveness of interventions for suicidal young men.

Participants in the Jordan *et al* (2012) study were acutely aware of the benefits they gained from meaningful (re)engagement with family and friends. As such, these findings support the importance of informal social networks in the process of helping young men to deal with their suicidality (Cleary, 2005; Oliver *et al*, 2005). In terms of service delivery, the value of promoting opportunities for such engagement, particularly over the longer term as young men move away from their immediate suicidal crisis, is suggested. Such thinking is supported by a series of recent reviews of the evidence concerning interventions relevant to suicide (youth) prevention that have highlighted the value of those which foster supportive relationships within families as well as significant others (Beautrais *et al*, 2005; Daniel and Goldston, 2009; see also Mishara *et al*, 2005).

Moving policy forward: micro and macro level policy amendments to enhance the care of suicidal people and enhance suicide prevention measures

In addition to the advancements and developments in policy alluded to in the preceding sections, the authors wish to advance the argument that there are some aspects of current suicide prevention policy that are fitting, appropriate and useful for informing the P/MH nursing care of the suicidal person (eg. development and promotion of effective clinical and professional practices, and additional training for caregivers to improve delivery of effective treatments). Others aspects are, in our view, in need of further thinking and development; we would argue that there would be merit in re-visiting suicide prevention policies (such as they are). These aspects are listed in Table 12.1 and some are explained in further detail below.

Re-visiting our policy emphasis on reducing access

Several authors have implored nurses to be more vigilant for, and conscious of, a range of means that people might use to attempt to take their own life. Anderson and Jenkins (2006), for example, draw specific attention to the risks of (over-dosing with) anti-psychotic and anti-depressant medication, train track 'hotspots' and ligature points (particularly within inpatient settings). As laudable as such exhortations may be (and we concur that more can be done by P/MH nurses to address the 'environmental risk reduction'), there is, in such literature, unfortunately little or no acknowledgement of the complexity of the relationship between access to means to take one's life and rates of suicide.

Notwithstanding the practical problems of trying to ensure a 'means-free environment', the international epidemiological evidence on this matter is equivocal. See for example the findings in Sinyor and Levitt's (2010) study of the effect of erecting a barrier on a suicide hotspot in Toronto Canada; the yearly rates were unchanged by this restricting access to means intervention. We have

Table 12.1 Suicide and suicide prevention – proposed policy initiatives and emphases.

1. Consider a suicide policy literature that reflects a less defensive, less risk management-oriented position
2. Consider a suicide policy literature that emphasises and reiterates the need for P/MH nurses involved in care of the suicidal person to receive appropriate clinical supervision
3. Consider a suicide policy literature that while being mindful of the physical environment and its associated access to means, reflects that this should be an adjunct to the more central aspects of P/MH nursing care of suicidal people
4. Consider a suicide policy literature that replaces 'Improving surveillance systems' with 'Improving the ability and capacity of P/MH nurses to engage with suicidal people'
5. Consider a suicide policy literature that indicates the need for additional postgraduate (post-basic) education and training in care of the suicidal person, that includes DBT, the work emanating from the University of Toronto, and the skills, attitudes and knowledge perhaps captured with the terms, engagement, co-presencing and inspiring hope

previously drawn attention to this issue, which originated from the UK, and to related data and findings emanating from Australia and New Zealand. Further related evidence can be found originating in Japan, where, during the 1930s, the most powerful suicide 'magnet' of its time was the volcano on the island of Oshima. Various attempts were made to reduce access to this volcano, including erecting barbed wire fences, the instigation of a 24 hour volcano watch, making travelling to the island with only a one-way ticket illegal, and infiltrating the passengers on the ferry that travelled to the island with 'plainclothes' detectives in order to arrest those hell bent on self-destruction (Colt, 1991). Despite all these efforts, 167 men and women still managed to jump to their deaths in 1934, and more worryingly 29 people who had been restrained dived off the ferry returning them to mainland Japan and subsequently drowned!

Furthermore, if one is serious about tackling the issue of access to means, the (seemingly unacknowledged) multi-layered, complicated relationship between access to means and completed suicides needs to be thought about in more detail. For example, there is evidence from the USA indicating a robust correlation between easy access to firearms and completed suicide, with several studies showing firearm death as the most common means used in suicides in the USA (especially for males). Then there is the number one location for suicide in the world – the Golden Gate Bridge, near San Francisco, California.

While there is little or no debate or dissent that both firearms and the Golden Gate Bridge can be couched as examples of 'means' to attempt/complete suicide, each example has a 'loud' lobby opposing any restrictions to access. For example, various methods to reduce the access to means associated with the Golden Gate Bridge have been touted, including closing the bridge to pedestrians at night and having staff patrolling the bridge. However two specific methods of reducing access have met with significant resistance in a variety of forms. Firstly, the notion of erecting a so-called suicide barrier (atop or in place of the existing safety railings[9]) was frustrated by oppositional arguments such as the engineering difficulties associated with such a construction; public opposition (especially with regard to the damage done to the bridge's aesthetic); and cost. Secondly, the notion of a safety net suspended below the bridge's main super structure was advanced from (at least) 2006 onwards.

> On October 10, 2008, the Golden Gate Bridge Board of Directors voted 14 to 1 to install a plastic-covered stainless-steel net below the bridge as a suicide deterrent. The net will extend 20 feet (6 m) on either side of the bridge and is expected to cost $40–50 million to complete. However, lack of funding could delay the net's deployment. (ref. Wikipedia, recovered 2012)

The safety net has yet to be built.

A variety of studies have been undertaken that consider the issue of gun control and suicide rates in an attempt to test the hypothesis that increased restrictions on firearms can reduce the annual suicide rate. There is evidence to support this hypothesis (see for example, Lester and Leenaars, 1993; Leigh and Neil, 2010; Department of Justice Canada, 1996; Klieve *et al*, 2009; Miller and Hemenway, 1999, 2001). Inversely, there is evidence that refutes the hypothesis (see for example, Department of Justice Canada, 1996; Kates and Mauser, recovered 2012). The preponderance of evidence in this area, according to the Harvard Injury Control Research Center (recovered 2012) indicates that (a) firearm availability is a risk factor for youth suicide in the USA; (b) the evidence that firearm availability increases the suicide rates of adults is credible, but is currently less compelling. However, any attempts to restrict gun access or introduce gun control are met with a vociferous and loud lobby from many advocacy groups – not least the National Rifle Association in the USA.

---

9 This method of reducing access has been implemented successfully in other parts of the word – see the Eiffel Tower and the Empire State Building.

Accordingly, while it is possible, if not probable, that a range of 'interventions' or policies to restrict/prevent access to means will have a positive effect on reducing some suicides in the short term (eg. especially those where suicide is an impulsive act, and those with high impulsivity); there is also evidence that such 'environmental focused interventions' offer but one piece of the answer. Such exhortations and efforts to reduce access to means will also have to be mindful that there is likely to be resistance from certain lobby groups; and that long-term substitution effects may bedevil these attempts to reduce suicide rates.

Re-thinking the contemporary hegemonic role of pharmacological interventions in the care of suicidal people

In many parts of the world the principal approach to 'treating and helping suicidal people' is a pharmacological one. Indeed, in some parts of the world, as Maris *et al* (2000a) and Campbell (2006) point out, it can be argued that the *only* treatment or help that suicidal people receive is pharmacologically-based. This is an entirely unacceptable position for us, given (a) the range of interventions available to practitioners for helping suicidal people; (b) the well-documented views of service users regarding the current over-use of pharmacological agents in mental healthcare, (c) the inconclusive evidence (such as it is) regarding the aetiology and/or causation of suicide and (d) the absence of any so-called 'anti-suicide' pill!

Those that champion a pharmacologically-driven approach to caring for suicidal people, such as Anderson and Jenkins (2006), present a somewhat narrow or one-dimensional view of the role of psychopharmacology in the 'management' of suicide. While we do not doubt that there appears to be some utility in certain anti-depressant medications for some suicidal people (see Jick *et al*, 2004), there is similarly evidence that SSRIs continue to be associated with increased rates of suicidal thinking and behaviour, mostly in children and adolescents (see for example, Healy and Whitaker, 2003; Healy 2005). Accordingly, to posit pharmacological agents for suicidal people as unequivocal, free from controversy and having a strong evidence base, appears to be misrepresenting our current knowledge base and may constitute further evidence of the 'biologising' of suicide; further evidence of the previously mentioned methodological sleight of hand. This prompts Shneidman (2001, p. 73) to assert:

> the biologizing of suicide is an integral part of the medicalization of what is essentially – so I believe – a phenomenological decision of the mind.

Despite the attempts of some to make the multi-dimensional experience of suicidality into little more than 'a depressed brain in need of a chemical' and the associated emphasis on pharmacology as the primary *modus operandi* for 'helping' suicidal people, a more balanced representation of the evidence suggests that we are far from having an effective pharmacological treatment for all suicidal people.

Moving education forward: training for caregivers to improve delivery of effective care and treatment

Given the alarmingly high rates of mental health inpatient suicide and the even more concerning rates of suicide in the period of time following discharge[10] it seems eminently logical to make the case for additional training/education for care givers who wish to provide care to/for suicidal people. In the view of the authors of this book, the issue is not whether or not additional training/education is needed, but what the nature of this additional training/education should/could be? Interestingly, perhaps the crux of this matter is whether this additional training/education should focus on tightening up current ineffective, defensive and containment orientated practices (such as observation) or if the training/education should be focused on the interventions/approaches described in this book as to how P/MH nurses can work with suicidal people. Further, this might be prefaced by an even more rudimentary need regarding training/education on how to care for suicidal people being included (and/or enhanced) in undergraduate/pre-registration/entry-level programmes.

Current preparation – what training?

It is worth looking at the current international situation regarding preparation of nurses and, more specifically, preparing these practitioners to work with suicidal people. Nursing curricula, whether pre- or post-graduation, and the vast majority of the nursing textbooks used in conjunction with such courses/programs, commonly make reference (to a greater or lesser extent) to suicide. Differences are common and not surprising between specialist and generic pre-registration curricula (Younge and Boschma, 2006). Restricted by constraints of time and space, and by the demands of competing areas of care/issues for nurses, generic programs often have less attention to suicide (and still less devoted to care of the suicidal person) than specialist programs. Yet specialist programs (eg. P/MH nursing) have no case for complacency and arguably are still severely limited in their preparation of P/MH nurses to care for suicidal people. Almost inevitably, the focus in such curricula is an introduction to the principal theories of suicide (rightly so) and then material on risk and risk assessment; very little attention is given to what P/MH

10 As pointed out and referenced above.

nurses might do by way of caring for suicidal people once the risk assessment is complete (other than perhaps assigning and instigating various forms of defensive practice, administering medication and some reference to no-suicide contracts.)

It may well be that the best one can achieve in basic (entry-level) nurse education is to equip students with risk assessment skills, familiarity with suicide risk tools, and some intervention skills, such as active listening, personal awareness raising of their own issues around death, dying and suicide, and the beginnings of the development of the required qualities. It may well be that additional specialist and/or postgraduate, advanced education and training would be required for those nurses who wish to focus on or specialise with working with suicidal people. Just as one would not expect newly graduated nurses to take on a caseload of people requiring specialist psychotherapy, the authors suggest it would be clinically prudent not to expect newly graduated nurses to take on a case load 'heavy' with highly suicidal people. This appears to be particularly logical and sensible given the previously mentioned complexity of suicide and the emotional requirements that such clients demand of their nurses. In the light of these foci, one might conclude that the current preparation of nurses to work with suicidal people is deficient in providing them with the skills, attitudes and knowledge necessary for delivering adequate, therapeutic, transformative care for suicidal people. Hence there is a clear need to provide additional education/training to address this matter.

Improving observations and tightening up policies

Some, such as Bowers and Park (2001), the Standing Nursing and Midwifery Advisory Committee (SNMAC) (1999), Gournay and Bowers (2000) and Bowers *et al* (2007), indicate that the education/training emphasis needs to be on improving so-called special observations and tightening up observations policies (and ensuring strict adherence to these policies). For example, Bowers and Park (2001, p. 777) argue that what is needed is a clear, agreed, workable, policy as this would facilitate basic training. However, in the same paper they also acknowledge that there seems to be no agreement about what observers are supposed to do during special observations and they find it hard to see what the content of such training should be. Perhaps Bowers and Park (2001, p. 777) feel that training nurses how to undertake observations while reading a newspaper should be part of this training as they also state:

> Although some authors decry the nurse who sits in the doorway of a patient's room reading a newspaper, even this might be appropriate at times and temporarily offers the patient a form of privacy of solitude.

Similarly, the Standing Nursing Midwifery Advisory Committee (1999, p. 6) advocate tightening up the observations policies and they offer what they believe to be the essential components of adequate training to carry out observations, these are listed in Box 12.1.

It is noteworthy that of these 11 elements, only two (perhaps three) make any reference to what nurses might actually do while enacting observations, and more importantly they say nothing about how a nurse might ease a suicidal person's psychache, promote a suicidal person's hope, or facilitate a reconnection with humanity. Gournay and Bowers (2000, p. 131) argue that nursing staff need to more strictly adhere to (observation) protocols and policies. And despite the admonishments of the UK Department of Health (2001) regarding the use of intermittent observations, Bowers *et al* (2007, p. 187) conclude their latest research with a number of recommendations, one of which states:

> Trusts should review their special observations policies to ensure that this form (intermittent observation) of containment is an available option for staff.

Bowers and some others have repeatedly purported that observation is not simply a custodial activity, but an opportunity to interact with the patient and that encouraging communication, listening and conveying to the patient that they are cared for are important components (see also for example SNMAC, 1999; Gournay

Box 12.1 Standing Nursing Midwifery Advisory Committee's essential components of adequate training in close observations

(a) Risk assessment
(b) Risk management
(c) Engagement of patients at risk of harming self and others
(d) Factors associated with self-harm/harm to others
(e) Indications for observation
(f) Levels of observation
(g) Therapeutic opportunities in observations
(h) Roles and responsibilities of the multidisciplinary team in relation to observation
(i) Making the observation safe
(j) Recording the observation
(k) The use of reviews and audit

and Bowers, 2000). Yet at the risk of sounding incredulous, it is difficult to see how any nurse can interact with, encourage communication with and listen to a suicidal person when they are checking in on them intermittently; for instance if they are following the SNMAC's (1999, p. 3) guidance and checking the patient's location every 15–30 minutes.

Training in engagement and meaningful ways to responding to suicidal people

As an alternative to focusing on defensive and/or containment orientated issues, in place of improving observations and tightening up policies we suggest the following emphasis regarding additional education/training. There are a number of (nursing) practices regarding helping suicidal people that have some supporting empirical evidence regarding their utility and effectiveness. These are dialectical behaviour therapy; the approach that focuses on de-escalating an individual's emotional (psychache) crisis and providing the person with an enhanced ability to identify/express their distressing emotions; and the approach that focuses on engagement, inspiring hope and reconnecting the person with humanity. It is these approaches where, for us, that our education/training emphasis must be.

Training in dialectical behaviour therapy (see Linehan 2007) and the approach that focuses on de-escalating an individual's emotional (psychache) crisis and providing the person with an enhanced ability to identify/express their distressing emotions (Bergman and Links, 2002; Bergman *et al*, 2007) have been covered previously (see Chapter 7); therefore we will concentrate on the approach the focuses on engagement, inspiring hope and reconnecting the person with humanity. For those authors contributing to the empirical literature on the nursing care of the suicidal person (see Cutcliffe *et al*, 2006; Cutcliffe and Stevenson, 2007; Sun *et al*, 2005; Talseth *et al*, 1997, 1999) and for key figures in the international suicidology academe (Joiner, 2005; Maris *et al* 2000a; Shneidman, 1997, 2001, to name but a few)[11] *the practice of working with suicidal people is essentially an interpersonal endeavour; one that is inherently concerned with listening and talking* (our emphasis). In order to do so, the nurse needs to be comfortable with co-presencing; needs to be able to sit with the suicidal patients' and their own emotions that surround the experience(s) of death, suicide and mortality. While some nurses may feel that they are already comfortable with this (and that may very well be the case), there is a body of evidence that shows how for many, dealing with emotionally charged experiences such as death and suicide

11 And for many P/MH authors, researchers and practitioners who have contributed to the debate

is often problematic and is sometimes avoided altogether. Evidence of this dynamic is evident in both 'vintage' and more contemporary literature.

Altschul's (1972) seminal contribution on the importance of interpersonal relations as the foundation of effective P/MH nursing found that P/MH nurses largely shunned any contact with patients, consistently spending their time in the office and only about 10% with patients. Altschul's conclusions about P/MH nursing are an echo of the earlier work of Menzies Lyth (1959) in relation to 'general' nurses' response to suffering and death, namely having great difficulty and thus avoiding this. More recently, Sanon-Rollins (recovered 2011) drew attention to a survey made of three hospitals. The findings revealed that regardless of institutional or demographic characteristics, nurses use avoidance as a primary strategy to resolve conflict, including their own internal conflict.

Similarly, even a cursory examination of the bereavement counselling literature will show that dealing with the issues or topics of death and dying often provokes feelings of discomfort in the listener (Lendrum and Syme, 1992; Raphael, 1983; Worden, 1988). Accordingly, it is not surprising that some nurses still have significant discomfort when talking about situations which are synonymous with death and dying. Coupled with these emotionally charged issues is the qualitatively different nature of death (or attempted death) by suicide (Jordan, 2001). *Thus, nurses working with a person who has made a serious suicidal attempt need to be thoroughly prepared to hear about death, dying and suicide and moreover, must not shy away from this; they should not be uncomfortable with the topic(s) nor discourage the suicidal person from talking openly about his/her suicidality, psychache and/or hopelessness* (our emphasis).

A similar argument has been postulated previously by Davidhizar and Vance (1993), who also stressed that when working with suicidal people nurses need to consider their own attitudes towards suicide in order that they can ensure that they do not distance themselves from the suicidal person. Such consideration clearly demands and requires that the nurse needs to possess a high degree of self-awareness and needs to have come to terms with his or her own mortality. Without so doing, the process of providing meaningful caring responses to suicidal people would be hindered if not actually thwarted. As a result, any additional training would have to include some attention to these issues.

Consideration of these approaches for caring for suicidal people allows the authors to highlight some of the key and/or minimum educational components for including in a post-basic program in equipping nurses to provide effective, meaningful caring responses to suicidal people.

Box 12.2 Minimum educational components for including in a post-basic program in equipping nurses to provide effective, meaningful caring responses to suicidal people

- Self-awareness training – specifically dealing with one's own mortality
- Cognitive re-framing techniques and skills
- Experiential work around being comfortable with stillness
- Monitoring one's self – particularly one's own level of hope
- Experiential work around hearing about death, dying and suicide
- Techniques and qualities associated with inspiring hope
- Techniques and qualities associated with presencing
- Listening (without prejudice or discomfort)
- Recognising limiting personal constructs, cognitive distortions (such as catastrophising, over-generalising, selective abstraction, arbitrary interference, magnification and minimising, emotional reasoning, use of 'shoulds and oughts', labelling and mislabelling)
- The use of gentle, implicit challenges
- Giving and receiving clinical supervision
- A basic understanding of and ability to detect transference and counter-transference
- Familiarity with and comfort using empathy-promoting interpersonal techniques: simple reflection, selective reflection, empathic building, paraphrasing, summarising, clarifying, open questions, closed questions, appropriate self-disclosure
- Creating a calming, peaceful external (physical) environment
- Experiential work on becoming comfortable with not having erudite answers
- Interventions and attitudes to build trust
- Interventions geared to explore and facilitate understanding of the meanings attached to the suicidal act (eg. catalytic interventions, empathic building, selective reflection)
- Role modelling and the use of simulators

Moving suicide research forward: the need for clinically-focused studies

As stated previously, despite the use of a range of interventions, the evidence is consistent in showing a decade by decade rise in the global rate of suicide since the

1950s (WHO, recovered 2012). The WHO (recovered 2012) state that,

> In the last 45 years suicide rates have increased by 60% worldwide

and that

> though traditionally suicide rates have been highest among the male elderly, rates among young people have been increasing to such an extent that they are now the group at highest risk in a third of countries, in both developed and developing countries.

Consequently, we can assert with some degree of empirical confidence (or authority) that our knowledge of suicide is far from complete; our interventions and suicide prevention endeavours have thus far met with only limited success and; suicide intervention and prevention need to become a more sophisticated process, perhaps tailored to the particular needs of certain cultures, populations and communities. It is also necessary, though perhaps a difficult point to acknowledge, that our research efforts to help reduce the global rate of suicide have also met with, at best, limited success.

One area where there appears to be broad consensus is that there are a range of times and opportunities where intervention to prevent suicide appears to be possible. This is particularly the case if one embraces or accepts the view that suicide, or a person's path to suicide, can be described as a trajectory (see for example, Morttunen *et al*, 1992; National Task Force on Suicide, 1994; Shneidman, 1993; Aldridge, 1998; Joiner, 2005). One of the implications from such a view is that healthcare practitioners have several 'windows of opportunity' in which they might be able to intervene and help a person avoid making a suicide attempt or completing suicide. For healthcare practitioners these opportunities are often couched in terms of primary, secondary and tertiary levels of (prevention) intervention. However, there remains much we do not know about the nature and efficacy of the interviews interventions (that we already have) at each of the levels of healthcare. Moreover, we still do not have a very clear understanding of the nature of the individual's suicidal experience(s). Consequently, it becomes evident that there is a clear and urgent requirement to gain a deeper understanding of the particular lived experiences of people who attempt suicide. This will help enable us to design specific and effective interventions for each of the identified levels. Indeed, such a position is highlighted in the words of Dr John Frank, Scientific Director, Canadian Institute of Population and Public Health where he states:

> One must understand how human health (and ill health) develops, in order to design effective programs and policies to protect and promote the

wellbeing of the public. (CIHR, Institute of Population and Public Health Website, 2002).

We need to ask such questions as: what leads these people to attempt suicide? What particular experiences, be they social (or societal), spiritual, psychological, or interpersonal, are involved in influencing younger males to consider taking their own life?

The case for studying the lived experiences of people who have attempted suicide

Having outlined the limitations of previous research endeavours and our current understanding of the 'trajectory' of suicide, the next logical step is to offer a viable alternative. It is important to point out that such an alternative does not *replace* (emphasis added) existing *methods but serves to augment and/or complement* (emphasis added) efforts understand to understand suicide. Consequently, it is necessary to outline the key philosophical and methodological underpinnings of phenomenology.

Phenomenology is a human science whose purpose is to describe and understand particular phenomena as lived experience. It is the rigorous, critical and systematic study of 'essences'. The purpose of which is to explicate the structure or essence of the lived experience of a phenomenon in the search for the 'unity meaning', which is the identification of the essence of the phenomenon, and its accurate description through everyday lived experience (van Manen, 1997).

The argument for suggesting phenomenology as the method most appropriate for the research endeavour in this substantive area is grounded in nursing's philosophical beliefs about humans and the holistic nature of healthcare practice. As a discipline, nursing has long encouraged detailed attention to the holistic care of humans (Peplau, 1952, 1988), purposefully avoiding attempts to 'reduce' a person into his or her constituent parts. As a result, nurses concern themselves with providing care for the mind, body, spirit, and social and environmental issues influencing the person's wellbeing. This results in providing care for the 'integrated whole' of the person. Such approaches to care have clear connections and commonality with phenomenological inquiry, given that phenomenology is equally concerned with understanding and exploring the integrated whole (Streubert and Carpenter, 1999). A holistic perspective and the study of experience as 'lived' serves as the foundations for phenomenological inquiry.

Furthermore, lived experience in the everyday world is the central focus of phenomenological inquiry (Schutz, 1972). Or to rephrase, those experiences that are central to human life are appropriate for phenomenological study, if not required to be studied using phenomenological methods. There can be few better examples of experiences that are central to human life than the experiences that lead a person to consider ending his or her life. While acknowledging the complex interaction of biological, genetic, interpersonal and sociological variables in contributing to a person's suicidal behaviour, there is utility in understanding suicide as a result of a person's life, his or her experiences and the situated contextual meaning that the person attributes to these experiences (Heidegger,1962).

In order to provide care/interventions, at all of the previously described levels, it is thus necessary to view the person and his or her situation holistically, and to understand the particular experiences or phenomena and situated meanings that lead these people to attempt suicide. Because there is a distinct need to design interventions and programs that specifically address the needs, problems and circumstances that usher people into attempting suicide (ie. the trajectory of suicide), such interventions and programs cannot be designed without the preliminary understanding of this trajectory.

Furthermore, as stated previously, understanding suicide clearly needs a multi-dimensional and multi-professional response. Accordingly, the authors argue that there is great merit and currency in constructing multi-professional research teams to address this issue. The authors further assert that no single professional group has all the answers to this problem, hence the utility of drawing on the expertise that each professional group can offer. Furthermore, the multi-disciplinary nature of such research teams means that each member would be able to bring his or her particular disciplinary experience and expertise to the data analysis, to the rewriting of the phenomenological text. Such multi-disciplinary analysis will provide a more comprehensive understanding of the lived experiences of suicidal males. Importantly, this deeper understanding will inform the potential interventions that could be provided by a variety of healthcare disciplines, each of whom is involved in the care and prevention of the suicidal male.

Specific clinically-focused future suicide research questions

In bringing this chapter and, correspondingly, the book to a close, we wish to focus on the future; especially the nature of future studies that we suggest are needed in order to better understand how (and what) needs to be done to better help suicidal people under our care.

In so doing we offer the following list:

- There is a need for a clinical trial comparing the therapeutic effects of healthcare units/centres that use custodial, containment-driven practices (eg. use of close observations) against other healthcare units/centres that use an engagement, hope-inspiring, model of care for suicidal people. Where 'conflicting' or contrary practice models exist, the logical step is to contrast such models with one another. Clearly, radical change to current practice can be anxiety-provoking for some (see Cutcliffe and Barker, 2002); resulting in some cases in catastrophic predictions of what could happen if engagement replaces observations. The authors argue that a clinical trial, undertaken on such a scale that would minimise any potential risk, could quite easily be designed.

- Evaluating specific suicide risk assessment instruments. Even while accepting the axiom that suicide risk assessment instruments are only one 'piece' of a comprehensive assessment, further studies that validate their accuracy are necessary. Some encouraging work has already been completed in Canada in this area (see Perlman *et al*, 2011) and while instruments often share common features (Perlman *et al*, 2011), the evidence indicates that some instruments have more utility and validity than others.
- There is a need to survey the current extent of formal education, training and preparation that clinical staff have received pertaining to the care of the suicidal person. The contemporary data on completed inpatient/outpatient suicides, and suicides following discharge, clearly suggest additional training and education are necessary. That being said, the full extent of the need for this training (or more accurately trainings), remains unclear. Determining where the gaps in knowledge, skills and attitudes exist perhaps helps inform where to target remedial and practice development efforts first.
- Perhaps a component of the aforementioned survey would be an attempt to establish the degree of confidence and competence that clinical staff possess when they are nursing suicidal people.
- Training for clinical staff to improve their care of suicidal people would have to be evaluated, perhaps revised and refined, and re-evaluated. Such iterative approaches to model (practice) testing appear to indicate the need for an 'action research' evaluation study.
- Given that a single study might be a random event (and thus is deemed to have little long-term predictive value), confirmation (or refutation – see Popper, 1965) of the original observation is necessary; thus more observations of the phenomenon of interest are sought. As a result, replicating the study that led to the first theory of how P/MH nurses care for suicidal people, described in Cutcliffe and Stevenson (2007), appears to be required.

- While there appears to be little or no doubt that (diminished) hope, and with that, hopelessness, are clearly key variables in the experiences of suicidal people, a deeper, more sophisticated understanding of how hope can be inspired, nurtured, instilled and maintained in suicidal people is clearly needed. Moreover, these induced theories would subsequently require testing and validating.
- Further testing and verification of other emerging models or interventions are necessary to develop and expand our evidence-base for effective suicide prevention and interventions. For example, further evaluations dialectic behavioural therapy, or/and the work emanating out of the PISA study, and interventions to prevent suicide post-discharge would be most welcome.

As part of a clinical and scientific community, we are only just beginning to unravel and understand one of the most compelling and yet mysterious human experiences – self-initiated death. There is little doubt that more lives could be saved and enhanced if we knew more and subsequently enacted how to help suicidal people move from a death-orientated place to a life-orientated place. While the evidence captured in this book indicates that we may have more 'tools' at our disposal than was previously the case, and that these (perhaps) preliminary tools may have some utility, we encourage clinicians of all disciplines to remain open to further discoveries, future validated theories and the findings of studies that have yet to be undertaken.

Acknowledgements

Parts of this chapter were originally published as

Cutcliffe JR, Stevenson C (2008) Never the twain? reconciling national suicide prevention strategies with the practice, educational and policy needs of Psychiatric/Mental Health Nurses: part two. *International Journal of Mental Health Nursing*, **17**: 351–62

and

Cutcliffe JR, Stevenson C (2008) A critique of Anderson and Jenkins' article 'The national suicide prevention strategy for England: the reality of a national strategy for the nursing profession'. *Journal of Psychiatric and Mental Health Nursing*, **15**: 154–60

and have been reproduced (and/or adapted) with the kind permission of Blackwell Science.

References

Aldridge D (1998) *Suicide: The Tragedy of Hopelessness*. Jessica Kingsley, London.
Altschul A (1972) *Patient–Nurse Interaction*. Churchill Livingstone, Edinburgh.

Anderson R (2000) Assessing the risk of self-harm in adolescents: a psychoanalytic perspective. *Psychoanalytic Psychotherapy*, **14**(1): 9–21.

Anderson M, Jenkins R (2006) The national suicide prevention strategy for England: the reality of a national strategy for the nursing profession. *Journal of Psychiatric and Mental Health Nursing*, **13**(6): 641–50.

Arsenault-Lapierre G, Kim C, Turecki G (2004) Psychiatric diagnoses in 3275 suicides: a meta-analysis. *BMC Psychiatry*, **4**: 4–37.

Barker P, Cutcliffe JR (1999) Clinical risk: a need for engagement not observation. *Mental Health Practice*, **2**(8): 8–12.

Barney LJ, Griffiths KM, Jorm AF, Christensen H (2006) Stigma about depression and its impact on help-seeking intentions. *Australian and New Zealand Journal of Psychiatry*, **40**: 51–4.

Barraclough B, Bunch J, Nelson P, Sainsbury P (1974) A hundred cases of suicide: clinical aspects. *British Journal of Psychiatry*, **125**: 355–73.

Beautrais A (2007a) Editorial: The contribution to suicide prevention of restricting access to methods and sites. *Crisis (Supplement 1 Controlling access to means of suicide*, **28**(suppl 1): 1–3.

Beautrais A (recovered 2007b) *Suicide Researchers Receives Top International Award*. http://www.chmeds.ac.nz/newsevents/articles/suicidetopaward.htm.

Beautrias AL, Collings SCD, Ehrhardt P, Henare K (2005) *Suicide Prevention: A Review of Evidence of Risk and Protective Factors and Points of Effective Intervention*. New Zealand Ministry of Health, Wellington.

Bergmans Y, Links P (2002) A description of a psychosocial/psychoeducational intervention for persons with recurrent suicide attempts. *Crisis*, **23**: 156–60.

Bowers L, Park A (2001) Special observations in the care of psychiatric inpatients: a literature review. *Issues in Mental Health Nursing*, **22**: 769–86.

Bowers L, Gournay K, Duffy D (2000) Suicide and self-harm in inpatient psychiatric units: a national survey of observation policies. *Journal of Advanced Nursing*, **32**(2): 437–44.

Bowers L, Whittington R, Nolan P, Parkin D, Curtis S, Bhui K, Hackney D, Allan T, Simpson A, Flood C (2007*) The City 128 Study of Observations and Outcomes on Acute Psychiatric Wards*, City University, London.

Bowles N, Dodds P, Hackney D, Sunderland C, Thomas P (2002) Formal observations and engagement: a discussion paper. *Journal of Psychiatric and Mental Health Nursing*, **9**(3): 255–60.

Buchanan-Barker P, Barker P (2005) Observation: the original sin of mental health nursing? *Journal of Psychiatric and Mental Health Nursing*, **12**: 541–9.

Burke S, McKeon P (2007) Suicide and the reluctance of young men to use mental health services. *Irish Journal of Psychiatric Medicine*, **24**(2): 67–70.

Campbell FR (2006) The aftermath of suicide: the clinician's role. In Simon RI, Hales RE (eds.) *The American Psychiatric Publishing Textbook of Suicide Assessment and Management*. American Psychiatric Publishing, Washington DC, pp. 459–76.

Canadian Institutes for Health Research (2002) http://wwwcihr-irscgcca/e/institues/ipph.

Cantor CH, Slater PJ (1995) The impact of firearm control legislation on suicide in Queensland: preliminary findings. *Medical Journal of Australia*, **162**(11): 583–5.

Cardell R, Pitula CR (1999) Suicidal inpatients' perceptions of therapeutic and non-therapeutic aspects of constant observation. *Psychiatric Services*, **20**(8): 1066–70.

Centre for Suicide Prevention (2007) *Men and Suicide: Part II Encouraging Help-Seeking and the Promise of Social Support*. SIEC Alert No 66, December 2007.

Charlton J, Kelly S, Dunnell K, Evans B, Jenkins R, Wallis R (1994) Trends in suicide deaths in England and Wales. In: Jenkins R, Griffiths S, Wylie I, Hawton K, Morgan G, Tylee A (eds.) *The Prevention of Suicide*. Department of Health, HMSO, London, pp. 5–12.

Cleary A (2005) Death rather than disclosure: struggling to be a real man. *Irish Journal of Sociology*, **14**(2): 155–76.

Colt GH (1991) *The Enigma of Suicide*. Summit Books, New York.

Connell RW, Messerschmidt J (2005) Hegemonic masculinity rethinking the concept. *Gender and Society*, **19**(6): 829–59.

Cutcliffe JR (2003) The differences and commonalities between United Kingdom and Canadian psychiatric/mental health nursing: a personal reflection. *Journal of Psychiatric and Mental Health Nursing*, **10**, 255–7.

Cutcliffe JR, Barker P (2002) Considering the care of the suicidal client and the case for 'engagement and inspiring hope' or observations. *Journal of Psychiatric and Mental Health Nursing*, **9**(5): 611–21.

Cutcliffe JR, Barker P (2004) The Nurses' Global Assessment of Suicide Risk (NGASR): developing a tool for clinical practice. *Journal of Psychiatric/Mental Health Nursing*, **11**: 393–400.

Cutcliffe JR, McKenna HP (2005) An introduction to concepts and their analysis. In: Cutcliffe JR, McKenna HP (eds.) *The Essential Concepts of Nursing*. Churchill Livingstone/Elsevier, pp. 1–13.

Cutcliffe JR, Stevenson C (2007) *Care of the Suicidal Person*. Elsevier, Edinburgh.

Cutcliffe JR, Stevenson C, Jackson S, Smith P (2006) A modified grounded theory study of how psychiatric nurses work with suicidal people. *International Journal of Nursing Studies*, **43**(7): 791–802.

Cutcliffe JR, McKenna HP, Keeney S, Jordan J, Stevenson C. (in press) 'Straight from the horse's mouth': rethinking and reconfiguring services in Northern Ireland in response to suicidal young men. *Journal of Psychiatric and Mental Health Nursing* (accepted August 2012).

Daniel SS, Goldston DB (2009) Interventions for suicidal youth: a review of the literature and developmental considerations. *Suicide and Life Threatening Behaviour*, **39**(3): 252–68.

Davidhizar R, Vance A (1993) The management of the suicidal patient in a critical care unit. *Journal of Nursing Management*, **1**: 95–102.

De Leo D, Dwyer J, Firman D, Neulinger K, Grad B (2003) Trends in hanging and firearm suicide rates in Australia: substitution of method? *Suicide and Life-Threatening Behavior*, **33**(2): 151–64.

Denzin N, Lincoln YS (1994) Introduction: Entering the field of qualitative enquiry. In: Denzin N, Lincoln YS (eds.) *Handbook of Qualitative Research*, Sage, London.

Department of Health (2001) *Safety First – Five Year Report of the National Confidential Inquiry into Suicides and Homicides by People with Mental Health Problems*. HMSO, London.

Department of Health (2002) *National Suicide Prevention Strategy for England*. Department of Health, London.

Department of Health (2005) *National Suicide Prevention Strategy for England (2nd) Annual Report on Progress*. HMSO, London.

Department of Justice Canada (1996) *A Statistical Analysis of the Impacts of the 1977 Firearms Control Legislation.*

Dodds P, Bowles N (2001) Dismantling formal observation and refocusing nursing activity in acute inpatient psychiatry: a case study. *Journal of Psychiatric and Mental Health Nursing*, **8**: 173–88.

Eastwood EA, Schectman J (1999) Direct observation nursing: adverse patient behaviours and functional outcomes. *Nursing Economics*, **17**(2): 96–102.

Favazza AR (1996) *Bodies Under Siege*. Johns Hopkins University Press, Baltimore.

Fletcher RF (1999) The process of constant observation: perspectives of staff and suicidal patients. *Journal of Psychiatric and Mental Health Nursing*, **6**(1): 9–14.

Fortune SA, Hawton K (2005) Suicide and deliberate self-harm in children and adolescents. *Current Paediatrics*, **15**: 575–80.

Geddes JR, Juszczak E (1995) Period trends in rate of suicide in first 28 days after discharge from psychiatric hospital in Scotland, 1968–92. *British Medical Journal*, **311**: 357–60.

Geddes JR, Juszczak E, O'Brien F, Kendrick S (1997) Suicide in the 12 months after discharge from psychiatric inpatient care, Scotland 1968–92. *Journal of Epidemiology and Community Health*, **51**: 430–4.

Goh S, Salmons P, Whittington R (1990) Hospital suicides: are there preventable factors? *British Journal of Psychiatry*, **154**: 247–9.

Gournay K, Bowers L (2000) Suicide and self-harm in in-patient psychiatric units: a study of nursing issues in 31 cases. *Journal of Advanced Nursing*, **32**(1): 124–31.

Gunnell D, Middelton N, Frankel S (2000) Method availability and the prevention of a suicide: a re-analysis of secular trends in England and Wales 1950–1975. *Social Psychiatry and Psychiatric Epidemiology*, **25**: 437–43.

Harden A, Sutcliffe K, Lempert T (2002) *Young Men and Suicide Prevention: A Scoping Exercise for A Review of the Effectiveness of Health Promotion Interventions of Relevance to Suicide Prevention in Young Men*. EPPI-Centre, Social Science Research Unit, Institute of Education, University of London.

Harvard Injury Control Research Center: Guns and Death (recovered 2012). http://www.hsph.harvard.edu/research/hicrc/firearms-research/guns-and-death/index.html.

Hawton K (2007) Restricting access to methods of suicide: rationale and evaluation of this approach to suicide prevention. *Crisis (Supplement 1 Controlling access to means of suicide*, **28**(suppl. 1): 4–9.

Hawton K, James A (2005) Suicide and deliberate self-harm in young people. *British Medical Journal*, **330**: 891–4.

Hawton K, Zahl D, Weatherall R (2003) Suicide following deliberate self-harm: long-term follow-up of patients who present to a general hospital. *British Journal of Psychiatry*, **182**: 537–42.

Healy D (2005) *Psychiatric Drugs Explained*, 4th edn. Churchill Livingstone, Edinburgh.

Healy D, Whitaker C (2003) Antidepressants and suicide: risk-benefit conundrums. *Journal of Psychiatry & Neuroscience*, **28**(5): 331–7.

Heidegger M (1962) *Being and Time*. Harper & Row, New York.

Heyman EN, Lombardo BA (1995) Managing costs: the confused, agitated or suicidal inpatient. *Nursing Economics*, **13**: 107–111, 118.

Ho TP (2003) The suicide risk of discharged psychiatric patients. *Journal of Clinical Psychiatry*, **64**: 702–7.

Holmes D, Kennedy S, Perron A (2004) The mentally ill and social exclusion: a critical examination of the use of seclusion from the patient's perspective. *Issues in Mental Health Nursing*, **25**(6): 559–78.

International Association for Suicide Prevention (2003) Press Release: *Celebrating the 1st World Suicide Prevention Day, 10th September, 2003 SUICIDE CAN BE PREVENTED!* (recovered 2007). http://www.med.uio.no/iasp/english/wspd/2003/wspd_text.html.

James K, Stewart D, Bowers L (2012) Self-harm and attempted suicide within inpatient psychiatric services: a review of the literature. *International Journal of Mental Health Nursing*. Article first published online: 16 FEB 2012, DOI: 10.1111/j.1447-0349.2011.00794.x.

Jick H, Kaye JA, Jick SS (2004) Antidepressants and the risk of suicidal behavior. *Journal of the American Medical Association*, **292**: 338–43.

Joiner T (2005) *Why People Die by Suicide*. Harvard University Press, Cambridge, MA.

Jones J, Ward M, Wellman N, Hall J, Lowe T (2000) Psychiatric inpatients' experiences of nursing observation: a United Kingdom perspective. *Journal of Psychosocial Nursing*, **38**(12): 10–19.

Jordan JR (2001) Is suicide bereavement different? A reassessment of the literature. *Suicide and Life-Threatening Behavior*, **31**: 91–102.

Jordan J, McKenna HP, Keeney SR, Cutcliffe JR, Stevenson C, Slater P, McGowan I (2012) Providing meaningful care: learning from the experiences of suicidal young men. *Qualitative Health Research*. Accepted for publication September 2011.

Kates DB, Mauser G (recovered 2012) Would banning firearms reduce murder and suicide? A review of international and some domestic evidence. *Harvard Journal of Law and Public Policy*. http://www.law.harvard.edu/students/orgs/jlpp/Vol30_No2_Kates-Mauseronline.pdf.

King EA, Baldwin DS, Sinclair JMA, Campbell MJ (2001) The Wessex recent in-patient suicide study, 2. Case-control study of 59 in-patient suicides. *British Journal of Psychiatry*, **17**: 537–42.

Klieve H, Sveticic J, De Leo D (2009) Who uses firearms as a means of suicide? A population study exploring firearm accessibility and method choice. *BMC Medicine*, **7**: 52. doi: 10.1186/1741-7015-7-52.

Leigh A, Neill C (2010) Do gun buybacks save lives? Evidence from panel data. *American Law and Economics Review*, **12**(2): 462–508. doi: 10.1093/aler/ahq013.

Leitner M, Barr W, Hobby L (2008) *Effectiveness of Interventions to Prevent Suicide and Suicidal Behaviour: A Systematic Review*. Health and Community Care Research Unit, Liverpool University/Info Tech UK Research: Scottish Government Social Research.

Lendrum S, Syme G (1992) *Gift of Tears: A Practical Approach to Loss and Bereavement Counselling*. Routledge, London.
Lester D, Murrell ME (1982) The preventive effect of strict gun control laws on suicide and homicide. *Suicide and Life-Threatening Behavior*, **12**(3): 131–40.
Lester J, Leenaars A (1993) Suicide rates in Canada before and after tightening firearms control laws. *Psychological Reports*, **72**: 791–810.
Loftin C, McDowall D, Wiersema B, Cottey TJ (1991) Effects of restrictive licensing of handguns on homicide and suicide in the District of Columbia. *New England Journal of Medicine*, **325**(23): 1615–20.
Luoma JB, Martin CE, Pearson JL (2002) Contact with mental health and primary care providers before suicide: a review of the evidence. *American Journal of Psychiatry*, **159**(6): 909–16.
MacKay I, Paterson B, Cassells C (2005) Constant or special observations of inpatients presenting a risk of aggression or violence: nurses' perceptions of the rules of engagement. *Journal of Psychiatric and Mental Health Nursing*, **12**(4): 464–71.
Maris RW (1981) *Pathways to Suicide*. Johns Hopkins University Press, Baltimore.
Maris RW (1997) Social forces in suicide: a life review, 1965–1995. In: Maris RW, Silverman MM, Canetto SS (eds.) *Review of Suicidology 1997*. Guilford Press, New York, pp. 42–60.
Maris RW (2007) Foreword. In: Cutcliffe JR, Stevenson C (2007) *Care of the Suicidal Person*. Elsevier, Edinburgh, p. xii.
Maris RW, Berman AL, Silverman MM (2000a) *Comprehensive Textbook of Suicidology*. Guilford Press, New York.
Maris, RW, Berman, AL, Silverman, MM and Farberow, N (2000b) Indirect self-destructive behavior In: Maris, RW, Berman, AL and Silverman, MM *Comprehensive textbook of suicidology* Guilford Press, New York, ps 427–55.
Menzies Lyth I (1959) The functions of social systems as a defence against anxiety: a report on a study of the nursing service of a general hospital. *Human Relations*, **13**: 95–102.
Miller M, Hemenway D (1999) The relationship between firearms and suicide: a review of the literature. *Aggression and Violent Behavior: a Review Journal*, **4**: 59–75.
Miller M, Hemenway D (2001) Gun prevalence and the risk of suicide: a review. *Harvard Health Policy Review*, **2**: 29–37.
Mishara BL, Weisstub DN (2005) Ethical and legal issues in suicide research. *International Journal of Law and Psychiatry*, **28**: 23–41.
Mishara BL, Houle J, Lavoie B (2005) Comparison of the effects of four suicide prevention programs for family and friends of high-risk suicidal men who do not seek help themselves. *Suicide and Life-Threatening Behavior*, **35**(3): 329–42.
Moore P, Berman K, Knight M, Devine J (1995) Constant observation: implications for nursing practice. *Journal of Psychosocial Nursing*, **33**(3): 46–50.
Morse JM (1999) Qualitative generalisability. *Qualitative Health Research*, **9**: 5–6.
Morttunen M, Aro H, Lonnqvist J (1992) Adolescent suicide: endpoint of long-term difficulties. *Journal of the American Academy of Child and Adolescent Psychiatry*, **31**(4): 649–54.
National Task Force on Suicide in Canada (1994) *Suicide in Canada: Update of the Report of the Task Force on Suicide in Canada*. Mental Health Division – Health Services Directorate, Health Programs and Services Branch, Health Canada.

Nordentoft M, Branner J, Drejer K, Mejsholm B, Hansen H, Petersson B (2005) Effect of a suicide prevention centre for young people with suicidal behaviour in Copenhagen. *European Psychiatry*, **20**(2): 121–8.

O'Brien L, Cole R (2003) Close-observation areas in acute psychiatric units: a literature review. *International Journal of Mental Health Nursing*, **12**: 165–76.

Oliver M, Pearson N, Coe N, Gunnell D (2005) Help-seeking behaviour in men and women with common mental health problems: cross-sectional survey. *British Journal of Psychiatry*, **186**: 297–301.

Peplau H (1952) *Interpersonal Relations in Nursing*. GP Putnam, New York.

Peplau H (1988) *Interpersonal Relations in Nursing*, 2nd edn. GP Putnam, New York.

Perlman CM, Neufeld E, Martin L, Goy M, Hirdes JP (2011) *Suicide Risk Assessment Inventory: A Resource Guide for Canadian Health Care Organizations*. Ontario Hospital Association and Canadian Patient Safety Institute, Toronto.

Pirkola S, Sohlman B, Wahlbeck K (2005) The characteristics of suicides within a week of discharge after psychiatric hospitalization – a nationwide register study. *BMC Psychiatry*, **5**: 32.

Pitula CR, Cardell R (1996) Suicidal inpatients' experiences of constant observation. *Psychiatric Services*, **47**(6): 6491–651.

Popper K (1965) *Conjectures and Refutations: The Growth of Scientific Knowledge*. Harper & Row, New York.

Powell J, Geddes J, Hawton K (2000) Suicide in psychiatric hospital in-patients. *British Journal of Psychiatry*, **176**(3): 266–72.

Public Health Agency (recovered 2012) PHA announce research findings – 'Suicide: providing meaningful care'. http://www.publichealth.hscni.net/news/pha-announce-research-findings-%E2%80%93-%E2%80%98suicide-providing-meaningful-care%E2%80%99.

Raphael B (1983) *The Anatomy of Bereavement*. Unwin Hyman, London.

Renaud J, Chagnon F, Balan B, Turecki G, McGirr A, Marquette C (2006) Psychiatric services utilisation in completed suicides of a youth centres population. *BMC Psychiatry*, **6**: 36.

Russell V, Gaffney P, Collins K, Bergin A, Bedford D (2004) Problems experienced by young men and attitudes to help-seeking in a rural Irish community. *Irish Journal of Psychiatric Medicine*, **21**(1): 6–10.

Sandelowski M (1998) The call to experts in qualitative research. *Research in Nursing and Health*, **21**: 467–71.

Sanon-Rollins G (recovered 2011) *Surviving Conflict on the Job*. http://nswebnursingspectrumcom/Articles/SurvivingConflictCFhtm.

Santa Mina EE, Gallop R (1998) Childhood sexual and physical abuse and adult self-harm and suicidal behaviour: a literature review. *Canadian Journal of Psychiatry*, **43**(8): 793–800.

Schutz A (1972) *The Phenomenology of the Social World*. Heinemann, London.

Shneidman E (1993) Commentary: suicide as psychache. *Journal of Nervous and Mental Disease*, **181**: 145–7.

Shneidman ES (1997) The suicidal mind. In: Maris RW, Silverman MM, Canetto SS (eds.) *Review of Suicidology*. Guilford Press, New York, pp. 22–41.

Shneidman ES (2001) *Comprehending Suicide: Landmarks in 20th-Century Suicidology*. American Psychological Association, Washington.

Silverman MM (1997) Current controversies in suicidology. In: Maris RW, Silverman MM, Canetto SS (eds.) *Review of Suicidology*. Guilford Press, New York, pp. 1–21.

Sinyor M, Levitt AJ (2010) Effect of a barrier at Bloor Street Viaduct on suicide rates in Toronto: natural experiment. *British Medical Journal*, **341**: 2884.

Speckens AEM, Hawton K (2005) Social problem-solving in adolescents with suicidal behaviour: a systematic review. *Suicide and Life-Threatening Behavior*, **35**: 365–87. doi: 10.1521/suli.2005.35.4.365.

Standing Nursing and Midwifery Advisory Committee (1999) *Practice Guidance: Safe and Supportive Observation of Patients at Risk: Mental Health Nursing – Addressing Acute Concerns*. Department of Health, London.

Stevenson C, Cutcliffe JR (2006) Problematizing special observation in psychiatry: Foucault, archaeology, genealogy, discourse and power/knowledge. *Journal of Psychiatric and Mental Health Nursing*, **13**: 713–21.

Stoff DM, Mann JL (eds.) (1997) *The Neurobiology of Suicide: From the Bench to the Clinic*. The New York Academy of Sciences, New York,

Streubert HJ, Carpenter DR (1999) *Qualitative Research in Nursing: Advancing the Humanistic Imperative*. Lippincott, Philadelphia.

Sun FK, Long A, Boore J, Tsao LI (2005) Nursing people who are suicidal on psychiatric wards in Taiwan: action and interaction strategies. *Journal of Psychiatric and Mental Health Nursing*, **12**(3): 275–82.

Talseth AG, Lindseth A, Jacobson L, Norberg A (1997) Nurses' narrations about suicidal psychiatric inpatients. *Nordic Journal of Psychiatry*, **51**: 359–64.

Talseth AG, Lindseth A, Jacobson L, Norberg A (1999) The meaning of suicidal in-patients' experiences of being cared for by mental health nurses. *Journal of Advanced Nursing*, **29**(5): 1034–41.

Tanney BL (2000) Psychiatric diagnoses and suicidal acts. In: Maris RW, Berman AL, Silverman MM (eds.) *Comprehensive Textbook of Suicidology*. Guilford Press, New York, pp. 311–40.

Treatment for Adolescents with Depression Study (TADS) (2007) Long-term effectiveness and safety outcomes. *Archives of General Psychiatry*, **64**(10).

Van Manen M (1997) *Researching Lived Experience: Human Science for Action Sensitive Pedagogy*. State University of New York Press, New York.

van Praag HM (2004) Stress and suicide: are we well-equipped to study this issue? *Crisis*, **25**(2): 80–5.

van Spijker B, van Straten A, Kerkhof AM (2010) The effectiveness of a web-based self-help intervention to reduce suicidal thoughts: a randomized controlled trial. *Trials*, **11**: 25.

Worden JW (1988) *Grief Counselling and Grief Therapy*. Tavistock/Routledge, London.

World Health Organization (recovered 2012) *Depression/Suicide*. Available from http://www.who.int/health_topics/suicide/en/.

Younge O, Boschma G (2006) Debating the integration of psychiatric/mental health nursing content in undergraduate nursing programmes. In: Cutcliffe JR, Ward M (eds.) *Key Debates in Psychiatric/Mental Health Nursing*. Churchill Livingstone, Edinburgh.

Zahl DL, Hawton K (2004) Repetition of deliberate self-harm and subsequent suicide risk: long-term follow-up study of 11 583 patients. *British Journal of Psychiatry*, **185**: 70–5.

Index